ECONOMIC ISSUES, PROBLEMS AND PERSPECTIVES

TARP ON THE U.S. AUTOMOTIVE INDUSTRY: IMPACT AND IMPLICATIONS

ECONOMIC ISSUES, PROBLEMS AND PERSPECTIVES

Additional books in this series can be found on Nova's website under the Series tab.

Additional E-books in this series can be found on Nova's website under the E-books tab.

AMERICAN POLITICAL, ECONOMIC, AND SECURITY ISSUES

Additional books in this series can be found on Nova's website under the Series tab.

Additional E-books in this series can be found on Nova's website under the E-books tab.

ECONOMIC ISSUES, PROBLEMS AND PERSPECTIVES

TARP ON THE U.S. AUTOMOTIVE INDUSTRY: IMPACT AND IMPLICATIONS

SAMANTHA E. WALCOTT
AND
JASON A. CAPALDI
EDITORS

Nova Science Publishers, Inc.
New York

Copyright © 2011 by Nova Science Publishers, Inc.

All rights reserved. No part of this book may be reproduced, stored in a retrieval system or transmitted in any form or by any means: electronic, electrostatic, magnetic, tape, mechanical photocopying, recording or otherwise without the written permission of the Publisher.

For permission to use material from this book please contact us:
Telephone 631-231-7269; Fax 631-231-8175
Web Site: http://www.novapublishers.com

NOTICE TO THE READER

The Publisher has taken reasonable care in the preparation of this book, but makes no expressed or implied warranty of any kind and assumes no responsibility for any errors or omissions. No liability is assumed for incidental or consequential damages in connection with or arising out of information contained in this book. The Publisher shall not be liable for any special, consequential, or exemplary damages resulting, in whole or in part, from the readers'use of, or reliance upon, this material. Any parts of this book based on government reports are so indicated and copyright is claimed for those parts to the extent applicable to compilations of such works.

Independent verification should be sought for any data, advice or recommendations contained in this book. In addition, no responsibility is assumed by the publisher for any injury and/or damage to persons or property arising from any methods, products, instructions, ideas or otherwise contained in this publication.

This publication is designed to provide accurate and authoritative information with regard to the subject matter covered herein. It is sold with the clear understanding that the Publisher is not engaged in rendering legal or any other professional services. If legal or any other expert assistance is required, the services of a competent person should be sought. FROM A DECLARATION OF PARTICIPANTS JOINTLY ADOPTED BY A COMMITTEE OF THE AMERICAN BAR ASSOCIATION AND A COMMITTEE OF PUBLISHERS.

Additional color graphics may be available in the e-book version of this book.

Library of Congress Cataloging-in-Publication Data

TARP on the U.S. automotive industry : impact and implications / editors, Samantha E. Walcott and Jason A. Capaldi.
  p. cm.
 Includes bibliographical references and index.
 ISBN 978-1-61324-363-3 (hardcover : alk. paper) 1. Automobile industry and trade--Government policy--United States. 2. Automobile industry and trade--Subsidies--United States. 3. Troubled Asset Relief Program (U.S.) I. Walcott, Samantha E. II. Capaldi, Jason A. III. Title: TARP on the United States automotive industry.
 HD9710.U52T37 2011
 338.4'76292220973--dc22
                           2011013406

Published by Nova Science Publishers, Inc. † New York

CONTENTS

Preface		vii
Chapter 1	An Update on TARP Support for the Domestic Automotive Industry *Congressional Oversight Panel*	1
Chapter 2	General Motors'Initial Public Offering: Review of Issues and Implications for TARP *Bill Canis, Baird Webel and Gary Shorter*	131
Chapter 3	Troubled Asset Relief Program: Automaker Pension Funding and Multiple Federal Roles Pose Challenges for the Future *United States Government Accountability Office*	155
Chapter 4	Troubled Asset Relief Program: Continued Stewardship Needed as Treasury Develops Strategies for Monitoring and Divesting Financial Interests in Chrysler and GM *United States Government Accountability Office*	209
Chapter Sources		239
Index		241

PREFACE

While it remains too early to tell whether Treasury's intervention in and reshaping of the U.S. automotive industry will prove to be a success, there can be no question that the government's ambitious actions have had a major impact and appear to be on a promising course. Even so, the companies that received automotive bailout funds continue to face uncertain futures, taxpayers remain at financial risk, concerns remain about the transparency and accountability of Treasury's efforts, and moral hazard lingers as a long-run threat to the automotive industry and the broader economy. This book examines the impact and implications of TARP on the U.S. automotive industry.

Chapter 1- Since the Panel's last comprehensive review of TARP support for the domestic automotive industry in September 2009, Treasury's automotive investments have, in financial terms, starkly improved. As of September 2009, the Congressional Budget Office (CBO) estimated that taxpayers would lose $40 billion on their automotive investments. Today, CBO has reduced its loss estimate to $19 billion, and the three largest recipients of automotive bailout funds – General Motors (GM), Chrysler, and GMAC/Ally Financial – all appear to be on the path to financial stability.

Chapter 2- On November 18, 2010, General Motors Company (GM) conducted an initial public offering (IPO) of stock to investors, once again becoming a publicly traded company.

General Motors Corporation (Old GM) was a publicly traded company from 1916 until its bankruptcy in 2009. As part of restructuring, GM and Old GM combined received over $50 billion in federal assistance through the federal Troubled Asset Relief Program (TARP). In exchange for this financial support, most of Old GM's assets were sold to General Motors Company, a new corporation owned by the U.S. Treasury, the United Autoworkers (UAW) retiree health care trust fund, the governments of Canada and Ontario, and a group of bondholders.

Chapter 3- Over $81 billion has been committed under the Troubled Asset Relief Program (TARP) to improve the domestic auto industry's competitiveness and long-term viability. The bulk of this assistance has gone to General Motors (GM) and Chrysler, who sponsor some of the largest defined benefit pension plans insured by the federal Pension Benefit Guaranty Corporation (PBGC). As part of GAO's statutorily mandated oversight of TARP, this report examines:

    the impact of restructuring on GM's and Chrysler's pension plans;
    the impact of restructuring on auto supply sector pension plans;

the impacts on PBGC and plan participants should auto industry pension plans be terminated; and

how the federal government is dealing with the potential tensions of its multiple roles as pension regulator, shareholder, and creditor.

Chapter 4- The Department of the Treasury (Treasury) provided $81.1 billion in Troubled Asset Relief Program (TARP) aid to the U.S. auto industry, including $62 billion in restructuring loans to Chrysler Group LLC (Chrysler) and General Motors Company (GM). In return, Treasury received 9.85 percent equity in Chrysler, 60.8 percent equity and $2.1 billion in preferred stock in GM, and $13.8 billion in debt obligations between the two companies.

As part of GAO's statutory responsibilities for providing oversight of TARP, this report addresses (1) steps Chrysler and GM have taken since December 2008 to reorganize, (2) Treasury's oversight of its financial interest in the companies, and (3) considerations for Treasury in monitoring and selling its equity in the companies. GAO reviewed documents on the auto companies' restructuring and spoke with officials at Treasury, Chrysler, and GM, and individuals with expertise in finance and the auto industry.

Chapter 1

AN UPDATE ON TARP SUPPORT FOR THE DOMESTIC AUTOMOTIVE INDUSTRY[*]

Congressional Oversight Panel

EXECUTIVE SUMMARY[*]

Since the Panel's last comprehensive review of TARP support for the domestic automotive industry in September 2009, Treasury's automotive investments have, in financial terms, starkly improved. As of September 2009, the Congressional Budget Office (CBO) estimated that taxpayers would lose $40 billion on their automotive investments. Today, CBO has reduced its loss estimate to $19 billion, and the three largest recipients of automotive bailout funds – General Motors (GM), Chrysler, and GMAC/Ally Financial – all appear to be on the path to financial stability.

While it remains too early to tell whether Treasury's intervention in and reshaping of the U.S. automotive industry will prove to be a success, there can be no question that the government's ambitious actions have had a major impact and appear to be on a promising course. Even so, the companies that received automotive bailout funds continue to face uncertain futures, taxpayers remain at financial risk, concerns remain about the transparency and accountability of Treasury's efforts, and moral hazard lingers as a long-run threat to the automotive industry and the broader economy.

Treasury is currently unwinding its stakes in GM, Chrysler, and GMAC/Ally Financial. Of those companies, GM is furthest along in the process of repaying taxpayers. It conducted an initial public offering (IPO) on November 18, 2010, and Treasury used the occasion to sell a portion of its GM holdings for $13.5 billion. This sale represents a major recovery of taxpayer funds, but it is important to note that Treasury received a price of $33.00 per share – well below the $44.59 needed to be on track to recover fully taxpayers' money. By selling

---

[*] This is an edited, reformatted and augmented version of a Congressional Oversight Panel's publication, dated January 13, 2011.

stock for less than this break-even price, Treasury essentially "locked in" a loss of billions of dollars and thus greatly reduced the likelihood that taxpayers will ever be repaid in full.

Treasury has explained its decision to sell at a loss by saying that it wished to unwind government ownership of the automobile industry as quickly as possible. This justification may very well be reasonable, but it is difficult to evaluate. Because Treasury has cited different, conflicting goals for its automotive interventions at different times – saying, for example, that it wished to save American jobs, to produce the best possible return to taxpayers, or to return the company to private ownership as rapidly as possible – it is difficult for the Panel or any outside observer to judge whether Treasury's results in fact qualify as successful.

The other major automotive manufacturer to receive government assistance, Chrysler, remains a private company. Because Treasury has already absorbed $3.5 billion in losses on loans made to the pre-bankruptcy Chrysler, the prospect for a full recovery of taxpayers' money depends upon Treasury's ability to sell its ownership of Chrysler at a profit. However, as Treasury owns only 10 percent of the company's stock, it has very limited ability to influence the timing of an eventual public offering. The remaining 90 percent of Chrysler was parceled out to several other parties, including the Italian automotive manufacturer Fiat, through the bankruptcy process – but while this approach may have saved Chrysler from liquidation, the result is that Treasury has little authority to act in taxpayers' interests. Another source of concern is Treasury's hasty unwinding of its position in Chrysler Financial, in which taxpayer returns appear to have been sacrificed in favor of an unnecessarily accelerated exit, further compounded by apparently questionable due diligence.

The final major recipient of automotive-related aid, GMAC/Ally Financial, represents a curious case. GMAC/Ally Financial is a financial company, not a manufacturer; it operates in many fields entirely unrelated to the automotive industry. Traditionally, however, the company has provided the bulk of financing to GM car dealerships, as well as significant financing to individual purchasers of GM vehicles. As such, Treasury saw the survival of GMAC/Ally Financial as critical to its broader automotive rescue.

Since the Panel's report on GMAC/Ally Financial in March 2010, the company has experienced three consecutive quarters of profits and has reduced the risk in its mortgage portfolio. Even so, taxpayers likely will not begin to recover their investment until GMAC/Ally Financial conducts an IPO. Treasury has had significant leverage over the IPO's timing due to its preferred stock holdings, but regrettably, Treasury has been inconsistent in acknowledging this leverage. Treasury's reluctance to recognize its own influence may represent an effort to claim a coherent "hands off" shareholder approach, despite the unique circumstances that apply to GMAC/Ally Financial.

The "hands off" approach may in itself raise questions. Treasury has asserted that, even if one of the automotive companies had announced an entirely unrealistic business plan, Treasury would not have intervened. In more practical terms, Treasury declined to block GM's purchase of AmeriCredit, a subprime financing company, even though AmeriCredit may ultimately compete against GMAC/Ally Financial and thus damage that company's ability to repay taxpayers. Although Treasury's "hands off" approach may have reassured market participants about the limited scope of government intervention, it may also have forced Treasury to leave unexplored options that would have benefited the public.

Treasury is now on course to recover the majority of its automotive investments within the next few years, but the impact of its actions will reverberate for much longer. Treasury's rescue suggested that any sufficiently large American corporation – even if it is not a bank – may be considered "too big to fail," creating a risk that moral hazard will infect areas of the economy far beyond the financial system. Further, the fact that the government helped absorb the consequences of GM's and Chrysler's failures has put more competently managed automotive companies at a disadvantage. For these reasons, the effects of Treasury's intervention will linger long after taxpayers have sold their last share of stock in the automotive industry.

SECTION ONE

A. Introduction

In late 2008 and early 2009, the federal government undertook the unprecedented rescue of two of the three major U.S.-based automobile manufacturers, as well as a major automotive financing company. These interventions were accomplished using resources from the Troubled Asset Relief Program (TARP), a program that Congress created with passage of the Emergency Economic Stabilization Act (EESA) in October 2008 and which was aimed primarily at preventing economic collapse by restoring stability in the financial sector. This month the Congressional Oversight Panel looks at what the TARP has accomplished in the automobile sector and the prospects for recovering the taxpayer's investments in the three rescued firms: General Motors, Chrysler, and GMAC/Ally Financial.[1]

The Panel first reviewed the actions of Treasury in rescuing GM and Chrysler in a September 2009 report. That report asked whether the actions taken to that point to rescue GM and Chrysler served merely to forestall a decision ultimately to liquidate those companies or to intervene with still more government assistance to make them viable. It remains too early to render a conclusive verdict on that question. But the events of the intervening 16 months allow a tentative judgment: GM and Chrysler are both more viable firms than they were in December 2008 with GM on a credible path to recovery but Chrysler's outlook more uncertain. Likewise, the degree to which Treasury will be successful in recovering the taxpayer's investment in these firms has become more apparent for GM than for Chrysler. The intervening time since the Panel's last report on the GM and Chrysler rescues has also allowed for some greater understanding of how Treasury would behave as an investor in both firms. What remains uncertain is whether the improvement in both companies is directly attributable to Treasury's intervention or to the more general improvement of the economy. In addition, there remains a great deal of uncertainty about the long-run impact of the government's significant intervention in the operations of these private firms.

In its March 2010 report, the Panel examined the actions of Treasury, closely related to its investments in GM and Chrysler, in supporting the auto financing firm GMAC/Ally Financial. That report noted that there were lingering unresolved issues related to GMAC/Ally Financial's emerging business strategy. In the 10 months since that report was issued, the firm's operating performance has improved considerably, but Treasury's exit strategy remains unclear.

The use of TARP resources to prevent the collapse of two of the three domestic automakers was and continues to be controversial. Policymakers confronting this situation in

November and December 2008 had several courses of action, ranging from doing nothing to full adoption of the rescue plans proposed by the companies. It is possible that private sector financial firms, such as private equity funds or hedge funds, may have stepped up to provide financing for some of GM's or Chrysler's more desirable assets at a later date. However, it is unclear to what extent broad-based private sector emergency funding to buy both firms in their entirety was a feasible option in the midst of the credit market crisis during the fall of 2008. It was the judgment of the Bush Administration, a judgment confirmed by many knowledgeable market participants at the time, that such a private sector intervention was unlikely. Hence, the Bush Administration chose a middle-of-the-road option, providing the firms with TARP-financed loans sufficient to tide them over for a few months but leaving it to a new administration to make its own assessments as to the long-term viability of GM and Chrysler and ultimately to choose to put the firms through expedited bankruptcy proceedings.

In contrast to its interventions in the financial sector, where assistance was provided to banks without requiring sweeping changes in their management and operations, government intervention in the auto sector has been noteworthy for the major restructuring that was required as a condition for receiving government financing. While it remains too early to tell whether Treasury's intervention in and reshaping of the U.S. auto industry will prove to be a success, there can be no question that the government's ambitious actions have had a major impact. Completion of an IPO of GM stock is an especially significant milestone that serves to highlight the timeliness of an updated assessment of the TARP's performance in rescuing the U.S. auto and auto financing industries. These favorable events, however, must be thoughtfully balanced against the moral hazard risks created by the taxpayer's bailout of the three institutions and the ongoing implicit guarantee of the government. By bailing out GM, Chrysler, and GMAC/Ally Financial, the government sent a powerful message to the marketplace – some institutions will be protected at all cost, while others must prosper or fail based upon their own business judgment and acumen. We regret that Treasury has focused solely on the apparent success of the GM IPO in assessing the rescues of the three institutions to the distinct exclusion of the moral hazard risks arising from the bailouts.

B. OVERVIEW OF GOVERNMENT INTERVENTION

1. Summary of Government Intervention in Auto Manufacturing and Financing Industries

a. Condition of the Domestic Auto Industry in 2008

Even prior to the onset of the financial crisis, the domestic automotive industry was facing severe challenges and strains. Not only had foreign competitors steadily increased their market share, and rising fuel prices softened demand, but Chrysler and GM faced additional challenges posed by legacy costs and a series of poor strategic decisions.

With the onset of the financial crisis, the challenges facing the auto industry – which now also included tightening credit markets, declining consumer confidence, decreased demand, and rising unemployment – became acute.[2] The tightened credit market was especially significant not only because it impacted the automakers' access to debt market/bank financing, but also because 90 percent of consumers finance automobile purchases through loans, either directly from the manufacturers' financing arms or through third-party financial institutions, all of which experienced increased difficulty in late 2008 in raising capital to finance such loans.[3] The particularly weak condition of Chrysler Financial and GMAC/Ally Financial exacerbated the plummeting sales at GM and Chrysler as the credit markets seized up.[4] Ford did not need government assistance in large part because it conducted a massive refinancing in 2006, which provided the company with a credit facility that it could draw down as needed as the credit markets tightened considerably for other auto makers.

b. Rescues of Chrysler and GM

By the beginning of December 2008, GM and Chrysler could no longer secure the credit they needed to conduct their day-to-day operations.[5] The CEOs of Chrysler and GM appeared before Congress and appealed for government assistance to help them remain in business, but they were unable to muster sufficient congressional support to get a rescue bill through the Senate. Unless they could raise billions of dollars in new financing from private investors, they faced bankruptcy and probable liquidation.

Typically, when a firm reaches a financial crisis as severe as the ones facing GM and Chrysler in the fall of 2008, the firm files for bankruptcy in federal court. This invokes a process where there are two possible courses of action: either the firm is salvaged but reorganized using interim debtor in possession (DIP) financing, or the firm is liquidated.[6] But the circumstances in the global credit markets in November and December 2008 were unlike any the financial markets had seen in decades. U.S. domestic credit markets were frozen in the wake of the Lehman bankruptcy, and international sources of funding were extremely limited. Cross-border lending was decreasing due to a domestic bias in lending, concerns over cross-currency and foreign exchange swap markets, and higher regulatory capital charges.[7] In September 2008, China had already reduced its holdings of U.S. subprime mortgage-backed securities by approximately $6 billion.[8] Furthermore, several sovereign wealth funds that had stepped in to provide funding for U.S. firms were beginning to face losses on their investments. For example, the Abu Dhabi Investment Authority purchased $7.5 billion worth of Citigroup convertible bonds in early November 2007,[9] only to see the share price plummet over the next 12 months.[10] Consequently, according to Treasury, bankruptcy with reorganization of the two auto companies using private DIP financing did not appear to be an option by late fall 2008, leaving liquidation of the firms as the more likely course of action absent a government rescue.

Facing the prospect of the collapse of GM and Chrysler, and with the option of a privately financed DIP bankruptcy proceeding foreclosed because of the extraordinary conditions in the credit markets, President George W. Bush on December 19, 2008 announced a government-funded rescue package for the automotive industry – the Automotive Industry Financing Program (AIFP). The rescue package broadened the allocation of TARP assistance to the domestic automotive industry.[11]

The White House estimated when it made the announcement that "the direct costs of American automakers failing and laying off their workers in the near term would result in a more than 1 percent reduction in real GDP growth and about 1.1 million workers losing their jobs, including workers for automotive suppliers and dealers."[12] This estimate was produced by the Council of Economic Advisors and reflected the direct job losses at GM and Chrysler, their suppliers, and dealerships over the short term, i.e., roughly six months.[13] Over the longer term, it is highly likely that the assets of these firms – particularly those related to the production of the more successful truck and minivan models – would have been brought back into production by competing firms such as Ford or the international auto manufacturers that build vehicles in the United States. Alternatively, the production capacity of the remaining firms might have been expanded to supply additional vehicles and employ additional workers. Likewise, while there would have been adjustments in supplier relationships and dealer networks, these changes would have created partially offsetting new employment, as those firms sought to fill the void created by the exit from the marketplace of two large auto manufacturers.

The AIFP called for an investment of $13.4 billion in GM and Chrysler by mid-January 2009 and additional funding for GM of up to $4.0 billion.[14] In announcing the plan, then-Treasury Secretary Henry Paulson stated that EESA provided him with the authority to make the investment, even as he acknowledged that "the purpose of [the TARP] program and the enabling legislation is to stabilize our financial sector."[15] This marked a reversal of the Administration's previous stance that automakers were ineligible to receive TARP assistance.[16]

The terms of the loans required both Chrysler and GM to demonstrate to the government their ability to achieve financial viability, and both companies submitted their viability plans on February 17, 2009.[17] The results of the Obama Administration's review of those plans were announced on March 30, 2009.[18] Both companies ultimately entered bankruptcy and, with the active involvement of the federal government, underwent radical restructurings through "363 sales" (conducted under Section 363(b) of the U.S. Bankruptcy Code), which allow a business to sell all or substantially all of its assets and leave only the remainder of the assets for distribution in a Chapter 11 plan.[19] Following those restructurings and after eventually providing a total of $63.1 billion in support, American taxpayers owned about 10 percent of what is now known as New Chrysler and 61 percent of New GM.[20]

c. Auto Suppliers and Warranties

The TARP's assistance to the automotive industry includes two additional initiatives. First, as a result of the downturn in the economy, automotive suppliers had great difficulty accessing credit. Consequently, on March 19, 2009, Treasury announced the Auto Supplier Support Program (ASSP), under which the government agreed to guarantee payment for products shipped by participating suppliers, even if the buyers went out of business.[21] Through the ASSP, Treasury committed $1.0 billion to Chrysler and $2.5 billion to GM, though each company drew down smaller amounts. Those funds have since been repaid. Second, the automotive companies' widely publicized vulnerability in late 2008 and early 2009 also raised concerns that consumers might not purchase Chrysler and GM automobiles for fear that the companies could not back their warranties. Accordingly, Treasury lent Chrysler $280 million and GM $361 million to backstop their new vehicle warranties. Both Chrysler and GM have since repaid those loans.

d. Rescues of Chrysler Financial and GMAC/Ally Financial

Treasury states that as it considered using TARP funds to rescue Chrysler and GM, it came to the conclusion that they could not survive without Chrysler Financial's and GMAC/Ally Financial's financial underpinning, respectively. Without access to "floorplan financing" – that is, loans to auto dealers to allow them to purchase their inventories – many dealers would have been forced to close their doors. In addition, despite the relatively competitive retail lending environment, GM and Chrysler relied on GMAC/Ally Financial and Chrysler Financial, respectively, for a substantial portion of their consumer auto financing.[22]

GMAC/Ally Financial's need for assistance in late 2008 arose from mortgage market investments that had incurred severe losses. On December 24, 2008, four days after President Bush announced the AIFP, the Federal Reserve Board approved GMAC/Ally Financial's application to become a bank holding company (BHC).[23] As part of this approval, the Federal Reserve required GMAC/Ally Financial to raise $7 billion in new equity. To satisfy this requirement, Treasury provided GMAC/Ally Financial with $5 billion in emergency funding under the AIFP on December 29, 2008, and GMAC/Ally Financial made an equity rights offering to its existing shareholders for $2 billion.[24]

Subsequently, GMAC/Ally Financial was one of 19 firms included in the government's "stress tests."[25] When the stress tests revealed that GMAC/Ally Financial needed to increase its capital, funding that it was unable to raise in the markets, the government extended further investments of $7.5 billion in May 2009 and $3.8 billion in December 2009.[26] Treasury's investment in GMAC/Ally Financial now consists of 73.8 percent of the company's common stock, $2.7 billion in trust-preferred securities, and $5.9 billion in mandatory convertible preferred (MCP) shares.

The assistance to Chrysler and Chrysler Financial was interwoven due to the common ownership of those two entities. On January 16, 2009, Treasury made a $1.5 billion loan directly to Chrysler Financial, which has since been repaid.[27] On January 2, 2009, as part of its broader assistance to Chrysler, Treasury provided a $4.0 billion loan to Chrysler Holding, an entity owned by Cerberus Management.[28] Both Chrysler and Chrysler Financial were subsidiaries of Chrysler Holding at the time. In connection with the loan to Chrysler Holding, Treasury was entitled to the first $1.375 billion of proceeds from Chrysler Financial that would have flowed to Chrysler Holding and 40 percent of any additional proceeds that Chrysler Financial paid to Chrysler Holding after certain other distributions were made.[29] As part of the bankruptcy process, $500 million of the $4.0 billion loan was assumed by New Chrysler, leaving Chrysler Holding with a $3.5 billion loan.

On May 17, 2010, Treasury announced that it had settled with Chrysler Holding and extinguished the loan for $1.9 billion in consideration for the government's 40 percent interest in Chrysler Financial, a settlement that it noted was above the valuation determined in an analysis by investment bank Keefe, Bruyette and Woods, but which would nevertheless result in a loss of $1.6 billion on the initial $3.5 billion loan.[30] Seven months later, on December 21, 2010, TD Bank Group announced that it had agreed to purchase Chrysler Financial from Cerberus Management for approximately $6.3 billion.[31] Using this sale price, Treasury's right to 40 percent of Chrysler Financial's equity would have been worth $2.5 billion, representing a $600 million difference from the $1.9 billion Treasury settled for in May 2010.

The rush to exit Chrysler Financial – compounded by incomplete due diligence – may have resulted in an unnecessarily subpar return for taxpayers, preventing Treasury from recouping more of its prior $1.6 billion loss. Presumably, Treasury's stance as a reluctant shareholder underscored the rationale for an expedited exit in this investment.[32] However, such an approach was still in marked contrast to Treasury's longer-term (and generally successful) investment mentality in other instances (for example, GMAC/Ally Financial, Chrysler). Further, Treasury apparently conducted limited valuation due diligence, focusing on the merits of the offer from Cerberus in the context of an expected wind-down of the Chrysler Financial platform. Cerberus had operated Chrysler Financial in run-off mode, and Treasury had valued it as such in the context of the offer from Cerberus. While Treasury relied primarily on a valuation premised on the wind-down assumption, Treasury also states that they considered other inputs to evaluate fully the offer from Cerberus. However, aside from providing an accompanying net-presentvalue analysis in response to subsequent Panel requests, Treasury was unable to provide any documentation to support this claim of a multi-pronged valuation exercise that encompassed a potential bid from a strategic buyer.

After this settlement, Treasury no longer had any interest in or claim on Chrysler Financial, leaving Cerberus as the sole owner of the company. Cerberus, recognizing the inherent value of the Chrysler Financial platform to potential strategic bidders (i.e., other financial institutions seeking a foothold in the auto lending market), sought to cash in on the value of the franchise. Thomas Gilman, CEO of Chrysler Financial, explained that, "During this time our origination engine was idling, but we knew we had a valuable franchise and so we continue[d] to make strategic investments in the core competencies of our operations in technology, process and talent."[33]

Following Treasury's sale, Chrysler Financial benefited from the lifting of restrictions associated with the TARP assistance provided to Chrysler Holding, as well as capital investments Cerberus made in order to enhance further the strategic options for company going forward.[34] As Mr. Gilman explained following the acquisition by TD Bank, "the ultimate solution for Chrysler Financial is to find a strong partner that could provide stable and long-term financing to support the needs of our customers and our dealers."[35]

e. Differences between Automotive Industry and Financial Institution Interventions

The Administration has articulated a set of uniform principles to govern its ownership interests in financial and automotive companies. One such set of principles is that in "exceptional cases" where the government feels it is necessary to respond to a company's request for substantial assistance, Treasury will reserve the right to establish upfront conditions as necessary including requirements for new viability plans as well as changes to boards of directors and management.[36] Treasury determined that seven institutions – AIG, Citigroup, Bank of America, GM, GMAC/Ally Financial, Chrysler, and Chrysler Financial – should be deemed "exceptional assistance" recipients.

In practice, however, there were clear differences between the treatment of banks and the automobile manufacturers that received TARP assistance, and even among those considered to be "exceptional cases." Both Chrysler and GM faced government-mandated restructurings. In comparison, Treasury has generally not forced TARP recipient financial institutions to reorganize, nor, with the exception of AIG, has it changed their boards and managements.[37] Treasury's assistance to Bank of America and Citigroup – two "exceptional assistance" recipients – was not conditioned on restructuring or management changes. Even in the case of GMAC/Ally Financial – a financial institution that, like GM and Chrysler, was assisted as part of the TARP's Auto Industry Financing Program – Treasury chose not to put the firm through bankruptcy.

Moreover, while Treasury has not generally exercised a significant role in restructuring the management of most of the financial institutions that received TARP capital investments, it has done so with the largest and most distressed TARP recipients, and this is particularly true of those assisted under the AIFP – GM, GMAC/Ally Financial, and Chrysler. Of course, in the cases of GM, AIG, and GMAC/Ally Financial, Treasury's ability to effect management changes may have been at least facilitated by its majority ownership positions. In contrast to the treatment of Chrysler and GM shareholders, who were wiped out, those with equity stakes in AIG, Citigroup, and GMAC/Ally Financial have seen their positions severely diluted by the government, but they have not been wiped out. Furthermore, unlike many creditors of the automotive companies, who were wiped out, companies with contractual ties to AIG, for instance those that owned AIG-originated credit default swap (CDS) contracts, were made whole.

f. Current State of Government's Investments

There are currently $51.5 billion in TARP funds outstanding under the AIFP.[38] Figure 1 shows the current state of TARP funds used to support the auto industry. In total, U.S. taxpayers spent $49.9 billion in support of GM, about $12.8 billion in support of Chrysler, and $17.2 billion in support of GMAC/Ally Financial. The assistance to automotive suppliers accounts for approximately $3.5 billion of TARP commitments, bringing the gross TARP support for the U.S. domestic automotive industry to approximately $84.8 billion.

	Total Invested	% of Total AIFP	Total Repaid	% of Investment Repaid	Total Lost\Extinguished	Assistance Currently Obligated
GMAC/Ally Financial	$17,174	21%	–	0%	–	[40] $17,174
General Motors	49,861	61%	$(22,717)	46%	–	2 7,144
Chrysler Financial	1,500	2%	(1,500)	100%	–	–
Chrysler	12,810	16%	(2,180)	17%	($3,488)	7,142
Total AIFP	$81,345	–	($26,397)	–	($3,488)	$ 51,459

Figure 1. AIFP Assistance by Company as of December 30, 2010 *(millions of dollars)*[39].

Figure 2 illustrates the proportion of TARP funds expended and repaid in support of the auto industry compared to the amounts used for other purposes.

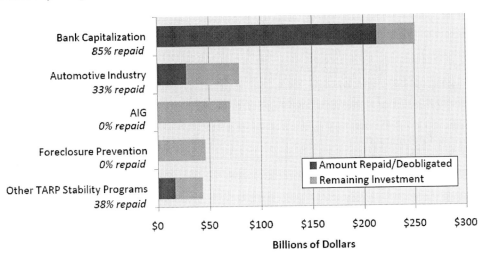

Figure 2. TARP Funds Repaid as a Portion of Total Expended by Program Type[41].

As shown above, a significant amount of the AIFP assistance remains outstanding, particularly in comparison to the bank recapitalizations conducted under the TARP. In addition, compared to the TARP bank recapitalization and other stability programs, it is generally taking Treasury a longer period of time to dispose of its AIFP investments. The longer disposition process is largely the result of the nature of Treasury's investments in each program. While most of Treasury's banking sector investments (with the exception of investments in Citigroup and a small number of other banks) were limited to purchases of senior preferred stock or subordinated debentures (the terms of which allowed the recipient the right to redeem at any time, subject to regulatory approval), Treasury's AIFP investments are a combination of loans, preferred stock, and common stock. Since common stock interests in GM, Chrysler, and GMAC/Ally Financial now form the majority of Treasury's remaining AIFP investments, the disposition of these ownership interests will depend on the condition of the equity capital markets, the state of the auto sector, and the broader economic outlook. As with the disposition of Treasury's investment in insurance giant AIG, the complete disposition of Treasury's AIFP investments could take place over several years.

At this point, it is impossible to determine whether Treasury's assistance through the AIFP will have a long-term financial cost or gain. The Panel examines this issue, as well as the context for government assistance and likely exit strategies for each company, in more depth below.

C. Current State of the Domestic Automotive Industry

U.S. auto companies have significantly improved their operating performance over the past year, moving from losses to profits in recent quarters. Automakers restructured during the global recession by cutting brands, closing factories, and laying off workers, positioning themselves for higher profits once consumer demand increased. Since the automakers have recently demonstrated that they can generate profits at a much lower level of sales, the industry may be well positioned to exploit any increased demand.[42] The industry's improved efficiency has allowed automakers to become more flexible and better able to meet changing consumer demands, while still remaining profitable. Improved production procedures and lower inventory have resulted in fewer discounts on new car sales, improving the profitability on each car sold. Investor enthusiasm for GM's IPO in November 2010 demonstrates a more favorable outlook for the auto companies since the restructurings of GM and Chrysler, in large part because of structural cost reductions, resulting in leaner and more efficient business models, and boosting optimism for the possibility of more sustainable profits over the long term.

These fundamental changes across the industry are outlined below. Restructuring efforts at the individual companies are outlined in more detail in the corresponding GM, Chrysler, and GMAC/Ally Financial sections of this report.

1. Capacity Reductions

Restructuring during the economic downturn has resulted in increased factory and labor usage and reduced vehicle inventory. As Figure 3 below illustrates, the North American production capacity of the big three automakers steadily declined from 2001 to 2004, before declining more sharply in recent years. In comparison, the utilization rate, a metric that measures the degree to which companies exploit their existing production capacity, is projected to increase from a trough of 47 percent in 2009 to 80 percent in 2012. The reduction in production capacity, combined with a more efficient use of inputs, demonstrates that the nation's largest three automakers have taken steps to align their size and production with a more subdued market backdrop.

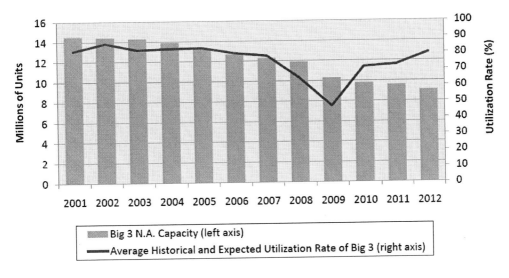

Figure 3. North American Capacity of Big 3 Automakers Compared to Capacity Utilization Rate[43].

2. Lower Labor Costs
Industry-wide labor costs are also substantially lower, primarily due to the following:

- A reduction in the number of salaried employees;[44]
- Salary declines resulting from the hiring of Tier 2 workers, who are new hires with average wages of $33 per hour. Tier 1 employees, who have been employed for longer, have average wages of $58 per hour;
- A shift in responsibility for employee health-care costs as a result of a 2007 agreement with the UAW;[45] and
- Streamlined job classifications, which help improve assembly line productivity.

Overall, the cost bases at Chrysler, Ford, and GM are some 35 percent lower in 2010 than they were in 2005 and 20 percent lower than they were in 2007.[46]

3. Resiliency in Market Share
Since the 1980s, American automakers have been losing ground in their home market, but they started to reverse that trend in 2010, at the expense of their Japanese rivals. This reflects gains in the U.S. auto market by Ford and a retreat by Toyota after a series of Toyota recalls over the past year. After shedding or eliminating four brands as part of its restructuring, GM's share has fallen from 19.7 percent in 2009 to 18.3 percent at present,[47] while Chrysler's share has slightly improved from 9.0 percent in 2009 to approximately 9.5

percent. Chrysler's improvement in market share has been aided by a shift to lower-margin sales of "fleet" vehicles to rental car agencies and other commercial buyers.

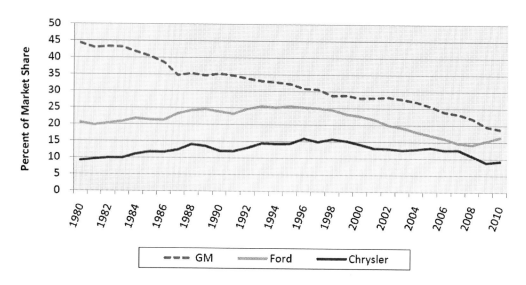

Figure 4. Big 3 Total U.S. Market Share, 1980 to 2010[48].

4. Pricing

Finally, the industry has also benefited from a reduction in sales promotions (as its inventory management has improved, in line with a more sustainable utilization rate), which has resulted in a steadily higher average transaction price per vehicle sold. Figure 5 below shows the average transaction price per vehicle as a percentage of the Manufacturer Suggested Retail Price (MSRP). This measure reached a trough of 75 percent in August of 2009 as the industry struggled to unload unsold inventory, but has since increased to 84 percent in October 2010, eclipsing pre-crisis levels.

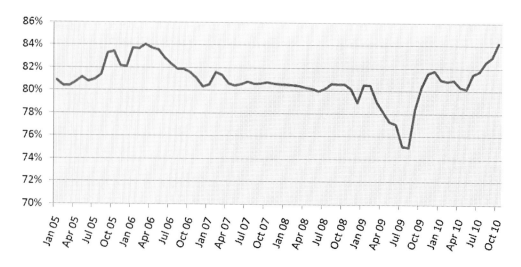

Figure 5. Transaction Price as a Percentage of MSRP[49].

5. Outlook

Putting all of the aforementioned factors together, the industry's financial outlook has improved considerably over the past two years. Despite a historically weak backdrop of U.S. sales, the industry is now reporting strong profits. The combination of greatly reduced capacity, generally stable market share, and improved pricing has more than offset persistently weak (but improving) demand. Thus, many industry observers believe that an improvement in the economy will result in a disproportionate increase in profitability, as the industry will be able to increase production without incurring meaningful new investment costs. Meanwhile, sales outside the United States – particularly in the emerging markets of Brazil, Russia, India, and China – are pacing an improving long-term sales outlook, as these markets overtake the United States as the key driver of incremental industry demand.

The auto industry's average U.S. seasonally adjusted annual rate (SAAR) for the year-to-date period through the end of December 2010 is 12.5 million sales. This compares to 11.1 million in the corresponding year-ago period.[50] However, this level is still 29 percent below the average SAAR of 16.3 million in the 10 years preceding 2006. Nonetheless, the industry's lower cost base has made it possible for the auto companies to return to profitability at this level.[51] Industry experts forecast improvements in sales of roughly one million units per year for both 2011 and 2012.[52]

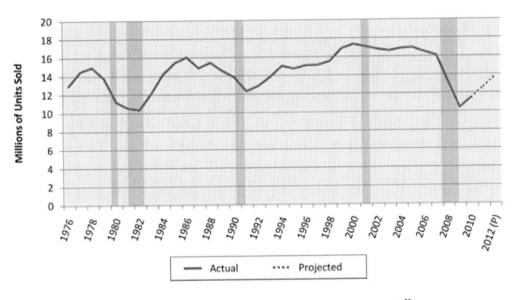

Figure 6. Light Vehicle Sales, Autos and Trucks, Millions of Units Sold (SAAR)[53].

As noted earlier, the auto industry is also benefitting from rising global sales. According to estimates by J.D. Power & Associates, worldwide light vehicle sales may rise to 71.1 million vehicles, surpassing the previous record of 70.3 million units in 2007. These forecasts highlight the importance of non-U.S. markets to the viability and profitability of the U.S. auto companies: GM sells far more cars outside the United States than it does domestically. While GM North America delivered 661,000 vehicles in the third quarter of 2010, GM delivered 567,000 vehicles in China alone, an additional 391,000 in Europe, and another 447,000 in the rest of the globe. GM holds 18.3 percent of Brazil's market share, same as its U.S. market share.[54] (However, earnings overall are still strongly driven by North America. GM reported in the third quarter of 2010 that $2.1 billion of its earnings before interest and taxes (EBIT) came from its North American branch, whereas its European branch lost $0.6 billion, and the rest of its international operations only earned $0.6 billion.) This global growth in sales has been paced by rapid increases in demand in Brazil, Russia, India, and China, which now account for 34 percent of industry sales, compared to 9 percent in 2000.[55] Within the next five years, the percentage of sales in these countries and other developing markets is forecast to outstrip that of mature markets (North America, Europe, and Japan).[56]

Some industry analysts are very bullish on the U.S. auto recovery, taking the view that improved capacity usage, reduced labor costs, and global platforms can produce sustainable profits.[57] The global auto industry, however, is highly cyclical and sensitive to changes in consumer sentiment, employment, interest rates, gasoline prices, and general economic activity.[58] In the absence of any improvements in the United States in employment, housing, credit-based spending, and the equity markets, a near-term recovery in demand for automobiles may be harder to achieve.[59]

D. General Motors

1. Context

a. Background and the Government Intervention

One of America's largest and most storied corporations, GM enjoyed a highly profitable stretch during the 1990s. Its stock price peaked above $93 in April 2000, up from $27.50 in late 1991. This decade of success was built largely on sales of GM's light trucks and sport utility vehicles (SUVs), as well as the high profit margins generated by GMAC/Ally Financial, a finance arm that initially focused on automobiles, but over time evolved into a more diversified financial services firm. By 2005, though, GM was losing money. High gasoline prices had dampened consumer demand for its vehicles, which lagged behind competitors in fuel efficiency, and its market share declined. GM was also hurt by an unsustainable cost structure, largely due to the high cost of its retiree health care and pension benefits. GM's investment in automobile design lagged behind competitors, which led to further erosion in the company's market share. It all added up to a spiral of decline.

In 2006, GM sold much of its ownership in GMAC/Ally Financial, which at the time remained profitable. The two firms remained highly interdependent under agreements that kept GMAC/Ally Financial as the largest financier of GM automobile purchases. But the sale of GMAC/Ally Financial proved to be a stop-gap measure for GM, since in 2007 the automaker posted a staggering loss of more than $38 billion. The recession that began in December 2007 took a toll on all manufacturers in the highly cyclical auto industry, but GM, with its high fixed costs and increasingly uncompetitive vehicles, was particularly vulnerable. In the fall of 2008, amid the credit crisis, the firm was unable to fund its operations using private-sector lenders, and appealed to Congress for an emergency bailout.

The Bush and Obama Administrations provided multiple rounds of TARP assistance to GM, culminating in a rapid bankruptcy restructuring in June 2009.[60] Out of this process, a new company emerged: General Motors Company (New GM).[61] This new entity shed Old GMs least valuable assets and most burdensome liabilities.[62] To help achieve the transition to a new, leaner company, Treasury invested a total of $49.9 billion in GM.[63]

b. Impact of Changes in Tax Rules

Like certain other TARP recipients, GM may receive additional benefits from the government as a result of certain Treasury-issued guidance[64] concerning the rules applicable to carrying forward net operating losses (NOLs).[65] The ability to carry forward an NOL allows corporations to offset future taxable income with losses from prior years, thereby reducing future tax liabilities.[66] However, the use of NOL carryforwards is subject to various limitations. One provision in the Internal Revenue Code limits the amount of taxable income that a corporation may offset in years following an ownership change.[67]

This limitation would have had a significant impact on numerous TARP recipients, since several of them experienced a change in ownership, as a result of government investments and the disposition of those investments. Treasury issued several notices that applied only to TARP recipients, and addressed the application of the ownership change rules in the context of the government's investment in TARP recipients.[68] These notices established the definition of "change in ownership" as applied to TARP recipients, in general ignoring changes in the government's equity ownership in determining whether a "change in ownership" has occurred. GM was a beneficiary of the tax notices, while Chrysler and GMAC/Ally Financial did not benefit because they were limited liability companies at the time they received government funds and were treated as pass-through entities for federal income tax purposes.

GM has reported approximately $9.1 billion in U.S. federal and state NOL carry-forwards.[69] The actual financial impact of Treasury's tax notices to GM is difficult to determine and will depend on the company's future income.[70] Nonetheless, the favorable rules provided in the notices are likely to affect GM's value.

It is important to note that the change-in-ownership restrictions were intended to prevent companies from buying other firms for the purpose of benefitting from their tax losses. GM's situation following the government rescue was a different case, since the government did not invest in GM with the purpose of benefitting from GM's tax losses. Nonetheless, the Panel has noted previously with respect to TARP-recipient banks that the favorable tax guidance pitted "Treasury's responsibilities as TARP administrator, regulator, and tax administrator against one another," and that these notices fuel "the perception that income tax flexibility is especially, and quickly, available for large financial institutions at a time of general economic difficulty."[71] This observation would appear to apply with equal validity to Treasury's rescue of GM. On the other hand, it is possible that the favorable tax guidance will contribute to greater profitability and market value of GM, which will in turn enhance the value, and improve the recovery, of the taxpayers' investment.[72]

2. More Recent Developments

Following the formation of New GM, approximately $39.3 billion of Treasury's original investment was converted into common equity, resulting in a government stake representing 60.8 percent of GM's common equity.[73] The remaining government investment was split between $7.1 billion in debt, $2.1 billion in New GM preferred stock, and $986 million in the form of a loan to Old GM. In a series of payments between July 2009 and April 2010, GM repaid the $7.1 billion in debt that it owed to Treasury.[74] New GM has also repurchased from Treasury the $2.1 billion in New GM preferred stock.[75] The $986 million government loan to Old GM remains outstanding.

After GM's bankruptcy, Treasury officials played a significant role in the selection of a new CEO, Edward Whitacre, Jr., who was named to the position on December 1, 2009.[76]

Treasury also appointed four members of the GM board.[77] On August 12, 2010, GM announced that Mr. Whitacre would step down as CEO on September 1, 2010 and be replaced by Daniel Akerson, a Treasury-appointed member of GM's board of directors.[78] As a recipient of "exceptional financial assistance," GM is also subject to the executive compensation determinations of Patricia Geoghegan, Treasury's Special Master of TARP Executive Compensation, who replaced Kenneth Feinberg as "pay czar."[79]

On July 22, 2010, GM announced the $3.5 billion acquisition of AmeriCredit, an automotive finance firm that specializes in subprime auto lending.[80] Several of GM's competitors, such as Ford and Toyota, have in-house financing divisions, which are often called "captive" financing arms. And following GM's sale of GMAC/Ally Financial in 2006, industry analysts cited GM's lack of a captive financing arm as a competitive disadvantage.[81] Now that GM has acquired AmeriCredit, GM says that it still considers GMAC/Ally Financial to be a key strategic partner, but that AmeriCredit provides GM with more financial alternatives, and that AmeriCredit provides an auto financing platform that GM can build out.[82]

Throughout much of 2010, GM was preparing for an initial public offering (IPO), a process that promised to allow Treasury to sell its stake in GM's common stock.[83] The final underwriting agreement consisted of 35 underwriters, both large and small firms.[84] Treasury negotiated an underwriting fee of 0.75 percent, as opposed to a more customary figure of 2 or 3 percent for an IPO of comparable size.[85] Although the IPO was expected to price at a range of between $26 and $29, strong investor enthusiasm during the company's road show presentations resulted in the offering being six times oversubscribed.[86] Subsequently, the price was increased to $33.[87]

The IPO took place on November 18, 2010, when GM common stock began trading under the ticker "GM" on the New York Stock Exchange (NYSE).[88] Total funds generated in this offering were $23.1 billion, before accounting for underwriting fees and commissions.[89] Based on total funds raised, the IPO was the largest IPO in U.S. history.[90]

GM's stock performed well throughout its first day of trading, with the common stock settling at a price of $34.19.[91] President Obama applauded the IPO, noting that "American taxpayers are now positioned to recover more than my administration invested in GM."[92] He stated that because GM's management had made the "tough decisions necessary to make themselves more competitive in the 21st century – the American auto industry – an industry that's been the proud symbol of America's manufacturing might for a century; an industry that helped to build our middle class – is once again on the rise."[93]

On November, 26, 2010, GM announced that its underwriters exercised in full their so-called over-allotment options to purchase an additional 71.7 million shares of common stock from the selling stockholders, for a total of $2.37 billion, plus an additional 13 million shares of mandatory convertible junior preferred stock from the company, for a total of $650 million.[94]

Original Investment Date	Original Assistance Amount	Original Investment Type	Exchange	Current Investment Type	Cumulative Investment Amount	Amount Repaid
12/29/2008	$884	Loan	Exchanged for GMAC Equity	—	—	
12/31/2008	13,400	Loan with additional notes	Old GM debt credit bid; New GM equity received	New GM common equity	$13,400	
4/22/2009	2,000	Loan with additional notes	Old GM debt credit bid; New GM equity received	New GM common equity	2,000	
5/20/2009	4,000	Loan with additional notes	Old GM debt credit bid; New GM equity received	New GM common equity	4,000	
5/27/2009	361	Loan with additional notes	Old GM debt credit bid; New GM equity received	New GM common equity	361	$361
6/3/2009	30,100	Loan with additional notes (see breakdown below)			30,100	
			Old GM debt credit bid; New GM equity received	New GM common equity	19,942	
			Became New GM loan	New GM loan	7,072	6,712
			Became New GM preferred stock	New GM preferred stock	2,100	2,139
			Remained Old GM loan	Old GM loan	986	
Total	$50,745				$49,861	[99]$22,717

Figure 7. TARP Investment in GM (millions of dollars).

Net proceeds from the sale of common stock for existing GM shareholders totaled $18.0 billion. Net proceeds from the sale of preferred stock were $4.9 billion, which compared favorably to GM's November 17 estimate of preferred stock proceeds of $3.9 billion-$4.4 billion,[95] bringing the total net proceeds to $22.9 billion. Some of GM's proceeds from the sale of the preferred shares went to redeem Treasury's $2.1 billion in preferred stock holdings. GM anticipates that it will contribute $2.0 billion in common stock to its U.S. hourly and salaried pension plans, in addition to a $4.0 billion cash contribution to the pension plans that it announced on December 2, 2010.[96]

In total, the sales of GM stock produced $13.5 billion in receipts to the Treasury.[97] Including exercise of the over-allotment option, Treasury sold over 412 million shares of the total 550 million shares sold. Treasury still holds more than 500 million shares, or 33.3 percent ownership of GM.[98] During its first three weeks on the NYSE, GM's stock traded at between $33.17 and $34.89 per share. Figure 7 shows the amount and current status of the government's various investments in GM. Of the $49.9 billion in government assistance, $27.2 billion currently remains outstanding.

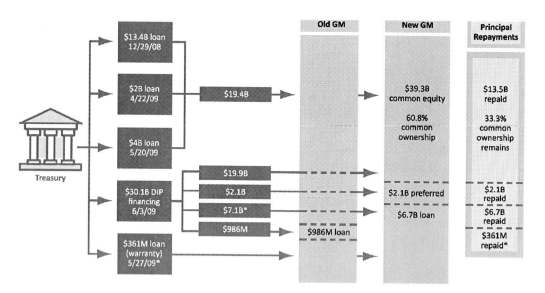

* The three boxes with asterisks were part of a transaction executed as part of GM's bankruptcy. The $361 million to Old GM, which was used to provide a government backstop on warranties for GM vehicles, was credit bid into New GM debt as part of the bankruptcy and then repaid on July 10, 2009, using funds from the $7.1 billion portion of the government's bankruptcy financing of GM.

Figure 8. TARP Funds Committed to GM.

3. *Outlook*

While Treasury's investment in GM provided a backstop for a company on the brink of failure, the rescue forced taxpayers to bear considerable risk, risk they will continue to bear until Treasury disposes of the remainder of its investment in the company. This section examines the viability of GM, an issue that will impact the outcome of the government's investment in the company.

a. GM's Emerging Business Model
GM's strategy for improving its business model focuses on four key areas:

(1) streamlining operations so as to improve capacity utilization;[100]
(2) reducing labor costs;
(3) strengthening competitiveness in international markets; and
(4) reducing financial leverage in order to improve the company's balance sheet.[101]

i. Streamlining Operations
GM is taking a number of steps in order to streamline its operations. First, it plans to reduce the total number of plants it operates in the United States from the 47 it had in 2008 to 34 by the end of 2010 and to 31 by 2012.[102]

Second, GM has reduced the number of brands it offers in the United States from eight to four. GM's four core brands are Chevrolet, GMC, Cadillac, and Buick, which is the fastest growing automotive brand in the United States.[103] GM has discontinued or divested Pontiac, Saturn, Saab, and Hummer.[104] October 2010 calendar-year-to-date retail sales for GM's four core brands were up 15 percent, and total sales were up 22 percent.[105] Year-to-date through October, GM's four core brands sold 85,737 more units than its eight brands sold during the same period in 2009.[106]

Third, GM has also announced a goal of reducing its number of domestic dealerships from approximately 5,000 as of September 30, 2010 to 4,500 by the end of 2010. GM expects these reductions to produce cost savings over time, but it also recognizes that they could also have the effect of reducing GM's U.S. market share.[107] Despite these closings, GM continues to maintain an independent international network of 21,000 dealers.[108]

As a result of these efforts, as well as an underlying improvement in sales, UBS estimates that GM's capacity utilization, which measures the company's actual output as a percentage of its potential output, will improve from 43 percent in 2009 to 74 percent in 2010.[109] UBS expects GM's capacity utilization to fall in 2011 before rising again in 2012 and beyond.[110]

ii. Reducing Labor Costs
GM has sought to use the restructuring to reduce the cost of its hourly labor force.[111] More specifically, it has reduced the number of its employees, restructured its labor agreement, and transferred its health care obligations to the UAW's Voluntary Employee Benefit Association (VEBA).[112] Overall, GM states that it has reduced its U.S. hourly labor costs from $16 billion in 2005 to $5 billion in 2010.[113] It also states that it has reduced the number of hourly employees in the United States from 111,000 in 2005 to 50,000 in 2010.[114] Since 2008, the company has reduced its global workforce by about 35,000 employees, including about 11,000 hourly employees in United States,[115] though the number of employees has risen since GM emerged from bankruptcy in 2009. The company believes, and industry analysts concur, that a more competitive cost structure will allow GM to compete better for market share.

iii. Improving International Competitiveness
GM also states that is enhancing its competitiveness in international markets. According to the presentation GM used in its retail road show,[116] it is refocusing on emerging markets, with a particular focus on Brazil, Russia, India, and China.[117] In 2009, 72 percent of GM's

total sales volume came from outside the United States, including 39 percent from emerging markets.[118]

GM's market share in Brazil, Russia, India, and China grew from 9.8 percent in 2004 to 12.7 percent in 2009.[119] It has the number one market share position in those four nations as a whole, and it occupies the top spot in China as well.[120] GM projects that Brazil, Russia, India, and China have the largest growth potential of any markets in the world.[121]

IV. Reducing Leverage

GM is seeking to reduce its leverage in order to lower the cost of servicing its debt and become less vulnerable to the ups and downs of the automotive industry's business cycle.[122] GM also intends to fund its pension plans fully. To that end, GM on December 2, 2010, announced the aforementioned voluntary $4 billion cash contribution to its U.S. pension plans.[123] More broadly, the company stated in its November 2010 public offering presentation that it has $24 billion in available liquidity, as compared to about $35 billion in underfunded pension obligations, debt, and perpetual preferred shares.[124] Reducing its debt burden should allow GM to strengthen its credit rating; the company is seeking to achieve a strong investment grade rating.[125]

b. Results

GM's most recent financial statements provide four key indicators of improvement in overall performance: revenue and sales, credit ratings, market share, and access to financing.[126] While it may be too soon in the business cycle to discern trends, GM's initial financial and operating ratios are improving. Both return on assets and return on sales have increased gradually through 2010.[127] In total, GM sold 8.2 million units worldwide during the 12-month period ending September 30, 2010.[128] Net revenue totals for each of the first three quarters of 2010 were more than $30 billion.[129] (These revenue totals are comparable to GM's revenue results in 2009. In the second half of 2009, GM's total net sales and revenue were $57.5 billion.)[130] However, as analysts have noted, the company is able to sell its products at higher prices and has improved its margins materially.[131] In North America specifically, sales in the third quarter of 2010 were $21.5 billion versus $14.4 billion in the same quarter a year prior.[132] In addition, GM expanded its North American operations by adding 3,000 employees between January 1 and September 30, 2010.[133] On November 30, GM announced plans to hire an additional 1,000 engineers and researchers in Michigan.[134]

On October 6, 2010, the credit rating agency Fitch gave GM the Issuer Default Rating[135] of BB-, non-investment grade or speculative, the same as Ford.[136] While GM has considerably less debt than Ford, Fitch noted that GM's large pension obligations dwarf those of Ford. GM is rated as having a stable outlook by four different credit agencies.[137] While it is not clear what GM's credit ratings would be absent government support, Standard & Poor's states that it does not give GM a ratings boost because of the government's investment.[138]

GM is seeking to lower its "breakeven point," the number of cars that the company needs in order for its revenues to equal its costs. Doing so, will enable GM to remain profitable even at the bottom of the business cycle. In its U.S. operations, GM has reduced its break-even point from an industry-wide sales total of 15.5 million units in the third quarter of 2007 to less than 11 million units in the fall of 2010.[139] In 2007, GM needed a 25 percent market share, or roughly 3.88 million vehicles sold out of a market of 15.5 million, in order to break even. Today, GM needs a market share of less than 19 percent, or approximately 2.09 million vehicles sold out of a market of 11 million.[140] In sum, GM is now able to break even with a smaller share of a smaller market. This improvement has been driven in part by the reduction in labor costs, in addition to improvements in vehicle pricing.[141] For example, average transaction prices for the Chevrolet Equinox are up $3,900 from 2009 to 2010, and Buick LaCrosse average transaction prices are up $7,500 over the same period.[142]

GM's overall market share has been falling in both the United States and Europe. In the United States, GM's market share fell from 28.6 percent in 2002 to 22.2 percent in 2008, and then to an estimated 19.0 percent in 2010. In Europe, GM's market share fell from 10.2 percent in 2000 to 9.3 percent in 2008, and then to 8.1 percent in 2010.[143] GM's post-bankruptcy declines in market share likely stem at least in part from the company's decision to discontinue certain brands and to reduce consumer incentives for vehicle purchases.

4. Treasury's Exit Strategy

Between April and November 2010, Treasury interacted closely with GM in an attempt to ensure that Treasury had all relevant market demand information prior to the IPO to help determine how much of its stock it should sell and at what price.[144] Treasury conducted due diligence, relying heavily on the input of its advisor, Lazard Ltd. Lazard also handled many of the direct interactions with the IPO's underwriters. In making determinations about the volume and price of its stock sales, Treasury states that it sought to abide by its shareholder principles, balancing the desire to exit as soon as practicable against its objective of maximizing the value of the taxpayers' investment. Consistent with these principles, according to Treasury, it sought to leave GM in charge of day-to-day management decisions, including the selection of underwriters and timing of the IPO. Treasury also worked closely with the underwriters – rather than the company – to determine the timing and pricing of the government's sale of GM stock.[145] GM states that it decided the timing of the IPO, though it did have discussions with Treasury about the issue. The company also states that Treasury's primary role was related to how many shares it would eventually choose to sell.[146]

Treasury sold nearly 40 percent of its equity stake through the IPO. Despite the possibility that the value of GM's equity could increase within the next year as a result of a continued market recovery, the seasoning of GM's management, and a slate of new automobiles due to be released, Treasury maintains that it decided not to postpone the sale of its shares – or revise the amount being offered – for several reasons. While market risk and execution risk were two significant concerns, Treasury also said that it was important to signal to the market that the government intended to exit its investment and return the funding of the company to private hands.[147]

After the offering, Treasury's total stake in the company fell from 60.8 percent to 36.9 percent. When the underwriters exercised their over-allotment option on November 26, Treasury's stake fell to 33.3 percent.[148] As is customary for many IPOs, Treasury will be unable to begin selling the remainder of its investment for 180 days following the IPO. After this lockup period ends, Treasury maintains that it will look to sell the remainder of its shares in accordance with its shareholder principles and subject to market events.[149]

a. Analysis of Treasury's Exit Strategy

The strong investor demand for GM's IPO stands in stark contrast to the company's predicament in the fall of 2008. Yet despite the improvements that GM has achieved in a relatively short period of time, there is still uncertainty regarding the taxpayers' investment in

GM. This section examines GM's efforts to transform itself into a far more viable entity. While the outlook is more positive than it was two years ago, the GM investment is still likely to result in an overall loss for taxpayers.

i. GM Emerged from the Restructuring as a Far More Viable Business

According to industry analysts, GM has emerged from the restructuring as a far more viable business, positioned to take advantage of its streamlined cost structure and a competitive labor situation to return to profitability.[150] That GM is a much improved business is evidenced by its results from the first three quarters of 2010,[151] as well as the strong demand for shares in the IPO.[152] The company has successfully executed many of its core objectives for the restructuring: streamlining its capacity, shedding labor costs, and refocusing its efforts on high-growth international markets. Although, significant uncertainty remains for the company, the company's efforts to refocus its business strategy and shed costs have substantially increased the likelihood that taxpayers will suffer minimal losses on their investment, or perhaps even be repaid in full.

ii. Uncertainty Remains

The Panel has identified three sources of uncertainty that could have a negative impact on GM's stock price: international markets, GM's long-term competitive viability, and GM's longterm obligations and legacy liabilities. From the perspective of U.S. taxpayers, this uncertainty is important because Treasury is likely to continue to hold a stake in GM through most of 2011 and perhaps into 2012.

International Markets

The company still faces uncertainty with respect to certain operating units going forward, particularly in Europe, which accounts for 22 percent of the company's sales.[153] GM has a restructuring plan for its European operations, similar to its U.S. plan, that seeks to cut European capacity by 20 percent, reduce labor costs by about $320 million per year, and improve the weak image of the Opel brand among European consumers.[154] But GM's restructuring plans in Europe are lagging behind its American efforts – the company will not complete the European restructuring for at least a year.[155] In the meantime GM is generating significant losses in Europe.[156]

In addition, competition will likely increase in many of GM's higher growth markets. GM's market share in developing nations has been growing: the company is first in Chinese market share, third in Brazilian market share, and third in Russian market share. But analysts believe that GM's foothold in these markets is somewhat unstable, given the sharp competition, and they project that GM's market share in Brazil and China will decline by 2015.[157] Early indicators suggest that this trend may have already begun, as reflected in a market share decline in Brazil from 19.9 percent to 18.3 percent during 2010.[158] Furthermore, the potential upside for GM in China is limited by the fact that it is required to operate as a joint venture that only takes a proportional share of the profits.[159] On the other hand, GM starts from a strong position in China, Brazil, and Russia, and any future losses in market share may be more than offset by the growth of those markets.

Competitive Viability

There are also questions about the competitive viability of GM over both the short term and the long term. In the short term, the questions involve what is generally seen as a lackluster product launch schedule in 2011, particularly in the United States, where its market share faces pressure from Ford.[160] GM launched 28 new vehicles in 2010, but just four of those launches were in the United States. The story for 2011 is similar, with 27 product launches planned, of which four are for the United States. GM's product lineup is expected to improve in later years, with 37 product launches, including 15 U.S. launches, planned for 2013.[161]

Over the long term, there are still questions about GM's ability to develop new products that respond to – or drive – market demand. In particular, the company must be able to compete in the development of fuel-efficient technologies. To that end, it is encouraging that the electric Chevrolet Volt was recently named Motor Trend's 2011 Car of the Year,[162] but the outcome of GM's large investment in the Volt remains unclear. The Volt will compete against an increasingly crowded field of fuel-efficient vehicles, including the new Nissan Leaf. It is unclear whether the Volt, which uses lithium batteries that will eventually need to be replaced, will prevail over the hybrid technology being pursued by competitors.[163]

Senior officials at GM expect the Chevrolet Cruze to become an alternative to the Ford Focus, Honda Civic, and Toyota Corolla in the small-car segment – traditionally a less profitable but rather large segment of U.S. car sales – but at this point the newly launched Cruze lacks a significant track record of sales in the United States. Moreover, while it is encouraging that average transaction prices have increased in GM's crossover segment – vehicles that combine elements of cars and SUVs – such increases have not been as widespread in GM's car and truck portfolios.[164]

Long-Term Obligations and Legacy Liabilities

While GM shed many of its most onerous liabilities during the restructuring, several long-term obligations remain. Estimates differ on how much money GM will need to contribute to underfunded pensions and other post-retirement employee benefits (OPEB) over the short and long term. The company has disclosed that as of September 30, 2010, its underfunded pension liability was $29.4 billon.[165] At the same time, GM's underfunded OPEB stood at $9.4 billion.[166] The company expects to disburse nearly $8.4 billion per year from 2011-2014 in net benefit payments for its U.S. pension plans, plus $1.4 billion per year for its non-U.S. pensions plans.[167]

Old GM, whose remaining assets include unsold manufacturing plants and equipment, also has significant legacy liabilities that could eventually impose costs on taxpayers. Old GM has created four separate trusts to pay off environmental claims, unsecured creditors, asbestos claims, and litigation claims. More than 70,000 claims for more than $275 billion have been made against all four Old GM trusts, but more than $150 billion in claims have been resolved or eliminated.[168] It is unclear what the recovery rate on claims will be. In August 2010, Old GM proposed a bankruptcy plan that would make $536 million available to handle environmental claims. In October 2010, Old GM agreed to a $773 million settlement to resolve its liabilities at 89 Old GM sites.[169] The company anticipates the majority of the environmental remediation will be completed or under way in five years.[170]

In the event that there are more than $35.0 billion in unsecured claims against Old GM, New GM will be obligated to issue shares of its common stock to Old GM, diluting

Treasury's and other shareholders'stakes in New GM.[171] Treasury also continues to have direct exposure to Old GM as a result of its $986 million loan to the company.

iii. Taxpayers Likely to Suffer Some Losses on Their Investment in GM

To date, Treasury has provided only aggregate data on projected losses across the auto sector, and it has not yet provided data on projected losses by each individual institution. On September 30, 2010, Treasury estimated an overall loss of $14.7 billion to the government from federal support of GM, Chrysler, and GMAC/Ally Financial.[172] Speaking more recently to the Automotive Press Association, Steven Rattner, former head of the Presidential Task Force on the Auto Industry, estimated Treasury's loss exposure on the entire automotive rescue at less than $10 billion.[173] While it is not clear precisely how much Treasury expects to lose on its GM investment specifically, its aggregate projections suggest that it envisions at least some losses on GM.[174]

Pricing the GM IPO far below the break-even price may have had the effect of greatly reducing the likelihood that taxpayers will be fully repaid, as full repayment will not be possible unless the government is able to sell its remaining shares at a far higher price. However, it is impossible to know if a longer-term investment horizon by the government (via an IPO at a later date) would have allowed Treasury to sell its shares at a more favorable price, closer to its break-even cost basis. Prior to the IPO, Treasury needed to sell each of its shares for an aggregate price of $44.59 in order to break even.[175] After the initial public offering and the exercising of the over-allotment option by the underwriters, Treasury will need to sell its remaining stake – 500,065,254 shares – for an average of $52.75 in order to recoup fully its investment.[176] If one subtracts out the value of GM's various dividend and interest payments to Treasury, the break-even share price rises to $54.28.

However, the Panel recognizes that it is impossible to time the market, and that delaying the IPO would have exposed Treasury to the risk that the price that buyers were willing to pay for GM stock would fall. Moreover, as detailed in Section H.1, retaining the stock for a long period could have conflicted with the government's stated objective of disposing of its shares "as soon as practicable." There was also the possibility that a delay would have resulted in uncertainty in the market, as Treasury was concerned about how Old GM bondholders – who received 10 percent of the stock in New GM – would exercise their rights in the wake of the restructuring.[177] Aside from a delay, Treasury had two additional alternatives: to sell a smaller percentage of its holdings in an IPO and a larger portion in subsequent secondary offerings, or to use the IPO to dispose of as many shares as possible, no matter the price.

While it is difficult to ascertain whether the government could have been more flexible in its timing, or whether a delayed timeline would have resulted in a higher return for taxpayers, the decision to sell a large number of shares below the break-even price decreased the chances that taxpayers will be repaid in full.[178]

E. Chrysler

1. Context

a. Background and the Government Intervention

Chrysler, long the smallest of the "Big Three" U.S. automakers, first faced bankruptcy and turned to the U.S. government for help in the late 1970s. At that time, Chrysler petitioned for and received $1.5 billion in federal government loan guarantees. The loans were then repaid in 1983, ahead of schedule. In 1984, Chrysler introduced the minivan, which has remained a major source of sales for the company ever since. In 1987, Chrysler bought American Motors Corporation (AMC), including the Jeep brand, another important contributor to the company's sales.[179] In 1997, following several years of strong performance, Chrysler was acquired by Daimler-Benz of Germany for $37 billion, in what was the largest foreign takeover of a U.S. firm to that date. In 2007, after several years of losses, Daimler effectively paid for Cerberus Capital, a U.S. private equity fund, to assume control of Chrysler, in an 80-20 partnership.

Following several years of losses, Chrysler faced imminent bankruptcy in late 2008, having lost $5.3 billion in the first three quarters of that year alone.[180] Chrysler's losses were due to its poor sales performance and high fixed costs. In December 2008, the Bush Administration announced that it would use the TARP to assist Chrysler.[181] On January 2, 2009, Treasury loaned $4 billion to Chrysler Holdings, the parent of Old Chrysler,[182] as a temporary measure, while Chrysler prepared a longer-term viability plan. The viability plan prepared by Chrysler was rejected by President Obama's Auto Task Force on March 30, 2009, which concluded that Chrysler required a partner to achieve long-term viability.[183] Fiat, the Italian automobile manufacturer, was selected to take management control of Chrysler.[184] As detailed further below, in order to entice Fiat to take control of Chrysler's management, Fiat was offered a path to majority ownership of the company through various agreements signed as part of the restructuring. Consequently, Fiat is very much in control of how Chrysler's continued viability and valuation will evolve.

As part of Chrysler's pre-planned bankruptcy, Treasury provided financing that ultimately reached $3.8 billion, of which $1.9 billion was disbursed.[185] To capitalize New Chrysler, which came into existence on June 10, 2009, Treasury provided an additional loan facility of $6.6 billion repayable in two tranches under the First Lien Credit Agreement.[186] In addition, New Chrysler assumed $500 million of the $4 billion loaned to Chrysler Holdings, bringing the total face value of the Treasury loan exposure to New Chrysler to $7.1 billion. Treasury has effectively written off $3.5 billion associated with its Chrysler investment. This total includes the $1.6 billion portion of the loan to Chrysler Holdings that was not assumed by New Chrysler due to bankruptcy law and financial reasons, as well as the entirety of the $1.9 billion in DIP financing.[187] Treasury received a 9.8 percent equity stake in New Chrysler pursuant to the restructuring agreements.[188]

As with its other AIFP investments, Treasury's current primary focus with respect to Chrysler is to recover the TARP funds it has provided to that firm. However, the manner in which the investment was structured limits Treasury's ability to control the course of events at Chrysler. In addition to Fiat and Treasury, there are two other participants in the Chrysler restructuring: the UAW's VEBA and the Canadian government. These actors have their own sets of interests and incentives, which adds an additional layer of complexity to the transaction and may further constrain Treasury's ability to exercise its rights fully. Moreover, as detailed below, the complex and interrelated contractual arrangements involving the various parties make it difficult to assess the level of recovery for the taxpayers under various possible future scenarios, including a potential Chrysler IPO.

The government is likely to recover the TARP loans provided to Chrysler directly,[189] but any additional recovery will depend on when and under what conditions Treasury will be able to sell its equity stake. This section examines the structure of the government's investment in Chrysler, as well as the most likely potential exit scenarios and their consequences.

For a table summarizing the monies paid to the various Chrysler entities over time, see Figure 9 below.

b. Current Ownership Structure and Possible Changes

Chrysler is currently owned by four parties: Treasury, the Canadian Government, the UAW's VEBA, and Fiat. Each of these parties contributed funds or resources to New Chrysler and received equity and/or debt claims on Chrysler in exchange for its contribution. Furthermore, several agreements between these four parties give specific parties the right to increase their equity stakes in Chrysler. In particular, Fiat has a variety of options to achieve majority ownership of the company.

Fiat owns a 20 percent equity stake, along with management control of Chrysler, which it received in exchange for Chrysler gaining access to various Fiat technologies and Fiat's international distribution networks.[194] Fiat did not make any cash contribution in exchange for this equity stake in Chrysler. The Canadian government invested in New Chrysler, through a $2.2 billion loan,[195] and received 2.5 percent of the equity.[196] Also as part of the restructuring, the UAW's VEBA took a note with a face value of $4.7 billion,[197] and 67.7 percent of the equity in New Chrysler,[198] in exchange for various concessions on wages and benefits,[199] and the assumption of responsibility for health care costs for retired UAW Chrysler workers. This initially left Treasury with the remaining 9.8 percent of equity.[200]

The four equity owners of Chrysler are all party to the Amended and Restated Limited Liability Company Operating Agreement of Chrysler Group LLC (Operating Agreement), which governs how Chrysler is currently being strategically managed.[201] This agreement, signed on June 10, 2009,[202] contains numerous clauses that can lead to a change in Chrysler's ownership structure. Several clauses give Fiat certain rights to increase its equity, while others grant certain rights to the other parties, including Treasury. These agreements work with each other, and actions by one party in some cases are necessary to trigger the right of other parties to exercise their respective options. Going forward, much will depend on whether and when a Chrysler IPO occurs.

i. Fiat's Options to Increase its Equity Share

Fiat may increase its equity ownership in Chrysler in a number of ways. It is important to note, however, that Fiat may only acquire a controlling interest after Chrysler repays all TARP and Canadian government loans extended to it. First, the Operating Agreement provides that Fiat's equity stake will increase by 5 percent if and when each of the following performance targets[203] is met:

- Chrysler builds a 40 mile-per-gallon (MPG) car in the United States;
- Chrysler builds a next-generation engine in a U.S. factory, based on Fiat technology;[204]
- Fiat sells Chrysler vehicles through its international distribution network.[205]

Original Investment Date	Original Assistance Amount	Original Investment Type	Exchange	Current Investment Type	Cumulative Investment Amount	Amount Repaid	Amount Lost
1/2/2009	$4,000	Debt Obligation w/	$500 million assumed by	Loan	$3,500	$1,900	$(1,600)
		Additional Note	New Chrysler on 5/27/09				
4/29/2009	280	Debt Obligation w/		Loan	280	280	
		Additional Note					
5/1/2009	1,888	Debt Obligation w/		Loan	1,888		[191](1,888)
		Additional Note					
5/27/2009	6,642	Debt Obligation w/	$500 million assumed by	Loan	[192]7,142		
		Additional Note	New Chrysler on 5/27/09				
Total	$12,810				$12,810	$2,180	$(3,488)

Figure 9. TARP Investments in Chrysler (millions of dollars).

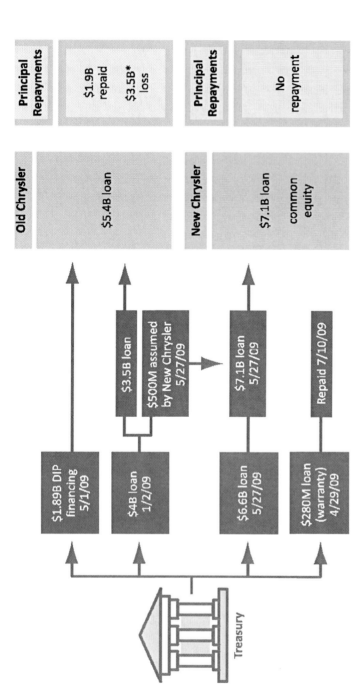

Figure 10. TARP Funds Committed to Chrysler[193].

If all three targets are met, then Fiat's equity stake will increase by 15 percent, and it will own 35 percent of Chrysler's equity – without having to make any payments to the other equity holders. As Fiat's ownership share increases to 35 percent, that of the other three owners will be diluted; the VEBA will then directly own 55 percent of the equity, Treasury 8 percent, and the Canadian government 2 percent.[206]

To date, the company has not met any of the targets that would trigger an increase in Fiat's equity stake of New Chrysler. However, it is generally expected that these targets will ultimately be reached.[207]

In addition to meeting these performance targets, Fiat has other avenues to increase its equity ownership, providing the opportunity to gain majority control of Chrysler. The following options are available to Fiat:

- Fiat has the right to increase its equity stake by up to 16 percent, under certain conditions, diluting the other three parties proportionally (the Incremental Equity Call Option).[208] The exercise of this option may occur before, simultaneous to, or after a Chrysler IPO, provided that Chrysler has repaid the TARP and Canadian government loans. The price for this option is set at a market-based formulaic price prior to the IPO or a market price after the IPO.
- Fiat also has a right to buy up to 40 percent of the VEBA's equity stake at a market-based formulaic price prior to the IPO or a market price after the IPO, subject to an adjustment for taxes (the VEBA Call Option).[209]
- Fiat has a right to buy any and all equity interest that Treasury may have in Chrysler (the Treasury Call Option).[210] This option may be exercised by Fiat during the 12-month period following the repayment in full of all TARP loans at an exercise price equal to a market price in the event that a Chrysler IPO takes place, or using a "dueling investment banks" method to determine the price otherwise.[211] Even though this agreement makes use of market prices in the event an IPO has happened, it nevertheless gives Fiat certain control over when Treasury could sell any remaining equity it might have. This could conflict with Treasury's ability to maximize its return from the investment, because Fiat controls the timing of the event.

ii. Treasury's Rights

The various options and rights granted to some of the parties in other agreements, beyond those mentioned above, mean that the current equity ownership percentages do not necessarily reflect the true economic interests of the various entities. One such agreement is the Equity Recapture Agreement, signed between Treasury and the UAW's VEBA on June 10, 2009. This agreement entitles Treasury to all proceeds from the sale of any of the VEBA's equity stake in Chrysler above a threshold amount, set at $4.25 billion and growing from January 1, 2010 at 9 percent per year (Threshold Amount).[212] The agreement also gives Treasury the right to acquire the entirety of the VEBA's equity stake for the then-applicable Threshold Amount.[213] This means that if the equity valuation of Chrysler exceeds a certain level, then Treasury and not the VEBA would be the majority economic beneficiary of such an increase in valuation.[214] As a practical matter, with the expiration of the TARP, Treasury does not currently have funds available to exercise its call option absent further congressional action to appropriate resources to Treasury's Auto Industry Financing Program.[215] As described above, Treasury will still passively benefit from any sales by the VEBA of its equity above the Threshold Amount, but in this case the VEBA will control the timing and volume of any sales. Hence, the expiration of the TARP may effectively preclude Treasury from following a more aggressive course of action to maximize the taxpayer's return on their investment in Chrysler. A private investor would likely choose the more aggressive path to maximizing profits. However, as described further below, Treasury, as a government entity, is not merely an investor and has a number of competing policy priorities to take into consideration.[216]

The accompanying box shows the various claims on Chrysler and among the four parties at the present time. It also illustrates how Fiat and the other stakeholders are likely to exercise the options they hold going forward over the next two years.

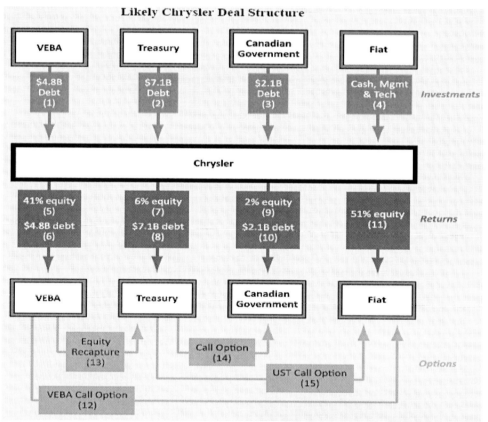

This diagram provides a summary of the various claims on Chrysler and among the four parties involved in the company's rescue. It illustrates each party's potential returns under the assumption that Fiat increases its equity stake to 51 percent by meeting the three performance targets – building a 40 MPG car in the United States, using Fiat technology to build a next-generation engine in a U.S. factory, and selling Chrysler vehicles through its international distribution network – and exercising the Incremental Equity Call Option. The following notes correspond to the numbers in parentheses and provide an explanation of each transaction in the diagram.

1) $4.8 billion in liabilities owed by Old Chrysler to the VEBA were assumed by New Chrysler.

2) Treasury committed financing. The total loan facility was $6.6 billion, of which $4.6 billion has been drawn down by Chrysler. New Chrysler also assumed $500 million of debt from Old Chrysler that was owed to Treasury.
3) The Canadian government contributed financing in parallel to that committed by Treasury. The total loan facility was $2.1 billion, of which $1.5 billion has been drawn down by Chrysler.
4) Fiat contributed management and technology to New Chrysler. Fiat did not contribute any financing. If Fiat exercises the Incremental Equity Call Option, as this graphic assumes, it will have to contribute money to Chrysler. This could be between $0.5 billion and $2 billion and will depend on several factors.
5) The 41 percent equity shown here assumes that Chrysler and Fiat meet all three of the performance targets and that Fiat exercises its rights under the Incremental Equity Call Option.
6) The VEBA Note is payable out to 2023, with most of the principal to be repaid after the U.S. and Canadian governments have been repaid.
7) The 6 percent equity shown here assumes that Chrysler and Fiat meet all three of the performance targets and that Fiat exercises its rights under the Incremental Equity Call Option.
8) $2.1 billion is due by December 10, 2011 and of the remainder, half is due on June 10, 2016, and the balance is due on June 10, 2017.
9) The 2 percent equity shown here assumes that Chrysler and Fiat meet all three performance targets and that Fiat exercises its rights under the Incremental Equity Call Option.
10) The Canadian loans are due on June 10, 2017. The U.S. dollar value of the debt fluctuates with the exchange rate between U.S. and Canadian dollars.
11) The 51 percent equity shown here assumes that Chrysler and Fiat meet all three performance targets and that Fiat exercises its rights under the Incremental Equity Call Option.
12) This option gives Fiat the right to buy 4.4 percent of Chrysler's diluted equity (assuming all three performance targets have been met) no more than once every six months, starting July 1, 2012 and running until either (1) June 30, 2016, (2) 22 percent of the equity has been so purchased, or (3) Treasury exercises its right to call the VEBA's equity under the Equity Recapture Agreement. The price is based on the Enterprise Value/Earnings Before Interest, Tax, Depreciation, and Amortization (EV/EBITDA) multiple method described in the Operating Agreement for the Incremental Equity Call Option, prior to an IPO, and a market price after an IPO. In either case, the amount is adjusted for any tax liability that Fiat might have to assume.
13) The Equity Recapture Agreement gives Treasury an economic interest in the VEBA's equity stake in Chrysler above a Threshold Amount of $4.25 billion, growing at 9 percent per year from January 1, 2010. Treasury can actively exercise this right by buying the VEBA's equity for the Threshold Amount less any proceeds received by the VEBA for equity already sold, or selling the rights to one or more third parties. Treasury can also passively benefit from this right, receiving all cash from sales of the VEBA's equity above the Threshold Amount.

14) The Canadian government is entitled to 20 percent of any proceeds received by Treasury under the Equity Recapture Agreement.

15) This option gives Fiat the right to buy any and all equity interest that Treasury may have in Chrysler. This option may be exercised by Fiat during the 12-month period following the repayment in full of all TARP loans at an exercise price equal to a market price in the event that a Chrysler IPO has taken place, or otherwise using a "dueling investment banks" method to determine the price.

2. Outlook

a. Company Business Plan

Chrysler has changed numerous aspects of its business as part of its emergence from bankruptcy and its new relationship with Fiat. It has restructured its brands, reduced its U.S. dealership network, introduced new models, improved its U.S. market share, reduced its capacity, and negotiated lower labor costs.[217] Following initial cutbacks, Chrysler has recently begun to add employees. All of these actions, together, have returned Chrysler to operational profitability, although it continues to report net losses stemming from the interest expense on the TARP loans.[218]

On November 4, 2009, Chrysler unveiled its five-year business plan.[219] Chrysler stated that it plans to have four brands – Dodge, Ram Trucks, Jeep, and Chrysler – but to have them sold through unified dealerships. Ram had been a sub-brand of Dodge for nearly 30 years. Unlike GM, Chrysler has not closed any of its pre-bankruptcy brands, although Chrysler had only three brands pre-bankruptcy, compared to eight at GM.

Like GM, Chrysler has reduced its number of dealers in the United States. The logic is that with fewer dealers, the remaining dealers will sell more vehicles, reach a higher level of profitability, and so be able to afford a greater level of investment in their dealerships. This investment, which Chrysler is pushing under the name "Project Genesis," aims to create more customer-friendly showrooms.[220]

Chrysler has introduced several new models since emerging from bankruptcy on June 10, 2009. The most significant from a revenue perspective has been the new Jeep Grand Cherokee introduced in May 2010.[221] This model has sold 66 thousand units to date.[222] Discussions have begun to use the same underlying platform to produce a luxury SUV under Fiat's Maserati brand.[223] Chrysler is also preparing to launch the Chrysler 200, which will replace the Chrysler Sebring. The Ram truck brand has had some critical success, notably winning Texas Truck of the Year,[224] but its sales performance has failed to match that of the GM and Ford pickup lines in 2010.[225] Overall truck sales for Chrysler are up 13 percent for the first 11 months of 2010 as compared to the same period in 2009. Equivalent sales, however, have increased 17 percent at GM and 22 percent at Ford for the same period.[226] Chrysler's minivan segment saw a revamped model introduced for model year 2011.

Figure 11 below shows the evolution over the last eight years of Chrysler's sales in the United States, by far its largest market. The importance to Chrysler of the light truck segment, which includes the minivan, pickup, and SUVs, is clear, as this segment has consistently been responsible for the majority of Chrysler's sales in the United States. Chrysler's market share has seen a slight uptick in 2010 year-to-date versus 2009, which has been driven by its performance in the car market.[227] Additionally, Chrysler's average transaction price has increased $1,900 since March 2009.[228]

Operationally, Chrysler now has one fewer plant than it did prior to bankruptcy, but it should be noted that this reflects both the closure of four major plants offset by Chrysler's purchase of a bankrupt supplier's three factories.[230] This capacity reduction, together with contractual changes that have reduced labor costs, has lowered the volume at which Chrysler breaks even to 1.65 million units.[231]

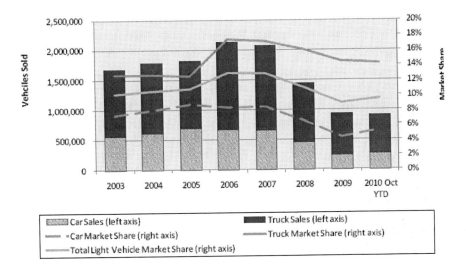

Figure 11. Chrysler U.S. Vehicle Sales by Segment, 2003 to Present[229].

Fiat has also begun its efforts to re-enter the U.S. market. On November 17, 2010, Chrysler announced 130 dealerships that have been selected to sell Fiat vehicles.[232] These dealerships will be distinct from the dealerships that sell the Chrysler family of vehicles, although some Fiat dealerships were sold to existing Chrysler dealers. Chrysler began building the Fiat 500, also known as the Cinquecento, in the fourth quarter of 2010, and will start selling the vehicles in North America in 2011.

Period	Vehicles Sold (000s)	Vehicles Sold, U.S. (000s)	Revenue (USD millions)	Modified EBITDA (USD millions)[235]	Net Income (USD millions)	Cash Flow (USD millions)	Employees at end of Period (000s)
8/4/07 to 12/31/07	1,081	828	26,561		(639)		76
2008	2,007	1,453	48,477		(16,844)		56
1/1/09-6/30/09[236]	656	471	11,082		(4,425)		50
Q4 2009	318	216	9,434	398	(2,691)		48
Q1 2010	334	235	9,687	787	(197)	1,498	50
Q2 2010	407	292	10,478	855	(172)	481	52
Q3 2010	401	293	11,018	937	(84)	419	52

Figure 12. Chrysler Financial and Operational Results, Mid-2007 to Q3 2010[234].

Since emerging from bankruptcy, Chrysler's financial performance has been burdened by the significant and costly debt it still carries, much of it related to the TARP.[233] Figure 12 below shows several key financial and operational metrics for Chrysler and how they have evolved before and after bankruptcy.

b. Government Exit Strategy

Treasury currently has both debt and equity claims on Chrysler. Treasury's total outstanding debt claims on New Chrysler, including additional notes and payment-in-kind interest considerations, have a total face value of $5.8 billion.[237] Furthermore, Chrysler still retains the right to draw up to an additional $2.1 billion in funding pursuant to the original loan agreement.[238] These loans are due to be paid back in tranches, with the last tranche due in 2017.[239] Given Chrysler's efforts to refinance its TARP loans,[240] its stated desire to repay the TARP loans by 2014,[241] its pending application for loans from Department of Energy's Advanced Technology Vehicles Manufacturing Loan Program (ATVM),[242] and the continued positive cash flow from the automotive business,[243] it is likely that all the loans extended to Chrysler under the TARP will be repaid, possibly in advance of the contractual due dates. Therefore, most of the uncertainty regarding Treasury's financial return on the Chrysler intervention stems from the unpredictability of Treasury's ultimate recovery from its equity stake.

Plans for the sale of Treasury's equity stake have not been formally divulged. Chrysler is currently a privately held company with no publicly traded equity against which to value Treasury's equity stake.[244] Sergio Marchionne, the CEO of Chrysler and Fiat, has publicly stated that he expects to take Chrysler public via an IPO sometime in 2011. How much, if any, of Treasury's stake could be sold at that point is unclear. The eventual monies received by Treasury for its investments in Chrysler will depend on Chrysler's financial and operational performance, if and when Chrysler's equity becomes publicly traded and, to a large degree, the actions of Fiat and the VEBA. If Chrysler's equity does not immediately become publicly traded after the TARP loans get repaid, then the return on investment will depend to an even bigger extent on the actions of Fiat and could be lower as a result.[245] In his most recent comments, the Fiat CEO has indicated that he considers it possible that Fiat will go over the 50 percent ownership mark in 2011.[246]

c. Valuing Chrysler's Equity

Determining an appropriate valuation for Chrysler's equity, in the absence of trading of its equity on a public exchange, is difficult and involves a large amount of subjective assessment.

However, there are ways of estimating a value: (1) the Operating Agreement contains a pricing formula for several of Fiat's options to buy additional equity of Chrysler, and (2) equity research analysts who cover Fiat have estimated values for Fiat's stake in Chrysler. Under most of these valuations, Treasury's rights under the Equity Recapture Agreement have positive value.

The Operating Agreement provides a valuation method to be used in the absence of public trading. The valuation is the product of the most recent four quarters' earnings and a market-assigned "multiple," which relies on valuations of other comparable automobile manufacturers, and deducts the company's debt according to certain rules.[247] Applying that valuation methodology to Chrysler's financial results for the third quarter of 2010 results in an estimate of Treasury's equity stake in Chrysler of $2.8 billion.[248]

This result is very sensitive to the earnings period and the pool of comparable firms. In particular, earnings for the fourth quarter of 2009 were particularly bad for Chrysler.[249] Further, the Operating Agreement provides that the multiple used for the valuation of Chrysler may not exceed Fiat's multiple,[250] which is currently the lowest in the industry.[251] This effectively limits the implied valuation of Chrysler. And according to analyst reports, certain plans announced by Fiat will further lower Fiat's – and in turn Chrysler's – multiple,[252] for the purposes of assessing how much Fiat must pay to acquire additional equity in Chrysler using several of the options it has.

Equity analysts who cover Chrysler provide another source of valuation estimates. Figure 13 below shows the values attributed to Fiat's stake in Chrysler in the most recent research notes published by four firms.

Firm	Date	Size of Fiat's Equity Stake	Valuation of Fiat's Stake (USD millions)	Valuation of Chrysler Equity (USD millions)
Goldman Sachs[253]	Sept. 24, 2010	35%	2,857	8,162
Kepler[254]	April 26, 2010	51%	5,225	10,245
Credit Agricole[255]	April 23, 2010	35%	4,319	11,459
Deutsche Bank[256]	April 22, 2010	35%	0	0

Figure 13. Analyst Evaluations of Chrysler Equity Value.

As for the debt owed by Chrysler, as part of the five-year business plan announced on November 4, 2009, Chrysler detailed its plan to repay its obligations to Treasury, as well as those owed to the Canadian government.[257] Chrysler projected repaying all TARP loans by the end of 2014. This would be several years in advance of when the loans mature. Chrysler's desire to end its connection with the TARP ahead of time reflects its desire to achieve a cheaper source of financing going forward.[258] However, the five-year business plan also projected that Chrysler would receive $3 billion in Department of Energy loans, $1 billion in each year from 2010 to 2012.[259]

If Chrysler succeeds in meeting its five-year business plan, and with potential help from any Department of Energy loans extended to Chrysler, the TARP will have all the debt owed to it repaid by 2014, in advance of Chrysler's contractual obligations.[260]

3. Analysis of the Government's Exit Strategy Based on Likely Repayment Scenarios

For a successful government exit to be carried out, all TARP loans would need to be repaid, and Treasury would need to divest its equity stake in Chrysler and recover sufficient value to compensate the taxpayer for the Chrysler-related losses of $3.5 billion. As noted earlier, much will depend on Treasury's ability to maximize its return from the sale of its equity stake and whether or not Chrysler has an IPO.

Treasury currently has debt instruments outstanding to Chrysler with a total face value of $5.8 billion. Under the scenarios laid out above, Treasury is likely to recover the full amount of its outstanding TARP loans to Chrysler ahead of time whether or not an IPO occurs.[261] In addition, Treasury has lost $3.5 billion on loans made to Old Chrysler. For Treasury to recover all the funds that it has invested in Chrysler, both Old and New, then all the loans have to be repaid, and Treasury's equity stake would have to yield at least $3.5 billion to make up for the losses to date. Based on just the 8 percent of Chrysler's equity that will be directly held by Treasury at the time of any potential sale, Chrysler would have to be valued at approximately $44 billion to cover the losses to date.[262] This is roughly in line with the amount reported in the Panel's September 2009 report, which calculated the break-even valuation of Chrysler at $57.5 billion.[263] For comparison, when Chrysler was acquired by Daimler in 1998, it was valued at $37 billion, which adjusted for inflation would equate to $49 billion today.[264] Prior to that acquisition, Chrysler had never been so highly valued.[265]

As discussed above, the Equity Recapture Agreement between Treasury and the VEBA may change the picture because of the additional economic interest it grants to Treasury. If Treasury were able to exercise fully its rights under this agreement, then Treasury's stake would be a considerably larger share of Chrysler. This in turn would mean that it would be possible for the valuation of Chrysler to be significantly lower in order for the TARP to recoup fully its investment and maximize return for the taxpayers.[266] Exact calculations are difficult as they depend on the date of sale. Assuming a January 1, 2012 sale date for the entire equity stakes of both Treasury and the VEBA, for example, Chrysler's equity would have to be valued at approximately $14.5 billion for Treasury to recoup the $3.5 billion that it has lost on Chrysler-related loans to date, which would make it easier for Treasury to recover all of its investments in Chrysler.

Figure 14 below includes the key dates when the various rights take effect to facilitate the following discussion of possible repayment scenarios.

Date	Event	Source
12/10/2011	$2.08 billion of loan to Chrysler from Treasury is due; $500 million CAD from Canadian loan is also due	Chrysler Group LLC financial statements
7/1/2012	VEBA Call Option activates, allowing Fiat to purchase up to 40 percent of VEBA's equity stake in Chrysler	VEBA Call Option Agreement
1/1/2013	Fiat's Class B rights, the performance targets, expire; after this date Fiat may acquire a stake equivalent to that it could have acquired under the Class B rights, but by paying a price equivalent to that of the Incremental Equity Call Option – this is the Alternative Call	Operating Agreement
1/1/2013	Starting on this date, a simple majority, 51 percent, of Chrysler's equity holders can force an IPO	Operating Agreement
6/10/2016	Half of the remaining balance on Treasury loans to Chrysler are due	Chrysler Group LLC financial statements
7/1/2016	VEBA Call Option expires	VEBA Call Option Agreement
6/10/2017	Remaining balance on Treasury loans to Chrysler are due	Chrysler Group LLC financial statements

Figure 14. Chrysler Timeline.

As noted above, Treasury does not currently have the ability to appropriate funds to acquire the VEBA's equity. If Chrysler does well financially and the VEBA's sales of equity reach the Threshold Amount, then any equity sales above that level will benefit Treasury.[267]

In this case, however, the VEBA and not Treasury will have control over the timing and execution of these sales. In addition, Fiat's ability to control the timing of the exercise of its option to buy Treasury's entire equity stake in Chrysler after repayment of the TARP loans could limit the ability of Treasury to recoup the maximum possible amount from its equity stake and its claims to the VEBA's equity stake.

a. Possible Scenarios for a Sale of Treasury's Equity Stake

It appears that Treasury has a chance to recover some or all of the previously lost amounts through gains on the equity stake. Treasury is guided by a number of different principles for its involvement in private companies and, as with GM, it needs to balance its desire to exit as soon as practicable against its objective of maximizing the value of the taxpayers investment.[268] The level of return Treasury can realize for the taxpayers, however, is uncertain at this point. In addition to unpredictable market developments, the complex nature of the restructuring transaction and the competing and potentially conflicting sets of interests among the parties may constrain Treasury's freedom to act in the best interest of the taxpayers. As noted earlier, much will depend on the conditions under which Treasury and the VEBA will be able to dispose of their equity stakes. Two possible scenarios are described below.

i. Large IPO Exit Scenario

As discussed above, repayment in full of Chrysler's government loans is a pre-condition for Fiat to gain majority control of the company. An IPO may happen whether or not Fiat has a majority ownership of Chrysler's shares, but if Fiat can reach a 51 percent equity stake in Chrysler before January 1, 2013, it will have sole control over the timing of a Chrysler IPO.[269] In Fiat's second quarter 2010 analyst call, its CEO stated that the priority for the IPO was to allow the VEBA to sell its stake in Chrysler for cash that it can use to invest and meet its obligations for the health care of the retired UAW workers.[270] Chrysler also expects the other equity owners eventually to sell their stakes.[271]

An IPO would likely take place in late 2011 or 2012.[272] Fiat would have the option to increase its equity stake to a majority by exercising the Incremental Equity Call Option either prior to or concurrently with the IPO. For this to happen, Chrysler would need to have repaid all of its government loans by that time. In a large IPO package scenario Fiat would exercise its option simultaneously with the IPO, and Treasury would be able to sell its entire direct equity stake at that time. The ultimate level of recovery for Treasury would depend on the market for Chrysler's shares and, to some degree, on the VEBA's actions.[273]

ii. Delayed IPO

As discussed earlier, Fiat has a number of ways to increase its equity stake to a majority position, which can precede a Chrysler IPO.[274] The main reason why Fiat may prefer to delay an IPO is to be able to have Chrysler repay its loans[275] and so allow Fiat to exercise the entire Incremental Equity Call Option more cheaply prior to an IPO.[276] This would save Fiat a significant amount of money because instead of paying Chrysler market price for the new equity, it would be able to purchase the stake (and dilute the other shareholders) at a far lower cost based on a valuation methodology tied to inputs that could artificially lower Chrysler's value as opposed to what the equity might sell for in an IPO.[277] According to analysts, exercising the option prior to an IPO would mean up to a $2 billion savings for Fiat,[278] which would translate into a corresponding loss for Chrysler. This in turn would lower the value of the company in a subsequent IPO and result in a loss for the other owners of Chrysler, including Treasury.[279] The Fiat CEO's most recent remarks implying that his company may go beyond a 50 percent ownership of Chrysler in 2011 has reinforced analyst opinions that Fiat would try to save money and acquire majority ownership by exercising the Incremental Equity Call Option prior to an IPO.[280]

The exit options available to Treasury underlie the fact that Treasury's intervention in Chrysler was done in a distinct manner within the TARP by giving Fiat significant rights and benefits at the outset. The Panel notes that this may have saved Chrysler from dissolution, but the conflicting interests inherent in the structure of the intervention going forward may restrict Treasury's ability to maximize return for the taxpayers as it unwinds the government's ownership position.

F. GMAC/Ally Financial

1. Context

a. Brief History of the Company

For most of its history, GMAC Financial Services/Ally Financial was a wholly owned subsidiary of GM. As GM's captive finance arm, GMAC/Ally Financial provided GM dealers with the financing necessary to acquire and maintain automobile inventories and to provide customers with a means to finance automobile purchases.[281] Over time, the company's operations expanded and diversified to include insurance, mortgages, commercial finance, and online banking.[282] However, the decline in the last decade in GM's credit rating negatively impacted GMAC/Ally Financial's credit ratings and increased the cost of financing GM automobile sales. These circumstances, coupled with GMAC/Ally Financial's branching out into other lending sectors outside the auto industry, called into question GMAC/Ally Financial's ownership and governance structure. As a result, on November 30, 2006, GM sold 51 percent of the equity in GMAC/Ally Financial to an investment consortium led by Cerberus Capital Management, L.P. (Cerberus) for about $14 billion. GMAC/Ally Financial emerged as an independent global financial services company, but GMAC/Ally Financial's operations continued to have many attributes of a captive finance arm's relationship with an automaker.[283]

b. What Precipitated Government Assistance?

A combination of factors led to the government's decision to provide assistance to GMAC/Ally Financial.[284] GMAC/Ally Financial reported a net loss of $2.5 billion for the third quarter of 2008,[285] bringing its losses over five consecutive quarters to $7.9 billion. By late 2008, Residential Capital, LLC (ResCap), GMAC/Ally Financial's global real estate finance business, was incurring debilitating losses due to the downturn in the housing market, especially due to its significant subprime mortgage exposure. Its automotive financing operations were severely weakened by the financial crisis and GM's precarious situation, both of which constricted credit, sharply reduced demand, and moved GMAC/Ally Financial closer toward insolvency.[286]

As detailed in the Panel's March 2010 report, Treasury presents a two-fold justification for its intervention in GMAC/Ally Financial. First, Treasury states that it acted because of GMAC/Ally Financial's significance to the automotive industry and to GM and Chrysler in particular. As Treasury considered using funds from the TARP to rescue GM and Chrysler in December 2008, it quickly came to the conclusion that GM could not survive without GMAC/Ally Financial's financial underpinning. In particular, GMAC/Ally Financial provided GM dealers with almost all of their "floorplan financing" – that is, loans to purchase their inventory. Without access to this credit, many dealers would have been forced to close their doors. Second, Treasury states that it acted because of GMAC/Ally Financial's inclusion in the stress tests, pursuant to which Treasury committed to provide funds for bank holding companies that could not raise funds privately.[287] Over time, Treasury states that it approached the issue of continuing to support GMAC/Ally Financial from the position that it must follow through on its commitments, even if the commitments are not legally enforceable, in order to maintain the credibility of the federal government. These rationales are circular, since GMAC/Ally Financial would not have been included in the stress tests had the government not intervened in December 2008 by expediting the company's application for bank holding company status in order to prevent General Motors from liquidating.

The particular issues associated with GMAC/Ally Financial's near-collapse make this government intervention unique. As the Panel discussed in its March 2010 report, the solvency issue that the company faced in late 2008 owed to poor management decisions related to mortgage market investments that rapidly collapsed once the housing market downturn began. Furthermore, unlike the legacy shareholders and creditors of GM and Chrysler – companies that underwent restructuring via the bankruptcy process – the legacy stakeholders of GMAC/Ally Financial (for example, Cerberus) were rescued along with the company because the government opted not to place GMAC/Ally Financial into bankruptcy.

c. Government Support Efforts

The U.S. government has spent a total of $17.2 billion to support GMAC/Ally Financial under the TARP. Currently, after Treasury's December 2010 conversion of $5.5 billion of its $11.4 billion in mandatory convertible preferred stock in Ally Financial into common stock, Treasury's remaining investment consists of $2.7 billion in trust preferred securities (TruPS), $5.9 billion in mandatory convertible preferred stock, and a 73.8 percent common equity ownership stake.[288] Conversion of Treasury's remaining MCPs would increase the government's equity ownership in the company to approximately 82 percent.

GMAC/Ally Financial received funds on three separate occasions: in December 2008, May 2009, and December 2009.[289] The government's support efforts are illustrated in Figure 15 below.

Original Investment Date	Original Assistance Amount	Original Investment Type	Exchange	Current Investment Type	Cumulative Investment Amount	Amount Repaid	Amount Lost
12/29/2008	5,000	Preferred Stock w/ Exercised Warrants	Exchange for convertible preferred stock	Convertible Preferred Stock	[291]$5,250		
12/29/2008	884	Loan to General Motors	Extinguished in consideration for 35.4 percent of GMAC/Ally Financial common stock	Common Stock	884		
5/21/2009	7,500	Convertible Preferred Stock w/ Exercised Warrants	$3 billion exchanged for common stock	Convertible Preferred Stock	[292]7,875		
12/30/2009	2,540	Trust Preferred Securities w/ Exercised Warrants		Trust Preferred Securities w/ Exercised Warrants	2,667		
12/30/2009	1,250	Convertible		Convertible	1,313		
		Preferred Stock w/ Exercised Warrants		Preferred Stock w/ Exercised Warrants			
Total	$17,174				$17,989		

Figure 15. TARP Investment in GMAC/Ally Financial *(millions of dollars)*[290].

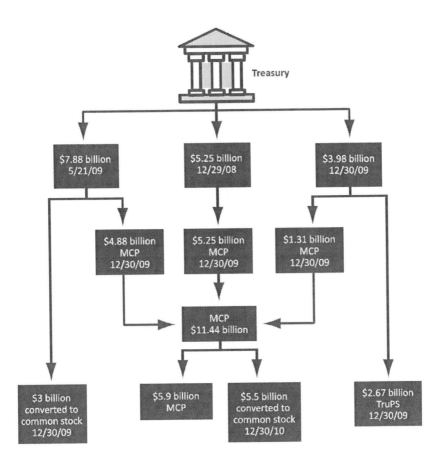

Figure 16. GMAC/Ally Financial Flowchart of Investments[293].

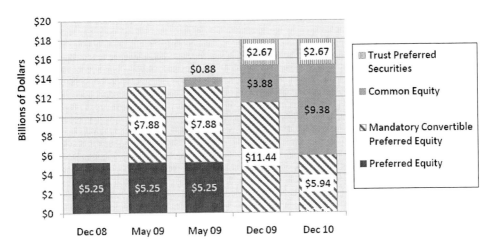

Figure 17. Treasury's Investments in GMAC/Ally Financial[294].

While Treasury holds a controlling interest in GMAC/Ally Financial, lesser interests are held by General Motors, the GM Trust (which was established as part of GM's bankruptcy and is managed by an independent trustee), the private equity company Cerberus, and third party investors, who purchased a portion of Cerberus' legacy stake.[295] The current ownership composition of GMAC/Ally Financial is illustrated in Figure 18 below.

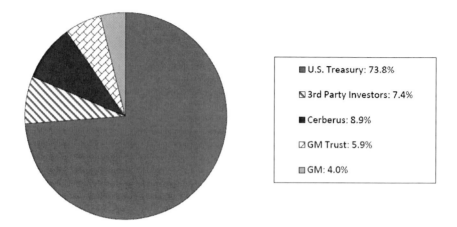

Figure 18. GMAC/Ally Financial's Current Ownership Structure (as of 12/30/2010)[296].

d. Current Company Structure

Since the beginning of 2010, GMAC/Ally Financial's operations have centered on three business segments:

- Dealer and retail automotive financing services (including insurance for consumers, automotive dealerships, and other businesses);
- Mortgage activities focusing primarily on the residential real estate market in the United States, with some international operations; this segment includes the operations of ResCap; and
- Commercial finance activities that provide secured lending products and other financing.

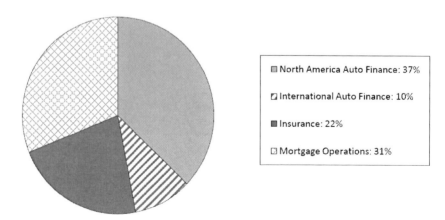

Figure 19. Third Quarter 2010 GMAC/Ally Financial Gross Revenue by Segment[297].

e. Recent Developments

GMAC/Ally Financial is one of the world's largest financial services companies with approximately $173.2 billion of assets as of September 30, 2010.[298] The third quarter of 2010 marked the third straight profitable quarter for GMAC/Ally Financial (net income of $278 million), with all segments and entities profitable, including ResCap and Ally Bank, which is GMAC/Ally Financial's online bank.[299]

According to its most recent quarterly earnings report, GMAC/Ally Financial has made progress on several important fronts since the Panel last provided an in-depth examination of the company in its March 2010 oversight report.[300] These recent developments are discussed in more detail below.

First, GMAC/Ally Financial's core auto finance business has now seen seven consecutive profitable quarters, primarily due to general improvement in the auto market and GMAC/Ally Financial's increased penetration of both GM and Chrysler consumer auto originations.[301]

As Chrysler is also now increasing its U.S. market share in the wake of the Toyota recalls and a downsized GM, GMAC/Ally Financial has potential for further growth in this market. On April 30, 2009, GMAC/Ally Financial entered into a legally binding term sheet with Chrysler to provide automotive financing products and services to Chrysler dealers and customers, which made GMAC/Ally Financial the "preferred provider of new wholesale financing for Chrysler dealer inventory."[302] On August 6, 2010, GMAC/Ally Financial entered into another agreement with Chrysler, which replaced and superseded the April 2009 term sheet. GMAC/Ally Financial is Chrysler's preferred provider of new wholesale financing for dealer inventory in the United States, Canada, Mexico, and other international markets. Chrysler is obligated to provide GMAC/Ally Financial with certain exclusivity privileges, including the use of GMAC/Ally Financial for designated minimum threshold percentages of certain of Chrysler's retail financing subvention programs. (A subvented loan is one where the auto manufacturer provides an incentive to the lender to offer a lower interest rate than it would otherwise offer.) The agreement extends through April 30, 2013, with automatic one-year renewals unless either GMAC/Ally Financial or Chrysler provides sufficient notice of nonrenewal. In addition, GMAC/Ally Financial was named the preferred lender for Fiat in the United States on September 30, 2010 (owing to its existing relationship with Chrysler).[303]

While its North American operations have continued to drive results, the performance of GMAC/Ally Financial's international operations has also improved. GMAC/Ally Financial is experiencing strong auto loan originations in China, Brazil, and the United Kingdom.[304] With a continued focus on streamlining its auto business, GMAC/Ally Financial's International Automotive Finance segment sold its Argentina auto finance business and signed an agreement to sell its Ecuador auto finance business during the third quarter of 2010.

Second, after recognizing approximately $18.3 billion in mortgage-related losses during the 2007-2009 period, GMAC/Ally Financial continues to make progress in liquidating legacy mortgage assets at levels above their sharply reduced carrying value. During the third quarter of 2010, ResCap sold approximately $11.0 billion worth of European mortgage assets and businesses to affiliates of hedge fund and private equity firm Fortress Investment Group.[305] This transaction means that GMAC/Ally Financial has effectively exited the European mortgage market. As of November 3, 2010, GMAC/Ally Financial sold $1.9 billion of held-for-sale legacy mortgage assets at gains. The company's management believes that it has "effectively de-risked the mortgage business."[306] GMAC/Ally Financial has stated that it is considering a number of strategic alternatives with respect to ResCap, including asset sales, spin-offs, or other potential transactions.[307]

In response to questions concerning irregularities in foreclosure document procedures, which have raised questions about the validity of foreclosures and led to new uncertainties in the mortgage industry, GMAC/Ally Financial states that it continues to monitor closely delinquency and claims trends as well as new repurchase requests, entered into settlements with Freddie Mac and Fannie Mae in 2010 under which it made one-time payments to the GSEs for the release of repurchase obligations, and increased its reserve for mortgage repurchases during the third quarter of 2010.

Finally, GMAC/Ally Financial continues to make progress in accessing the capital markets, improving its funding profile and reducing legacy costs. Ally Bank has taken on a more prominent funding role within the company. The bank's deposits and certificate of deposit (CD) retention rate have increased, and the overall firm's cost of funds has declined by over 100 basis points, or 1 percentage point, since becoming a bank holding company.[308]

2. Outlook

a. Company Strategy/Business Plan

A greatly improved market backdrop and a longer-term investment mentality on the part of Treasury, GMAC/Ally Financial's principal shareholder, have facilitated a strategy aimed at repaying the government and cultivating a sustainable independent business strategy. At the beginning of 2010 (several months into the tenure of new CEO Michael A. Carpenter), GMAC/Ally Financial announced six objectives for the company, which include becoming the leading global auto finance provider for dealers and consumers, improving its liquidity position and access to the capital markets, reducing the risk in its mortgage operations, improving cost structure, and transitioning fully into a bank holding company.[309]

At a high level, GMAC/Ally Financial's business plan is focused on achieving these six objectives, which are designed to position the company toward profitability and stability through a combination of higher earnings, reductions in balance sheet risk, the shedding of unproductive businesses, and improved access to the capital markets (at a lower cost of capital). The status of the company's progress on each of these fronts is discussed in more detail below.

Auto Finance. GMAC/Ally Financial has become the number one U.S. new car lender (according to AutoCount, an automotive industry data source), and the company expects to maintain that position.[310] GMAC/Ally Financial's auto finance franchise also has nearly three times the market share of its five largest competitors.[311]

GMAC/Ally Financial's U.S. penetration for the third quarter of 2010 currently stands as follows:[312]

- 84 percent of GM dealer stock (as compared to 73 percent for the third quarter of 2009);
- 76 percent of Chrysler dealer stock (as compared to 67 percent for the third quarter of 2009);
- 34 percent of GM consumer sales (as compared to 32 percent for the third quarter of 2009); and

- 49 percent of Chrysler consumer sales (as compared to 21 percent for the third quarter of 2009).

While GMAC/Ally Financial is a leader in floorplan finance (as evidenced by the figures listed above), it states that it is also repositioning its auto finance franchise balance sheet to both reduce the scope of its subvented business with GM and to focus on a more balanced origination and leasing mix. See Figure 20 below.[313] GMAC/Ally Financial has also increased its lending to consumers with super-prime and prime credit ratings, while reducing its near-prime and non-prime exposures.[314] Going forward, one of GMAC/Ally Financial's major focuses will be to expand its presence in the used vehicle market, which is approximately twice the size of the new vehicle market in terms of volume,[315] but where borrowers generally have weaker credit quality.

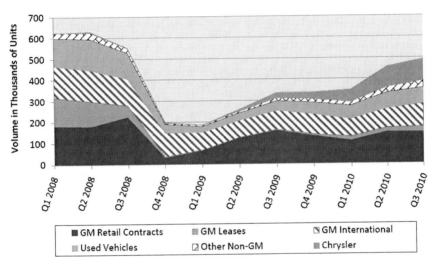

Figure 20. GMAC/Ally Financial Consumer Auto Financing Volume by Sector[316].

Access to Capital Markets

A core component of GMAC/Ally Financial's viability going forward (and a precursor to an IPO) is its ability to access the capital markets. For calendar year 2010, GMAC/Ally Financial had completed approximately $36 billion of new secured, unsecured funding and asset-backed securities (ABS) transactions in 2010 (and excluding growth in deposits).[317]

Mortgage Operations

The company has completed a strategic review of its mortgage operations. Since it marked $2.0 billion in mortgage assets to fair value in the fourth quarter of 2009 (due to the reclassification of certain international mortgage assets and businesses and domestic mortgage assets from held-for-investment (HFI) to held-for-sale (HFS), and management's intent to sell certain mortgage-related assets and thereby reduce volatility in GMAC/Ally Financial's financial results), GMAC/Ally Financial has made continued progress in reducing its legacy mortgage risk. The remaining mortgage assets are predominantly noneconomic exposures and assets supporting its agency origination and servicing business.[318] As reflected in Figure 21 below, the total assets in GMAC/Ally Financial's mortgage operations portfolio have declined from $147 billion to $41 billion (with $20.5 billion remaining at ResCap) between 2006 and the end of the third quarter of 2010, while the slight uptick seen in asset values over the course of 2010 reflects the improved market backdrop for mortgage assets.[319]

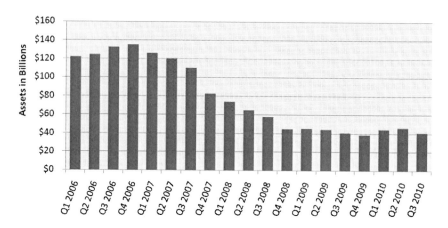

Figure 21. ResCap and Mortgage Operations Assets[320].

Ally Bank

With respect to increasing the importance of Ally Bank within the overall company's funding structure, Ally Bank increased its deposit base by $1.8 billion in the third quarter (a 29 percent increase, year-over-year) and achieved an 88 percent CD retention rate. Banking operations now comprise 29 percent of GMAC/Ally Financial's total funding.[321]

GMAC/Ally Financial expects that Ally Bank will continue to expand to represent a greater proportion of GMAC/Ally Financial's funding over time.

Cost Reductions

GMAC/Ally Financial has also made progress with respect to its objective of reducing controllable expenses by approximately $600 million during 2010. Its quarterly expenses for the third quarter of 2010 were $146 million less than those of the prior year period.[322]

b. Government Exit Strategy

As discussed above, Treasury's outstanding investment in GMAC/Ally Financial is $17.2 billion, which includes $5.9 billion in MCPs, $2.7 billion in TruPs, and 73.8 percent of the common equity of GMAC/Ally Financial.[323]

Treasury has identified four tasks with which GMAC/Ally Financial must continue to demonstrate progress in order for any government exit strategy to be successful.[324] First, GMAC/Ally Financial must demonstrate consistent access to secured and unsecured funding sources. Second, GMAC/Ally Financial must demonstrate a consistent track record of profitability. Third, GMAC/Ally Financial must mitigate market concerns regarding the risk related to its mortgage operations. Finally, GMAC/Ally Financial must be able to demonstrate to equity investors that its bank franchise will continue to grow at an attractive rate.

As with Chrysler (and until recently with GM) Treasury's stake in GMAC/Ally Financial – common, TruPs, and MCPs[325] – is fundamentally illiquid. Accordingly, Treasury's large common stock position in GMAC/Ally Financial, a non-public company, can be sold only in private sales unless and until GMAC/Ally Financial launches an IPO. Hence, the U.S. government's exit strategy for GMAC/Ally Financial relies primarily upon an IPO tentatively scheduled, per GMAC/Ally Financial management, for 2011. Treasury intends to sell its interests in a timely and orderly manner that "minimizes financial market and economic impact," under what it determines to be appropriate market conditions.[326] Consistent with its approach overall, Treasury's goal is to "dispose of the government's interests as soon as practicable consistent with EESA goals."[327] When asked at the Panel's recent hearing about the timetable for a GMAC/Ally Financial IPO, Secretary Geithner stated that it would happen "[a]s quickly as we can do it," emphasizing that Treasury is "going to move as quickly as we can to replace the government's investments with private capital, take those firms public, and figure out a way to exit as quickly as we can. And we're working very hard with the management and board of Ally to achieve that outcome."[328] While noting that he does not know how soon the IPO will happen, Secretary Geithner stated that "it's going to be much sooner than we thought six months ago."[329]

As it has done with its stake in Citigroup, and as it plans to do for its stake in AIG, Treasury recently converted $5.5 billion of its MCP interest (nearly half of its preferred shares) into common stock.[330] In addition to providing more clarity on the government's equity stake (and potential shareholder dilution),Treasury's conversion also helps GMAC/Ally Financial in two significant ways.[331] First, as a result of the conversion and the consequent dilution of the equity interest in GMAC/Ally Financial held by or on behalf of GM, the Federal Reserve has determined that Ally Bank and GM will no longer be treated as "affiliates" for purposes of Sections 23(a) and 23(b) of the Federal Reserve Act, which, among other things, impose limitations on transactions between banks and their affiliates.[332] Since Ally Bank is a source of cheap financing in part because it is the beneficiary of federal deposit insurance, it is cheaper and more cost-effective for GMAC/Ally Financial to use its bank as the core piece of its auto finance operations. This Federal Reserve decision will allow GMAC/Ally Financial to use Ally Bank to fund an increasing amount of GM retail and dealer loans.[333] Second (and, according to Treasury, the more important ramification), the conversion was intended to strengthen GMAC/Ally Financial's capital structure by increasing the proportion of equity in the form of common stock (and, therefore, conforming GMAC/Ally Financial's equity account to that more typical of a bank holding company and improving its leverage ratios). This factor largely determined the timing of Treasury's conversion, as Treasury determined it would be beneficial to allow the company to conform its capital structure to that of a more typical bank holding company before it starts to market itself to investors ahead of an upcoming IPO.[334]

The conversion helps GMAC/Ally Financial raise equity in the capital markets in the future, and improves GMAC/Ally Financial's ability to raise debt financing as loss-absorbing common equity increases.[335] GMAC/Ally Financial's management is pleased with the timing and terms of Treasury's conversion and believes that there are no other steps the government would need to take before the company pursues an IPO. It remains too early, however, to speculate on the impact of this transaction on an IPO and Treasury's exit strategy because Treasury still retains $5.9 billion in MCPs and $2.7 billion in TruPS.[336] At this time, Treasury's strategy for the disposition of those interests remains unclear.

Alternatively, Treasury has noted that it would be impossible to rule out a sale of GMAC/Ally Financial.[337] The company would entertain any bids that might come in, and

Treasury, as the majority shareholder, would have a significant influence on any discussions and the decision on whether to accept such a bid.[338] Treasury has stated, however, that only a small number of institutions could digest an acquisition of this magnitude, so this course of action appears less feasible than an IPO exit strategy.[339]

As part of its exit strategy, Treasury should ensure that legacy private sector stakeholders in GMAC/Ally Financial do not see any return until U.S. taxpayers recoup their entire investment.

c. Valuing GMAC/Ally Financial's Equity

Since GMAC/Ally Financial is a private company, and its business platform is unique, it is difficult to conduct a clear analysis of its current value. As comparables, Treasury currently uses for the GMAC/Ally Financial valuation 35 publicly traded companies across the bank, thrift, and specialty lender sectors.[340] Through an analysis of the market performance of these comparables, by using the average price-to-book value for this imperfect peer group, it is possible to estimate a market capitalization for GMAC/Ally Financial.[341] During 2010, the 35 comparable firms traded between 102 and 132 percent of their book value. Applying this range of multiples to GMAC/Ally Financial – with a reported book value of $21 billion as of the third quarter of 2010 – values the equity of the entire firm between $21.4 billion and $27.7 billion.[342] Hence, this methodology values the Treasury's 73.8 percent equity stake between $15.8 billion and $20.4 billion.[343] However, as noted, this is a crude yardstick given that GMAC/Ally Financial has a differentiated business model focused on the auto finance sector. Further, the company's book value calculation is likely to change before an IPO.

In conversations with Panel staff, Mr. Carpenter and other senior officers from GMAC/Ally Financial's management stated that its public offering, if priced at or near book value, could help facilitate the conversion of the Treasury's remaining MCPs, which would help the company ultimately repay the government in full.[344] As Figure 22 below illustrates, the average price-to-book of Treasury's 35 comparables has recovered dramatically from its 2009 trough and has remained above 100 percent for the entirety of 2010. The performance of these comparables, which are used by Treasury's Office of Financial Supervision (OFS) to monitor the value of its investments,[345] appears to be positive for GMAC/Ally Financial, signaling a market perception at this time that comparable companies are valued at a multiple high enough to provide for full Treasury repayment. While the comparables show a positive trend in the market valuation of their businesses, there is a clear disparity between the performance of the broader universe of Treasury comparables and that of a more specifically tailored peer group, which may provide a closer – but still imperfect – representation of the value of GMAC/Ally Financial. As demonstrated in Figure 22 below, the average price-to-book ratios of the nation's four largest banks (Bank of America, JPMorgan, Citigroup, and Wells Fargo), as well as CIT Group, a large specialty lender, have traded within a relatively narrow band over the past 12 months, underperforming a larger universe of financial firms. As of December 31, 2010, the price-tobook ratio of those five larger financial sector companies was 25 percent lower than that of the universe of smaller companies.

Figure 22. Price-to-Book Ratio of GMAC/Ally Financial Comparables[346].

3. Analysis of Intended Exit Strategy

a. The Timetable for Treasury's Exit Strategy

As discussed above, GMAC/Ally Financial has taken steps to mitigate some of the poor management decisions made in the past (most notably with respect to the company's substantial mortgage market exposure). As economic conditions have improved, the potential for Treasury to recoup its investment increased as market prices for capital transactions improved throughout 2010. In recent conversations with Panel staff, Treasury representatives have expressed confidence about the progress the company has made over the course of 2010 and the prospects for the taxpayers to be repaid pending the completion of an IPO.

Treasury pointed to three key developments that underscore their optimism.[347]

- First, they noted the improvements in the company's liquidity profile, with approximately $30 billion of new secured and unsecured funding transactions and an increase in the number of deposits at Ally Bank.
- Second, they noted that the outlook for GMAC/Ally Financial has become more favorable as the valuations for financial companies have increased since the early part of 2010.[348]
- Finally, Treasury discussed how the company's core business has remained profitable for three consecutive quarters.

Treasury's cause for optimism on both the company's progress and an upcoming IPO, however, might be premature. As discussed above, the Panel notes that the valuations for financial companies have not improved as much as Treasury stated. It is likely that mortgage market valuations have had the biggest impact on GMAC/Ally Financial (largely as a result of the company's efforts to stem the bleeding at ResCap). While GMAC/Ally Financial has now had three consecutive quarters of overall profitability, this likely owes more to the improvements in the ResCap mortgage portfolio than to anything else.

Moreover, with respect to GMAC/Ally Financial's improved liquidity, an analysis of GMAC/Ally Financial's five-year credit default swap (CDS) spreads, a market indicator of perceived risk of a company's default, provides insight into the market's perception of the company's health. Using Ford Motor Credit (FMCC), a better capitalized company without the same degree of mortgage exposure, as a comparable provides a basis of comparison. The movement in GMAC/Ally Financial's CDS spread illustrates the dramatic improvement in market sentiment towards the company following the announcement that the Treasury would provide assistance to the company on December 29, 2008. The 14.8 percent decline in GMAC/Ally Financial's CDS spread between December 30, 2010 and January 5, 2011, as compared to the 2.0 percent decline in Ford Motor Credit's CDS spread during the same period, further demonstrates the improvement in market opinion following Treasury's conversion of $5.5 billion of preferred interests in GMAC/Ally Financial into common stock.[349] However, the current low spreads on its CDS, and its position relative to Ford Motor Credit – a company with a stronger balance sheet – show that GMAC/Ally Financial is apparently still benefitting from the support provided by Treasury as well as a market belief that the support will remain intact for the foreseeable future (which helps it secure funding at a lower cost).

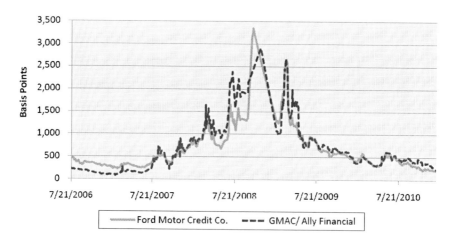

Figure 23. Credit Default Spreads on GMAC/Ally Financial and Ford Motor Credit[350].

b. Key Variables/Risks Going Forward that Might Impact the Exit Strategy and Government Returns

As with its ownership stakes in GM and Chrysler, there are certain variables and risks associated with Treasury's ability to divest its ownership stake in GMAC/Ally Financial successfully. As detailed below, the exit strategy timetable for GMAC/Ally Financial is somewhat complicated because the company's outlook is tied substantially to two key sectors – the auto industry and mortgage market – and the outlook for both remains uncertain. A successful exit strategy will, however, continue to depend upon positive – and improving – earnings as well as greater clarity about the company's medium-term strategy to grow Ally Bank, manage the GM relationship, maintain a mortgage portfolio with a more conservative risk/reward calculus, and seize other growth opportunities. Since a public offering is the most likely method for recovery of taxpayers'money, if GMAC/Ally Financial experiences delays or obstacles in accessing the equity capital markets, this will prolong Treasury's involvement as a shareholder and could potentially impact GMAC/Ally Financial's ability to repay its government assistance.

i. Performance of U.S. Auto Retail Market

Given how the largest percentage of GMAC/Ally Financial's net revenue during the third quarter of 2010 was related to North American auto finance, GMAC/Ally Financial faces the classic monoline concentration risk – it is a company that focuses primarily on operating in one specific financial area. The company's viability and future profitability are, therefore, intimately tied to the performance of the U.S. retail auto market.[351]

On one hand, GMAC/Ally Financial's efforts to increase lending to consumers with super-prime and prime credit ratings (while reducing its near-prime and non-prime exposures), as discussed above, have resulted in higher quality originations that will likely minimize the risk of delinquencies and necessitate lower loss provisions (at least in the short term). Additionally, it might be at least somewhat prudent for a company to have such a disproportionate exposure to the auto finance business, since this asset class category is very attractive from a risk point of view, and has been one of the most resilient asset classes in the banking business.

On the other hand, however, the global auto industry is highly cyclical and sensitive to changes in consumer sentiment, employment, gasoline prices, interest rates, and general economic activity.[352] GMAC/Ally Financial's focus on this sector – and its continued close relationships with GM and Chrysler – concentrates the risk to GMAC/Ally Financial of any decline in the automotive industry. The success of GMAC/Ally Financial's auto finance franchise (and, in large part, that of GMAC/Ally Financial as a company), therefore, in large part depends upon credit quality and the pace of auto sales growth, which is tied to the rate of economic recovery, consumer sentiment, and the outlook for housing and employment in the United States. Further, GMAC/Ally Financial's prior major effort at diversification (albeit under an earlier management team) beyond the automotive industry, ResCap, was clearly not successful. While GMAC/Ally Financial has started to focus on building a presence in the used-car sector, where prices are currently at an all-time high,[353] it is unclear what level of revenue this sector will generate for GMAC/Ally Financial going forward, but it will become less valuable if prices decline.

ii. Relationship with GM

GM recently acquired AmeriCredit, an auto finance company with total assets of $10 billion, to meet customer demand for leasing and non-prime financing for GM vehicles. GMAC/Ally Financial's auto finance franchise focuses on prime retail and dealer financing, while AmeriCredit focuses on subprime retail financing exclusively.[354] If GM changes AmeriCredit's business model and expands its financing operations, however, GMAC/Ally Financial would lose some of its GM market share to AmeriCredit. While GMAC/Ally Financial continues to emphasize how it maintains an "important, mutually beneficial relationship" with GM,[355] GM's acquisition of AmeriCredit raises the question as to whether GMAC/Ally Financial will continue to be uniquely positioned to serve GM dealers and customers.

GMAC/Ally Financial's current relationship with GM is shaped by the shared historical relationship between the two entities since 1919. Until 2006, GMAC/Ally Financial was a wholly owned subsidiary of GM, functioning as GM's captive financing arm with the interests of both entities very closely aligned. As part of the 2006 sale, GMAC/Ally Financial and GM entered into several service agreements that "codified the mutually beneficial historic relationship between the companies."[356] One of these agreements was the United States Consumer Financing Services Agreement (USCFSA), which provided that GM would use GMAC/Ally Financial exclusively whenever it offered vehicle financing and leasing incentives to customers.[357] The parties agreed to maintain this relationship for 10 years. As consideration for this arrangement, GMAC/Ally Financial pays GM an annual exclusivity fee and agrees to meet specified targets with respect to consumer retail and lease financings of new GM vehicles. On December 29, 2008, after the Federal Reserve approved GMAC/Ally Financial's application to become a bank holding company, GM and GMAC/Ally Financial agreed to modify certain terms and conditions of the USCFSA.[358] The modified USCFSA is in effect until December 24, 2013, but certain provisions terminate in January 2011.[359] In addition, the subvention agreements between GM and GMAC/Ally Financial have been continued through these contractual agreements.[360]

These contractual modifications mean that GMAC/Ally Financial will be engaging in a sizeable renegotiation with its biggest operating partner in the near future. While the USCFSA relates mainly to subvented GM financing, GMAC/Ally Financial's share of which is proportionately less important now than what it once was, it is likely that before GMAC/Ally Financial can pursue an IPO, potential investors would like further clarification on GMAC/Ally Financial's relationship with GM going forward, especially given how critical GMAC/Ally Financial's relationships with GM dealers and customers are to its balance sheet.[361] This may include a renegotiated operating agreement between GM and GMAC/Ally Financial that would explicitly prevent AmeriCredit from overtaking GMAC/Ally Financial's floorplan and consumer financing, at least for the indefinite future.[362]

While GM's AmeriCredit acquisition does not pose a near-term threat to GMAC/Ally Financial's business, it could represent a longer-term strategy by GM to grow its own captive financing arm organically.[363] GM currently benefits from its relationship with GMAC/Ally Financial because Ally Bank (as a federally insured depository institution) has a lower cost of capital than captive finance companies such as Ford Motor Credit, leading some industry analysts to conclude that this remains an excellent arrangement for GM.[364] As the Panel stated in its March 2010 report, however, "it would not be unreasonable for a potential equity investor to question whether [GMAC/Ally Financial]'s relationship with GM is designed to serve GM's rather than [GMAC/Ally Financial]'s shareholders' interests."[365] In that context, GMAC/Ally Financial's non-captive status subjects it to greater risk from GM: the relationship could sour, and GMAC/Ally Financial could lose its preferred provider role, and/or GM could, in fact, form its own, new captive finance company.[366] If any of this were to happen, investor enthusiasm for a potential GMAC/Ally Financial IPO might be dampened, absent any evidence of other tangible growth opportunities. GMAC/Ally Financial has become the preferred finance company in the United States for Saab, Suzuki, Thor Industries (the world's largest manufacturer of recreational vehicles), and Fiat over the course of 2010, but it is unclear how much business these relationships will generate for GMAC/Ally Financial going forward, and it appears that current revenue projections are fairly small. An IPO requires a prospective investor to believe either that GMAC/Ally Financial's relationship with GM is sufficiently stable to sustain it as a separate company, or that GMAC/Ally Financial can expand adequately (through growth strategies for Ally Bank, Chrysler, other automotive companies, the used car market, or otherwise) to handle the risk of a reduced relationship with GM. The public equity markets have never had an opportunity to evaluate this question, and their assessment remains unknown.

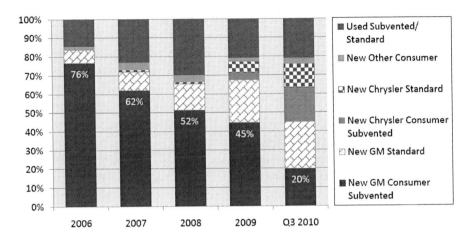

Figure 24. GMAC/Ally Financial's Auto Finance Loan Originations through December 20, 2010 (Percent of Units Originated)[367].

iii. Turmoil in the Mortgage Market

GMAC Mortgage, a subsidiary of GMAC/Ally Financial, is the fifth largest U.S. mortgage servicer.[368] As the Panel discussed in its November 2010 report, in the fall of 2010, reports began to surface of problems with foreclosure documentation.[369] GMAC Mortgage announced on September 24, 2010 that it had identified irregularities in its foreclosure document procedures, which have raised questions about the validity of some of its foreclosures. GMAC/Ally Financial temporarily suspended evictions and foreclosure sales by GMAC Mortgage in 23 states during September after an employee testified that he signed foreclosure documents without ensuring their accuracy.

These developments raise two important issues: (1) the validity of some of GMAC Mortgage's foreclosures given the irregularities in its documentation procedures; and (2) the amount of exposure GMAC/Ally Financial could face from mortgage repurchases.

With respect to the first issue, as of November 3, 2010, GMAC Mortgage has reviewed 9,523 foreclosure affidavits and, where necessary, has re-executed some.[370] Fewer than 15,500 additional affidavits are being reviewed and, when necessary, will be remediated.[371] According to GMAC/Ally Financial, the review has shown "no evidence of inappropriate foreclosure to date," and GMAC Mortgage "is confident that the decisions behind foreclosure proceedings were sound."[372] Corrective actions will be taken as necessary, according to the company, and company management expects that the vast majority of cases will be remediated over the next few months.

With respect to the second issue, GMAC Mortgage, like other underwriters/issuers, is required to make representations and warranties about the mortgage loans to the purchaser or securitization trust when selling mortgage loans through whole-loan sales or securitizations. This may require it to repurchase mortgage loans as a result of borrower fraud or if a payment default occurs on a mortgage loan shortly after its origination. Over the course of 2010, GMAC/Ally Financial entered into settlements with Fannie Mae and Freddie Mac, under which it made one-time payments to Fannie Mae and Freddie Mac for the release of repurchase obligations relating to mortgage loans sold to the GSEs.[373] This means that its remaining exposure is to potential repurchase obligations related to mortgage loans sold to private institutions to be securitized. Estimates of potential repurchase claims are subject to change as GMAC Mortgage provides more clarity on its exposure. Some analysts see GMAC/Ally Financial as a "well capitalized company with considerable liquidity and earnings power," despite the risk of negative publicity surrounding mortgage uncertainties.[374] Furthermore, while the company's current repurchase reserve might not be sufficient to resolve all future claims, these issues will likely take years to settle, which would thereby spread the impact of the liability over a period of time and mitigate capital outflows.[375] The repurchase exposure is the primary concern of both GMAC/Ally Financial's management and investors, rather than the foreclosure irregularities issue.[376] Because the 2009 stress tests considered the ability of financial institutions to remain well-capitalized only until the end of 2010, however, the stress tests offer limited reassurance that major bank holding companies like GMAC/Ally Financial will remain well-capitalized in the months and years to come, especially if the economic recovery remains sluggish. Even the prospect of such losses could damage GMAC/Ally Financial's reputation, its ability to raise capital, and its ability to pursue an IPO.[377] If the company is unable to assuage investor concerns on this front, the timing of a potential IPO could be impacted.

In conversations with Panel staff, Treasury representatives noted that they believe GMAC/Ally Financial's exposure is manageable, and asserted that the risk profile of GMAC Mortgage is no worse or better than that of its peers.[378] In addition, they stated that they have not dictated GMAC/Ally Financial's response to the foreclosure irregularities issue, but have handled the issue in a "routine" manner, consistent with its core principles as a "reluctant shareholder."[379] According to GMAC/Ally Financial, however, Mr. Carpenter has met with Treasury Acting Assistant Secretary for Financial Stability Tim Massad regularly on this topic.[380] While GMAC/Ally Financial management concurs that Treasury has not told the company how to respond to this issue, they note that Treasury remains a "very concerned shareholder" on this topic.[381]

iv. Has GMAC/Ally Financial Sufficiently Reduced the Risk in its Mortgage Portfolio?

As discussed above, one of GMAC/Ally Financial's core goals has been to review the mortgage strategy and reduce the risk in its mortgage operations business. During the earnings call for the third quarter of 2010 (and in conversations with Panel staff), Mr. Carpenter stated that the company has "effectively de-risked the mortgage business."[382] While ResCap was again profitable in the third quarter of 2010 (with net income of $38 million) and has required no additional capital or liquidity support, there continues to be a risk that ResCap will not be able to meet its debt service obligations.[383] Although GMAC/Ally Financial's mortgage operations proved to be a poor strategy in the past, its plans to retain and expand its mortgage servicing/origination business (rather than selling off the entire ResCap business) are much less balance sheet intensive and lower risk than mortgage originations. It remains unclear whether GMAC/Ally Financial has reduced the risk in its mortgage portfolio completely, in large part because the company's outstanding contingent liabilities (including repurchase claims) and any remaining legal exposure could present risks going forward.[384]

v. Maintaining a Robust Liquidity Profile

As noted above, GMAC/Ally Financial faces multiple impediments to profitability, especially amid a fragile economic and market recovery. At the parent company level, GMAC/Ally Financial must maintain sufficient liquidity to support its non-bank asset originations, debt maturities, interest and dividends, and investments/loans to operating subsidiaries. GMAC/Ally Financial must continue to demonstrate unfettered and non-government-sponsored access to the third-party credit markets, including wholesale financing markets, and must continue to make headway in reducing its cost of capital.

A key challenge facing GMAC/Ally Financial will be maintaining robust liquidity. GMAC/Ally Financial suffers from significant amounts of maturing debt, as reflected below in Figure 25. GMAC/Ally Financial has $21.5 billion coming due in 2011 and $19.8 billion in 2012. In the second quarter of 2009, the company received approval to issue debt up to $7.4 billion under the FDIC's Temporary Liquidity Guarantee Program (TLGP).[385] Pursuant to the program, it issued $4.5 billion of unsecured long-term debt, which included $3.5 billion of senior fixed-rate notes and $1.0 billion of senior floating rate notes. Both types of notes are due in December 2012.[386] On October 30, 2009, GMAC/Ally Financial issued an additional $2.9 billion of unsecured debt in the form of senior fixed-rate notes. These notes are due in October 2012.[387] If GMAC/Ally Financial is unable to refinance at affordable rates or has insufficient cash to cover its maturing obligations, it may face even higher borrowing costs, possibly resulting in renewed liquidity problems.

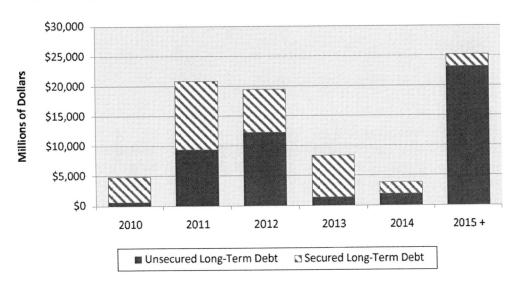

Figure 25. Long-Term Debt Maturities as of September 30, 2010 - Ally Financial (excluding ResCap)[388].

vi. Ally Bank's Strategy is a Work in Progress

As discussed above, Ally Bank provides GMAC/Ally Financial with a source of liquidity in both the retail and wholesale markets. Ally Bank also provides diversified funding (including deposits) for the automotive financing unit. This strategy has several components. GMAC/Ally Financial is simultaneously integrating Ally Bank with the auto lending business while expanding its retail banking offerings. GMAC/Ally Financial is aware that its combination of retail online banking and wholesale automotive financial services is untested but believes that it offers good value to Ally Bank's customers while simultaneously involving Ally Bank effectively in the automotive lending side of the business.

GMAC/Ally Financial has been engaged in an aggressive marketing campaign for Ally Bank. Among other things, Ally Bank has been attempting to interest depositors by offering CD rates that have been and remain among the highest available nationally.[389] Some analysts also believe that there is long-term uncertainty with Ally Bank's funding strategy due to both the risks associated with changing its operational and funding model to one focused on banking and those risks associated with whether an internet banking platform can meet the funding requirements of a large-scale company such as GMAC/Ally Financial.[390] In addition, since Ally Bank's current deposit mix is rate sensitive, GMAC/Ally Financial could be subject to some amount of volatility due to the potential for loss of customers and deposit amounts due to rate shifts.[391] In order to support Ally Bank's expansion and sustain its capital strength, the GMAC/Ally Financial parent company will "probably need to inject significant cash capital over the next few years."[392] The extent to which GMAC/Ally Financial will need to provide Ally Bank with cash infusions remains unclear.

Ultimately, Ally Bank appears to be both critical to GMAC/Ally Financial and is very much a work in progress. The Panel notes that Ally Bank may ultimately need to move toward a more traditional banking model (with a branch network) and broaden its footprint via other offerings. These possibilities, however, are not on the immediate horizon and would be impractical for the company to accomplish before the government's exit.[393]

G. Auto Supplier Support Program

1. Background

Generally, automotive suppliers ship parts to auto manufacturers and receive payment 45-60 days later. Under normal market conditions, suppliers can either sell or borrow against the payment commitments, known as receivables. In early 2009, the downturn in the economy and uncertainty regarding the future of GM and Chrysler resulted in tightening credit for auto suppliers. Banks stopped providing credit against supplier receivables. On March 19, 2009, in order to address this situation and to provide overall structural support for the auto industry, Treasury announced the creation of the Auto Supplier Support Program (ASSP).[394]

2. TARP Intervention

When the ASSP was created, up to $5 billion in financing was made available through the TARP. Participating suppliers could access a government-backed guarantee of eligible receivables or sell receivables into the program. A fee was charged for participation in the ASSP, and receivables were sold into the program at a discount.[395] While all domestic automotive manufacturers were eligible for the program, only Chrysler and GM participated.

Two special-purpose vehicles (SPVs), GM Supplier Receivables LLC and Chrysler Receivables SPV LLC, were created to administer the program for GM and Chrysler, respectively. Originally, $3.5 billion was committed to the GM SPV, and $1.5 billion was dedicated to the Chrysler counterpart. On July 1, 2009, Treasury reduced the total amount available under the ASSP to $3.5 billion, with $2.5 billion being reserved for GM's SPV and

$1 billion for the Chrysler SPV. As Figure 26 details, through the life of the program, only $413.1 million of the $3.5 billion in available funding was drawn down. Treasury's commitment to lend to the SPVs terminated in April 2010.[396] All funds outstanding under the ASSP were repaid, and

Treasury earned a total of $14.9 million in interest as well as $101.1 million in proceeds from additional notes.[397]

	Original Commitment	Adjusted Commitment	Amount Drawn Down	Interest Paid	Proceeds from Additional Notes
GM Receivables LLC	$3,500	$2,500	$290.0	$9.1	$56.5
Chrysler Receivables SPV LLC	1,500	1,000	123.1	5.8	44.5
Total	$5,000	$3,500	$413.1	$14.9	$101.1

Figure 26. Auto Supplier Support Program Metrics *(millions of dollars)*.

3. Current Status of Auto Supplier Industry

Standard indicators appear to show a stabilization in the automotive supplier industry as industry-wide consolidation increases. While there were 62 automotive supplier bankruptcies in 2009, there were only 5 failures in 2010.[398] Furthermore, the auto supplier industry's capacity utilization rate, an indicator of the degree to which an enterprise uses its ability to produce, is currently 60.5 percent. While this figure is significantly higher than it was at its trough of 45.9 percent during the crisis, it remains notably lower than the pre-crisis level, when it was typically above 70 percent.[399] This has led to ongoing consolidation of the supplier industry. Ford, GM, and Chrysler have announced reductions of 53, 30, and 50 percent, respectively, in their direct supply bases.[400]

H. Analysis of Treasury's Interaction with all Three Companies in Light of Government's Objectives

1. Summary of Principles upon which Government Says it Will Conduct its Involvement in Private Companies

In numerous hearings, reports, and statements to the press, Treasury has articulated four guiding principles for its involvement in private industry in the wake of the financial crisis, and specifically for its involvement with the automotive industry.

First, the government has cast itself as a "reluctant shareholder." It has stated that: "[t]he government has no desire to own equity stakes in companies any longer than necessary, and will seek to dispose of its ownership interests as soon as practicable. Our goal is to promote strong and viable companies that can quickly be profitable and contribute to economic growth and jobs without government involvement."

Second, Treasury has said that it will "reserve the right to set upfront conditions to protect taxpayers, promote financial stability, and encourage growth. When necessary, these conditions may include restructurings similar to that now underway at GM as well as changes to ensure a strong board of directors that selects management with a sound long-term vision to restore their companies to profitability and to end the need for government support as quickly as is practically feasible."

Third, Treasury has stated its commitment to "managing its ownership stake in a hands-off, commercial manner." This includes a commitment not to "interfere with or exert control over day-to-day company operations." To the extent that Treasury appoints any board members, it has stated that "[n]o government employees will serve on the boards or be employed by these companies."

Finally, Treasury has stated that it will vote its shares only "on core governance issues, including the selection of a company's board of directors and major corporate events or transactions."[401]

Put together, these principles illustrate an approach to government intervention that seeks to minimize the government's role, dampen any leverage the government has simply by virtue of its unique authority as sovereign, and present itself as a shareholder that behaves in most cases as a private shareholder would, while still protecting the assets of the people of the United States.[402]

Given the principles Treasury has laid out for its own involvement with the American automobile industry, three questions arise: (1) has Treasury abided by its own principles; (2) has Treasury used its limited powers effectively; and (3) was Treasury correct in establishing these guidelines as an act of prudent government restraint, or did the guidelines unnecessarily tie Treasury's hands at a time when greater government action, or at least shareholder activism, was necessary.

2. Has Treasury Abided by its own Principles?

As to the first question, the answer seems to be a qualified yes. According to the information the Panel has received from Treasury and the companies, it seems that Treasury has kept to the guidelines it established for itself. It is unclear, however, whether given its status, the government can actually be a passive investor. On the whole, Treasury's involvement in the companies has been restricted to participation in periodic calls with management to obtain information, appointing directors as permitted by the shares Treasury holds, and voting on a limited number of issues. At present, Treasury staff speaks with management at GM and Chrysler at least monthly and with management at GMAC/Ally Financial on a regular basis. In most cases, it is the companies that contact Treasury to convey new information such as earnings reports, or other relevant data. During these calls, company management provides Treasury with updated information on current operations and financial information, including updates on revenue, market share, domestic and international sales, and any corporate highlights as well as a review and analysis of the companies' balance sheets.[403] Treasury maintains that these calls are one-way; Treasury's role is to listen to the information provided by management, and does not respond with any directives or requests of management.[404] In the wake of allegations of irregularities in GMAC/Ally Financial's mortgage foreclosures, however, Treasury did take the initiative to contact the company for additional information regarding the irregularities.

Treasury has described these calls as the type that any large shareholder might have with company management, although it is unlikely that a large private shareholder would actually be as passive as Treasury describes. For the most part, the companies also describe their interactions with Treasury as being similar to interactions with other major shareholders. For example, Chrysler has stated that it provides all of its owners, including Treasury, with the same information about its operations and financial results each month. GM has stated that Treasury expressed a desire to be kept apprised of progress but had no intention to influence the company's progress, and that Treasury has stayed true to that intent. Moreover, GM has confirmed that Treasury's role in determining the timing of its IPO was extremely limited and that Treasury left the decision in the hands of GM management. Chrysler has similarly stated that Treasury has not provided input on the proposed timing for that company's IPO.

Treasury has said that, in the period preceding the GM IPO, its interactions with GM were much more frequent than they had been previously.[405] This increased activity, however, Treasury has attributed solely to its need to perform due diligence as a large shareholder. GM has affirmed this view, and has also confirmed Treasury's position that the decision about when to have the IPO was made primarily by the company. Treasury and the Canadian government both had demand rights that would have enabled them to force an IPO by a certain date if the company had not begun the process, but the need to exercise those rights did not arise. Treasury has acknowledged that waiting a year or 18 months may have given GM time to improve its value even further, but noted that the company had determined that it was ready for an IPO.[406]

In general, GMAC/Ally Financial has described its interactions with Treasury in the same way. Preparations for GMAC/Ally Financial's potential IPO, however, have presented some challenges that have led to a different dynamic in the interactions between GMAC/Ally Financial and Treasury with regard to this issue. As the Panel discussed in its March 2010 report, Treasury's treatment of GMAC/Ally Financial has not adhered as firmly to the principles on which Treasury has claimed to base all of its TARP investment decisions.[407] For Treasury to suggest otherwise in conversations with Panel staff may reveal a bias to present a consistent narrative regarding its shareholder principles, rather than acknowledging the unique circumstances that its stake in GMAC/Ally Financial may present.

This is illustrated by the rigidity with which Treasury articulates these principles in explaining its interactions with the company – descriptions that often lack the transparency that would illustrate the unique factors that understandably impact Treasury's GMAC/Ally Financial exit strategy.

Treasury initially informed the Panel on November 22, 2010 that the timing of a potential IPO was entirely up to GMAC/Ally Financial. However, this assertion neglected to acknowledge the practical impact of the continued uncertainty regarding the potential conversion status of the Treasury's MCPs, and the obvious hurdle this would present in terms of proceeding with an IPO. Although Treasury later acknowledged that the timing of the conversion would impact the timing of the IPO, Treasury still maintained that the conversion of its MCP holdings was not a prerequisite for the company to proceed with an IPO. After a portion of the MCPs were converted, however, Treasury finally cited this move as a necessary step towards the IPO during a conversation with oversight bodies on January 5, 2011, and now appears somewhat more hesitant to reassert its prior claims of GMAC/Ally Financial's independence to pursue its IPO on its own timetable.[408] Treasury's stated rationale for timing the conversion tacitly confirms the fact that a GMAC/Ally Financial IPO would be impeded by a delay on Treasury's part in converting its MCPs into common shares, and seems to contradict Treasury's earlier statement that GMAC/Ally Financial could hold its IPO without waiting for Treasury to convert the MCPs.[409] In any case, the Panel recognizes that this may be a prudent (but belated) acknowledgement of the unique factors that understandably complicate the IPO process for GMAC/Ally Financial.

Treasury, in its role as shareholder, has also appointed a number of new members to the board of each company. At GM, Treasury has appointed 10 of the current 12 board members, including Dan Akerson, who was later named CEO by the company's directors. Treasury has appointed four members to the Chrysler board, and three to GMAC/Ally Financial's board, with an additional member currently undergoing the vetting process for appointment. As a result of converting a portion of its GMAC/Ally Financial MCPs into common shares, Treasury has also acquired the right to appoint two more members to the company's board. In seeking candidates for these positions, Treasury used private search companies, such as might be used by a private shareholder seeking to appoint directors to a large corporation.

As a common stockholder, Treasury has the right to vote its shares on various issues. In accordance with its commitment to vote only on "core governance issues," Treasury has exercised its right three times, all at GM: the appointment of board members; a stock split that immediately preceded the IPO; and a charter amendment for the preservation of tax assets. These actions fall squarely within the category of "core governance issues" and are the type on which a large private shareholder would usually vote. Treasury has never voted its shares in Chrysler or GMAC/Ally Financial.

Based on the information that Treasury has provided to the Panel, it appears that Treasury has been following its guidelines and has taken no action that a private shareholder could not take. This does not mean, however, that Treasury's position as a majority shareholder, or even as a shareholder at any level, has had no impact on the companies. It may be impossible for a government agency to hold a stake in a private company without having a greater impact than a private shareholder. First, Treasury's stake is more visible than that of any other shareholder. Because the American people have a direct interest in the companies, the companies' every movement is of potential interest to the press. Second, Treasury makes larger waves with each of its movements than a private investor does. The fact that Treasury intends to have a "hands-off" approach does not mean that its voice does not seem louder to the companies than those of other shareholders.

Treasury's ownership stake may have both a positive and negative impact on the companies' share prices. For example, there may be a perception in the market – particularly among debt investors – that the government stands behind the companies, regardless of whether the government has that intention, thereby making credit available to the companies on more favorable terms than they would have otherwise received. As discussed in Section F.3.a, the current spreads on GMAC/Ally Financial credit default swaps support this assumption. On the negative side, potential investors may fear that Treasury would wield influence disproportionate to its holdings, and that Treasury's presence is not a positive backstop, but an ongoing sign of the companies' inherent weaknesses.[410]

3. Has Treasury Used its Limited Authority Effectively?

To analyze the success of Treasury's intervention in the automotive industry, there must first be a definition of "success." Treasury has provided its own views on what would constitute a success. In testimony before the Panel, senior Treasury advisor Ronald Bloom defined success as primarily a question of return on investment: "the greater percentage of the money that we invested that we get back, the greater success."[411] The investment was not, however, made purely for the purpose of seeing a return on those funds. Mr. Bloom also testified to the importance of job preservation and listed a number of other measures for determining whether the program was successful, including the question of "whether these companies have addressed the long-term problems that we identified," such as "a declining market share, a poor profitability profile" and failing to increase their ability to provide "good, stable jobs."[412] Austan Goolsbee, Chairman of the Council of Economic Advisers, appeared in a recent video released by the White House to explain the "Rebirth of the American Auto Industry." According to Mr. Goolsbee, although taxpayers may soon see a return of the funds invested, the investment "was never really about the stock market. It was about saving American jobs."[413]

If the success of the overall automotive rescue, and of the government's means of implementing that program in accordance with the principles listed in Section H.1, above, is measured by Treasury's ability to meet its own definition of success, the program must: (1) provide a return on investment; (2) create or at least preserve jobs that would have otherwise been lost; and (3) set the companies on a path toward ongoing stability. Treasury's challenge, given its goals, lies not only in the difficulty of the goals themselves, but also in the fact that they may be mutually exclusive at times. For example, the best way to improve the return on investment and shore up the companies for the future may be to cut jobs. Also, to the extent that these companies have conflicting interests, Treasury may be placed in an untenable position. Historically, GMAC/Ally Financial has had close to a monopoly position in providing financing for GM dealers as well as a large share of the GM consumer financing market. This position is beneficial to GMAC/Ally Financial but not to GM and may have led to borrowers receiving more expensive loans than they might have obtained in a more competitive market. Treasury, as a stakeholder in both GM and GMAC/Ally Financial, can support neither GMAC/Ally Financial's dominant market position nor the entrance of greater competition without potentially undermining its investment in one company or the other. Moreover, judging Treasury solely by its ability to meet goals it set for itself may lead to a result that is overly favorable to Treasury. The goals articulated by Treasury may include certain assumptions about the proper role of government and the needs of the American economy that are not shared by all.

As described in detail elsewhere in this report,[414] the likelihood that taxpayers will receive a full return of their money depends on a variety of market factors that are impossible to predict with perfect accuracy. A certain portion of the funds have already been repaid, however, and the current prospect for a significant return is more favorable than it was as of the Panel's September 2009 report on the automotive industry. Using Mr. Bloom's yardstick, therefore, the program has been more successful than many had predicted.

Additional repayment at this point, however, turns in large part on Treasury's ability to sell off its entire stake in each company, including its sizeable remaining stake in GM. As discussed in Sections D, E, and F, above, Treasury faces challenges in each case. In the case of GM, Treasury still holds a substantial share of the common stock, which it must sell at a price approximately 64 percent above the IPO price to realize a profit on the government's overall investment. Investor interest in GM must therefore remain high enough to absorb such a large number of shares. GMAC/Ally Financial faces various uncertainties before investors are likely to welcome an IPO. And, in the case of Chrysler, the earliest an IPO is likely to occur is 2012, making it difficult to predict both Treasury's ability to sell its entire stake and the amount Treasury is likely to receive in such a sale. In any case, $3.5 billion of Treasury's investment in Chrysler has already been written off, so even a very successful IPO is unlikely to recoup all of the money invested in that company. Moreover, as discussed in Section E above, Treasury holds only an 8 percent equity stake in Chrysler and is unlikely to be able to exercise its call option to obtain more. This leaves Treasury with a stake that is too small either to command a control premium or to exercise any control over the timing of the IPO. Finally, it is not clear whether the market will have an appetite for shares of another large American auto company soon after the GM IPO.

The case of Chrysler Financial may provide an example of the government forgoing potential upside in order to exit an investment as quickly as possible. The issue is not that the implied value of Chrysler Financial increased by 33 percent in the seven months following the sale of Treasury's stake to Cerberus in May 2010. The Panel acknowledges that there is no exact science to determining the most opportune time to exit an investment. Rather, the government's exercise of due diligence in response to the overture from Cerberus to buy out its stake appears to have been surprisingly limited and did not envision other valuation scenarios for Chrysler Financial that would involve a strategic buyer for the asset. Clearly, both Cerberus and Chrysler Financial, on the other hand, recognized the value in the platform and subsequently sought to maximize the value of the business following the government's exit in preparation for a sale to a strategic buyer.

As the Panel has discussed in earlier reports, the cost of any program initiated under EESA cannot be measured solely by the amount of money returned to the public coffers.[415] The cost must also include a calculation of the risk that the American people assumed while the loans or investments were outstanding.[416] And it must include some accounting of the potential future effects on the industry and the wider economy, such as the heightened risk of moral hazard among American automobile companies, or among any large corporations, leading these companies and the market to assume that they have an implicit guarantee from the government (i.e., that they are "too big to fail," or at least will receive generous government support to ease the bankruptcy process). Even if such effects cannot be determined until years into the future, their potential must be taken into account when measuring the success of the automobile programs.

It is also difficult to determine how many jobs were saved through the government's intervention. In the aforementioned White House video presentation, Mr. Goolsbee states that hundreds of thousands of American workers are currently employed at GM plants, dealerships, and auto suppliers instead of "going out and looking for new work."[417] But, as discussed in Sections C and D, above, GM has also shed thousands of jobs as part of its bid to return to profitability. It is likely true that, had the company faced a prolonged disruption in operations as part of the bankruptcy process, either because the company was liquidated or because there was a significant delay in finding DIP financing, a much larger number of GM employees, if not all, may have been laid off.[418] The exact number of jobs ultimately saved is difficult to determine.

For example, some of the workers included in Mr. Goolsbee's calculation, such as those working for suppliers, may have served customers in addition to GM and may not have been laid off in the event of a GM liquidation. In addition, if the rescue of the automotive industry ultimately proves unsuccessful, then these jobs were not truly saved; instead, unemployment for these workers was delayed at a cost to the American taxpayers.[419] It is likely, however, that, had GM's bankruptcy been a more prolonged process, a larger number of workers would likely have lost their jobs.[420]

The final issue with respect to the effectiveness of the government's intervention is whether these companies are now on the path to long-term stability. Because the issues that determine long-term stability are often the same issues that determine a company's valuation, these factors overlap substantially with the question of whether and to what extent Treasury may recover its investment and exit its positions in these companies. As discussed in prior sections of this report, GMAC/Ally Financial has been profitable for the last three quarters, GM's earnings have increased in each of the last four quarters, and Chrysler has been consistently repaying its debts. GM and Chrysler nonetheless face a number of challenges. Both are seeking additional market share in the small-car sector, which is extremely competitive. Both must also convince consumers that they are creating reliable, quality cars, since their reputation in this area has been declining in recent years.[421] GMAC/Ally Financial must overcome its current trouble with foreclosure irregularities, and must establish a stable business model for automotive financing and leasing, one that is not overly dependent on GM in light of GM's acquisition of AmeriCredit. GMAC/Ally Financial also faces uncertainty related to its heavy concentration in the automotive industry. Even if the three companies' financials are relatively sound now, the domestic automotive sector as a whole must make a strong comeback in order for them to thrive.

4. Was Treasury Right in Establishing These Guidelines for Itself?

Treasury's determination to set and abide by its own guidelines may be an exemplary exercise in government restraint, or it may be an unnecessary and harmful restriction on government in a time when government intervention was necessary. The guidelines, to the extent that they were followed, provided some reassurance to the markets that Treasury's actions would be circumscribed and no more unpredictable than those of the average private investor. Moreover, given the public's preference for free-market commerce instead of government-owned enterprise, the guidelines may have assuaged some objections to Treasury's actions. They also may have provided a check on Treasury at times when the temptation to take more aggressive action arose and ensured that rules established with a cooler head prevailed.

On the other hand, Treasury created certain risk for the American people by imposing restrictions on its actions. The American people had a large amount of money at stake in private companies. Treasury arguably had a duty to protect those resources to the best of its ability, and voluntarily refraining from action could have been a way of doing less than that. Treasury staff has said that even if one of the companies had taken a step that, even to an industry outsider, would appear foolhardy, Treasury would not have stepped in to prevent the company from pursuing its plan. It does not appear that any of the companies involved with the TARP has had any intention of taking highly risky or questionable marketing or investment decisions, let alone actually having done so. Hence, Treasury's self-restraint does not seem to have ultimately had any harmful effects in practice.

There are, however, other opportunities that may have been lost. As discussed in the Panel's March 2010 report on GMAC/Ally Financial, it appears that the option to merge the company back into GM, making GMAC/Ally Financial again a captive finance arm, was not considered, despite certain potential advantages. The Panel has no opinion on whether merging the companies would actually have been the correct course, but it is disconcerting that the option was not thoroughly examined. This lack of consideration raises questions about whether other options that may have maximized benefits to the taxpayer were also left unexplored due to Treasury's avowed hands-off stance.

I. Conclusions and Recommendations

The financial crisis laid bare the challenges facing the domestic U.S. auto industry. The cumulative impact of a series of strategic and competitive missteps over the preceding decade came to the fore in the fall of 2008. While the Panel has previously questioned the government's perception of its policy choices during various stages of the crisis, there is little doubt that in the absence of massive government assistance, GM, Chrysler, and GMAC/Ally Financial faced the prospect of bankruptcies and potential liquidation, given the apparent dearth of available financing from the private sector. In the context of a fragile economy and the financial crisis (which severely restricted both corporate and consumer credit), the failure of these companies could have had significant near-term consequences in terms of job losses and the performance of the broader U.S. economy. Although the assets of GM and Chrysler (plants and equipment, employees, brand recognition) would have had value to other firms over the longer term, it was in the context of these adverse near-term consequences that both the Bush and Obama Administrations provided assistance to the auto sector.

The Panel takes no position on the decision to support the auto industry, a topic addressed in our September 2009 report. All told, the Bush and Obama Administrations provided $81.4 billion in assistance to these three companies (as well as $3.5 billion for auto suppliers). Unlike assistance to the banks, much of the government's investment still hangs in the balance, with 66 percent of overall assistance still outstanding. Treasury is now on course to recover the majority of its automotive investments within the next few years, but the impact of its actions will reverberate for much longer. Treasury's rescue suggested that any sufficiently large American corporation may be considered "too big to fail," broadening moral hazard risk from its TARP rescue actions beyond the financial sector. Further, the fact that the government helped absorb the consequences of GM's and Chrysler's failures has put more competently managed automotive companies at a disadvantage. Still, while the government perhaps set a dangerous precedent of expanding the notion of "too-big-to-fail" to the non-financial sector, the terms on which this support was provided offered considerably less comfort to legacy shareholders and creditors, at least to those of Chrysler and GM, than it did to the equity and debt holders of rescued financial firms.

While the outlook for the return on taxpayer funds has improved considerably over the past 12 months, there is still a long road ahead, particularly for GMAC/Ally Financial and Chrysler. Improving industry fundamentals – signified by GM's recent IPO – highlight a more hospitable backdrop since the Panel's last report on the auto sector in September 2009. This backdrop corresponds with improved operating fundamentals, as GM and Chrysler have shed costs and positioned themselves to produce profits at much lower levels of output. Market shares have generally stabilized, as has vehicle pricing since manufacturers no longer need to offer generous incentives to reduce overladen inventories. GMAC/Ally Financial has benefited from an improving backdrop for mortgage assets, allowing the firm to reduce the crushing overhang of its mortgage exposure, as well as reverse at least a portion of prior asset write-downs.

Against this improving backdrop, GM has reported improving earnings in each of the past four quarters. GMAC/Ally Financial is now in the black after reporting losses throughout 2009, and Chrysler's performance has improved materially with the help of its alliance with Fiat. (While operationally profitable, interest payments on TARP loans have prevented a bottom-line return to profitability at Chrysler.)

Treasury's calculations of potential taxpayer losses of $14.7 billion on total assistance of $81.3 billion to these three firms could ultimately prove conservative, but significant risks remain, given that the amount recovered will depend heavily on public market valuations of each firm's shares into 2011 and beyond.[422] Below is a brief summary of the status of Treasury's investments in GM, Chrysler, and GMAC/Ally Financial.

- GM: Of the $49.9 billion in total assistance, the government has thus far recouped $22.7 billion.[423] As of December 31, 2010, the government's unsold stake is valued at $18.4 billion, which would represent a total taxpayer loss of $7.9 billion.
- Chrysler: Only $2.2 billion in total assistance has been recouped,[424] and $3.5 billion in loans are considered a loss. However, the improved financial performance of the company indicates that Treasury's remaining loans to Chrysler may in fact be ultimately recovered. As discussed in Section E, for the government to recoup losses already incurred to Old Chrysler, the equity value of a potential IPO would have to exceed $14.5 billion.[425]
- GMAC/Ally Financial: Significant equity investments in GMAC/Ally Financial imply greater risk and more uncertainty in the lead-up to a potential IPO in 2011, although the improved operating performance – similar to that of GM and Chrysler – bodes well for a meaningful return on the $17.2 billion in total assistance to GMAC/Ally Financial. This being said, GMAC/Ally Financial is now the last TARP recipient standing – after the accelerated Citigroup exit and recent announcements about exiting AIG – for which the government has control of its exit and not articulated a clear exit strategy.

These rescue efforts by the government employed differentiated strategies with varying levels of risk to the taxpayer. While GM and Chrysler were put through bankruptcy, GMAC/Ally Financial was not, to the relative benefit of its legacy shareholders and creditors. Whereas the government shouldered the entire rescue of GM, it enlisted Fiat as a partner for Chrysler, which is a smaller and less economically significant automobile manufacturer than GM.

While the Panel has outlined various scenarios that could see taxpayers recover a meaningful amount of this assistance over the next two years, the financial returns on these investments do not tell the entire story and should not overshadow the Administration's broader objectives in providing assistance to the auto industry.

Unlike the intervention in the financial sector, the government in this case sought a broad restructuring of the underlying industry, and it was able to pursue this objective given its controlling stake in some of the impacted companies. Given the broader restructuring aims – as well as countering the threat of imminent and massive job losses – it is perhaps not surprising that the government has offered various benchmarks beyond a strict tally of the full return of the taxpayer's assistance to measure its success in this endeavor. While senior Treasury advisor Ronald Bloom once defined success solely in monetary terms – "the greater percentage of the money that we invested that we get back, the greater success",[426] – on other occasions Mr. Bloom and others in the Administration have cited the dual mandates of jobs preservation and effecting lasting fundamental reform of the auto sector.

As outlined in this report, there are examples of conflict – some inevitable, others not – between Treasury's core principles. In particular, the government has sought to present a consistent narrative of its role as a reluctant shareholder. In the case of GMAC/Ally Financial, transparency that would illustrate the unique circumstances of specific investments and explain certain actions by Treasury has sometimes been sacrificed in favor of retaining the appearance of a consistent narrative. This unnecessarily undermines the spirit of transparency critical to the effectiveness of the TARP.

Another recent example of this conflict between Treasury's principles involves Chrysler Financial, where meaningful incremental taxpayer returns appear to have been sacrificed in favor of an unnecessarily accelerated exit, further compounded by apparently questionable due diligence. The Panel notes that questions stemming from this transaction are not motivated by the fact that seven months following Treasury's exit, Chrysler Financial sold at a price that was 33 percent higher than the value of the company implied by Treasury's settlement price. Rather, the government's due diligence on the sale of its stake to Cerberus was surprisingly limited in scope. Treasury focused on the merits of the offer at hand and apparently neglected to contemplate more favorable valuation scenarios that may have resulted from a competitive bidding process of eager strategic buyers looking to acquire and invest in the Chrysler Financial platform. Given the apparent success of the longer-term investment mindset that has characterized the government's management of its AIG and GMAC/Ally Financial investments, Treasury's haste to exit Chrysler Financial is perplexing.

A final tally on the return of taxpayer assistance and a report card on longer-term reform efforts remain premature. Early returns indicate that the government's intervention in the auto sector – leaving aside any assessment of the relative merits of providing that assistance in the first place – has been surprisingly successful, both in terms of financial returns from assistance and the rebound in the companies' performance. The Panel notes that GM and Chrysler are now *adding* jobs after their initial downsizings. However, as noted, a more robust scorecard, one that weighs the positives from government intervention, such as the near-term preservation of jobs and prevention of a deeper contraction in the economy, versus the negatives, including the investment of substantial taxpayer dollars and the precedent set by government intervention into the private sector, is required to evaluate fully the government's actions. Nonetheless, this longer-term assessment should not obscure the near-term focus on recovering as much value as possible for the taxpayer. At the same time, the Panel recognizes that absent sustainable reform that produces a smaller auto industry subject to the discipline of the private capital markets, improved returns on taxpayer assistance could mask longer-term risks.

Likewise, the relatively improved outlook should not overshadow serious questions that prevent a more transparent assessment of the government's efforts. These questions arise from the fact that, having intervened on a massive scale and outlined sweeping mandates for the reform of the industry, the government – by its own account – then chose largely to retreat to the sidelines, performing run-of-the-mill oversight of its investments and leaving the heavy lifting to the government's designees on the companies' boards of directors.

Treasury has consistently (and often vociferously) asserted that it will not interfere or otherwise seek to influence the strategic management of the companies in which it holds a stake. The Panel recognizes the importance of a hands-off approach to day-to-day business operations and recognizes that crossing this line in certain instances can raise troubling questions regarding the government's role in the private sector. However, many would argue that this line had long since been crossed, given the government's initial decision to provide assistance to the auto industry, and to pretend otherwise today begs credulity.

In the case of GMAC/Ally Financial, the Panel recommended previously that Treasury explore the possibility of value-enhancing strategic arrangements that would seek to maximize the government's aggregate stake in both GM and GMAC/Ally Financial. Subsequently, rather than seeking a closer relationship with GMAC/Ally Financial, GM has chosen to build its own auto financing subsidiary via the acquisition of AmeriCredit. While such a move may seemingly make strategic sense for GM, it is not clear if the value to the government, as a shareholder in GM, outstrips the potential negative impact of this acquisition to the government's stake in GMAC/Ally Financial. Treasury's deliberate refusal to take a portfolio investment approach to managing its holdings across the auto sector appears to be inconsistent with the rationale for its decision to rescue GMAC/Ally Financial, which was to help GM continue to finance car sales, particularly to its dealership network.[427]

The Panel recognizes two potential positive developments from Treasury's hands-off approach. Namely, GM's efforts to establish its own captive auto finance subsidiary will likely improve the competitive dynamics in this market by reducing the company's reliance on GMAC/Ally Financial. Further, any residual moral hazard in the marketplace related to the perception that GMAC/Ally Financial is too interconnected with GM to be allowed to fail would likely be mitigated by GM's development of its own captive financing subsidiary.

The Panel makes the following recommendations:

- The Administration should enhance disclosure in the budget and financial statements for the TARP by reporting on the valuation assumptions ("credit reform" subsidy rates) for the individual companies included in the overall subsidy rate for the AIFP.
- The Panel recognizes that it is in the private sector's and the government's interest for Treasury to exit its investments as soon as practicable. However, Treasury should be cognizant that this may not in all instances be in the taxpayer's best interest. The Panel urges Treasury to consult independent third parties to assess these determinations in the future to identify instances where a longer investment horizon may meaningfully improve the outlook for the taxpayer's return on its investment.
- Treasury sought to assure the Panel during its February 2010 hearing on GMAC/Ally Financial that legacy private sector stakeholders in the company would not see any return until and if the U.S. taxpayer recoups its entire investment. The Panel recommends that Treasury expand on this assertion, clarifying its approach to the treatment of legacy shareholders in GMAC/Ally Financial as the government's exit plan moves forward. Aside from the consequences to the taxpayer's interest, clarifying the treatment of legacy shareholders will help preserve market discipline going forward.
- Given the scale of government intervention and the desire not to repeat this episode, it may be in the taxpayer's interest that Congress commission independent researchers to periodically assess the long-term fallout from the collapse of the auto industry and the subsequent government intervention, including the risk to taxpayers stemming from future disruptions to the auto market from economic, credit market or other potential threats. Related to these efforts, Congress should also follow up by contracting with independent researchers and market analysts to develop more credible estimates of the impact of the bailout of GM, GMAC/Ally Financial, and Chrysler on economic performance and employment.

SECTION TWO: ADDITIONAL VIEWS

A. J. Mark McWatters and Professor Kenneth R. Troske

We concur with the issuance of the January report and offer the additional observations below. We appreciate the efforts the Panel and staff made incorporating our suggestions offered during the drafting of the report.

We wish to make the following points.

- In the closing days of 2008 when GM, Chrysler, and GMAC/Ally Financial faltered, the American taxpayers – not the Department of Treasury – stood as the last safe-haven for these distressed institutions. In return for their generosity the CBO estimates that the taxpayers stand to lose approximately $19 billion on their investments.[428] This is real money, enough to finance the construction of over four Nimitz-class aircraft carriers (at $4.5 billion each) or fund approximately 25 years of NIH-sponsored breast cancer research (at $765 million per year).[429]
- Treasury's primary role in the restructuring of GM, Chrysler, and GMAC/Ally Financial was to act as a funding conduit for the taxpayer sourced capital infusions. These institutions have, not surprisingly, performed reasonably well over the past several months due to the strength of their foreign markets, the recovery of their domestic markets, the replacement of their directors and senior management, the de-leveraging of their balance sheets, the renegotiation of their collective bargaining agreements, the recovery of the capital markets, the tepid recovery of the general economy, and, of course, the "gift" of $19 billion or so of taxpayer funds. It remains to be seen, however, if these companies can remain on the path to financial recovery and independence from taxpayer-sourced subsidies.
- The Panel concludes in the report: "there is little doubt that in the absence of massive government assistance, GM, Chrysler, and GMAC/Ally Financial faced the prospect of bankruptcies and potential liquidation."[430]

While bankruptcy did follow for GM and Chrysler and probably should have followed for GMAC/Ally Financial, we remain skeptical that the companies would have been liquidated and sold off for scrap value absent direct intervention by the government. The brisk turn-around of the three institutions over the past two years indicates that even in the last quarter of 2008 substantial inherent value existed within each company. Despite claims to the contrary, we still have trouble concluding that Chevrolet, Cadillac, Buick, GMC trucks, and Jeep, as well as GMAC/Ally Financial's auto finance business, among others, were worth next to nothing in the closing days of 2008 and, but for the taxpayer-funded bailouts, would have failed and left hundreds of thousands temporarily unemployed. It would have been preferable for these institutions to have been reorganized by private sector participants, with, perhaps, debtor-in-possession financing guaranteed to a limited extent by the government. It is difficult to accept that private sector strategic buyers, private equity firms, hedge funds, and sovereign wealth funds were not willing and able to orchestrate the successful reorganizations or restructurings of the three distressed companies. Once the government entered the picture and signaled its intent to bail out the institutions with its unlimited taxpayer-financed checkbook, it is hardly surprising that private sector participants demurred. Under such circumstances, it is not possible for even the most sophisticated, motivated, and financially secure of private sector firms to prevail.

- The Panel states in the report:

Treasury is now on course to recover the majority of its automotive investments within the next few years, but the impact of its actions will reverberate for much longer. Treasury's rescue suggested that any sufficiently large American corporation – even if it is not a bank – may be considered "too big to fail," creating a risk that moral hazard will infect areas of the economy far beyond the financial system. Further, the fact that the government helped absorb the consequences of GM's and Chrysler's failures has put more competently managed automotive companies at a disadvantage. For these reasons, the effects of Treasury's intervention will linger long after taxpayers have sold their last share of stock in the automotive industry.[431]

The Panel states in the report:

These favorable events, however, must be thoughtfully balanced against the moral hazard risks created by the taxpayer's bailout of the three institutions and the ongoing implicit guarantee of the government. By bailing out GM, Chrysler, and GMAC/Ally Financial, the government sent a powerful message to the marketplace – some institutions will be protected at all cost, while others must prosper or fail based upon their own business judgment and acumen. We regret that Treasury has focused solely on the apparent success of the GM IPO in assessing the rescues of the three institutions to the distinct exclusion of the moral hazard risks arising from the bailouts.[432]

The Panel also states in the report:

As the Panel has discussed in earlier reports, the cost of any program initiated under EESA cannot be measured solely by the amount of money returned to the public coffers. The cost must also include a calculation of the risk that the American people assumed while the loans or investments were outstanding. And it must include some accounting of the potential future effects on the industry and the wider economy, such as the heightened risk of moral hazard among American automobile companies, or among any large corporations, leading these companies and the market to assume that they have an implicit guarantee from the government (i.e., that they are "too big to fail," or at least will receive generous government support to ease the bankruptcy process). Even if such effects cannot be determined until years into the future, their potential must be taken into account when measuring the success of the automobile programs.[433]

In our view, the above passages represent the most significant analysis provided in the report. The TARP has all but created an expectation, if not an emerging sense of entitlement, that certain financial and non-financial institutions are simply "too-big-or-too-interconnected-to-fail" and that the government will promptly honor the implicit guarantee issued for the benefit of any such institution that suffers a reversal of fortune. This is the enduring legacy of the TARP. Unfortunately, by offering a strong safety net funded with unlimited taxpayer resources, the government has encouraged potential recipients of such largess to undertake inappropriately risky behavior secure in the conviction that all profits from their endeavors will inure to their benefit and that large losses will fall to the taxpayers. The placement of a government sanctioned thumb-on-the-scales corrupts the fundamental tenets of a market economy – the ability to prosper *and the ability to fail.*

Following the bailouts of GM, Chrysler, and GMAC/Ally Financial and the potential loss of $19 billion or more of taxpayer-sourced funds, is it realistic to expect that the government will permit these companies to fail the next time around? We have our doubts. More significantly, the directors, managers, and employees of these institutions most likely appreciate the benefits afforded by the government's implicit guarantee, but it remains to be seen whether they also appreciate the attendant moral hazard risks.

- Although not the subject of this report, we would be remiss if we did not note that commentators have questioned the treatment of certain classes of creditors in the GM and Chrysler bankruptcies as well as certain procedures adopted by and rulings of the bankruptcy courts.[434]

Regarding this matter, Barry E. Adler, the Petrie Professor of Law and Business, New York University, offered the following testimony to the Panel:

> The rapid disposition of Chrysler in Chapter 11 was formally structured as a sale under §363 of the Bankruptcy Code. While that provision does, under some conditions, permit the sale of a debtor's assets, free and clear of any interest in them, the sale in Chrysler was irregular and inconsistent with the principles that undergird the Code.
> The most notable irregularity of the Chrysler sale was that the assets were not sold free and clear ... That is, money that might have been available to repay these secured creditors was withheld by the purchaser to satisfy unsecured obligations owed the UAW. Thus, the sale of Chrysler's assets was not merely a sale, but also a distribution – one might call it a diversion – of the sale proceeds seemingly inconsistent with contractual priority among the creditors.
> Given the constraint on bids, it is conceivable that the liquidation value of Chrysler's assets exceeded the company's going-concern value but that no liquidation bidder came forward because the assumed liabilities – combined with the government's determination to have the company stay in business – made a challenge to the favored sale unprofitable, particularly in the short time frame afforded. It is also possible that, but for the restrictions, there might have been a higher bid for the company as a going concern, perhaps in anticipation of striking a better deal with workers. Thus, the approved sale may not have fetched the best price for the Chrysler assets. That is, the diversion of sales proceeds to the assumed liabilities may have been greater than the government's subsidy of the transaction, if any, in which case the secured creditors would have suffered a loss of priority for their claims. There is nothing in the Bankruptcy Code that allows a sale for less than fair value simply because the circumstances benefit a favored group of creditors.[435]

In addition, with respect to the bailout of GMAC/Ally Financial, the Panel offered the following observations in its March 2010 report:

> Although the Panel takes no position on whether Treasury should have rescued GMAC, it finds that Treasury missed opportunities to increase accountability and better protect taxpayers' money. Treasury did not, for example, condition access to TARP

money on the same sweeping changes that it required from GM and Chrysler: it did not wipe out GMAC's equity holders; nor did it require GMAC to create a viable plan for returning to profitability; nor did it require a detailed, public explanation of how the company would use taxpayer funds to increase consumer lending.

Moreover, the Panel remains unconvinced that bankruptcy was not a viable option in 2008. In connection with the Chrysler and GM bankruptcies, Treasury might have been able to orchestrate a strategic bankruptcy for GMAC. This bankruptcy could have preserved GMAC's automotive lending functions while winding down its other, less significant operations, dealing with the ongoing liabilities of the mortgage lending operations, and putting the company on sounder economic footing. The Panel is also concerned that Treasury has not given due consideration to the possibility of merging GMAC back into GM, a step which would restore GM's financing operations to the model generally shared by other automotive manufacturers, thus strengthening GM and eliminating other money-losing operations.[436]

SECTION THREE: TARP UPDATES SINCE LAST REPORT

A. Ally Financial Mandatory Convertible Preferred Exchange to Common Stock

On December 30, 2010, Treasury converted $5.5 billion of its total convertible preferred stock in GMAC/Ally Financial into 531,850 shares of common stock of the company, following the terms of conversion. Treasury currently holds $5.9 billion of GMAC/Ally Financial's convertible preferred stock, $2.7 billion in Trust Preferred securities, and 73.8 percent of the common stock.

B. Metrics

Each month, the Panel's report highlights a number of metrics that the Panel and others, including Treasury, the Government Accountability Office (GAO), the Special Inspector General for the Troubled Asset Relief Program (SIGTARP), and the Financial Stability Oversight Board, consider useful in assessing the effectiveness of the Administration's efforts to restore financial stability and accomplish the goals of EESA. This section discusses changes that have occurred in several indicators since the release of the Panel's December 2010 report.

1. Financial Indices

Financial Stress
The St. Louis Financial Stress Index, a proxy for financial stress in the U.S. economy, has decreased by more than half since the Panel's December 2010 report. The index has decreased more than 80 percent since its post-crisis peak in June 2010. Furthermore, the recent trend in the index suggests that financial stress continues moving toward its long-run norm. The index has decreased by more than four standard deviations since EESA was enacted in October 2008.

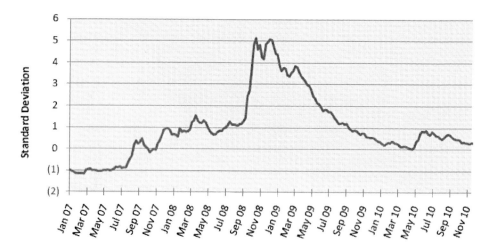

Figure 27. St. Louis Federal Reserve Financial Stress Index[437].

Stock Market Volatility

Stock market volatility, as measured by the Chicago Board Options Exchange Volatility Index (VIX), continues to decrease. The VIX has fallen by more than half since its post-crisis peak in May 2010 and has declined 18 percent since the Panel's December 2010 report. As of January 3, 2011, volatility was 13 percent higher than its post-crisis low on April 12, 2010.

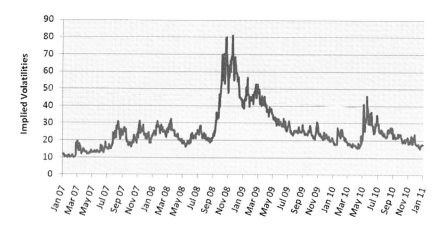

Figure 28. Chicago Board Options Exchange Volatility Index[438].

Interest Rates

As of January 3, 2011, the 3-month and 1-month London Interbank Offer Rates (LIBOR), the prices at which banks lend and borrow from each other, were 0.30 and 0.26, respectively.[439] Both rates have decreased slightly since the Panel's December 2010 report. The 3-month and 1-month LIBOR remain below their post-crisis highs in June 2010. Over the longer term, interest rates remain extremely low relative to pre-crisis levels, reflecting the impact of the actions of central banks and institutions' perceptions of reduced risk in lending to other banks.

Indicator	Current Rates	Percent Change from Data Available at Time of Last Report (12/1/2010)
3-Month LIBOR[440]	0.30	(0.2)%
1-Month LIBOR[441]	0.26	(1.8)%

Figure 29. 3-Month and 1-Month LIBOR Rates (as of January 3, 2011).

Interest Rate Spreads

As of January 3, 2011, the conventional mortgage rate spread, which measures the difference between 30-year mortgage rates and 10-year Treasury bond yields, decreased by 8 percent since the Panel's December 2010 report.[442] The TED spread, which captures the difference between the 3-month LIBOR and the 3-month Treasury bill rates, serves as an indicator for perceived risk in the financial markets.[443] As of January 3, 2011, the spread was 18.3 basis points, increasing almost 30 percent in December.

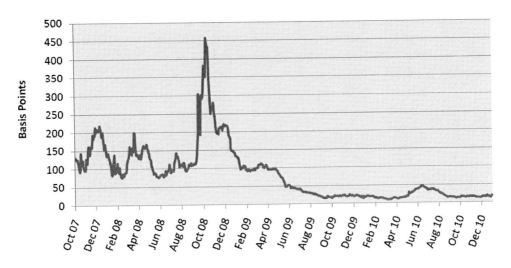

Figure 30. TED Spread[446].

The LIBOR-OIS (Overnight Index Swap) spread serves as a metric for the health of the banking system, reflecting what banks believe to be the risk of default associated with interbank lending.[444] The spread increased over threefold from early April to July 2010, before falling in mid-July.[445] The LIBOR-OIS spread grew approximately 13 percent since the Panel's December 2010 report. The decrease in both the LIBOR-OIS spread and the TED spread from the middle of 2010 suggests that hesitation among banks to lend to counterparties has receded. As shown in Figures 30 and 31 below, these spreads remain below pre-crisis levels.

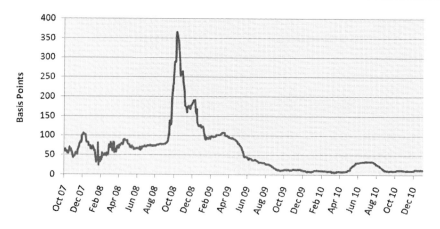

Figure 31. LIBOR-OIS Spread[447].

The interest rate spread on AA asset-backed commercial paper, which is considered mid-investment grade, decreased by almost 20 percent since the Panel's December 2010 report. The interest rate spread on A2/P2 commercial paper, a lower grade investment than AA asset-backed commercial paper, increased by approximately 10 percent. Both interest rate spreads remain below pre-crisis levels.

Indicator	Current Spread	Percent Change Since Last Report (12/1/2010)
Conventional mortgage rate spread[448]	1.44	(7.7)%
TED Spread (basis points)	18.28	27.5%
Overnight AA asset-backed commercial paper interest rate spread[449]	0.06	(19.4)%
Overnight A2/P2 nonfinancial commercial paper interest rate spread[450]	0.14	9.7%

Figure 32. Interest Rate Spreads (as of January 3, 2011).

Corporate Bonds

The spread between Moody's Baa Corporate Bond Yield Index and 30-year constant maturity U.S. Treasury Bond, which indicates the difference in perceived risk between corporate and government bonds, doubled from late April to mid-June 2010. During December, the spread declined approximately 10 percent, and has fallen almost 30 percent since its post-crisis peak in mid-June. The declining spread could indicate waning concerns about the riskiness of corporate bonds.

2. Bank Conditions

Net Charge-Offs and Nonperforming Loan Rates

Data on net charge-offs and nonperforming loans are beginning to reflect stabilizing loan quality in domestic banks loan charge-offs represented 2.8 percent of all loans at the end of the third quarter of 2010, falling 10 percent from the first quarter of 2010. Nonperforming loans as a percentage of all commercial bank loans have also declined. Nonperforming loans include loans that are in default for 90 or more days and nonaccrual loans.[452] Since the beginning of 2010, this percentage has fallen from 5.6 percent to 5.2 percent at the end of the third quarter of 2010.

Despite the recent decline, these two percentages remain well above their respective levels in October 2008. At the time, total net loan charge-offs accounted for only 1.2 percent of all loans, and nonperforming loans represented 2.3 percent of all loans.

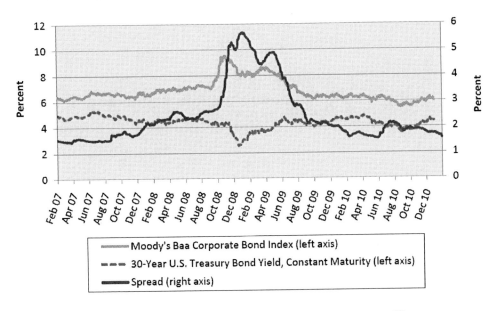

Figure 33. Moody's Baa Corporate Bond Index and 30-Year U.S. Treasury Yield[451].

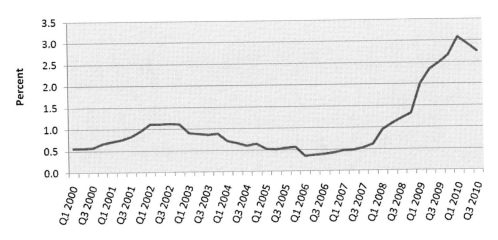

Figure 34. Net Loan Charge-Offs as a Percentage of Total Loans (as of Q3 2010)[453].

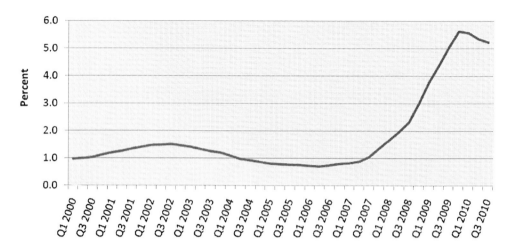

Figure 35. Nonperforming Loans as a Percentage of Total Loans (as of Q3 2010)[454].

Bank Failures

In 2010, a total of 157 banks failed and were placed into receivership, with eight institutions failing in December. Despite exceeding the total number of bank failures for 2009, banks that failed in 2010 had $92.1 billion in total assets, which represents approximately half of the total assets of failed institutions in 2009.[455] Most failures in 2010 involved institutions that held less than $10 billion in assets.

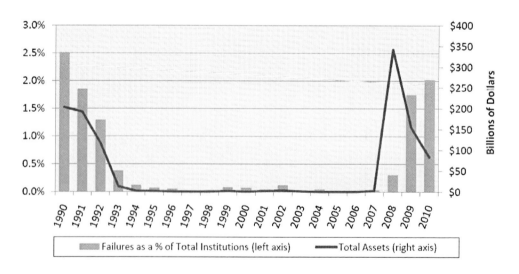

Figure 36. Bank Failures as a Percentage of Total Banks and Bank Failures by Total Assets (1990-2010)[456].

3. Housing Indices

Home Sales

Both new and existing home sales saw a month-over-month increase in November 2010, increasing 2 percent during the month. New home sales, as measured by the U.S. Census Bureau, increased 2 percent to 290,000 during the month. With respect to existing home sales, the National Association of Realtors estimates a 6 percent month-over-month increase in November, to an annual rate of 4.4 million homes sold. Although existing home sales in November remain below the ten-year historical average, current levels are above the July 2010 level, when existing home sales reached their lowest point in more than a decade.

Figure 37. New and Existing Home Sales (2000-2010)[457].

Foreclosures

Foreclosure actions, which consist of default notices, scheduled auctions, and bank repossessions, decreased 21 percent in November 2010 to 262,339, marking the first month since February 2009 that foreclosure filings have been below 300,000.[458] However, it is important to note that much of the decline could be attributed to a number of loan servicers suspending foreclosures in the fall of 2010 as they conducted internal reviews of their foreclosure procedures.[459] Since the enactment of EESA, there have been approximately 8.4 million foreclosure filings.[460]

Home Prices

With respect to housing price indices, the Case-Shiller Composite 20-City Composite Home Price Index decreased by less than 1 percent, while the FHFA Housing Price Index increased by less than 1 percent in October 2010. The Case-Shiller and FHFA indices are approximately 8 percent and 5 percent below their respective October 2008 levels.[461]

Case-Shiller futures prices indicate a market expectation that home-price values for the major Metropolitan Statistical Areas (MSAs) will decrease through 2011.[462] These futures are cash-settled to a weighted composite index of U.S. housing prices in the top ten MSAs, as well as to those specific markets. They are used to hedge by businesses whose profits and losses are related to a specific area of the housing industry, and to balance portfolios by businesses seeking exposure to an uncorrelated asset class. As such, futures prices are a composite indicator of market information known to date and can be used to indicate market expectations for home prices.

Indicator	Most Recent Monthly Data	Percent Change from Data Available at Time of Last Report	Percent Change Since October 2008
Monthly foreclosure actions[463]	262,339	(21.0)%	(6.2)%
S&P/Case-Shiller Composite 20 Index[464]	143.52	(0.1)%	(8.2)%
FHFA Housing Price Index[465]	190.83	0.2%	(5.4)%

Figure 38. Housing Indicators.

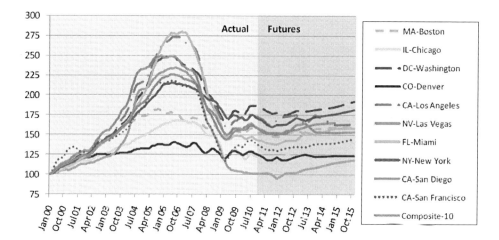

Figure 39. Case-Shiller Home Price Index and Futures Values[466].

C. Financial Update

Each month, the Panel summarizes the resources that the federal government has committed to the rescue and recovery of the financial system. The following financial update provides: (1) an updated accounting of the TARP, including a tally of dividend income, repayments, and warrant dispositions that the program has received as of November 30, 2010; and (2) an updated accounting of the full federal resource commitment as of December 30, 2010.

1. The TARP

a. Program Updates[467]

Treasury's spending authority under the TARP officially expired on October 3, 2010. Though it can no longer make new funding commitments, Treasury can continue to provide

An Update on TARP Support for the Domestic Automotive Industry

funding for programs for which it has existing contracts and previous commitments. To date, $396.2 billion has been spent under the TARP's $475 billion ceiling.[468] Of the total amount disbursed, $240.4 billion has been repaid. Treasury has also incurred $6.1 billion in losses associated with its Capital Purchase Program (CPP) and Automotive Industry Financing Program (AIFP) investments. About two-thirds of the $149.8 billion in TARP funds currently outstanding relates to Treasury's investments in AIG and assistance provided to the automotive industry.

CPP Repayments

As of December 30, 2010, 131 of the 707 banks that participated in the CPP have fully redeemed their preferred shares either through capital repayment or exchanges for investments under the Community Development Capital Initiative (CDCI). During December 2010, Treasury received the funds from the sale of the final outstanding Citigroup shares, equaling full repayment of the $25 billion investment as well as an additional $6.9 billion in profit from the sale of these shares.[469] An additional 14 banks fully repaid their remaining CPP capital, returning $3.3 billion in principal to Treasury. See Figure 40 below for repayment amounts.

Bank	Amount Repaid	Remaining Investment
First Horizon National Corporation	$866,540,000	Warrants
Huntington Bancshares	1,398071,000	Warrants
Heritage Financial Corporation	24,000,000	Warrants
First PacTrust Bancorp, Inc.	19,300,000	Warrants
East West Bancorp	406,546,000	Warrants
Wintrust Financial Corporation	250,000,000	Warrants
Capital Bancorp, Inc.	4,700,000	None
Surrey Bancorp	2,000,000	None
1st Source Corporation	111,000,000	None
California Oaks State Bank	3,300,000	None
The Bank of Currituck	1,742,850	None
Haviland Bancshares, Inc.	425,000	None
Signature Bancshares, Inc.	1,700,000	None
Nationwide Bankshares, Inc.	2,000,000	None
Total	$3,332,871,850	

Figure 40. Banks that Fully Repaid Their CPP Loans in December 2010[470].

Additionally, during December 2010, United Financial Banking Companies, Inc. made a partial repayment of $3 million, and The Bank of Kentucky Financial Corporation made a partial repayment of $17 million. A total of $167.9 billion has been repaid under the program, leaving $34.4 billion in funds currently outstanding.[471]

b. Income: Dividends, Interest, and Warrant Sales

In conjunction with its preferred stock investments under the CPP and the Targeted Investment Program (TIP), Treasury generally received warrants to purchase common equity.[472] As of December 30, 2010, 46 institutions have repurchased their warrants from Treasury at an agreed-upon price. Treasury has also sold warrants for 15 other institutions at auction. To date, income from warrant dispositions totals $8.2 billion.

In addition to warrant proceeds, Treasury also receives dividend payments on the preferred shares that it holds under the CPP, 5 percent per year for the first five years and 9 percent per year thereafter.[473] For preferred shares issued under the TIP, Treasury received a dividend of 8 percent per year.[474] In total, Treasury has received approximately $30.3 billion in net income from warrant repurchases, dividends, interest payments, profit from the sale of stock, and other proceeds deriving from TARP investments, after deducting losses.[475] For further information on TARP profit and loss, see Figure 42.

c. TARP Accounting

Program	Maximum Amount Allotted	Actual Funding	Total Repayments/ Reduced Exposure	Total Losses	Funding Currently Outstanding	Funding Available
Capital Purchase Program (CPP)	$204.9	$204.9	[ii]$(167.9)	[iii]$(2.6)	$34.4	$0
Targeted Investment Program (TIP)	40.0	40.0	(40.0)	0	0	0
Asset Guarantee Program (AGP)	5.0	[iv]5.0	[v](5.0)	0	0	0
AIG Investment Program (AIGIP)	69.8	[vi]47.5	0	0	47.5	22.3
Auto Industry Financing Program (AIFP)	81.3	81.3	(26.4)	[vii](3.5)	[viii]51.4	0
Auto Supplier Support Program (ASSP)[ix]	0.4	0.4	(0.4)	0	0	0
Term Asset-Backed Securities Loan Facility (TALF)	[x]4.3	[xi]0.1	0	0	0.1	4.2
Public-Private Investment Program (PPIP)[xii]	22.4	[xiii]15.1	[xiv](0.6)	0	14.5	7.4
SBA 7(a) Securities Purchase Program	0.4	[xv]0.4	0	0	0.4	[xvi]0
Home Affordable Modification Program (HAMP)	29.9	0.8	0	0	0.7	29.1
Hardest Hit Fund (HHF)	[xvii]7.6	[xviii]0.1	0	0	0.1	7.5

Program	Maximum Amount Allotted	Actual Funding	Total Repayments/ Reduced Exposure	Total Losses	Funding Currently Outstanding	Funding Available
FHA Refinance Program	8.1	[xix]0.1	0	0	0.1	8.0
Community Development Capital Initiative (CDCI)	0.8	[xx]0.6	0	0	0.6	0
Total	$475.0	$396.2	$(240.4)	$(6.1)	$149.8	$78.5

Figure 41. TARP Accounting (as of December 30, 2010) *(billions of dollars)*[i].

TARP Initiative[xxi]	Dividends[xxii] (as of 11/30/2010)	Interest[xxiii] (as of 11/30/2010)	Warrant Disposition Proceeds[xxiv] (as of 12/30/2010)	Other Proceeds (as of 11/30/2010)	Losses[xxv] (as of 12/30/2010)	Total
Total	$17,345	$1,083	$8,160	$9,801	($6,066)	$30,353
CPP	10,169	59	6,905	[xxvi]6,852	(2,578)	21,407
TIP	3,004	–	1,256	–	–	4,260
AIFP	[xxvii]3,729	931	–	xxviii15	(3,488)	1,217
ASSP	–	15	–	[xxix]101	–	116
AGP	443	–	–	[xxx]2,246	–	2,689
PPIP	–	76	–	[xxxi]310	–	386
SBA 7(a)	–	3	–	–	–	3
Bank of America Guarantee	–	–	–	[xxxii]276	–	276

Figure 42. TARP Profit and Loss *(millions of dollars)*.

d. CPP Unpaid Dividend and Interest Payments[476]

As of November 30, 2010, 140 institutions have missed at least one dividend payment on outstanding preferred stock issued under the CPP.[477] Among these institutions, 111 are not current on cumulative dividends, amounting to $151.5 million in missed payments. Another 29 banks have not paid $9.7 million in non-cumulative dividends. Of the $49.5 billion currently outstanding in CPP funding, Treasury's investments in banks with non-current dividend payments total $7.2 billion. A majority of the banks that remain delinquent on dividend payments have under $1 billion in total assets on their balance sheets. Also, there are 21 institutions that no longer have outstanding unpaid dividends, after previously deferring their quarterly payments.[478]

Twelve banks have failed to make six dividend payments, six banks have missed seven quarterly payments, and one bank has missed all eight quarterly payments. These institutions have received a total of $897.2 million in CPP funding. Under the terms of the CPP, after a bank fails to pay dividends for six periods, Treasury has the right to elect two individuals to the company's board of directors.[479] Figure 43 below provides further details on the distribution and the number of institutions that have missed dividend payments.

In addition, eight CPP participants have missed at least one interest payment, representing $4.0 million in cumulative unpaid interest payments. Treasury's total investments in these non-public institutions represent less than $1 billion in CPP funding.

Number of Missed Payments	1	2	3	4	5	6	7	8	Total
Cumulative Dividends									
Number of Banks, by asset size	17	28	20	20	14	9	3	0	111
Under $1B	10	21	17	16	9	6	1	0	80
$1B-$10B	6	6	3	3	5	3	2	0	28
Over $10B	1	1	0	1	0	0	0	0	3
Non-Cumulative Dividends									
Number of Banks, by asset size	6	1	6	6	3	3	3	1	29
Under $1B	5	1	6	5	3	3	3	1	27
$1B-$10B	0	0	0	1	0	0	0	0	1
Over $10B	1	0	0	0	0	0	0	0	1
Total Banks Missing Payments									140
Total Missed Payments									470

Figure 43. CPP Missed Dividend Payments (as of November 30, 2010)[480].

e. CPP Losses

As of December 30, 2010, Treasury has realized a total of $2.6 billion in losses from investments in five CPP participants. CIT Group Inc. and Pacific Coast National Bancorp have both completed bankruptcy proceedings, and the preferred stock and warrants issued by the South Financial Group, TIB Financial Corp., and the Bank of Currituck were sold to third-party institutions at a discount. Excluded from Treasury's total losses are investments in institutions that have pending receivership or bankruptcy proceedings, as well as an institution that is currently the target of an acquisition.[481] Settlement of these transactions and proceedings would increase total losses in the CPP to $3.0 billion. Figure 44 below details settled and unsettled investment losses from CPP participants that have declared bankruptcy, been placed into receivership, or renegotiated the terms of their CPP contracts.

Institution	Investment Amount	Investment Disposition Amount	Warrant Disposition Amount	Dividends & Interest	Possible Losses/ Reduced Exposure	Action
Cadence Financial Corporation	$44,000,000	$38,000,000	—	$2,970,000	$(6,000,000)	10/29/2010: Treasury agreed to sell preferred stock and warrants issued by Cadence Financial to Community Bancorp LLC for $38 million plus accrued and unpaid dividends. Completion of the sale subject to fulfillment of certain closing conditions.
Capital Bank Corporation[483]	41,279,000	—	—	3,457,117	(20,639,500)	11/9/2010: Capital Bank Corp. is seeking to enter an agreement with Treasury pursuant to which the company will repurchase outstanding TARP preferred shares at 50 percent of liquidation value, plus accrued unpaid dividends. The company will use cash proceeds from its acquisition by North American Financial Holdings Inc. As of Nov. 30, 2010, no agreement has been reached between Capital Bank Corp. and Treasury.
CIT Group Inc.*	2,330,000,000	—	—	43,687,500	(2,330,000,000)	12/10/2009: Bankruptcy reorganization plan for CIT Group Inc. became effective. CPP preferred shares and warrants were extinguished and replaced with contingent value rights (CVR). On Feb. 8, 2010, the CVRs expired without value.
Midwest Banc Holdings, Inc.	89,388,000	—	—	824,289	(89,388,000)	5/14/2010: Midwest Banc Holdings, Inc. subsidiary, Midwest Bank and Trust, Co., placed into receivership. Midwest Banc Holdings is currently in bankruptcy proceedings.
Pacific Coast National Bancorp*	4,120,000	—	—	18,088	(4,120,000)	2/11/2010: Pacific Coast National Bancorp dismissed its bankruptcy proceedings without recovery to creditors or investors. Investments, including Treasury's CPP investments, were extinguished.
Pierce County Bancorp	6,800,000	—	—	207,948	(6,800,000)	11/5/2010: Pierce County Bancorp subsidiary, Pierce Commercial Bank, placed into receivership.
Sonoma Valley Bancorp	8,653,000	—	—	347,164	(8,653,000)	8/20/2010: Sonoma Valley Bancorp subsidiary, Sonoma Valley Bank, placed into receivership.
South Financial Group*	347,000,000	130,179,219	$400,000	16,386,111	(216,820,781)	9/30/2010: Preferred stock and warrants sold to Toronto-Dominion Bank.

Figure 44. (Continued)

The Bank of Currituck*	4,021,000	1,742,850		169,834	(2,278,150)	12/3/2010: The Bank of Currituck completed its repurchase of all preferred stock (including preferred stock received upon exercise of warrants) issued to Treasury.
TIB Financial Corp.*	37,000,000	12,119,637	40,000	1,284,722	(24,880,363)	9/30/2010: Preferred stock and warrants sold to North American Financial Holdings.
Tifton Banking Company	3,800,000			223,208	(3,800,000)	11/12/2010: Tifton Banking Company placed into receivership.
UCBH Holdings, Inc.	298,737,000			7,509,920	(298,737,000)	11/6/2009: United Commercial Bank, a wholly owned subsidiary of UCBH Holdings, Inc., was placed into receivership. UCBH Holdings is currently in bankruptcy proceedings.
Total	$3,214,798,000	$182,041,706	440,000	77,085,901	$(3,012,116,794)	

Figure 44. CPP Settled and Unsettled Losses[482].

An Update on TARP Support for the Domestic Automotive Industry   85

f. Rate of Return

As of January 3, 2011, the average internal rate of return for all public financial institutions that participated in the CPP and fully repaid the U.S. government (including preferred shares, dividends, and warrants) remained at 8.4 percent, with only one institution, Central Jersey Bancorp, exiting the program in December.[484] The internal rate of return is the annualized effective compounded return rate that can be earned on invested capital.

g. Warrant Disposition

Institution	Investment Date	Warrant Repurchase Date	Warrant Repurchase/ Sale Amount	Panel's Best Valuation Estimate at Disposition Date	Price/ Estimate Ratio	IRR
Old National Bancorp	12/12/2008	5/8/2009	$1,200,000	$2,150,000	0.558	9.3%
Iberiabank Corporation	12/5/2008	5/20/2009	1,200,000	2,010,000	0.597	9.4%
Firstmerit Corporation	1/9/2009	5/27/2009	5,025,000	4,260,000	1.180	20.3%
Sun Bancorp, Inc.	1/9/2009	5/27/2009	2,100,000	5,580,000	0.376	15.3%
Independent Bank Corp.	1/9/2009	5/27/2009	2,200,000	3,870,000	0.568	15.6%
Alliance Financial Corporation	12/19/2008	6/17/2009	900,000	1,580,000	0.570	13.8%
First Niagara Financial Group	11/21/2008	6/24/2009	2,700,000	3,050,000	0.885	8.0%
Berkshire Hills Bancorp, Inc.	12/19/2008	6/24/2009	1,040,000	1,620,000	0.642	11.3%
Somerset Hills Bancorp	1/16/2009	6/24/2009	275,000	580,000	0.474	16.6%
SCBT Financial Corporation	1/16/2009	6/24/2009	1,400,000	2,290,000	0.611	11.7%
HF Financial Corp.	11/21/2008	6/30/2009	650,000	1,240,000	0.524	10.1%
State Street	10/28/2008	7/8/2009	60,000,000	54,200,000	1.107	9.9%
U.S. Bancorp	11/14/2008	7/15/2009	139,000,000	135,100,000	1.029	8.7%
The Goldman Sachs Group, Inc.	10/28/2008	7/22/2009	1,100,000,000	1,128,400,000	0.975	22.8%
BB&T Corp.	11/14/2008	7/22/2009	67,010,402	68,200,000	0.983	8.7%
American Express Company	1/9/2009	7/29/2009	340,000,000	391,200,000	0.869	29.5%
Bank of New York Mellon Corp	10/28/2008	8/5/2009	136,000,000	155,700,000	0.873	12.3%
Morgan Stanley	10/28/2008	8/12/2009	950,000,000	1,039,800,000	0.914	20.2%
Northern Trust Corporation	11/14/2008	8/26/2009	87,000,000	89,800,000	0.969	14.5%

Institution	Investment Date	Warrant Repurchase Date	Warrant Repurchase/ Sale Amount	Panel's Best Valuation Estimate at Disposition Date	Price/ Estimate Ratio	IRR
Old Line Bancshares Inc.	12/5/2008	9/2/2009	225,000	500,000	0.450	10.4%
Bancorp Rhode Island, Inc.	12/19/2008	9/30/2009	1,400,000	1,400,000	1.000	12.6%
Centerstate Banks of Florida Inc.	11/21/2008	10/28/2009	212,000	220,000	0.964	5.9%
Manhattan Bancorp	12/5/2008	10/14/2009	63,364	140,000	0.453	9.8%
CVB Financial Corp.	12/5/2008	10/28/2009	1,307,000	3,522,198	0.371	6.4%
Bank of the Ozarks	12/12/2008	11/24/2009	2,650,000	3,500,000	0.757	9.0%
Capital One Financial	11/14/2008	12/3/2009	148,731,030	232,000,000	0.641	12.0%
JPMorgan Chase & Co.	10/28/2008	12/10/2009	950,318,243	1,006,587,697	0.944	10.9%
CIT Group Inc.	12/31/2008	—	—	562,541	—	(97.2)%
TCF Financial Corp.	1/16/2009	12/16/2009	9,599,964	11,825,830	0.812	11.0%
LSB Corporation	12/12/2008	12/16/2009	560,000	535,202	1.046	9.0%
Wainwright Bank & Trust Company	12/19/2008	12/16/2009	568,700	1,071,494	0.531	7.8%
Wesbanco Bank, Inc.	12/5/2008	12/23/2009	950,000	2,387,617	0.398	6.7%
Union First Market Bankshares Corporation (Union Bankshares Corporation)	12/19/2008	12/23/2009	450,000	1,130,418	0.398	5.8%
Trustmark Corporation	11/21/2008	12/30/2009	10,000,000	11,573,699	0.864	9.4%
Flushing Financial Corporation	12/19/2008	12/30/2009	900,000	2,861,919	0.314	6.5%
OceanFirst Financial Corporation	1/16/2009	2/3/2010	430,797	279,359	1.542	6.2%
Monarch Financial Holdings, Inc.	12/19/2008 10/28/2008[485] 1/9/2009[486]	2/10/2010	260,000	623,434	0.417	6.7%
Bank of America	1/14/2009[487]	3/3/2010	1,566,210,714	1,006,416,684	1.533	6.5%
Washington Federal Inc./Washington Federal Savings & Loan Association	11/14/2008	3/9/2010	15,623,222	10,166,404	1.537	18.6%

Institution	Investment Date	Warrant Repurchase Date	Warrant Repurchase/ Sale Amount	Panel's Best Valuation Estimate at Disposition Date	Price/ Estimate Ratio	IRR
Signature Bank	12/12/2008	3/10/2010	11,320,751	11,458,577	0.988	32.4%
Texas Capital Bancshares, Inc.	1/16/2009	3/11/2010	6,709,061	8,316,604	0.807	30.1%
Umpqua Holdings Corp.	11/14/2008	3/31/2010	4,500,000	5,162,400	0.872	6.6%
City National Corporation	11/21/2008	4/7/2010	18,500,000	24,376,448	0.759	8.5%
First Litchfield Financial Corporation	12/12/2008	4/7/2010	1,488,046	1,863,158	0.799	15.9%
PNC Financial Services Group Inc.	12/31/2008	4/29/2010	324,195,686	346,800,388	0.935	8.7%
Comerica Inc.	11/14/2008	5/4/2010	183,673,472	276,426,071	0.664	10.8%
Valley National Bancorp	11/14/2008	5/18/2010	5,571,592	5,955,884	0.935	8.3%
Wells Fargo Bank	10/28/2008	5/20/2010	849,014,998	1,064,247,725	0.798	7.8%
First Financial Bancorp	12/23/2008	6/2/2010	3,116,284	3,051,431	1.021	8.2%
Sterling Bancshares, Inc./ Sterling Bank	12/12/2008	6/9/2010	3,007,891	5,287,665	0.569	10.8%
SVB Financial Group	12/12/2008	6/16/2010	6,820,000	7,884,633	0.865	7.7%
Discover Financial Services	3/13/2009	7/7/2010	172,000,000	166,182,652	1.035	17.1%
Bar Harbor Bancshares	1/16/2009	7/28/2010	250,000	518,511	0.482	6.2%
Citizens & Northern Corporation	1/16/2009	8/4/2010	400,000	468,164	0.854	5.9%
Columbia Banking System, Inc.	11/21/2008	8/11/2010	3,301,647	3,291,329	1.003	7.3%
Hartford Financial Services Group, Inc.	6/26/2009	9/21/2010	713,687,430	472,221,996	1.511	30.3%
Lincoln National Corporation	7/10/2009	9/16/2010	216,620,887	181,431,183	1.194	27.1%
Fulton Financial Corporation	12/23/2008	9/8/2010	10,800,000	15,616,013	0.692	6.7%

Figure 45. (Continued)

Institution	Investment Date	Warrant Repurchase Date	Warrant Repurchase/ Sale Amount	Panel's Best Valuation Estimate at Disposition Date	Price/ Estimate Ratio	IRR
The Bancorp, Inci The Bancorp Bank	12/12/2008	9/8/2010	4,753,985	9,947,683	0.478	12.8%
South Financial Group, Inci Carolina First Bank	12/5/2008	9/30/2010	400,000	1,164,486	0.343	(34.2)%
TIB Financial Corp/TIB Bank	12/5/2008	9/30/2010	40,000	235,757	0.170	(38.0)%
Central Jersey Bancorp	12/23/2008	12/1/2010	319,659	1,554,457	0.206	6.3%
Total			$8,148,651,825	$8,001,397,712	1.018	8.4%

Figure 45. Warrant Repurchases/Auctions for Financial Institutions that have fully Repaid CPP Funds (as of January 3, 2011).

Financial Institutions with Warrants Outstanding	Warrant Valuation (millions of dollars)		
	Low Estimate	High Estimate	Best Estimate
Citigroup, Inc.[488]	$53.80	$1,070.04	$168.61
SunTrust Banks, Inc.	15.38	186.09	78.14
Regions Financial Corporation	11.40	199.48	106.32
Fifth Third Bancorp	137.43	428.31	228.42
KeyCorp	33.05	183.96	93.42
AIG	1,064.98	2,516.60	1,652.69
All Other Banks	684.87	1,786.36	1,203.84
Total	$2,000.91	$6,370.84	$3,531.44

Figure 46. Valuation of Current Holdings of Warrants (as of January 3, 2011).

2. Federal Financial Stability Efforts

a. Federal Reserve and FDIC Programs

In addition to the direct expenditures Treasury has undertaken through the TARP, the federal government has engaged in a much broader program directed at stabilizing the U.S. financial system. Many of these initiatives explicitly augment funds allocated by Treasury under specific TARP initiatives, such as FDIC and Federal Reserve asset guarantees for Citigroup, or operate in tandem with Treasury programs. Other programs, like the Federal Reserve's extension of credit through its Section 13(3) facilities and special purpose vehicles

(SPVs) and the FDIC's Temporary Liquidity Guarantee Program (TLGP), operate independently of the TARP.

b. Total Financial Stability Resources

Beginning in its April 2009 report, the Panel broadly classified the resources that the federal government has devoted to stabilizing the economy through myriad new programs and initiatives such as outlays, loans, or guarantees. With the reductions in funding for certain TARP programs, the Panel calculates the total value of these resources to be approximately $2.5 trillion. However, this would translate into the ultimate "cost" of the stabilization effort only if: (1) assets do not appreciate; (2) no dividends are received, no warrants are exercised, and no TARP funds are repaid; (3) all loans default and are written off; and (4) all guarantees are exercised and subsequently written off.

With respect to the FDIC and Federal Reserve programs, the risk of loss varies significantly across the programs considered here, as do the mechanisms providing protection for the taxpayer against such risk. As discussed in the Panel's November 2009 report, the FDIC assesses a premium of up to 100 basis points, or 1 percentage point, on TLGP debt guarantees.[489] In contrast, the Federal Reserve's liquidity programs are generally available only to borrowers with good credit, and the loans are over-collateralized and with recourse to other assets of the borrower. If the assets securing a Federal Reserve loan realize a decline in value greater than the "haircut," the Federal Reserve is able to demand more collateral from the borrower. Similarly, should a borrower default on a recourse loan, the Federal Reserve can turn to the borrower's other assets to make the Federal Reserve whole. In this way, the risk to the taxpayer on recourse loans only materializes if the borrower enters bankruptcy.

c. Mortgage Purchase Programs

On September 7, 2008, Treasury announced the GSE Mortgage Backed Securities Purchase (MBS) Program. The Housing and Economic Recovery Act of 2008 provided Treasury with the authority to purchase MBS guaranteed by government-sponsored enterprises (GSEs) through December 31, 2009. Treasury purchased approximately $225 billion in GSE MBS by the time its authority expired.[490] As of December 2010, there was approximately $144.4 billion in MBS still outstanding under this program.[491]

In March 2009, the Federal Reserve authorized purchases of $1.25 trillion MBS guaranteed by Fannie Mae, Freddie Mac, and Ginnie Mae, and $200 billion of agency debt securities from Fannie Mae, Freddie Mac, and the Federal Home Loan Banks.[492] The intended purchase amount for agency debt securities was subsequently decreased to $175 billion.[493] All purchasing activity was completed on March 31, 2010. As of January 6, 2010, the Federal Reserve held $992 billion of agency MBS and $147 billion of agency debt.[494]

d. Federal Reserve Treasury Securities Purchases[495]

On November 3, 2010, the Federal Open Market Committee (FOMC) announced that it has directed the Federal Reserve Bank of New York (FRBNY) to begin purchasing an additional $600 billion in longer-term Treasury securities. In addition, FRBNY will reinvest $250 billion to $300 billion in principal payments from agency debt and agency MBS in Treasury securities.[496] The additional purchases and reinvestments will be conducted through the end of the second quarter of 2011, meaning the pace of purchases will be approximately $110 billion per month. In order to facilitate these purchases, FRBNY will temporarily lift its

System Open Market Account per-issue limit, which prohibits the Federal Reserve's holdings of an individual security from surpassing 35 percent of the outstanding amount.[497] As of January 6, 2010, the Federal Reserve held $1.03 trillion in Treasury securities.[498]

Program (billions of dollars)	Treasury (TARP)	Federal Reserve	FDIC	Total
Total	$475.0	$1,311.6	$690.9	$2,477.5
Outlays[xxxiv]	201.4	1,166.0	188.9	1,556.3
Loans	23.6	145.6	0	169.6
Guarantees[xxxv]	4.3	0	502	506.3
Repaid and Unavailable TARP Funds	245.8	0	0	245.8
AIG[xxxvi]	69.8	81.7	0	151.4
Outlays	[xxxvii]69.8	[xxxviii]26.4	0	96.2
Loans	0	[xxxix]55.2	0	55.2
Guarantees	0	0	0	0
Citigroup	0	0	0	0
Outlays	[xl]0	0	0	0
Loans	0	0	0	0
Guarantees	0	0	0	0
Capital Purchase Program (Other)	34.4	0	0	34.4
Outlays	[xli]34.4	0	0	34.4
Loans	0	0	0	0
Guarantees	0	0	0	0
Capital Assistance Program	N/A	0	0	[xlii]N/A
TALF	4.3	38.7	0	43.0
Outlays	0	0	0	0
Loans	0	[xliv]38.7	0	38.7
Guarantees	[xliii]4.3	0	0	4.3
PPIP (Loans)[xlv]	0	0	0	0
Outlays	0	0	0	0
Loans	0	0	0	0
Guarantees	0	0	0	0
PPIP (Securities)	[xlvi]22.4	0	0	22.4
Outlays	7.4	0	0	7.4
Loans	15.1	0	0	15.1
Guarantees	0	0	0	0
Making Home Affordable Program/ Foreclosure Mitigation	45.6	0	0	45.6
Outlays	[xlvii]45.6	0	0	45.6
Loans	0	0	0	0
Guarantees	0	0	0	0
Automotive Industry Financing Program	[xlviii]51.4	0	0	51.4
Outlays	43.3	0	0	43.3
Loans	8.1	0	0	8.1
Guarantees	0	0	0	0
Automotive Supplier Support Program	0.4	0	0	0.4

Program (billions of dollars)	Treasury (TARP)	Federal Reserve	FDIC	Total
Outlays	0.37	0	0	0.37
Loans	0	0	0	0
Guarantees	0	0	0	0
Community Development Capital Initiative	[i]0.57	0	0	0.57
Outlays	0	0	0	0
Loans	0.57	0	0	0.57
Guarantees	0	0	0	0
Temporary Liquidity Guarantee Program	0	0	502.0	502.0
Outlays	0	0	0	0
Loans	0	0	0	0
Guarantees	0	0	[lii]502.0	502.0
Deposit Insurance Fund	0	0	188.9	188.9
Outlays	0	0	[liii]188.9	188.9
Loans	0	0	0	0
Guarantees	0	0	0	0
Other Federal Reserve Credit Expansion	0	1,191.3	0	1,191.3
Outlays	0	[liv]1,139.6	0	1,139.6
Loans	0	[lv]51.7	0	51.7
Guarantees	0	0	0	0

Figure 47. Federal Government Financial Stability Effort (as of December 30, 2010)[xxxiii].

SECTION FOUR: OVERSIGHT ACTIVITIES

The Congressional Oversight Panel was established as part of the Emergency Economic Stabilization Act (EESA) and formed on November 26, 2008. Since then, the Panel has produced 26 oversight reports as well as a special report on regulatory reform, issued on January 29, 2009, and a special report on farm credit, issued on July 21, 2009. Since the release of the
Panel's December oversight report, the following developments pertaining to the Panel's oversight of the TARP took place:

- The Panel held a hearing in Washington on December 16, 2010 with Secretary Geithner, his fifth appearance before the Panel. The Secretary had the opportunity to discuss the economic impact and ultimate cost of the TARP, the challenges that remain in supporting the financial system and the housing market now that the TARP's authority has expired, and other topics related to the Panel's recently published oversight reports.

Upcoming Reports and Hearings

The Panel will release its next oversight report in February. The report will discuss executive compensation restrictions for companies that received TARP assistance, expanding upon the Panel's hearing on the topic on October 21, 2010.[499]

SECTION FIVE: ABOUT THE CONGRESSIONAL OVERSIGHT PANEL

In response to the escalating financial crisis, on October 3, 2008, Congress provided Treasury with the authority to spend $700 billion to stabilize the U.S. economy, preserve home ownership, and promote economic growth. Congress created the Office of Financial Stability (OFS) within Treasury to implement the TARP. At the same time, Congress created the Congressional Oversight Panel to "review the current state of financial markets and the regulatory system." The Panel is empowered to hold hearings, review official data, and write reports on actions taken by Treasury and financial institutions and their effect on the economy. Through regular reports, the Panel must oversee Treasury's actions, assess the impact of spending to stabilize the economy, evaluate market transparency, ensure effective foreclosure mitigation efforts, and guarantee that Treasury's actions are in the best interests of the American people. In addition, Congress instructed the Panel to produce a special report on regulatory reform that analyzes "the current state of the regulatory system and its effectiveness at overseeing the participants in the financial system and protecting consumers." The Panel issued this report in January 2009. Congress subsequently expanded the Panel's mandate by directing it to produce a special report on the availability of credit in the agricultural sector. The report was issued on July 21, 2009.

On November 14, 2008, Senate Majority Leader Harry Reid and the Speaker of the House Nancy Pelosi appointed Richard H. Neiman, Superintendent of Banks for the State of New York, Damon Silvers, Director of Policy and Special Counsel of the American Federation of Labor and Congress of Industrial Organizations (AFL-CIO), and Elizabeth Warren, Leo Gottlieb Professor of Law at Harvard Law School, to the Panel. With the appointment on November 19, 2008, of Congressman Jeb Hensarling to the Panel by House Minority Leader John Boehner, the Panel had a quorum and met for the first time on November 26, 2008, electing Professor Warren as its chair. On December 16, 2008, Senate Minority Leader Mitch McConnell named Senator John E. Sununu to the Panel. Effective August 10, 2009, Senator Sununu resigned from the Panel, and on August 20, 2009, Senator McConnell announced the appointment of Paul Atkins, former Commissioner of the U.S. Securities and Exchange Commission, to fill the vacant seat. Effective December 9, 2009, Congressman Jeb Hensarling resigned from the Panel, and House Minority Leader John Boehner announced the appointment of J. Mark McWatters to fill the vacant seat. Senate Minority Leader Mitch McConnell appointed Kenneth Troske, Sturgill Professor of Economics at the University of Kentucky, to fill the vacancy created by the resignation of Paul Atkins on May 21, 2010. Effective September 17, 2010, Elizabeth Warren resigned from the Panel, and on September 30, 2010, Senate Majority Leader Harry Reid announced the appointment of Senator Ted Kaufman to fill the vacant seat. On October 4, 2010, the Panel elected Senator Kaufman as its chair.

End Notes

* The Panel adopted this report with a 4-0 vote on January 12, 2011.
[1] Effective May 15, 2010, GMAC Financial Services changed its name to Ally Financial Inc. Except where the distinction is otherwise significant, this report refers to this company as "GMAC/Ally Financial."
[2] For a discussion of the factors leading up to the government's decision to support the automotive industry, *see* Congressional Oversight Panel, *September Oversight Report: The Use of TARP Funds in the Support and Reorganization of the Domestic Automotive Industry*, at 7-23 (Sept. 9, 2009) (online at cop.senate.gov/documents/cop-090909-report.pdf) (hereinafter "September 2009 Oversight Report").
[3] House Judiciary, Subcommittee on Administrative Law, Written Testimony of Ron Bloom, senior advisor, U.S. Department of the Treasury, *Ramifications of Automotive Industry Bankruptcies, Part II*, at 1 (July 21, 2009) (online at judiciary.house.gov/hearings/pdf/Bloom090721.pdf).
[4] GMAC/Ally Financial and Chrysler Financial were spun off from their parents in 2006 and 2007, respectively, but their enduring operational and economic interdependence is illustrated by the largely stable share of GM dealer financing provided by GMAC/Ally Financial and Chrysler dealer financing provided by Chrysler Financial (until GMAC/Ally Financial took over Chrysler Financial's floorplan business in May 2009). Relying on outside industry estimates, Treasury stated that the impact of letting GMAC/Ally Financial and Chrysler Financial fail (together with credit conditions at the time) would likely have been a further immediate decline of 1.5 to 2.5 million domestic automobile sales, primarily because of these companies' roles in providing floorplan financing to GM and Chrysler dealers. Treasury believes that such a decline in sales would, in turn, have immediately threatened the economic viability of GM and Chrysler. Treasury conversations with Panel staff (Feb. 2, 2010); Congressional Oversight Panel, Joint Written Testimony of Ron Bloom, senior advisor to the Secretary of the Treasury, and Jim Millstein, chief restructuring officer, U.S. Department of the Treasury, *COP Hearing on GMAC Financial Services*, at 3 (Feb. 25, 2010) (online at cop.senate.gov/documents/testimony-022510- treasury.pdf).
[5] Senate Committee on Banking, Housing and Urban Affairs, Written Testimony of Robert Nardelli, chairman and chief executive officer, Chrysler LLC, *The State of the Domestic Automobile Industry, Part II* (Dec. 4, 2008) (online at banking.senate.gov/public/index.cfm?FuseAction=Files.View&FileStore_id=c41857b2-7253-4253-95e3-5cfd7ea81393).
[6] Debtor-in-possession financing is a loan made to a firm in bankruptcy to allow it to continue operating. The DIP loan is senior to the other claims on the firm in bankruptcy.
[7] International Monetary Fund, *Global Financial Stability Report: Responding to the Financial Crisis and Measuring Systemic Risk*, at 8 (Apr. 2009) (online at www.imf.org/External/Pubs/FT/GFSR/2009/01/pdf/text.pdf).
[8] As of June 30, 2007, the Bank of China Limited, a state-owned commercial bank, held $8.97 billion of U.S. subprime ABS. By the end of the third quarter 2008, this amount dropped to $3.3 billion. Bank of China Limited, *Interim Report 2007*, at 23 (online at www.boc.cn/en/invester/ir3/200812/P020081212710228274350.pdf) (accessed Jan. 11, 2011); Bank of China Limited, *Report for the Third Quarter ended 30 September 2008*, at 9 (online at www.boc.cn/en/invester/ir3/200812/P020081212712640132355.pdf) (accessed Jan. 11, 2011).
[9] Citigroup, Inc., *Press Release: Citi to Sell $7.5 Billion of Equity Units to Abu Dhabi Investment Authority* (Nov. 26, 2007) (online at www.citigroup.com/citi/press/2007/071126j.htm).
[10] Data accessed through Bloomberg Data Service (Jan. 11, 2011).
[11] Then-Secretary Paulson did not use the name "Automotive Industry Financing Plan" at the time of the announcement. *See generally* U.S. Department of the Treasury, *Secretary Paulson Statement on Stabilizing the Automotive Industry* (Dec. 19, 2008) (online at www.financialstability.gov/latest/hp1332.html) (hereinafter "Secretary Paulson Statement on Stabilizing the Automotive Industry"). Nonetheless, the investments to GM and Chrysler were made under this program. *See generally* U.S. Department of the Treasury, *Troubled Asset Relief Program Transactions Report for Period Ending February 1, 2010*, at 15 (Feb. 3, 2010) (online at

www.financialstability.gov/docs/transaction-reports/2-3-10%20Transactions%20Report%20as%20of%202-1-10.pdf).

[12] *See* George W. Bush White House Archives, *Fact Sheet: Financing Assistance to Facilitate the Restructuring of Auto Manufacturers to Attain Financial Viability* (Dec. 19, 2008) (online at georgewbush-whitehouse.archives.gov/news/releases/2008/12/20081219-6.html) (hereinafter "George W. Bush White House Archives Fact Sheet").

[13] Panel conversations with Edward Lazear, Professor of Economics, Stanford University, and Chairman of the President's Council of Economic Advisors, 2006-2009 (Jan. 4, 2011).

[14] *See* U.S. Department of the Treasury, *Indicative Summary of Terms for Secured Term Loan Facility [GM]*, at Appendix A (Dec. 19, 2008) (online at www.treasury.gov/press-center/pressreleases/Documents/gm%20final%20term%20_%20appendix.pdf); U.S. Department of the Treasury, *Indicative Summary of Terms for Secured Term Loan Facility [Chrysler]*, at Appendix A (Dec. 19, 2008) (online at www.treasury.gov/press-center/press-releases/Documents/chrysler%20final% 20term%20_%20 appendix.pdf).

[15] Secretary Paulson Statement on Stabilizing the Automotive Industry, *supra* note 11 ("Treasury will make these loans using authority provided for the Troubled Asset Relief Program. While the purpose of this program and the enabling legislation is to stabilize our financial sector, the authority allows us to take this action. Absent Congressional action, no other authorities existed to stave off a disorderly bankruptcy of one or more auto companies"); September 2009 Oversight Report, *supra* note 2, at Section G.1.

[16] House Committee on Financial Services, Testimony of Henry M. Paulson, Jr., secretary, U.S. Department of the Treasury, *Transcript: Oversight of Implementation of the Emergency Economic Stabilization Act of 2008 and of Government Lending and Insurance Facilities: Impact on the Economy and Credit Availability*, at 18-19 (Nov. 18, 2008) (online at frwebgate.access.gpo.gov/cgi-bin/getdoc.cgi?dbname= 110_house_hearings&docid=f:46593.pdf) (stating that "[t]he TARP was aimed at the financial system. That is what the purpose is. That is what we talked about with the TARP ... I don't see [preventing the failure of one or more automotive companies] as the purpose of the TARP. Congress passed legislation that dealt with the financial system's stability.").

[17] *See* George W. Bush White House Archives Fact Sheet, *supra* note 12. The loans also imposed conditions related to operations, expenditures, and reporting.

[18] The Administration concluded that Chrysler could not achieve viability as a stand-alone company and that it would have to develop a partnership with another automotive company or face bankruptcy. As for GM, the Administration concluded that the automaker's financial viability plan relied on overly optimistic assumptions about the company and future economic developments.

[19] In GM's 363 sale, certain assets of Old GM (the automotive company that went into bankruptcy) were purchased by New GM (the company formed to buy the assets and financed by Treasury). As a part of this transaction, New GM also assumed certain liabilities of Old GM. Chrysler also engaged in a similar 363 sale. For a discussion of the details of the bankruptcy, *see* September 2009 Oversight Report, *supra* note 2, at 7-8.

[20] As a result of the GM IPO on November 17, 2010, Treasury has reduced its ownership stake in GM to 33 percent. For further discussion concerning the government's exit strategy for GM, see Section D.4, *infra*.

[21] In order to unlock credit further, participating suppliers could also sell their receivables into the program (run through American automotive manufacturers that agreed to participate in the program) at a discount before maturity. The supplier would pay a small fee for the right to participate in the program. Although all domestic automotive manufacturers were eligible, only Chrysler and GM chose to participate.

[22] For further discussion concerning the relationship between GM and GMAC/Ally Financial and Chrysler and Chrysler Financial, *see* Congressional Oversight Panel, *March Oversight Report: The Unique Treatment of GMAC Under the TARP*, at 57-74 (Mar. 10, 2010) (online at cop.senate.gov/documents/cop-031110-report.pdf) (hereinafter "March 2010 Oversight Report").

[23] Board of Governors of the Federal Reserve System, *Order Approving Formation of Bank Holding Companies and Notice to Engage in Certain Nonbanking Activities*, at 2 (Dec. 24, 2008) (online at www.federalreserve.gov/newsevents/press/orders/orders20081224a1.pdf).

[24] Treasury made a loan commitment to GM, which already owned a stake in GMAC/Ally Financial, of up to $1 billion in order to participate in the equity rights offering; however, only $884 million was drawn and used. U.S. Department of the Treasury, *Troubled Asset Relief Program Transactions Report for the Period Ending December 30, 2010*, at 18-19 (Dec. 30, 2010) (online at www.financialstability.gov/docs/transaction-

reports/12-30- 10%20Transactions%20Report%20as%20of%2012-30-10.pdf) (hereinafter "Treasury Transactions Report").

[25] The stress tests were designed to ensure that the nation's largest financial institutions could withstand a sharp economic downturn.

[26] Of the $7.5 billion investment provided in May 2009, $4.0 billion was provided to GMAC/Ally Financial related to its partial acquisition of Chrysler Financial in May 2009. Treasury explained that it began to orchestrate the transfer of most of Chrysler Financial's business into GMAC/Ally Financial because it realized in the spring of 2009 that by July 2009, Chrysler Financial would be unable to meet its financing requirements. Treasury conversations with Panel staff (Feb. 2, 2010).

[27] Treasury Transactions Report, *supra* note 24, at 18-19.

[28] Treasury Transactions Report, *supra* note 24, at 18-19; Cerberus Capital Management, L.P., *Company Profiles: Chrysler Holding LLC* (online at webcache.googleusercontent.com/search?q= cache:bcyLZou JF04J:www.cerberuscapital.com/profiles/chrysler.html+cerberus+chrysler+holdings&cd=4&hl=en&ct=clnk&gl=us) (accessed Jan.1, 2011).

[29] Treasury Transactions Report, *supra* note 24, at 18-19.

[30] U.S. Department of the Treasury, *Chrysler Financial Parent Company Repays $1.9 billion in Settlement of Original Chrysler Loan* (May 17, 2010) (online at www.financialstability.gov/latest/pr_05172010c.html).

[31] Toronto-Dominion Bank, *TD Bank Group to Acquire Chrysler Financial* (Dec. 21, 2010) (online at mediaroom.tdbank.com/index.php?s=43&item=271). The $6.3 billion sale price included $400 million of goodwill.

[32] With GMAC/Ally Financial moving quickly into the business of providing Chrysler financing, Treasury announced in late 2009 that Chrysler Financial had begun to wind down the minimal portion of its operations not assumed by GMAC/Ally Financial and aimed to complete the process by December 31, 2011. *See* Letter from Kenneth R. Feinberg, special master for TARP executive compensation, to Tracy Hackman, vice president, general counsel and secretary, Chrysler Financial, *Proposed Compensation Payments and Structures for Senior Executive Officers and Most Highly Compensated Employees*, Annex A, at A5 (Oct. 22, 2009) (online at www.financialstability.gov/docs/20091022%20Chrysler%20 Financial%202009%20Top%2025%20Determination.p df).

[33] Toronto-Dominion Bank, *Acquisition of Chrysler Financial by Toronto-Dominion Bank* (Dec. 21, 2010) (hereinafter "Acquisition of Chrysler Financial by Toronto-Dominion Bank"). Transcript provided by SNL Financial. During a recent interview, Chrysler Financial CEO Tom Gilman said the company was in liquidation mode and winding down its loan portfolio for most of 2010. The company currently has 1,850 employees after eliminating over 50 percent of its staff (about 2,000 positions) during the last two years, and its loan portfolio balance declined from $50 billion to under $10 billion as it generally stopped underwriting new loans over the past year. David Shepardson, *TD Bank to buy Chrysler Financial*, Detroit News (Dec. 21, 2010) (online at detnews.com/article/20101221/AUTO01/12210375).

[34] Acquisition of Chrysler Financial by Toronto-Dominion Bank, *supra* note 33. Transcript provided by SNL Financial. (Thomas Gilman, Chrysler Financial CEO, said "[W]e paid all debt and we paid all the U.S. government TARP funds that we received. Obviously, any restrictions related to TARP have now been lifted."). Restriction associated with the loan included the limitation of new business lines and major investments. U.S. Department of the Treasury, *Loan and Security Agreement By and Between The Borrower Listed on Appendix A as Borrower and The United States Department of the Treasury as Lender*, at 56 (Dec. 31, 2008) (online at www.financialstability.gov/docs/AIFP/Chrysler%20LSA%20as%20of%2005-26-10.pdf) ("No Loan Party will engage to any substantial extent in any line or lines of business activity other than the businesses generally carried on by the Loan Parties as of the Effective Date or businesses reasonably related thereto."); *Id.* at 58 ("No Loan Party intends to make any Investment, except Permitted Investments. If any Loan Party shall make a Permitted Investment not in the ordinary course of business in an amount greater than $100,000,000, such Loan Party shall comply with provisions").

[35] Acquisition of Chrysler Financial by Toronto-Dominion Bank, *supra* note 33. Transcript provided by SNL Financial.

[36] Congressional Oversight Panel, Written Testimony of Ron Bloom, senior advisor, U.S. Department of the Treasury, *COP Field Hearing on the Auto Industry* (July 27, 2009) (online at cop.senate.gov/documents/testimony-072709-bloom.pdf); The White House, *Fact Sheet: Obama Administration Auto Restructuring Initiative General Motors Restructuring* (June 30, 2009) (online at

financialstability.gov/latest/05312009_gm-factsheet.html) (hereinafter "White House Fact Sheet on General Motors Restructuring").

[37] As with the automotive companies, some of AIG's management has been replaced and the company has undergone a restructuring that has resulted in two of its profitable foreign insurance divisions being spun-off and its financial products division significantly cut back. However, the Federal Reserve and Treasury chose not to use the Bankruptcy Code to restructure AIG.

[38] This figure is composed of the $81.3 billion in total assistance provided to the automotive companies less the $26.4 billion in repayments and less the $3.5 billion in losses associated with the AIFP. Treasury Transactions Report, *supra* note 24, at 18-19.

[39] Treasury Transactions Report, *supra* note 24, at 18.

[40] As of December 30, 2010, Treasury had converted $9.4 billion of its investment in GMAC/Ally Financial into common stock. For further information regarding these conversions, see Section F.2.b of this report.

[41] The "Foreclosure Prevention" category includes the Home Affordable Modification Program (HAMP), the Hardest Hit Fund, and the Federal Housing Administration (FHA) Short Refinance program. It should be noted that these programs were not designed to solicit repayment. The "Other Stability programs" category includes the Term Asset-Backed Loan Facility (TALF), the Public-Private Investment Partnership (PPIP), and the Small Business Administration 7(a) Securities Purchase Program.

[42] For further discussion concerning the outlook for the auto industry, see Section C.5, *infra*.

[43] Capacity is defined here as two 8-hour work shifts per day times the average number of work days (240) per year at the maximum possible facility line rate (vehicles produced per hour). Utilization is production divided by capacity. Data provided by CSM.

[44] For example, GM's U.S. salaried headcount is currently 24,000, versus 30,000 in 2008 and 34,000 in 2007 (down 20 percent and 29 percent, respectively). GM's U.S. hourly workforce, which is almost completely made up of UAW members, is currently 46,000, down from 62,000 in 2008 and 78,000 in 2007. (Deutsche Bank Investment Research).

[45] In large part due to the shifting of healthcare costs to the UAW in the 2007 agreement, hourly labor costs within Chrysler, Ford, and GM have now declined to approximately $58 per hour, approaching the levels at U.S. plants operated by Japanese automakers and falling below historical levels of $65 per hour. Colin Langan, *10% Margins in the "New" US Auto Industry*, UBS Investment Research, at 5 (Nov. 15, 2010) (hereinafter "UBS Investment Research Paper").

[46] *Id.* at 1. UBS states that automakers "are now profitable at very low levels of utilization, which bodes well for operating leverage as sales demand continues to recover."

[47] General Motors Company, *Q3 2010 Results*, at 6 (Nov. 10, 2010) (online at media.gm.com /content/dam/Media/gmcom/investor/2010/Q3-Chart-Set.pdf) (hereinafter "GM Q3 2010 Results").

[48] Data provided by Wards Auto.

[49] Data compiled by CNW Research. MSRP is defined as Manufacturer Suggested Retail Price. The MSRP is the average sticker price of vehicles sold; Transaction Price excludes taxes, fees, and aftermarket products.

[50] Bureau of Economic Analysis, *Supplemental Data: Auto Vehicles* (Instrument: Light Total – seasonally adjusted at annual rates (Millions)) (online at www.bea.gov/national/xls/gap_hist.xls) (accessed Jan. 11, 2011). Standard & Poor's views on the extent of the sales rebound are conservative given the sluggish economic recovery, but it expects sales to improve again in 2011 to approximately 12.8 million units. Despite the improvement, this figure is still below the 2008 sales numbers. PricewaterhouseCoopers (PwC), while noting concerns about the "waning strength" of an economic recovery and "dimming prospects for marked improvement in 2011," states that North America's light vehicle landscape has continued to produce "convincing signs of near-term stability in terms of sales and assembly." PricewaterhouseCoopers, *North America Analyst Briefing* (Nov. 2010). For its part, Goldman Sachs is forecasting 2011 and 2012 sales at 13 million and 14 million, respectively, as it believes that additional pent-up demand "will help drive a steeper recovery in auto sales as some of these macro concerns abate." The Goldman Sachs Group, Inc., *Americas: Automobiles: See Upside to 3Q Consensus Post Our Volume Driven Est. Revisions* (Oct. 19, 2010) (hereinafter "Goldman Sachs Estimate Revisions"). In late October, Goldman Sachs also projected a 2013 SAAR estimate of 15 million. It is important to underscore, however, that these levels are still well below historic "normalized" sales.

[51] Standard & Poor's anticipates that recovering light vehicle sales and inventory rebuilding in the United States will boost production volumes by more than 10 percent in 2010. Standard & Poor's, *Industry Report Card: Busy Production Lines Are Fueling Global Automakers'Operating Profits And Credit Quality* (Oct. 4, 2010).

[52] An average of five analyst forecasts for SAAR improves from 11.6 million vehicles sold in 2010 to 12.6 million in 2011. The same analysts estimate that the 2012 SAAR will be 13.8 million vehicles. Averages are comprised of forecasts from PricewaterhouseCoopers Autofacts, CSM Worldwide, IHS Global Insight, J.D. Power, and IRN. Original Equipment Suppliers Association, *The State of the Supplier Industry*, at 8 (Nov. 10, 2010) (hereinafter "The State of the Supplier Industry").

[53] Bureau of Economic Analysis, *Auto and Truck Seasonal Adjustment Data* (Dec. 2, 2010) (online at bea.gov/national/xls/gap_hist.xls); Shaded areas reflect periods of economic recession as defined by the National Bureau of Economic Research. *See* National Bureau of Economic Research, *U.S. Business Cycle Expansions and Contractions* (online at www.nber.org/cycles/cyclesmain.html) (accessed Jan. 11, 2011). 2011 and 2012 data is an average projection comprised of SAAR projections from PricewaterhouseCoopers Autofacts, CSM Worldwide, IHS Global Insight, J.D. Power & Associates, and IRN. The State of the Supplier Industry, *supra* note 52.

[54] GM Q3 2010 Results, *supra* note 47, at 6, 11, 15.

[55] UBS Investment Research, *US (not BRIC) is Key NT Growth Market* (Nov. 11, 2010) (hereinafter "UBS Investment Research Paper on Growth Market").

[56] As recently as 2006, the United States accounted for more than a quarter of the global market, whereas in 2010, the United States accounted for a mere 16.3 percent of global demand. J.D. Power & Associates, however, predicts that China's share of the world market will climb from 10 percent in 2006 to 21 percent in 2013. Efraim Levy, *Industry Surveys: Autos & Auto Parts*, Standard & Poor's Research, at 15-16 (June 24, 2010).

[57] UBS points out that "significant structural changes made by the U.S. auto market in the last year have already resulted in enhanced operating margins, despite the low levels of sales." While the United States has not historically been a profitable market for domestic automakers, UBS estimates profitability will be approximately 10 percent for the industry going forward, based on the combination of capacity reductions, reduced labor costs, and improved outlook. In UBS'view, "[c]ombined with the ongoing sales recovery, these cost cuts paint a very bright picture for the 'new'North American auto industry over the next five years." UBS Investment Research Paper on Growth Market, *supra* note 55; UBS Investment Research Paper, *supra* note 45.

[58] Goldman Sachs concludes that the key risk for the auto sector "remains the pace of sales growth whose outlook is tied intimately to consumer sentiment and the outlook for housing and employment in the U.S." PricewaterhouseCoopers notes that while consumer credit has thawed substantially over the past year, and lending standards have eased, many consumers "are voluntarily and involuntarily absent from the new vehicle market," due in large part to widespread deleveraging and lenders'limited capacity to extend financing to potential buyers with "newly tarnished credit." Goldman Sachs Estimate Revisions, *supra* note 50. *See also* UBS Investment Research Paper, *supra* note 45.

[59] PricewaterhouseCoopers, North America Analyst Briefing (Nov. 2010).

[60] September 2009 Oversight Report, *supra* note 2, at 3,19.

[61] The company effectively came into being on July 10, 2009, when GM sold its "good" assets under Section 363 of the Code to a new, government-owned entity, General Motors Company (New GM). Order (I) Authorizing Sale of Assets Pursuant to Amended and Restated Master Sale and Purchase Agreement with NGMCO, Inc., a Treasury-Sponsored Purchaser; (II) Authorizing Assumption and Assignment of Certain Executory Contracts and Unexpired Leases in Connection with the Sale; and (III) Granting Related Relief, In Re General Motors Corp., S.D.N.Y. (No. 09-50026 (REG)) (July 5, 2009) (online at docs.motorsliquidationdocket.com/pdflib/2968_order.pdf). *See also* September 2009 Oversight Report, *supra* note 2, at 19.

[62] *See* White House Fact Sheet on General Motors Restructuring, *supra* note 36. For purposes of this report, the General Motors that existed prior to the 2009 restructuring is referred to as "Old GM." Its formal name is now Motors Liquidation Company.

[63] This figure includes investments in both Old GM and New GM. Treasury Transactions Report, *supra* note 24, at 18-19. Foreign governments provided assistance as well. The governments of Canada and Ontario invested a net of $9.5 billion in loans to GM, resulting in an 11.7 percent ownership stake. GM also arranged a revolving bridge facility with the German federal government with a commitment amount of €1.5 billion, equivalent at the time to $2.1 billion. That loan was repaid, in full, and extinguished on November 24, 2009. September 2009 Oversight Report, *supra* note 2, at 31; General Motors Company, *Amendment No. 9 to Form S-1: Preliminary Prospectus*, at 61 (Nov. 17, 2010) (online at www.sec.gov/Archives/edgar/data/1467858/000119312510262471/ds1a.htm) (hereinafter "GM Amendment No. 9 to Form S-1: Preliminary Prospectus").

[64] The so-called EESA Notices, in reference to the law that established the TARP, include: Notice 2008- 100, which concerned recipients of TARP funds under the Capital Purchase Program; Notice 2009-14, which extended the guidance in Notice 2008-100 to instruments issued under the Targeted Investment Program and the Automotive Industry Financing Program; Notice 2009-38, which extended the prior guidance to the Asset Guarantee Program and the Systemically Significant Failing Institutions Program, among other actions; and Notice 2010-2, which in part provides guidance on the impact of Treasury's sale of stock that it was issued under the TARP programs covered by the prior guidance. In the American Recovery and Reinvestment Act of 2009, Congress provided an exception to the section 382 limitations on loss carryovers for certain ownership changes of certain TARP recipients, including GM. *See American Recovery and Reinvestment Act of 2009*, Pub. L. No. 111-5, at § 382(n) (2009).

[65] A net operating loss (NOL) is the excess of a corporation's deductions over its taxable income. The future benefit of an NOL is considered a deferred tax asset for financial accounting purposes.

[66] Under Section 172 of the Internal Revenue Code, a corporation is allowed to carry forward the amount of any unrecognized net operating loss in the current taxable year to be recognized in future taxable years. In general, Section 172 provides that a net operating loss for the current taxable year may be carried back two taxable years, and carried forward for up to 20 taxable years. For financial accounting purposes, limitations on the use of an NOL carryforward may reduce the amount a corporation is able to reflect as a deferred tax asset on its financial statements, and in turn could negatively affect value of such corporation.

[67] In general, an ownership change occurs if the percentage of a corporation's stock owned by one or more "5-percent shareholders" increases by more than 50 percentage points over the lowest percentage of stock of such corporation owned by such shareholders at any time during the three-year period that ends on the date of the triggering event. Some events that can increase the percentage of stock owned by a 5-percent shareholder include a merger or acquisition of the corporation, sales of stock to 5-percent shareholders, redemptions, and new issuances of stock. A "5 percent shareholder" is any shareholder that owns 5 percent or more of the stock of the corporation. The stock owned by all shareholders who are not 5-percent shareholders is treated as being owned by one or more "public groups," which may be treated as 5-percent shareholders.

[68] The Secretary possesses the authority to issue income tax notices under 12 U.S.C. § 5211(c)(5). In addition, Section 382(m) specifically authorizes the Secretary to issue "such regulations as may be necessary or appropriate to carry out the purposes of this section." 26 U.S.C. § 382(m). *See also* Congressional Oversight Panel, *January Oversight Report: Exiting TARP and Unwinding Its Impact on the Financial Markets*, at 16-20 (Jan. 13, 2010) (online at cop.senate.gov/documents/cop-011410-report.pdf) (hereinafter "January 2010 Oversight Report").

[69] Total operating loss and tax credit carryforwards as of December 31, 2009 were $18.9 billion, of which $9.1 billion related to U.S. federal and state net operating loss carryforwards. General Motors Company, *Amendment No. 5 to Form S-1: Preliminary Prospectus*, at F-123 (Nov. 3, 2010) (online at www.sec.gov/Archives/edgar/data/1467858/000119312510246019/ds1a.htm) (hereinafter "GM Amendment No. 5 to Form S-1: Preliminary Prospectus").

[70] *See* January 2010 Oversight Report, *supra* note 68, at 16-22.

[71] January 2010 Oversight Report, *supra* note 68, at 22. The Special Inspector General for the Troubled Asset Relief Program (SIGTARP) has initiated an evaluation of Treasury's decision-making process in providing TARP recipients a waiver from the NOL carry-forward rules. SIGTARP seeks to determine the rationale behind the waiver, whether Treasury was aware of any tax effect that might result from the waiver, the identity of the decision-makers involved in issuing the waiver, and the extent to which Treasury's policy to dispose of TARP investments in a timely manner factored into the decision to issue a waiver. Office of the Special Inspector General for the Troubled Asset Relief Program, *Engagement Memo – Review of the Section 382 Limitation Waiver for Financial Instruments Held by Treasury* (Aug. 10, 2010) (online at www.sigtarp.gov/reports/audit/2010/Engagement%20Memo%20-%20Review%20of%20the%20Section%20382%20Limitation%20Waiver%20for%20Financial%20Instruments%20Held%20by%20Treasury.pdf).

[72] In addition, although the notices permit certain TARP recipients to enjoy a tax benefit that they would have otherwise been denied, other carry-forward benefits have been denied to TARP recipients. As discussed in more detail in the Panel's May 2010 report, TARP recipients were excluded from the extension of the NOL benefit that was included in the Worker, Homeownership, and Business Assistance Act of 2009. The Act permitted taxpayers with net operating losses in 2008 and 2009 to apply those losses to tax payments made in five preceding tax years, rather than only to payments made in the two preceding tax years. As the Panel

noted, this exclusion may have contributed to the development of the TARP "stigma," as "bank industry sources have stated that when banks accepted TARP funds, they had no reason to anticipate that their status as TARP recipients would cause them to be denied access to subsequent benefits afforded to their non-TARP competitors." Congressional Oversight Panel, *May Oversight Report: The Small Business Credit Crunch and the Impact of the TARP*, at 71 (May 13, 2010) (online at cop.senate.gov/documents/cop-051310-report.pdf). *See also* Internal Revenue Service, *Questions and Answers for The Worker, Homeownership, and Business Assistance Act of 2009 – Section 13 5-year Net Operating Loss (NOL) Carryback* (Feb. 24, 2010) (online at www.irs.gov/newsroom/article/0,,id=217370,00.html).

[73] September 2009 Oversight Report, *supra* note 2, at 64, 69.

[74] Treasury Transactions Report, *supra* note 24, at 18-19.

[75] U.S. Department of the Treasury, *General Motors Repays Taxpayers $2.1 Billion, Completing Repurchase of Treasury Preferred Stock* (Dec. 15, 2010) (online at www.financialstability.gov/latest/pr_12152010.html). The preferred stock was Series A fixed-rate cumulative perpetual, which paid a 9 percent dividend. General Motors Company, *Form 10-Q for the Quarterly Period Ended September 30, 2010*, at 36 (Nov. 10, 2010) (online at www.sec.gov/Archives/edgar/data/1467858/000119312510255233/d10q.htm) (hereinafter "GM Form 10-Q").

[76] *See* Steven Rattner, *Overhaul*, at 250 (2010).

[77] Following the bankruptcy proceedings, five new members were appointed to the 12-member board of New GM. Treasury's four appointments were Daniel Akerson (now GM's CEO), managing director of the private equity firm Carlyle Group; David Bonderman, co-founding partner of TPG Capital; Robert Krebs, retired chairman and chief executive of Burlington Northern Santa Fe railroad; and Patricia Russo, former chief executive of telecommunications company Alcatel-Lucent. To represent its stake, the Canadian government appointed Carol Stephenson, dean of Richard Ivey School of Business at the University of Western Ontario, to the Board. GM Amendment No. 9 to Form S-1: Preliminary Prospectus, *supra* note 63, at 196.

[78] Mr. Akerson had served on the board since July 2009 and had previously served as a managing director of the Carlyle Group. General Motors Company, *GM Announces CEO Succession Process* (Aug. 12, 2010) (online at media.gm.com/content/media/us/en/news/news_detail.brand_gm.html/content/Pages/news/us/en/2010/Aug/08 12_tra nsition).

[79] In addition, the Special Master will continue to oversee GM's compensation practices until the company repays all of the funds it received under the AIFP. *See TARP Standards for Compensation and Corporate Governance*, 31 CFR § 30.1 (June 15, 2009) (online at ecfr.gpoaccess.gov/cgi/t/text/text-idx?c=ecfr&sid=188bec27fb299580f359697139ae586a&rgn=div5&view=text&node=31:1.1.1.1.28&idno=31) (defining "exceptional financial assistance" as "any financial assistance provided under the Programs for Systemically Significant Failing Institutions, the Targeted Investment Program, the Automotive Industry Financing Program, and any new program designated by the Secretary as providing exceptional financial assistance."). The Special Master had authority to render individual compensation determinations for the top 25 most highly paid employees at GM, as well as to review compensation structures for the next 75 employees. On October 23, 2009, he released his determinations for the top 25, which reduced cash compensation by 31 percent compared to 2008 and by 46 percent compared to 2007. Total direct compensation decreased by 24.7 percent compared to 2008. Letter from Kenneth R. Feinberg, special master for TARP executive compensation, to Gregory E. Lau, executive director for Global Compensation, General Motors, *Proposed Compensation Payments and Structures for Senior Executive Officers and Most Highly Compensated Employees*, at Exh. 1 (Oct. 22, 2009) (online at www.financialstability.gov/docs/20091022%20GM%202009%20Top%2025%20Determination.pdf).

[80] General Motors Company, *GM to Acquire AmeriCredit* (July 22, 2010) (online at media.gm.com/content/media/us/en/news/news_detail.brand_gm.html/content/Pages/news/us/en/2010/July/07 22_a mericredit). The deal closed effective October 1, 2010. General Motors Company, *General Motors Announced Its Acquisitions of AmeriCredit Corp. Will Close Effective October 1, 2010* (Sept. 29, 2010) (online at www.gm.com/investors/announcements-events/event.jsp?id=3533539). SIGTARP has initiated an audit that will look at Treasury's role in reviewing, approving, or otherwise participating in GM's decision to acquire AmeriCredit. Office of the Special Inspector General for the Troubled Asset Relief Program, *Engagement Memo – Review of Treasury's Investment in General Motors Company* (Oct. 26, 2010) (online at www.sigtarp.gov/reports/audit/2010/Engagement%20Memo%20-%20Review%20of%20Treasury%27s%20Investment%20in%20General%20Motors%20Company.pdf).

[81] See Congressional Oversight Panel, Testimony of Michael Ward, analyst, Soleil-Ward Transportation Research, *Transcript: COP Hearing on GMAC Financial Services*, at 87 (Feb. 25, 2010) (online at frwebgate.access.gpo.gov/cgi-bin/getdoc.cgi?dbname=111_senate_hearings&docid=f:56723.pdf).

[82] General Motors Company conversations with Panel staff (Dec. 3, 2010).

[83] An initial public offering (IPO) occurs when a private company issues stock to the public for the first time. Prior to the IPO, the issuing institution works with an underwriting firm to determine the type of security to issue, the price, and the timing of the offering.

[84] Underwriters market shares to their clients. The underwriting syndicate included Morgan Stanley, J.P. Morgan, Merrill Lynch, Citigroup, Barclays Capital, Credit Suisse, Deutsche Bank, Goldman Sachs & Co., RBC Capital Markets, Banco Bradesco BBI, CIBC World Markets, Commerz Markets, BNY Mellon Capital Markets, ICBC International Securities, Itau BBA USA Securities, Lloyds TSB Bank, China International Capital Corporation HK Securities, Loop Capital Markets, Williams Capital Group, Soleil Securities Corporation, Scotia Capital (USA), Piper Jaffray & Co., SMBC Nikko Capital Markets, Sanford C. Bernstein & Co., Cabrera Capital Markets, Castle Oak Securities, CF Global Trading, C.L. King & Associates, FBR Capital Markets, Gardner Rich, Lebenthal & Co., M.R. Beal & Company, Muriel Siebert & Co. and Samuel A. Ramirez & Company. UBS was omitted from the final list amid reports that a sales analyst within the firm distributed an unauthorized e-mail to an institutional client regarding the valuation of GM. Morgan Stanley and J.P. Morgan Securities served as the primary book runners.

[85] Bill Canis, Baird Webel, and Gary Shorter, *General Motors'Initial Public Offering: Review of Issues and Implications for TARP*, Congressional Research Service, at 12-13 (Nov. 10, 2010) (online at www.crs.gov/Products/R/PDF/R41401.pdf) (hereinafter "GM's Initial Public Offering: Implications for TARP").

[86] GM Amendment No. 5 to Form S-1: Preliminary Prospectus, *supra* note 69. See General Motors Company, *General Motors Announces Increase in Size of Public Offering of Common Stock* (Nov. 17, 2010) (online at media.gm.com/content/media/us/en/news/news_detail.brand_gm.html/content/Pages/news/global/en/2010/111 7_am endment). See also GM's Initial Public Offering: Implications for TARP, *supra* note 85, at 12. According to press reports, in the run-up to the IPO, senior officials within the company marketed the IPO to a wide range of international investors in order to attract the broadest investor base possible. These investors included GM's partner in China – SAIC – as well as several sovereign wealth funds. See David Welch and Jeffrey McCracken, *GM Said to Approach Sovereign Wealth Funds to Boost Stock Sale*, Bloomberg News (Oct. 5, 2010) (online at www.bloomberg.com/news/2010-10-05/gm-is-said-to-approach-sovereign-wealth-funds-to-boost-initial-stocksale.html); Clare Baldwin, Soyoung Kim, and Philipp Halstrick, *GM IPO Multiple Times Oversubscribed*, International Business Times (Nov. 12, 2010) (online at www.ibtimes.com/articles/81505/20101112/gm-ipomultiple-times-oversubscribed-sources.htm).

[87] General Motors Company, *Amendment No. 8 to Form S-1: Preliminary Prospectus* (Nov. 16, 2010) (online at www.sec.gov/Archives/edgar/data/1467858/000119312510261467/ds1a.htm).

[88] GM also began trading under "GMM" on the Toronto Stock Exchange.

[89] In addition to $18.1 billion in common equity, the company issued $5.0 billion in preferred stock. The preferred stock issuance consisted of Series B mandatory convertible junior preferred shares, which pay a dividend of 4.75 percent. Data accessed from Bloomberg on Nov. 19, 2010.

[90] While the GM common stock offering was second only to Visa's 2008 IPO, the total funds raised by GM exceeded those raised by Visa. See Visa Investor Relations, *Visa Inc., Largest IPO in US History* (Mar. 19, 2008) (online at phx.corporate-ir.net/phoenix.zhtml?c=129145&p=irol-newsArticle&ID=1120295&highlight=).

[91] Shares of preferred stock closed at $50.45. Data accessed from Bloomberg on November 19, 2010.

[92] The White House, *Remarks by the President on General Motors* (Nov. 18, 2010) (online at www.whitehouse.gov/the-press-office/2010/11/18/remarks-president-general-motors).

[93] *Id.*

[94] General Motors Company, *General Motors Announces Underwriters'Exercise of Over-allotment Options* (Nov. 26, 2010) (online at www.gm.com/news-article.jsp?id=/content/Pages/news/ us/en/2010/Nov/ 1126_exercise.html).

[95] GM Amendment No. 9 to Form S-1: Preliminary Prospectus, *supra* note 63, at 9.

[96] GM anticipated that it would use approximately 43 percent of the preferred proceeds to purchase Treasury's Series A preferred holdings. It planned to use the remainder of the proceeds – supplemented with cash on hand – to make the cash pension contribution. See General Motors Company, *Form 424B1: Final Common*

Prospectus, at 38 (Nov. 18, 2010) (online at www.sec.gov/Archives/edgar/data/1467858/000119312510263484/d424b1.htm) (hereinafter "GM Form 424B1: Final Common Prospectus"); General Motors Company, *GM Makes $4 Billion Pension Plan Contribution* (Dec. 2, 2010) (online at www.gm.com/news-article.jsp?id=/content/Pages/news/us/en/2010/Dec/1202_pension.html) (hereinafter "GM Makes $4 Billion Pension Plan Contribution").

[97] U.S. Department of the Treasury, *Taxpayers Receive Additional $1.8 Billion in Proceeds from GM IPO* (Dec. 2, 2010) (online at www.financialstability.gov/latest/pr_12022010.html).

[98] An over-allotment option is an agreement between an issuer and its underwriter granting the underwriter the option to purchase and then resell additional shares to the investing public. Usually the over-allotment option is exercised by the underwriter if the demand before and after pricing is strong. Treasury's 33.3 percent ownership stake in GM is calculated on a basic – not fully diluted – share basis.

[99] This figure includes $13.5 billion in proceeds from the GM IPO that are not directly tied to a particular tranche of investment made in GM prior to its bankruptcy. Therefore, these funds are not accounted for as a line item, but instead are credited solely to the total line.

[100] The capacity utilization rate measures the amount of output currently being produced by the firm relative to the maximum amount of output it could produce given its current inputs.

[101] *See* General Motors Company, *GM Retail Roadshow*, at 5, 10, 17 (Nov. 18, 2010) (online at cop.senate.gov/documents/gm-publicoffering.pdf) (hereinafter "GM Retail Roadshow"); GM conversations with Panel staff (Dec. 3, 2010). GM's CEO and CFO have stated in the media that their goal is to get GM to zero debt. *See* CNBC, *GM Aiming for No Debt on Balance Sheet: CEO* (Nov. 18, 2010) (online at classic.cnbc.com/id/40251271/). GM's CFO, Chris Liddell, stated that this goal could realistically be reached in three to five years. *See* The Inside Track with Deirdre Bolton & Erik Schatzker, *Interview with GM CFO Chris Liddell*, Bloomberg News (Nov. 18, 2010) (findarticles.com/p/news-articles/ceo-wire/mi_8092/is_20101118/chrisliddell-bloomberg-tv/ai_n56320173/?tag=content;col1).

[102] GM Form 424B1: Final Common Prospectus, *supra* note 96, at 55, 60.

[103] General Motors Company, *Q2 2010 Results*, at 6 (Aug. 12, 2010) (online at media.gm.com/content/dam/Media/gmcom/investor/2010/Q2-Chart-Set.pdf) (hereinafter "GM Q2 2010 Results").

[104] GM Form 424B1: Final Common Prospectus, *supra* note 96, at 19.

[105] General Motors Company, *Form 8-K for the Period Ended November 3, 2010*, at 5 (Nov. 5, 2010) (online at www.sec.gov/Archives/edgar/data/1467858/000119312510249908/d8k.htm).

[106] *Id.* at 5.

[107] GM Form 424B1: Final Common Prospectus, *supra* note 96, at 19. These closings are substantially fewer in number than GM initially announced. *See* Office of the Special Inspector General for the Troubled Asset Relief Program, *Factors Affecting the Decisions of General Motors and Chrysler to Reduce Their Dealership Networks*, at 1 (July 19, 2010) (SIGTARP 10-008) (online at www.sigtarp.gov/reports/audit/2010/Factors%20Affecting%20the%20Decisions%20of%20General%20Motors%20 and%20Chrysler%20to%20 Reduce%20Their%20Dealership%20Networks%207_19_2010.pdf) (stating that GM announced on June 2, 2009 that it planned to "wind down" 1,454 of its 5,591 dealerships by October 2010).

[108] GM maintains that the scale of this dealer network strengthens its ability to compete in markets outside the United States. *See* GM Form 424B1: Final Common Prospectus, *supra* note 96, at 3.

[109] UBS Investment Research Paper, *supra* note 45, at 4.

[110] UBS Investment Research, *General Motors Company: Why Buy Now?* (Dec. 15, 2010) (hereinafter "UBS Investment Research Paper").

[111] GM Form 424B1: Final Common Prospectus, *supra* note 96, at 3.

[112] GM Form 424B1: Final Common Prospectus, *supra* note 96, at 3.

[113] The 2010 labor cost figure is an estimate that GM used in its retail roadshow. GM Retail Roadshow, *supra* note 101, at slide 17. *See also* Moody's Investors Service, *Credit Opinion: General Motors Company* (Oct. 29, 2010) (hereinafter "Moody's Credit Opinion: General Motors Company") ("This shift in the industry's operating structure has been the result of significant headcount reductions, the elimination of excess capacity, and the implementation of a new UAW contract.").

[114] The 2010 employee figure is an estimate that GM used in its retail roadshow. GM Retail Roadshow, *supra* note 101, at slide 17.

[115] UBS Investment Research Paper, *supra* note 110, at 6.

[116] A roadshow is a presentation to potential institutional or retail investors prior to the initial stock offering.

[117] GM Retail Roadshow, *supra* note 101, at slide 10.
[118] GM Form 424B1: Final Common Prospectus, *supra* note 96, at 1.
[119] GM Form 424B1: Final Common Prospectus, *supra* note 96, at 3.
[120] In the BRIC countries, GM had a share of 13 percent in 2009, compared to 11 percent for Volkswagen, 4 percent for Toyota, and 3 percent for Ford. The company's market share in China, specifically, was 13.3 percent in 2009. GM Retail Roadshow, *supra* note 101, at slide 9; GM Form 424B1: Final Common Prospectus, *supra* note 96, at 3.
[121] GM Retail Roadshow, *supra* note 101, at slide 10.
[122] General Motors Company conversations with Panel staff (Dec. 3, 2010).
[123] GM Makes $4 Billion Pension Plan Contribution, *supra* note 96.
[124] The $35 billion consists of $13 billion in underfunded U.S. pension obligations, $10 billion in underfunded non-U.S. pension obligations, $7 billion in perpetual preferred stock, and $5 billion in debt. GM Retail Roadshow, *supra* note 101, at slide 19.
[125] GM Retail Roadshow, *supra* note 101, at slide 19.
[126] In its presentation to retail investors for its upcoming IPO, the company presented guidance for the following metrics: earnings before interest and taxes (EBIT), EBIT margin, and free cash flow for both the middle of the business cycle and at the high end of the cycle. These projections provide insight into how management foresees GM's performance in 2011 and beyond. The company's EBIT mid-point projections are $12 billion at mid-cycle and $18 billion at high-cycle. The company's midpoint projections for free cash flow are $9 billion at mid-cycle and $15 billion at high cycle. GM Retail Roadshow, *supra* note 101, at slide 18.
[127] *See* General Motors Company, *Q3 Financial Highlights*, at 6, 7 (2010) (online at media.gm.com/content/dam/Media/gmcom/investor/2010/Q3-Financial-Highlights.pdf); General Motors Company, *Q2 Financial Highlights*, at 6, 7 (2010) (online at media.gm.com/content/dam/Media/gmcom/investor/2010/Q2- Financial-Highlights.pdf); GM Form 10-Q, *supra* note 75, at 1, 2. Return on assets is defined as net income divided by total assets. Profit margin is defined as net income divided by sales. These metrics are computed by taking the following data points from the quarterly filings: net income, total assets, and net sales.
[128] GM Retail Roadshow, *supra* note 101, at slide 9.
[129] GM Q3 2010 Results, *supra* note 47, at 2.
[130] General Motors Company, *Form 10-K for the Fiscal Year Ended December 31, 2009*, at 39 (Apr. 7, 2010) (online at www.sec.gov/Archives/edgar/data/1467858/000119312510078119/d10k.htm).
[131] David Whiston, *General Motors Company Has Reinvented Itself*, Morningstar, at 5, 15 (Nov.18, 2010).
[132] Joseph Amaturo, *A Lot of "Old" GM in the "New" GM*, Buckingham Research Group, at 47 (Dec. 6, 2010) (hereinafter "Buckingham Research Group Paper").
[133] GM Form 424B1: Final Common Prospectus, *supra* note 96, at 190.
[134] General Motors Company, *GM to Add 1,000 Electric Vehicle Engineering and Development Jobs in Michigan* (Nov. 30, 2010) (online at media.gm.com/content/media/us/en/news/news_detail.brand_gm.html/content/Pages/news/us/en/2010/Nov/1130_jo bs.html).
[135] The issuer default rating is an indicator given by credit rating agencies to potential investors of debt securities, which estimates the likelihood of default and relative creditworthiness of securities issued by a certain company.
[136] Fitch Ratings, *Fitch Assigns Initial [BB-] IDR to General Motors* (Oct. 6, 2010) (online at www.businesswire.com/news/home/20101006006853/en/Fitch-Assigns-Initial-BB--IDR-General-Motors).
[137] The ratings agencies include DBRS, Fitch, Moody's, and Standard & Poor's. GM Form 424B1: Final Common Prospectus, *supra* note 96, at 134.
[138] Standard & Poor's does, however, refer to GM as a government-related entity, albeit one whose importance to the government is limited because of the expectation that the government will reduce its ownership in GM. Standard & Poor's, *Global Credit Portal RatingsDirect: General Motors Co.*, at 2-3 (Nov. 11, 2010); E-mail from Standard & Poor's to Panel staff (Dec. 9, 2010).
[139] GM Form 424B1: Final Common Prospectus, *supra* note 96, at 3. *See also* Moody's Credit Opinion: General Motors Company, *supra* note 113, at 1 ("GM's Ba2 CFR reflects the company's strong position in developing markets, a competitive cost structure in North America, an improving domestic product portfolio, and a significantly stronger balance sheet and liquidity position as a result of the bankruptcy reorganization process.").
[140] *See* GM Retail Roadshow, *supra* note 101, at slide 16.

[141] GM Q3 2010 Results, *supra* note 47, at 10.
[142] GM Retail Roadshow, *supra* note 101, at slide 6.
[143] UBS Investment Research Paper, *supra* note 110, at 11-15.
[144] For a more detailed discussion of the government's shareholder principles and their implementation, see Section B, *infra*.
[145] Treasury conversations with Panel staff (Nov. 22, 2010).
[146] General Motors Company conversations with Panel staff (Dec. 3, 2010).
[147] See Moody's Investors Service, *GM's IPO – A Better Balance Sheet and Maybe Even More Car Customers*, at 1 (Nov. 22, 2010) (hereinafter "Moody's Paper on GM's Balance Sheet"); Treasury conversations with Panel staff (Nov. 22, 2010). Treasury also expressed concern that shareholders from Old GM could disrupt the pricing process had they gained control of their shares before the IPO.
[148] GM Form 424B1: Final Common Prospectus, *supra* note 96, at 236.
[149] Treasury conversations with Panel staff (Nov. 22, 2010).
[150] See, e.g., Moody's Paper on GM's Balance Sheet, *supra* note 147, at 1 ("This progress on the product portfolio front is supported by the IPO's positive messages about both the improving financial health of GM and the reduction in government ownership of the company.").
[151] See Section D.3.b.
[152] See Section D.2.
[153] Buckingham Research Group Paper, *supra* note 132, at 2.
[154] *See* UBS Investment Research Paper, *supra* note 110, at 11-12.
[155] Moody's Credit Opinion: General Motors Company, *supra* note 113, at 2.
[156] *See* Moody's Credit Opinion: General Motors Company, *supra* note 113, at 2.
[157] UBS Investment Research Paper on Growth Market, *supra* note 55, at 11-12.
[158] GM Q3 2010 Results, *supra* note 47, at 15.
[159] *See* UBS Investment Research Paper on Growth Market, *supra* note 55, at 1.
[160] *See* UBS Investment Research Paper, *supra* note 110, at 1-3.
[161] GM Retail Roadshow, *supra* note 101, at slide 13.
[162] Motor Trend, *2011 Motor Trend Car of the Year: Chevrolet Volt* (online at www.motortrend.com/oftheyear/car/1101_2011_motor_trend_car_of_the_year_chevrolet_volt/index.html).
[163] *See* Buckingham Research Group Paper, *supra* note 132, at 30-31.
[164] Average Transaction Price (ATP) increases are as follows: crossovers are 11 percent, cars are 9 percent, and trucks are 6 percent. GM Q2 2010 Results, *supra* note 103, at 8.
[165] GM Q3 2010 Results, *supra* note 47, at 20.
[166] GM Q3 2010 Results, *supra* note 47, at 20.
[167] GM Form 424B1: Final Common Prospectus, *supra* note 96, at 138.
[168] Motors Liquidation Company, *Motors Liquidation Company Files Joint Chapter 11 Plan*, at 1-2 (Aug. 31, 2010) (online at www.motorsliquidation.com/PressReleases.aspx) (hereinafter "Motors Liquidation Company Files Joint Chapter 11 Plan").
[169] U.S. Environmental Protection Agency, *Motors Liquidation Company (f/k/a General Motors (GM) Corporation) Bankruptcy Settlement* (Oct. 20, 2010) (online at www.epa.gov/compliance/resources/cases/cleanup/cercla/mlc/index.html).
[170] Motors Liquidation Company Files Joint Chapter 11 Plan, *supra* note 168, at 2.
[171] The $35.0 billion threshold refers specifically to unsecured claims that do not have a priority on Old GM's assets and are allowed as part of the bankruptcy proceeding. GM Amendment No. 5 to Form S-1: Preliminary Prospectus, *supra* note 69, at 11. Of course, the dilution to Treasury would occur only if Treasury remains a shareholder at that point.
[172] U.S. Department of the Treasury, *Office of Financial Stability Agency Financial Report: Fiscal Year 2010*, at 11 (Nov. 15, 2010) (online at www.financialstability.gov/docs/2010%20OFS%20AFR%20Nov%2015.pdf) (hereinafter "OFS Agency Financial Report").
[173] *See* Christine Tierney, David Shepardson, and Christina Rogers, *Rattner Predicts "Huge Success" for GM IPO*, The Detroit News (Nov. 16, 2010) (online at detnews.com/article/20101116/AUTO01/11160370/Rattner-predicts-%E2%80%98huge-success%E2%80%99-for-GM-IPO).
[174] Treasury maintains that it does not expect that the IPO will change the loss rate on the AIFP because Treasury had carried GM at book value on its books. Treasury conversations with Panel staff (Nov. 22, 2010).

[175] Panel staff estimates are derived from the amount of debt converted to equity divided by the common shares given to Treasury.

[176] Panel staff estimates. The break-even price includes underwriting commissions and discounts paid in order to sell Treasury's common shares in the initial public offering (IPO) of GM in November. The break-even price also includes dividend and interest payments on the debt and preferred stock portion of Treasury's investment, payments received from Motors Liquidation Company, GM Supplier program, and the premium paid to redeem its Series A preferred stock.

[177] Treasury conversations with Panel staff (Nov. 22, 2010).

[178] Estimating the likelihood and size of losses may be complicated by GM's reporting practices. In its recent regulatory filings, the company disclosed that internal controls relating to its financial reporting may present a risk going forward. It stated that "[w]e have determined that our disclosure controls and procedures and our internal control over financial reporting are currently not effective. The lack of effective internal controls could materially adversely affect our financial condition and ability to carry out our business plan." GM Form 424B1: Final Common Prospectus, *supra* note 96, at 30. Treasury maintains that it is comfortable with the sufficiency of the company's reporting, that investors did not raise concerns about this issue during the roadshow, and that the company's board and management are devoting time and energy to addressing the issue. Treasury conversations with Panel staff (Nov. 22, 2010).

[179] Chrysler Group LLC, *Chrysler Historical Timeline* (online at www.media.chrysler.com/newsrelease.do?id=2210&mid=) (accessed Jan. 11, 2011).

[180] Data provided by Chrysler (Jan. 11, 2011).

[181] See Section B for a description of the initial decision to support the automakers.

[182] Old Chrysler is used to refer to the automaker before June 10, 2009. The assets that did not carry over to New Chrysler, including the Chrysler name, remained in a company now known as Old Carco.

[183] The White House, *Determination of Viability Summary: Chrysler, LLC* (Mar. 30, 2009) (online at www.whitehouse.gov/assets/documents/Chrysler_Viability_Assessment.pdf).

[184] The White House, *Obama Administration New Path to Viability for GM & Chrysler* (Mar. 30, 2009) (online at www.whitehouse.gov/assets/documents/Fact_Sheet_GM_Chrysler.pdf).

[185] Treasury Transactions Report, *supra* note 24. On April 29, 2009, an additional $280,130,642 was lent to Chrysler Holdings to support a Special Purpose Vehicle (SPV) for Chrysler's warranties.

[186] Treasury Transactions Report, *supra* note 24; Chrysler Group LLC, *Consolidated Financial Statements as of December 31, 2009 and for the Period from June 10, 2009 to December 31, 2009*, at 20 (Apr. 21, 2010) (online at www.chryslergroupllc.com/pdf/news/2009_q4_year_end.pdf). Two billion dollars is due on December 10, 2011 and pays an interest rate of the London Interbank Offered Rate (LIBOR) plus 5 percent; this is referred to as the Tranche B loan. Of the remaining $4.6 billion, half is due on June 10, 2016 and the remainder on June 10, 2017. This remainder pays an interest rate of LIBOR plus 7.91 percent, and is referred to as the Tranche C Commitments.

[187] U.S. Department of the Treasury, *First Lien Credit Agreement Between Chrysler Group LLC and the U.S. Department of the Treasury* (June 10, 2009) (online at www.financialstability.gov/docs/AIFP/New%20Chrysler%20through%20Fourth%20Amendment.pdf); Treasury conversations with Panel staff (Dec. 22, 2010); Treasury Transactions Report, *supra* note 24.

188 U.S. Department of the Treasury, *Amended and Restated Limited Liability Company Operating Agreement of Chrysler Group LLC,* at 86 (June 10, 2009) (online at www.financialstability.gov/docs/AIFP/Binder1%20-%20Chrysler%20redacted%20corporate%20docs%20as%20posted%2012-09.pdf) (hereinafter "Chrysler LLC Operating Agreement").

[189] See Section E.3 for a detailed discussion.

[190] Treasury Transactions Report, *supra* note 24.

[191] While Treasury does not account for this loan as a loss due to potential recoveries in the future, it has stated that it does not expect material returns. As of December 30, 2010, $48.1 million has been recovered from asset sales associated with this loan. Treasury Transactions Report, *supra* note 24.

[192] As of September 30, 2010, $4.6 billion of this total has been drawn down and is outstanding. Chrysler Group LLC, *Unaudited Interim Condensed Consolidated Financial Statements as of September 30, 2010 and for the Three and Nine Months Ended September 30, 2010*, at 15 (Nov. 8, 2010) (online at www.chryslergroupllc.com/pdf/business/q3_2010_financial_statements.pdf) (hereinafter "Chrysler Consolidated Financial Statements").

[193] Treasury Transactions Report, *supra* note 24.

[194] This discussion does not reflect the impact of the January 10, 2011 announcement that Chrysler has met one of three incentive goals and thereby Fiat has increased its equity ownership position from 20 to 25 percent. Chrysler Group LLC, *Chrysler Group LLC Meets First of Three Performance Events; Fiat Increases Ownership to 25 percent* (Jan. 10, 2011) (online at www.media.chrysler.com/newsrelease.do?id=10453&mid=2) (hereinafter "Chrysler Meets First of Three Performance Events").

[195] U.S. Department of the Treasury, *Obama Administration Auto Restructuring Initiative* (Apr. 30, 2009) (online at www.financialstability.gov/latest/tg_043009.html). For every three U.S. dollars that Treasury loaned Chrysler, the Canadian government loaned one Canadian dollar to the company. The U.S. dollar amount of the Canadian government loan has fluctuated over time with changes in the exchange rate between the U.S. and Canadian dollars.

[196] Chrysler LLC Operating Agreement, *supra* note 188, at 86.

[197] Chrysler Consolidated Financial Statements, *supra* note 192, at 11.

[198] Chrysler LLC Operating Agreement, *supra* note 188, at 86.

[199] The White House, *Obama Administration Auto Restructuring Initiative* (Apr. 30, 2009) (online at www.whitehouse.gov/the-press-office/obama-administration-auto-restructuring-initiative) (hereinafter "Obama Administration Auto Restructuring Initiative").

[200] Chrysler LLC Operating Agreement, *supra* note 188, at 86.

[201] Chrysler LLC Operating Agreement, *supra* note 188, at 86.

[202] The Equity Subscription Agreement, The VEBA Call Option Agreement, The UST Call Option Agreement, The Equity Recapture Agreement, The Master Transaction Agreement, and The First Lien Credit Agreement were also signed on June 10, 2009 and collectively determine the interests, rights, and obligations of all the parties under the various possible scenarios.

[203] These performance targets are referred to as "Class B Events." *See* Chrysler LLC Operating Agreement, *supra* note 188, at Section 3.4.

[204] This discussion does not reflect the impact of the January 10, 2011 announcement that Chrysler has met one of three incentive goals and thereby Fiat has increased its equity ownership position from 20 to 25 percent. Chrysler Meets First of Three Performance Events, *supra* note 194.

[205] Obama Administration Auto Restructuring Initiative, *supra* note 199.

[206] Chrysler LLC Operating Agreement, *supra* note 188, at 86.

[207] This discussion does not reflect the impact of the January 10, 2011 announcement that Chrysler has met this incentive goal and thereby Fiat has increased its equity ownership position from 20 to 25 percent. Chrysler Meets First of Three Performance Events, *supra* note 194. All analyst reports on Fiat reviewed in Section E.2.c., for example, assume Fiat's stake to be at least 35 percent. Chrysler has indicated that it believed the three targets would be reached. Chrysler Group LLC conversations with Panel staff (Dec. 8, 2010).

[208] Chrysler LLC Operating Agreement, *supra* note 188, at Section 3.5.

[209] *VEBA Call Option Agreement* (June 10, 2010). This option gives Fiat the right to buy up to 4.4 percent of Chrysler's diluted equity (assuming all Class B events have occurred) no more than once every six months, starting July 1, 2012 and running until either (1) June 30, 2016, (2) 22 percent of the equity has been so purchased, or (3) the Treasury exercises its right to call the VEBA's equity under the Equity Recapture Agreement.

[210] U.S. Department of the Treasury, *UST Call Option Agreement Regarding Equity Securities of New Carco Acquisition LLC*, at 183 (June 10, 2009) (online at www.financialstability.gov/docs/AIFP/Chrysler%20LLC%20Corporate%20as%20of%2012-01-10.pdf).

[211] *Id.* at 183. The "dueling investment banks" method is as follows: both the buyer and seller select an investment bank to value the claim. If the two valuations are within 10 percent of each other, then the average is taken as the sale price. If the two estimates differ by more than 10 percent, then a third investment bank is appointed and the average of the closest two valuations is used as the sale price.

[212] U.S. Department of the Treasury, *Equity Recapture Agreement*, at 161 (June 10, 2009) (online at www.financialstability.gov/docs/AIFP/Chrysler%20LLC%20Corporate%20as%20of%2012-01-10.pdf) (hereinafter "Equity Recapture Agreement"). The Equity Recapture Agreement also gives Treasury the right to receive payments in 2014, 2016, and 2018 from the VEBA based on the value of the option, if the Threshold Amount has not yet been reached at those dates.

[213] Under the terms of the agreement, Treasury can buy the asset, the VEBA's equity in Chrysler, at any time for the Threshold Amount, less any cash already received by the VEBA for Chrysler equity sold. However, an agreement between Treasury and the Canada Development Investment Corporation (CDIC) requires that 20

percent of any receipts to Treasury under the Equity Recapture Agreement be transferred to the CDIC. U.S. Department of the Treasury, *April 30, 2009 Letter Agreement*, at 178 (June 10, 2009) (online at www.financialstability.gov/docs/AIFP/Chrysler%20LLC%20Corporate%20as%20of%2012-01-10.pdf).

[214] For example, if the equity valuation of Chrysler reaches a required multiple of the Threshold Amount (approximately $10 billion on January 1, 2012), then Treasury would be entitled to the benefit of 52 cents for each subsequent dollar increase in Chrysler's valuation. In other words, should Chrysler succeed and be valued at such a level, or higher, Treasury would be the marginal beneficiary of 80 percent of the VEBA's 55 percent equity interest (with CDIC owning 20 percent of this interest), which would bring Treasury's total economic interest in Chrysler to 52 percent, a majority.

[215] U.S. Department of the Treasury, *Troubled Asset Relief Program – Two year Retrospective* (Oct. 2010) (online at www.financialstability.gov/docs/TARP%20Two%20Year%20Retrospective_ 10%2005%2010_transmittal%20letter. pdf) ("October 3, 2010 marked the second anniversary of the Emergency Economic Stabilization Act that created the Troubled Asset Relief Program (TARP) and the end of the authority to make new financial commitments").

[216] See analysis in Section E.

[217] For exact figures, see Section E.

[218] Chrysler Consolidated Financial Statements, *supra* note 192, at 2.

[219] Chrysler Group LLC, *Our Plan Presentation* (Nov. 4, 2009) (online at www.chryslergroupllc.com/business/) (hereinafter "Chrysler Plan Presentation").

[220] Chrysler Group LLC, *Our Plan Presentation: Presentation 9 – U.S. Network Development* (Nov. 4, 2009) (online at www.chryslergroupllc.com/pdf/business/us_network_development.pdf).

[221] Chrysler Group LLC, *Chrysler Group LLC Celebrates Production Launch of All-new 2011 Jeep® Grand Cherokee at Detroit Plant; Announces Second Shift* (May 21, 2010) (online at www.chryslergroupllc.com/news/archive/2010/05/21/chrysler_celebrates_prod_launch_2011jgc_05212010).

[222] Data provided by Chrysler for full year 2010 worldwide sales (Jan. 10, 2011).

[223] Chrysler Plan Presentation, *supra* note 219.

[224] Chrysler Group LLC, *Ram, Jeep Bring Home High Honors at Texas Truck Rodeo* (Oct. 24, 2010) (online at blog.chryslergroupllc.com/blog.do?id=1215&p=entry).

[225] UBS Investment Research, *Retail & Fleet Registrations Q3 2010*, at 15 (Dec. 16, 2010).

[226] Automotive News, *Data Center* (Instrument: U.S. light-vehicle sales by nameplate, Nov. & YTD) (Dec. 1, 2010) (hereinafter "Automotive News Data Center").

[227] *Id.* As of November, 2010, Chrysler's U.S. car market share was 5.1 percent, up from 4.3 percent in 2009. On the other hand, Chrysler's U.S. truck market share actually declined from 14.4 percent in 2009 to 14.1 percent as of November, 2010.

[228] As of June 2010,the average transaction price was $27,300. Data provided by Chrysler (Jan. 10, 2011).

[229] The 2010 data includes information through November 2010. Automotive News Data Center, *supra* note 226.

[230] Data provided by Chrysler (Jan. 10, 2011).

[231] Chrysler Group LLC, *Our Plan Presentation: Presentation 16 – Financial Review* (Nov. 4, 2009) (online at www.chryslergroupllc.com/pdf/business/financial_review.pdf) (hereinafter "Chrysler Plan Presentation: Presentation 16 – Financial Review").

[232] Chrysler Group LLC, *Chrysler Group LLC Selects Dealers to Represent Fiat Brand in the U.S.* (Nov. 17, 2010) (online at www.media.chrysler.com/newsrelease.do?id=10325&mid=2).

[233] Chrysler's TARP loans have a weighted, based on carrying value, average effective interest rate of 9.36 percent. Chrysler Consolidated Financial Statements, *supra* note 192, at 12.

[234] Data provided by Chrysler (Jan. 11, 2011).

[235] Chrysler Group LLC, *Q3 2010 Results Review*, at 4 (Nov. 8, 2010) (online at www.chryslergroupllc.com/pdf/business/q3_2010_webcast_presentation.pdf).

[236] The following metrics for this time period are as of June 9, 2009: vehicles sold, revenue, and net income data. Data provided by Chrysler (Jan. 11, 2011).

[237] Chrysler Consolidated Financial Statements, *supra* note 192, at 12.

[238] Chrysler Consolidated Financial Statements, *supra* note 192, at 15. In addition to the $500 million in debt New Chrysler assumed from Old Chrysler, the company has drawn $4.6 billion of the $6.6 billion made available to the company on May 27, 2009, leaving $2.1 billion available for the company to draw down.

[239] Chrysler Consolidated Financial Statements, *supra* note 192, at 12.

[240] Chrysler Plan Presentation, *supra* note 219.

[241] Chrysler Plan Presentation: Presentation 16 – Financial Review, *supra* note 231.
[242] See footnote 259, *infra*, for a discussion of the ATVM loan program and Chrysler's application for funds from the program.
[243] Chrysler Consolidated Financial Statements, *supra* note 192, at 4.
[244] As of December 30, 2010, Treasury held 9.8 percent of the equity in Chrysler, but this will be diluted to 8 percent if and when Chrysler and Fiat meet the performance targets for Fiat's increased equity stake. Treasury also has an effective economic interest in 80 percent of the VEBA's 55 percent equity stake, see Section E.1.b.ii for details.
[245] For analysis of Treasury's likely exit scenarios, see Section E.3, *infra*.
[246] Bloomberg Data Service, *Fiat May Increase Chrysler Stake to 51% Before IPO* (Jan. 3, 2011) (hereinafter "Bloomberg Data Service") ("I think it is possible. I don't know whether it is likely, but it is possible that we'll go over the 50 percent mark if Chrysler decides to go to the markets in 2011," Sergio Marchionne, 58, told reporters at the Milan stock exchange today. "It will be advantageous if that happens.").
[247] Chrysler LLC Operating Agreement, *supra* note 188 (see the Definitions Addendum).
[248] Calculations were done based on the formula in the Operating Agreement, using third quarter 2010 (Q3 2010) financial results for Chrysler and other automotive manufacturers, as subsequently described. The average EV/EBITDA T12M (Enterprise Value to Earnings Before Interest, Tax, Depreciation, and Amortization on a Trailing 12 Month basis) (the market "multiple") for all Reference Automotive Manufacturers is 7.96 through Q3 2010. Excluding the outliers, as per the Operating Agreement formula, lowers the figure to 6.84, which is still higher than the Fiat EV/EBITDA T12M Multiple of 4.68 as of the end of the third quarter of 2010. Bloomberg Financial Service. Chrysler's EBITDA in the 12 months prior to the end of the third quarter of 2010 were $2,977 million ($398 million + $787 million + $855 million + $937 million). Chrysler Group LLC, *Unaudited Interim Condensed Consolidated Financial Statements as of September 30, 2010 and for the Three and Nine Months Ended September 30, 2010*, at 15 (Nov. 8, 2010) (online at www.chryslergroupllc.com/pdf/business/q3_2010_financial_statements.pdf); Chrysler Group LLC, *Chrysler Group LLC Reports Financial Results for the Period Ended March 31, 2010* (Apr. 21, 2010) (online at www.chryslergroupllc.com/news/archive/2010/04/21/2010_q1_press_release). Applying the 4.68 Fiat Multiple to Chrysler's EBITDA of $2,977 million yields an enterprise value of $13,932 million, less net debt of $3,766 million, which gives a total equity value for Chrysler of $10,166 million. The value to Treasury is the 9.8 percent of $10,166 million, or $1.0 billion for the direct equity, and approximately $1.8 billion for the proceeds to Treasury under the Equity Recapture Agreement.
[249] Chrysler Group LLC, *Chrysler Group LLC First Quarter (Q1) 2010 Financial Results Analyst Webcast*, at 2 (May 10, 2010) (online at www.chryslergroupllc.com/pdf/business/may10_presentation.pdf).
[250] Chrysler LLC Operating Agreement, *supra* note 188 (see the Definitions Addendum).
[251] Bloomberg Data Service.
[252] On April 21, 2010, Fiat announced its plans to "demerge" its industrial goods divisions from the automotive divisions. *See* Sergio Marchionne, *Fiat Investor Day: The Five Year Plan* (online at www.fiatgroup.com/en-us/mediacentre/press/Documents/2010/THE%20FIVE%20YEAR%20PLAN%20-%20Adress%20 from%20Sergio%20Marchionne.pdf) (accessed Jan. 11, 2011). Analysts predict this will further lower the overall multiple applied to Fiat. The Goldman Sachs Group, Inc., *Breaking Up is Easy to Do; Reiterating Conviction Buy*, at 32 (Sept. 24, 2010) (hereinafter "Goldman Sachs Paper on Fiat"). A lower multiple for Fiat would further limit the implied valuation of Chrysler under the Operating Agreement. Fiat's possible divestment of Ferrari would also lower the Fiat multiple. Barclays Capital, *Fiat SPA – Crystallising Option Value – Move to 1- OW*, at 8 (Dec. 7, 2010) (hereinafter "Barclays Capital Paper on Fiat"). Treasury has not discussed this with any of the Operating Agreement parties, including Fiat. Treasury conversations with Panel staff (Nov. 28, 2010).
[253] Goldman Sachs Paper on Fiat, *supra* note 252, at 32. Figures converted from Euros to U.S. dollars using the U.S. Treasury's rate of exchange as of December 31, 2010. U.S. Department of the Treasury, *Treasury Reporting Rates of Exchange* (Instrument: Euro Zone – Euro) (accessed Jan. 11, 2011) (online at www.fms.treas.gov/intn.html#rates) (hereinafter "Treasury Reporting Rates of Exchange").
[254] Kepler Research, *Wishful Thinking*, at 6 (Apr. 26, 2010).
[255] Cheuvreux: Credit Agricole Group, *A New Fiat in the Making*, at 2 (Apr. 23, 2010) (online at www.borsaitaliana.it/bitApp/viewpdf.bit?location=/media/star/db/pdf/86353.pdf). Figures converted from Euros to U.S. dollars using the U.S. Treasury's rate of exchange as of December 31, 2010. Treasury Reporting Rates of Exchange, *supra* note 253.

[256] Deutsche Bank, *The Great Divide – Initial Thoughts*, at 3 (Apr. 22, 2010) (online at www.borsaitaliana.it/media/star/db/pdf/88399.pdf).

[257] Chrysler Plan Presentation: Presentation 16 – Financial Review, *supra* note 231. Chrysler has reiterated this plan in conversations with Panel staff. Chrysler conversations with Panel staff (Dec. 10, 2010).

[258] Chrysler conversations with Panel staff (Dec. 10, 2010).

[259] The loans, under the Advanced Technology Vehicle Manufacturing (ATVM) program, charge an interest rate equivalent to Treasury's cost of funds, which is lower than interest on the TARP loans. *See* U.S. Department of Energy, *Advanced Technology Vehicles Manufacturing Incentive Program*, 73 Federal Register 66721 (Nov. 12, 2008) (interim final rule). Based on the current difference between these interest rates, the cost savings to Chrysler, and the associated loss to Treasury, would be worth approximately $180 million per year. The ATVM loans have the potential to extend beyond 2017, the current date by which Chrysler must repay all of its obligations to the TARP.

[260] When Sergio Marchionne was asked about the use of ATVM funds on an analyst call he said: "As you well know, cash is fungible. So to the extent that we produce cash from operations, cash can be used, not to be redeployed in the investment cycle, but to go back and repay existing indebtedness. So at the end of the day, we need to have those funds [ATVM loans] targeted for capital and engineering and development efforts, but in the scheme of things, they will all end up in the same pot and how we use that cash to repay who is really up to Chrysler." Chrysler Plan Presentation, *supra* note 219, at 61st minute. The Panel notes that if ATVM funds were used to repay TARP loans, this result would reflect policy choices made pursuant to the ATVM program and does not appear to violate either the terms of the ATVM program or the terms of EESA, even though it may raise concerns regarding Chrysler's financial health.

[261] See Section E.2.b, *supra*, for a discussion.

[262] This figure is derived as follows: ($3.5 billion (amount written off on Old Chrysler and Chrysler Holdings loans) / 8 percent (Treasury's equity stake, assuming all three performance targets are met)). Consideration of the time value of money and/or the riskiness of the securities held by Treasury would push the break-even point higher.

[263] September 2009 Oversight Report, *supra* note 2, at 46. The difference is due to Chrysler-related losses being lower than were expected in 2009.

[264] This calculation uses Consumer Price Index data for May 1998 and October 2010. U.S. Department of Labor, *Consumer Price Index: All Urban Consumers* (Nov. 17, 2010) (online at ftp://ftp.bls.gov/pub/special.requests/cpi/cpiai.txt).

[265] Bloomberg Data Service.

[266] See Section E.1.b for an analysis of the various exit strategies and their respective costs and benefits to the taxpayers.

[267] For a discussion of Treasury's rights to the VEBA's equity, see Section E.1.b, *supra*.

[268] See a summary of Treasury's principles in Section H.1, *infra*.

[269] Chrysler LLC Operating Agreement, *supra* note 188, at Section 14.1. Starting January 1, 2013 a simple majority of Chrysler's equity owners can force the company to have an IPO.

[270] Chrysler Plan Presentation, *supra* note 219.

[271] Chrysler Group LLC conversations with Panel staff (Dec. 9, 2010).

[272] Chrysler Group LLC conversations with Panel staff (Dec. 9, 2010).

[273] The VEBA is unlikely to be able to dispose of its entire equity stake at once, but since Treasury gets the benefit of the VEBA sales above the Threshold Amount, it will be affected by the volume and timing of these sales. For a discussion see Section E.1.b. Treasury's right to receive income from such sales survives its exit as a shareholder of Chrysler. Moreover, as noted above, if Treasury did increase its equity stake by exercising its rights under the VEBA option agreement, Treasury could realize a higher return on its investment. VEBA's actions are not under Treasury's control, but the Panel notes that the lack of resources for Treasury to exercise fully its rights may limit the level of return to the taxpayer.

[274] See Section E.1.b, *supra*.

[275] To prepay the TARP and Canadian government loans, Chrysler would need the approval of a simple majority of its Board of Directors. Assuming that all three performance targets are met, Fiat would only need the agreement of one more director, either the VEBA director, the Canadian director, or one of the three Treasury directors. Chrysler LLC Operating Agreement, *supra* note 188, at Sections 5.1 and 5.8.

[276] Chrysler LLC Operating Agreement, *supra* note 188, at Section 3.5. This gives Fiat the right to buy 16 percent of the equity using either a public market price or the valuation formula described in E.2.c. This option can only

be exercised once Chrysler has repaid the monies borrowed from the TARP and from the Canadian Government. Funds received by Chrysler for the Incremental Equity Call Option can be used simultaneously to repay the TARP loans. Recent reports from analysts covering Fiat indicate that Fiat may float some of its interest in Ferrari and Marelli, a parts supplier, ahead of a Chrysler flotation. A possible explanation for floating these two components of Fiat is to raise the necessary funds to exercise the Incremental Equity Call Option.

[277] As described in Section E.2.c, *supra*, the Operating Agreement's formula for the valuation of Chrysler uses a market "multiple" tied to that of Fiat, which is the lowest in the industry, to calculate the value of Chrysler. See footnote 248, *supra*, for a detailed discussion on the calculation of market multiples.

[278] Barclays Capital Paper on Fiat, *supra* note 252, at 8. ("We estimate a pre-IPO transaction could save Fiat between $1.0bn and $2.7bn compared to a post IPO deal. Adjusted for debt assumed by Fiat, we calculate ROI in a 40-100% range."); UBS Investment Research, *Chrysler: Pre vs Post IPO Take-over*, at 1 (Dec. 15, 2010) (hereinafter "UBS Investment Research Paper on IPO").

[279] A similar logic applies to Fiat's rights under the VEBA Call Option Agreement. *VEBA Call Option Agreement* (June 10, 2010). This also has implication for Treasury's return due the Equity Recapture Agreement. Equity Recapture Agreement, *supra* note 212, at 161.

[280] Bloomberg Data Service, *supra* note 246 ("It looks cheaper for Fiat to get 51 percent of Chrysler before the IPO," said Philippe Houchois, a London-based analyst at UBS AG, who estimates that Fiat could save $1 billion to $2.7 billion if it exercises the option before a Chrysler listing. "It's a positive scenario for Fiat shares."). For analysis, *see* UBS Investment Research Paper on IPO, *supra* note 278, at 1.

[281] Captive financing organizations can be structured as legally separate subsidiaries or distinct business lines, but they exist primarily as extensions of their corporate parents. Their purpose is to facilitate the parent corporation's sale of goods or services by providing debt and/or lease financing to the parent's customers. *See* Standard & Poor's, *Captive Finance Operations* (Apr. 17, 2009) (online at www2.standardandpoors.com/spf/pdf/media/Captive_Finance_Operations.pdf).

[282] For further discussion concerning GMAC/Ally Financial's diversification efforts, *see* March 2010 Oversight Report, *supra* note 22, at 11-13.

[283] While GMAC/Ally Financial may no longer be a captive in the legal sense after it became an independent finance company in 2006, it maintains close ties with GM in many ways as a result of the contractual codification of its historical relationship with GM. For example, as part of the 2006 sale, GMAC/Ally Financial and GM entered into several service agreements that codified the mutually beneficial historic relationship between the companies. One of these agreements was the United States Consumer Financing Services Agreement (USCFSA), which, among other things, provided that GM would use GMAC/Ally Financial exclusively whenever it offered vehicle financing and leasing incentives to customers. (As described below, this agreement was modified when GMAC/Ally Financial became a bank holding company in December 2008.) For further discussion of the USCFSA, see Section F.3.b, *infra*. GMAC/Ally Financial also remains the leading floorplan finance franchise for GM dealers.

[284] For further discussion concerning the factors that precipitated government assistance, *see* March 2010 Oversight Report, *supra* note 22, at 11-17, 32-42.

[285] GMAC LLC, *GMAC Financial Services Reports Preliminary Third Quarter 2008 Financial Results* (Nov. 5, 2008) (online at media.gmacfs.com/index.php?s=43&item=286).

[286] For further discussion concerning GMAC/Ally Financial's business and why it was failing, *see* March 2010 Oversight Report, *supra* note 22, at 11-17, 32-42.

[287] *See* March 2010 Oversight Report, *supra* note 22, at 57-78.

[288] U.S. Department of the Treasury, *Treasury Converts Nearly Half of Its Ally Preferred Shares to Common Stock* (Dec. 30, 2010) (online at www.treasury.gov/press-center/press-releases/Pages/tg1014.aspx) (hereinafter "Treasury Converts Ally Preferred Shares to Common Stock").

[289] For further discussion concerning the government's "staged" investments in GMAC/Ally Financial, *see* March 2010 Oversight Report, *supra* note 22, at 42-57. On December 29, 2008, Treasury purchased $5 billion in GMAC/Ally Financial Senior Preferred Stock and also received warrants for an additional $250 million in preferred equity. Second, Treasury made an additional purchase of $7.5 billion of GMAC/Ally Financial Mandatory Convertible Preferred Stock on May 21, 2009, increasing its investment to $12.5 billion. Additionally, on May 29, 2009, Treasury accepted Old GM's 35.4 percent equity stake in GMAC/Ally Financial in exchange for the $884 million loan given to Old GM in December 2008. Finally, Treasury authorized an additional investment of $3.8 billion in the form of $2.54 billion of Trust Preferred Securities

(TruPs) and $1.25 billion of MCPs on December 30, 2009. At this time, $3 billion of the initial December 2008 investment was converted to common stock, bringing Treasury's control of GMAC/Ally Financial to 56.3 percent. In May 2009, the terms of the MCPs specified that GMAC/Ally Financial could convert the stock at any time, but if the conversion would result in Treasury owning more than 49 percent of the company, then GMAC/Ally Financial would need Treasury's approval or an order from the Federal Reserve. The terms of this MCP were revised in exchange for Treasury's additional investment in December 2009. After the December 2009 investment, GMAC/Ally Financial could only convert the MCPs if it received prior written approval from Treasury or an order from the Federal Reserve. As part of the terms of its December 2009 investment, Treasury also acquired "a 'reset' feature on the entirety of its MCP holdings such that the conversion price under which its MCPs can be converted into common equity will be adjusted in 2011, if beneficial to Treasury, based on the market price of private capital transactions occurring in 2010." U.S. Department of the Treasury, *Treasury Announces Restructuring of Commitment To GMAC* (Jan. 5, 2010) (online at www.financialstability.gov/latest/pr_1052010.html) (hereinafter "Treasury Announces Restructuring of Commitment To GMAC"). *See also* U.S. Department of the Treasury, *Contract [GMAC]*, at 482 (May 21, 2009) (online at www.financialstability.gov/docs/AIFP/Posted%20to%20AIFP%20Website%20-%20GMAC%202009.pdf) ("The Series F-2 shall be convertible to common stock, in whole or in part, at the applicable Conversion Rate at the option of the holder upon specified corporate events, including any public offering of GMAC's common stock, certain sales, mergers or changes of control at GMAC"). This feature preserves Treasury's ability to assess whether it is advantageous to Treasury to convert considering all the facts and circumstances available at the time. On December 30, 2010, Treasury announced it is converting $5.5 billion of its MCP holdings in GMAC/Ally Financial into common stock. *See* Treasury Converts Ally Preferred Shares to Common Stock, *supra* note 288.

[290] Treasury Transactions Report, *supra* note 24, at 18-19.

[291] Includes exercised warrants.

[292] Includes exercised warrants.

[293] These figures include the exercised warrants associated with each investment. Treasury obtained a 35 percent equity stake on May 29, 2009, when it exercised its option to exchange its $884 million loan (to GM) for the ownership interest GM had purchased. Including all preferred to common stock conversions, Treasury holds 73.8 percent of the GMAC/Ally Financial's common stock as of December 30, 2010. Treasury Transactions Report, *supra* note 24, at 18.

[294] Warrants for MCPs and Preferred Equity were immediately exercised and are included. Treasury Announces Restructuring of Commitment To GMAC, *supra* note 289; Treasury Transactions Report, *supra* note 24, at 18-19.

[295] Although the third-party investors received their share in distributions from Cerberus, they are not Cerberus affiliates and will not necessarily act in concert with Cerberus. As part of the conditions to the approval of the BHC application, none of these third-party investors own, hold, or control more than 5 percent of the voting shares or 7.5 percent of the total equity of GMAC/Ally Financial. The Federal Reserve describes them as sophisticated investors who are independent of Cerberus and each other. Board of Governors of the Federal Reserve System, *GMAC LLC; IB Finance Holding Company, LLC: Order Approving Formation of Bank Holding Companies and Notice to Engage in Certain Nonbanking Activities*, Federal Reserve Bulletin, Vol. 95, Legal Developments: Fourth Quarter, 2008 (May 29, 2009) (online at www.federalreserve.gov/pubs/bulletin/2009/legal/q408/order6.htm). As private equity investors, none of these parties are required to disclose their identities publicly under applicable law, and Cerberus generally avoids the spotlight whenever possible. Cerberus Institutional Partners, L.P., *Letter to Investors*, at 6 (Jan. 22, 2008) (online at online.wsj.com/public/resources/documents/WSJ-LB-cerberus080214.pdf).

[296] Ally Financial Inc., *Ally Financial Announces Conversion of Certain U.S. Treasury Investments into Common Equity* (Dec. 30, 2010) (online at media.ally.com/index.php?s=43&item=438).

[297] Not reflected in this pie chart is the fact that the Corporate Segment recorded a $535 million loss for the third quarter of 2010. The Corporate segment is composed of the Commercial Finance Group, certain equity investments, other corporate activities, the residual impacts from corporate funds transfer pricing and treasury asset liability management activities, and reclassifications and eliminations between the reportable operating segments. Ally Financial Inc., *Form 10-Q For the Quarterly Period Ended September 30, 2010*, at 80 (Nov. 9, 2010) (online at www.sec.gov/Archives/edgar/data/40729/000119312510252419/d10q.htm) (hereinafter "Ally Financial Form 10- Q").

[298] *Id.* at 79.

[299] *Id.* at 82, 94.
[300] Ally Financial Inc., *3Q10 Earnings Review*, at 3 (Nov. 3, 2010) (online at phx.corporate-ir.net/External.File?item=UGFyZW50SUQ9MzQ2Nzg3NnxDaGlsZElEPTQwMjMzOHxUeXBlPTI=&t=1) (hereinafter "Ally Financial 3Q10 Earnings Review").
[301] While GMAC/Ally Financial's share of GM-subvented financing has declined from 76 percent in 2006 to 20 percent as of the third quarter of 2010, GMAC/Ally Financial's share of Chrysler-subvented financing has increased since 2009, along with its shares of GM and Chrysler direct-to-consumer loans.
[302] GMAC LLC, *GMAC Financial Services Enters Agreement to Provide Financing for Chrysler Dealers and Customers* (Apr. 30, 2009) (online at gmacfs.mediaroom.com/index.php?s=43&item=324). The April 2009 term sheet contemplated a more definitive agreement.
[303] Ally Financial 3Q10 Earnings Review, *supra* note 300, at 3.
[304] Ally Financial 3Q10 Earnings Review, *supra* note 300, at 17.
[305] Ally Financial Inc., *Ally Financial Completes Sales of European Mortgage Assets and Operations* (Oct. 1, 2010) (online at media.ally.com/index.php?s=43&item=419).
[306] Ally Financial Inc., *Transcript: Q3 2010 Earnings Call*, at 5 (Nov. 3, 2010) (hereinafter "Ally Financial Transcript: Q3 2010 Earnings Call").
[307] Ally Financial Inc., *Form 10-Q for the Quarterly Period Ended June 30, 2010*, at 10 (Aug. 6, 2010) (online at www.sec.gov/Archives/edgar/data/40729/000119312510181437/d10q.htm); Ally Financial Form 10-Q, *supra* note 297, at 10-11. It does not appear, however, that GMAC/Ally Financial will completely dispose of ResCap, since it plans to shift its mortgage operations to focus on agency servicing and originations.
[308] *See* Ally Financial 3Q10 Earnings Review, *supra* note 300, at 3; Ally Financial Inc., *2Q10 Earnings Review*, at 26 (Aug. 3, 2010) (online at phx.corporate-ir.net/External.File?item=UGFyZW50SUQ9 MzI0MjM1M3x DaGlsZElEPTM5MTY3NXxUeXBlPTI=&t=1) (hereinafter "Ally Financial 2Q10 Earnings Review"); GMAC Financial Services, *Preliminary 2010 First Quarter Results* (May 3, 2010) (online at phx.corporate-ir.net/External.File?item=UGFyZW50SUQ9NDQxMjF8Q2hpbGRJRD0tMXxUeXBlPTM=&t=1); GMAC Financial Services, *Preliminary 2009 Fourth Quarter Results* (Feb. 4, 2010) (online at phx.corporateir.net/External.File?item=UGFyZW50SUQ9MjkzNTh8Q2hpbGRJRD 0tMXxUeXBlPTM=&t=1).
[309] Ally Financial 2Q10 Earnings Review, *supra* note 308, at 28. Ally Financial Transcript: Q3 2010 Earnings Call, *supra* note 306, at 1. During the third quarter 2010 earnings call, Mr. Carpenter stated that the company believes it has "become a fully-fledged bank holding company," so it will no longer report on its progress relating to that objective anymore.
[310] Ally Financial Transcript: Q3 2010 Earnings Call, *supra* note 306, at 1. This statistic reflects data for the first half of 2010.
[311] Ally Financial 3Q10 Earnings Review, *supra* note 300, at 6.
[312] Ally Financial 3Q10 Earnings Review, *supra* note 300, at 6.
[313] General Motors may elect to sponsor incentive programs (on both retail contracts and leases) by supporting financing rates below standard rates at which GMAC/Ally Financial purchases retail contracts. Subvention is the manner in which GM pays for exclusive promotions offered through GMAC/Ally Financial. This practice is akin to a marketing expense.
[314] Ally Financial Transcript: Q3 2010 Earnings Call, *supra* note 306, at 9.
[315] Ally Financial Transcript: Q3 2010 Earnings Call, *supra* note 306, at 3.
[316] Ally Financial Form 10-Q, *supra* note 297.
[317] Ally Financial 3Q10 Earnings Review, *supra* note 300, at 3.
[318] Ally Financial 3Q10 Earnings Review, *supra* note 300, at 8.
[319] Ally Financial 3Q10 Earnings Review, *supra* note 300, at 8.
[320] Ally Financial Form 10-Q, *supra* note 297.
[321] Ally Financial Transcript: Q3 2010 Earnings Call, *supra* note 306.
[322] Ally Financial Transcript: Q3 2010 Earnings Call, *supra* note 306.
[323] If Treasury were to convert its remaining $5.9 billion of MCPs prior to an IPO at the same conversion terms used in the December 2010 conversion (i.e., same conversion price and conversion ratio), its common equity ownership percentage would increase to 81.7 percent.
[324] Treasury conversations with Panel staff (Nov. 18, 2010).
[325] TruPs have elements of both common equity and debt, are senior to all other common equity of GMAC/Ally Financial, and have no contractual restrictions on transfer (other than requirements that certificates bear certain

legends and other similar restrictions set forth in the Declaration of Trust for the Trust), while MCPs, which are convertible at the Federal Reserve's option, would require conversion before they can be marketed. *See* Treasury Announces Restructuring of Commitment To GMAC, *supra* note 289; U.S. Department of the Treasury, *Decoder* (online at www.financialstability.gov/roadtostability/decoder.htm) (accessed Jan. 11, 2011); U.S. Department of the Treasury, *The Treasury Capital Assistance Program and the Supervisory Capital Assessment Program*, Joint Statement by Secretary of the Treasury Timothy F. Geithner, Chairman of the Board of Governors of the Federal Reserve System Ben S. Bernanke, Chairman of the Federal Deposit Insurance Corporation Sheila Bair, and Comptroller of the Currency John C. Dugan (May 6, 2009) (online at www.financialstability.gov/latest/tg91.html); GMAC, Inc., *Summary of Trust Preferred Securities and Warrant Terms* (May 21, 2009) (online at financialstability.gov/docs/AIFP/Posted%20to%20 AIFP%20 Website%20- %20GMAC%202009.pdf).

[326] U.S. Department of the Treasury, *Office of Financial Stability Agency Financial Report: Fiscal Year 2009* at 40 (Dec. 10, 2009) (online at www.treasury.gov/about/organizationalstructure/offices/Mgt/Documents/ OFS%20AFR%2009_24.pdf) (hereinafter "OFS FY2009 Agency Financial Report"); Treasury conversations with Panel staff (Nov. 18, 2010).

[327] OFS FY2009 Agency Financial Report, *supra* note 326, at 44. Given that Treasury currently holds 73.8 percent of GMAC/Ally Financial's common equity, it is likely to take one to two years following the IPO for Treasury to dispose completely of its ownership stake. Treasury conversations with Panel staff (Jan. 5, 2011).

[328] Congressional Oversight Panel, Testimony of Timothy F. Geithner, secretary, U.S. Department of the Treasury, *Transcript: COP Hearing with Treasury Secretary Timothy Geithner* (Dec. 16, 2010) (online at cop.senate.gov/hearings/library/hearing-121610-geithner.cfm) (publication forthcoming).

[329] *Id.*

[330] Treasury Converts Ally Preferred Shares to Common Stock, *supra* note 288.

[331] Treasury conversations with Panel staff (Jan. 5, 2011).

[332] Transactions between Ally Bank and GM will, however, continue to be subject to regulation and examination by the bank's primary federal regulator, the Federal Deposit Insurance Corporation. Ally Financial Inc., *Form 8-K* (Dec. 30, 2010) (online at www.sec.gov/Archives/edgar/data/40729/000119312510291571/d8k.htm). After it became a bank holding company, GMAC/Ally Financial requested on two occasions that the Federal Reserve Board grant Ally Bank an exemption from Section 23(a) of the Federal Reserve Act. Section 23(a) restricts the amount of "covered transactions" between a bank and its affiliates. According to the Federal Reserve Board, the "twin purposes of section 23(a) are (i) to protect against a depository institution suffering losses in transactions with affiliates and (ii) to limit the ability of an institution to transfer to its affiliates the subsidy arising from the institution's access to the federal safety net." Board of Governors of the Federal Reserve System, *Transactions Between Member Banks and Their Affiliates*, 67 Fed. Reg. 76560, 76560 (Dec. 12, 2002) (final rule). The safety net consists of deposit insurance, the Federal Reserve's discount window, and other banking regulatory tools designed to protect financial markets and participants. Section 23(a), however, authorizes the Board to grant an exemption if it finds that doing so is in the public interest and consistent with the statute's purposes. 12 U.S.C. § 371c(f)(2); 12 CFR § 223.43(a). On December 24, 2008, the Board granted GMAC/Ally Financial's request for an exemption for retail loans, and on May 21, 2009, it granted GMAC/Ally Financial's extended request for an exemption for both retail and dealer loans. For further details and discussion concerning Section 23(a) of the Federal Reserve Act and GMAC/Ally Financial's receipt of Section 23(a) waivers, *see* March 2010 Oversight Report, *supra* note 22, at 23-25.

[333] In the company's view, the Section 23(a) limitations were impacting their business with GM. GMAC/Ally Financial conversations with Panel staff (Jan. 5, 2011).

[334] In addition to seeking an improved capital structure prior to the company's efforts to market itself to investors, Treasury also stated that were other factors that influenced the timing of its December 2010 conversion. First, by year-end 2010, GMAC/Ally Financial had demonstrated a track record of overall profitability for three consecutive quarters. Second, GMAC/Ally Financial made headway in reducing the risk in its mortgage portfolio during 2010. By year-end 2010, GMAC/Ally Financial had entered into settlements with Fannie Mae and Freddie Mac to resolve potential repurchase exposure related to mortgage loans sold to the GSEs. In addition, the company sold its European mortgage operations, representing approximately $11.0 billion of assets. Treasury conversations with Panel staff (Jan. 5, 2011).

[335] According to JPMorgan Chase, if Treasury converts its GMAC/Ally Financial preferred stake into common equity, GMAC/Ally Financial should be able to lower its leverage as preferred dividends could decline by $1 billion. A conversion of some or all of Treasury's preferred stake into common equity should likely "further

improve Ally's leverage ratios in the event of an IPO." J.P. Morgan, North America Credit Research, *Ally Financial Inc.: 3Q10 Preview* (Nov. 1, 2010) (hereinafter "Ally Financial 3Q10 Preview").

[336] While investor confidence and interest in an IPO has presumably been increased because the recent conversion provides some reassurance to the markets that Treasury does not intend to retain its ownership stake in GMAC/Ally Financial over the long term, some investors might be hesitant to buy shares that could later be substantially diluted through a conversion by the government. As part of the terms of Treasury's December 2010 conversion, GMAC/Ally Financial also agreed to assist Treasury in the sale of a portion of its holdings of TruPs on terms acceptable to Treasury and GMAC/Ally Financial as soon as practical, subject to certain conditions. GMAC/Ally Financial's working assumption is that the company will redeem Treasury's remaining MCPs as part of the IPO, meaning that GMAC/Ally Financial will need to raise additional equity to pay back Treasury. GMAC/Ally Financial conversations with Panel staff (Jan. 5, 2011).

[337] Treasury conversations with Panel staff (Nov. 18, 2010).

[338] Treasury conversations with Panel staff (Nov. 18, 2010).

[339] Treasury conversations with Panel staff (Nov. 18, 2010).

[340] Treasury conversations with Panel staff (Jan. 10, 2011). Treasury requested that the identity of the 35 companies be withheld.

[341] The book value of a company, in this instance, is the difference between a company's assets and its liabilities. The market capitalization is broadly defined as the dollar value of a company.

[342] Bloomberg Data Service; SNL Financial. This analysis is based on GMAC/Ally Financial's third quarter 2010 total asset figure of $173.2 billion, its total liabilities of $152.2 billion and its implied book value, the difference between assets and liabilities, of $21.0 billion. The analysis uses the price-to-book ratios of the 35 comparables and averages the results for each trading day for the full-year 2010. The implied trading ranges for the comparables are as follows: low estimate (102 percent), median estimate (113 percent), average estimate (114 percent), and high estimate (132 percent).

[343] As discussed in Section B.1.d, Treasury has converted or exchanged $9.4 billion (both a loan and preferred stock) of its investment in GMAC/Ally Financial for the 73.8 percent equity stake it currently holds, therefore valuing Treasury's common interests in the company above the amount it invested to receive those interests. This does not, however, account for the remaining debt instruments Treasury holds in the company, or the difficulty in liquidating such a large equity position.

[344] GMAC/Ally Financial conversations with Panel staff (Dec. 6, 2010).

[345] Treasury conversations with Panel staff (Nov. 18, 2010).

[346] Bloomberg Data Service. Note that Large Cap Comparables refers to Bank of America, Citigroup, Wells Fargo, JPMorgan Chase, and CIT Group.

[347] Treasury conversations with Panel staff (Nov. 18, 2010).

[348] Noting that although there is no company that is a perfect match against which to measure GMAC/Ally Financial's prospects, Treasury is nonetheless pleased with the general improvements in valuation of companies that are at least somewhat comparable to GMAC/Ally Financial. Treasury conversations with Panel staff (Nov. 18, 2010).

[349] On the day prior to the announcement – December 29, 2010 – GMAC/Ally Financial's 5-year CDS spread was 270.9 basis points and Ford Motor Credit's was 218.5 basis points. On January 5, 2011, these metrics were 230.8 and 214.1 basis point, respectively. Bloomberg Data Service.

[350] Bloomberg Data Service.

[351] Treasury conversations with Panel staff (Nov. 18, 2010). *See also* Ally Financial Form 10-Q, *supra* note 297, at 80.

[352] See Section C.5, *supra*.

[353] Decreased consumer confidence in the economy is driving more people to purchase used cars, putting increased pricing pressure on a limited supply of vehicles. Inventory is low due to the current shortage of lease returns and trade-ins for vehicles of this type.

[354] Ally Financial 2Q10 Earnings Review, *supra* note 308, at 7. However, there is room for competition between the two in the leasing market, as the economy recovers, and some lease programs may be more suitable to a captive financier.

[355] Ally Financial 2Q10 Earnings Review, *supra* note 308, at 7.

[356] GMAC LLC, *Form 10-K for the Fiscal Year Ended December 31, 2008*, at 40 (Feb. 27, 2009) (online at www.sec.gov/Archives/edgar/data/40729/000119312509039567/d10k.htm) (hereinafter "GMAC Form 10-K").

[357] *Id.* at 40.

[358] *Id.* at 40.

[359] *Id.* at 40. These amendments include the following: The parties agreed that for a two-year period (until 2011), GM could offer retail financing incentive programs through an alternative financing source under certain conditions. Following that two-year period, GM would be able to offer any incentive programs on a graduated basis through alternative financing sources, along with GMAC/Ally Financial, provided that the pricing satisfies certain requirements. The parties agreed to eliminate the requirement that GMAC/Ally Financial satisfy certain lending and underwriting targets in order to remain the exclusive underwriter of special promotional loan programs offered by GM. GM offered GMAC/Ally Financial the right to finance these special programs for retail consumers for a five-year period. The parties eliminated the exclusivity arrangement with respect to promotional programs for GM dealers, and this change will be phased out over time. The parties agreed that GMAC/Ally Financial would no longer have an obligation to lend to a particular wholesale or retail customer, provide operating lease financing products, or be required to pay a penalty or receive lower payments or incentives for refusing to lend to a customer or for failing to satisfy individual or aggregate lending targets. GMAC/Ally Financial can also make loans to any third party and will use its own underwriting standards in making loans, including GM-related loans.

[360] *See, e.g.,* GMAC Form 10-K, *supra* note 356, at 162; GMAC, Inc., *Form 10-K for the Fiscal Year Ended December 31, 2009,* at 43-44 (Mar. 1, 2010) (online at www.sec.gov/Archives/edgar/data/ 40729/ 000119312510043252/d10k.htm) (hereinafter "GMAC Form 10-K").

[361] Industry analyst conversations with Panel staff (Nov. 16, 2010).

[362] Industry analyst conversations with Panel staff (Nov. 16, 2010).

[363] Although a substantial loss in GM business would have a meaningful impact on GMAC/Ally Financial's ongoing viability because the company's auto finance platform has not yet undergone sufficient diversification, it is likely that an unwinding of GM's relationship with GMAC/Ally Financial would happen over the long term, which would allow for the impact of the loss to be spread over a period of time.

[364] Industry analyst conversations with Panel staff (Dec. 3, 2010).

[365] March 2010 Oversight Report, *supra* note 22, at 108-109.

[366] The Panel also notes that GM might be further incentivized to form its own new captive finance company (or build AmeriCredit's platform) because it is beneficial to have a finance arm particularly during very tough markets, as it provides some protection if other lenders walk away. Industry analyst conversations with Panel staff (Nov. 10, 2010).

[367] Data from GMAC/Ally Financial.

[368] House Financial Services, Subcommittee on Housing and Community Opportunity, Written Testimony of Thomas Marano, chief executive officer, Mortgage Operations, Ally Financial Inc., *Robo-Signing, Chain of Title, Loss Mitigation, and Other Issues in Mortgage Servicing,* at 1 (Nov. 18, 2010) (online at financialservices.house.gov/Media/file/hearings/111/Marano111810.pdf) (hereinafter "Thomas Marano Testimony") (stating that GMAC Mortgage "is currently the fifth largest residential mortgage servicer in the United States ...").

[369] *See* Congressional Oversight Panel, *November Oversight Report: Examining the Consequences of Mortgages Irregularities for Financial Stability and Foreclosure Mitigation,* at 7-8 (Nov. 16, 2010) (online at cop.senate.gov/documents/cop-111610-report.pdf) (hereinafter "November 2010 Oversight Report").

[370] Ally Financial 3Q10 Earnings Review, *supra* note 300, at 10.

[371] Ally Financial 3Q10 Earnings Review, *supra* note 300, at 10.

[372] Ally Financial 3Q10 Earnings Review, *supra* note 300, at 10. *See also* Thomas Marano Testimony, *supra* note 368, at 1.

[373] In March 2010, GMAC/Ally Financial's subsidiaries, GMAC Mortgage and Residential Funding Company, LLC, made a one-time payment to Freddie Mac for the release of repurchase obligations relating to mortgage loans sold to Freddie Mac prior to January 1, 2009. The release does not cover any of GMAC/Ally Financial's potential repurchase obligations related to mortgage loans sold to Freddie Mac after January 1, 2009 or GMAC/Ally Financial's potential repurchase obligations related to "private-label" mortgage securities (mortgage loans sold to private institutions to be securitized). This agreement also does not cover any of GMAC/Ally Financial's obligations with respect to loans where its subsidiary Ally Bank is the owner of the servicing. Ally Financial Form 10-Q, *supra* note 297, at 77. On December 27, 2010, GMAC/Ally Financial announced that ResCap and certain ResCap subsidiaries reached a settlement with Fannie Mae for the release of repurchase obligations relating to mortgage loans sold to Freddie Mac. The agreement covers loans serviced

by GMAC Mortgage on behalf of Fannie Mae prior to June 30, 2010, and all mortgage-backed securities that Fannie Mae purchased prior to the settlement, including private-label securities. "The settlement was for approximately $462 million and releases ResCap and its subsidiaries from liability related to approximately $292 billion of original unpaid principal balance (and $84 billion of current UPB) on these loans." ResCap and Fannie Mae also reached an arrangement with respect to "ResCap's payment of mortgage insurance proceeds where mortgage insurance coverage is rescinded or canceled." This agreement does not cover other contractual obligations that ResCap has with Fannie Mae (e.g., those that may arise in connection with mortgage servicing), and excludes Ally Bank. Ally Financial Inc., *Ally Financial's Mortgage Subsidiaries Reach Agreement With Fannie Mae on Repurchase Exposure* (Dec. 27, 2010) (online at media.ally.com/index.php?s=43&item=437).

[374] Ally Financial 3Q10 Preview, *supra* note 335. Based upon assumptions of delinquency rates, put-back rates, put-back acceptance, and loss severity on the $310.6 billion of loans originated by GMAC/Ally Financial during 2006-2008, JPMorgan Chase estimated in November 2010 that mortgage put-backs will cost the company $1.4 billion of incremental capital. While this potential magnitude is significant, JPMorgan Chase believes GMAC/Ally Financial can "easily fund potential liabilities" with its existing liquidity or estimated 2010 net income and notes that the firm increased its mortgage repurchase reserve by $1 billion in 2009 to end the year with a $1.2 billion reserve.

[375] Ally Financial 3Q10 Preview, *supra* note 335, at 2.

[376] GMAC/Ally Financial conversations with Panel staff (Dec. 6, 2010); Industry analyst conversations with Panel staff (Dec. 1, 2010).

[377] Moody's Investors Service, *Issuer Comment: Problems at GMAC Servicing and Ally Financial Are Credit Negative* (extracted from *Moody's Weekly Credit Outlook*) (Sept. 27, 2010) (noting that GMAC/Ally Financial may need to increase its marketing expense to help offset or overcome the reputational damage associated with these developments).

[378] Treasury conversations with Panel staff (Nov. 18, 2010).

[379] Treasury conversations with Panel staff (Dec. 21, 2010).

[380] These meetings have been requested by both GMAC/Ally Financial and Treasury. GMAC/Ally Financial conversations with Panel staff (Dec. 14, 2010). The Panel also notes the company's recent testimony on this topic. *See, e.g.,* Thomas Marano Testimony, *supra* note 368.

[381] GMAC/Ally Financial conversations with Panel staff (Dec. 13, 2010).

[382] Ally Financial Transcript: Q3 2010 Earnings Call, *supra* note 306; Ally Financial 3Q10 Earnings Review, *supra* note 300, at 40.

[383] Ally Financial Form 10-Q, *supra* note 297, at 10.

[384] Industry analyst conversations with Panel staff (Dec. 1, 2010).

[385] GMAC Form 10-K, *supra* note 360, at 83.

[386] GMAC Form 10-K, *supra* note 360, at 83.

[387] GMAC Form 10-K, *supra* note 360, at 83.

[388] Regarding ResCap long-term debt, $716 million is set to mature in 2011, $358 million is set to mature in 2012, $1,236 million is set to mature in 2013, $809 million is set to mature in 2014, and $1,011 million is set to mature during and after 2015. There was no ResCap long-term debt scheduled to mature in 2010. These amounts exclude ResCap debt held by GMAC/Ally Financial and collateralized borrowings in securitized trusts. Ally Financial Form 10-Q, *supra* note 297, at 31.

[389] Bankrate.com, *CD Investment Rates* (online at www.bankrate.com/cd.aspx) (accessed Jan. 11, 2011). This strategy has been politically contentious as regulators view unusually high rates as an indication of instability. For example, in the summer of 2009, Ally Bank's rates were more than double the national average. This prompted the American Bankers Association (ABA) to write a letter of complaint to the FDIC and the FDIC to issue new regulations setting a variety of standards for the interest rates permissible for insured depository institutions that are not well capitalized. For further discussion concerning the controversy surrounding Ally Bank's interest rates and the viability of Ally Bank's strategy going forward, *see* March 2010 Oversight Report, *supra* note 22, at 105-107. *See also* Bankrate.com, *CD Investment Rates* (online at www.bankrate.com/funnel/cd-investments/cd-investment-results.aspx?local=false&tab=CD&prods=15&icjd=CR_searchCDNational_cd_1yrCD_V1) (accessed Jan. 11, 2011).

[390] Moody's Investors Service, Global Credit Research, *Liquidity Risk Assessment: Ally Financial Inc.*, at 1 (Oct. 15, 2010) (hereinafter "Moody's Liquidity Risk Assessment").

[391] *Id.* at 1. While Ally Bank has demonstrated strong CD retention rates, Moody's believes that "these deposits are rate sensitive and therefore less sticky than demand deposits offered through traditional branch networks." Given the very limited product suite at Ally Bank, some analysts believe that Ally Bank's deposits function more like brokered deposits (or "hot money") than core deposits at more conventional banks. Industry analyst conversations with Panel staff (Dec. 1, 2010). Brokered deposits are large deposits that deposit brokers shop among depository institutions looking for high rates and are usually viewed as risky for the depository institution. They are short-term investments, which have been associated with high rates of bank failures. *See* Mindy West and Chris Newbury, *Brokered and High-Cost Deposits*, FDIC Interagency Minority Depository Institutions National Conference Presentation, at 33, 40 (July 2009) (online at www.fdic.gov/regulations/resources/minority/events/interagency2009/Presentations/Brokered.pdf). *See also* L.J. Davis, *Chronicle of a Debacle Foretold*, Harper's Magazine, at 53-54 (Sept. 1990). One analyst considers Ally Bank's proportion of brokered deposits and lack of restrictions on deposit withdrawals to be a warning sign of bank instability. *See* Congressional Oversight Panel, Written Testimony of Christopher Whalen, senior vice president and managing director, Institutional Risk Analytics, *COP Hearing on GMAC Financial Services*, at 18 (Feb. 25, 2010) (online at cop.senate.gov/documents/testimony-022510- whalen.pdf); Congressional Oversight Panel, Testimony of Christopher Whalen, senior vice president and managing director, Institutional Risk Analytics, *Transcript: COP Hearing on GMAC Financial Services*, at 91-98 (Feb. 25, 2010) (online at frwebgate.access.gpo.gov/cgi-bin/getdoc.cgi?dbname=111_senate_ hearings& docid=f:56723.pdf).

[392] Moody's Liquidity Risk Assessment, *supra* note 390, at 1.

[393] GMAC/Ally Financial conversations with Panel staff (Dec. 6, 2010).

[394] U.S. Department of the Treasury, *Auto Supplier Support Program: Stabilizing the Auto Industry at a Time of Crisis* (Mar. 19, 2009) (online at www.treasury.gov/press-center/pressreleases/Documents// supplier_support_program_3_18.pdf).

[395] The credit insurance cost participants 2 percent, while selling receivables into the program carried a 3 percent cost. U.S. Department of Commerce, Office of Transportation and Machinery, *On the Road: U.S. Automotive Parts Industry Annual Assessment*, at 19 (2010) (online at trade.gov/wcm/groups/ internet/documents/article/auto_reports_parts2010.pdf).

[396] The GM SPV closed on April 5, 2010, and the Chrysler SPV closed on April 7, 2010. Treasury Transactions Report, *supra* note 24, at 19.

[397] The additional notes were financial instruments that Treasury took from the Chrysler and GM SPVs as part of their agreement to participate in the program; the notes provided Treasury the opportunity to recognize upside gains on its investments. As dictated in the legislation that created the TARP, the Emergency Economic Stabilization Act, financial instruments such as warrants were to be provided to Treasury in consideration for its investment in participating institutions. As the law states, instruments such as warrants, or additional debentures in the case of the ASSP, were created "to provide for reasonable participation by the Secretary, for the benefit of taxpayers, in equity appreciation in the case of a warrant or other equity security, or a reasonable interest rate premium, in the case of a debt instrument." 12 U.S.C. § 5223(d)(2)(A)(i).

[398] Data provided by the Original Equipment Suppliers Association in response to a Panel request (Nov. 30, 2010).

[399] Data provided by the Original Equipment Suppliers Association in response to a Panel request (Jan. 7, 2011).

[400] The State of the Supplier Industry, *supra* note 52, at 17. This measure is based on number of direct suppliers each manufacturer states it will use going forward. For example, Ford has stated that it will have 750 direct suppliers in the future as compared to the 1,600 it currently relies upon.

[401] White House Fact Sheet on General Motors Restructuring, *supra* note 36.

[402] Whether the use of the TARP for the support of the automotive industry is a legitimate use of TARP funds is an issue that the Panel has addressed at length. September 2009 Oversight Report, *supra* note 2, at 70-79.

[403] Data provided by Treasury (Dec. 9, 2010).

[404] Treasury conversations with Panel staff (Nov. 18 and 22, 2010).

[405] Treasury conversations with Panel staff (Nov. 22, 2010).

[406] The exact timing of the IPO was impacted by the holiday season. Treasury has stated that there was a consensus that if the IPO did not happen by mid-November 2010, it would have to wait until after the holidays and possibly until the spring for a receptive market. Treasury conversations with Panel staff (Nov. 22, 2010). As discussed in Sections C and D, *supra*, the company has taken several steps in the course of restructuring that have made it a more attractive investment, including streamlining its operations and improving its efficiency.

[407] March 2010 Oversight Report, *supra* note 22.

[408] In something of a departure from its involvement in GM, Treasury would not state unequivocally that the timing of a GMAC/Ally Financial IPO is solely in company management's hands. Treasury conversations with Panel staff (Jan. 5, 2011).

[409] Treasury also cited the need to bolster GMAC/Ally Financial's capital structure and its recent settlement with Fannie Mae on mortgage repurchase claims as affecting the timing of the conversion. During the same meeting, Treasury articulated, for the first time, the need to conduct the conversion in order to remove GMAC/Ally Financial from the strictures of section 23(a) of the Federal Reserve Act, which limits the transactions between a bank and its non-bank affiliates (in this instance, GM). Treasury conversations with Panel staff (Jan. 5, 2011). GMAC/Ally Financial was granted an exemption from this rule in 2008 and in 2009. *See* March 2010 Oversight Report, *supra* note 22, at 23-25.

[410] *See* September 2009 Oversight Report, *supra* note 2, at 80-102 (discussing the tensions inherent in government ownership of private enterprise). Moreover, GM has indicated that it believes that some potential consumers may be disinclined to buy automobiles from the companies due to dissatisfaction with the government's policies. The company was unwilling to provide documentation to support this claim, as it views this analysis as confidential and proprietary.

[411] Congressional Oversight Panel, Testimony of Ron Bloom, senior advisor, U.S. Department of the Treasury, *Transcript: COP Field Hearing on the Auto Industry*, at 38 (July 27, 2009) (online at cop.senate.gov/documents/transcript-072709-detroithearing.pdf) (hereinafter "Transcript: Testimony of Ron Bloom").

[412] *Id.* at 38-39.

[413] The White House, *The White House Whiteboard: The Rebirth of the American Auto Industry*, at 3:15 (Nov. 18, 2010) (online at www.whitehouse.gov/photos-and-video/video/2010/11/18/white-house-white-boardrebirth-american-auto-industry) (hereinafter "The White House Whiteboard: The Rebirth of the American Auto Industry").

[414] See Sections D, E, and F.

[415] *See, e.g.,* Congressional Oversight Panel, *September Oversight Report: Assessing the TARP on the Eve of Its Expiration*, at 95-104 (Sept. 16, 2010) (online at cop.senate.gov/documents/cop-091610-report.pdf).

[416] In addition, Treasury has already written off $3.5 billion in funds invested in the domestic automotive industry. See Figure 1.

[417] The White House Whiteboard: The Rebirth of the American Auto Industry, *supra* note 413, at 3:36. An earlier White House estimate placed the figure at 1.1 million jobs saved by the entire automobile industry rescue. George W. Bush White House Archives Fact Sheet, *supra* note 12.

[418] For a full discussion of the bankruptcy options available to GM and Chrysler, *see* September 2009 Oversight Report, *supra* note 2.

[419] To the extent that the rescue of the automotive industry is viewed as a job preservation program, it is not clear that such a program aimed solely at a single industry was the best use of funds for this purpose. The Panel takes no position on this issue, however.

[420] On the other hand, it should be noted that employment in the motor vehicle and parts industry declined by 40 percent between November 2006 and November 2010, from 1.1 million to 650,000.

[421] As discussed in Sections D and E above, though, both have made definite strides in this area.

[422] OFS Agency Financial Report, *supra* note 172, at 11; Treasury Transactions Report, *supra* note 24, at 18-19.

[423] Total funds recovered to date excludes dividends and interest of $766 million paid to Treasury through December 31, 2010.

[424] Total funds recovered to-date excludes interest of $580 million paid to Treasury through December 31, 2010.

[425] Certain assumptions apply to this estimate. See Section E.3 for a fuller discussion.

[426] Transcript: Testimony of Ron Bloom, *supra* note 411, at 38.

[427] A similar portfolio analysis might have been undertaken at the time of the initial decision to rescue Chrysler, exploring the alternative of letting Chrysler fail in order to bolster the prospects of the remaining domestic auto manufacturers, particularly GM.

[428] *See* Congressional Budget Office, *Report on the Troubled Asset Relief Program – November 2010*, at 5 (Nov. 18, 2010) (online at www.cbo.gov/ftpdocs/119xx/doc11980/11-29-TARP.pdf).

[429] *See* U.S. Navy, *Fact File: Aircraft Carriers* (online at www.navy.mil/navydata/fact_display.asp?cid=4200&tid=200&ct=4) (accessed Jan. 12, 2011); U.S. Department of Health and Human Services, *National Institutes of Health, Estimates of Funding for Various Research, Condition and Disease Categories (RCDC)* (Feb. 1, 2010) (online at report.nih.gov/rcdc/categories/).

[430] See Section I, *supra*.

[431] See Section I, *supra*.

[432] See Section A, *supra*.

[433] See Section H.3, *supra*.

[434] *See* September 2009 Oversight Report, *supra* note 2, at 148 (from the Additional Views of former Panel member Congressman Jeb Hensarling).

[435] Congressional Oversight Panel, Written Testimony of Barry E. Adler, Charles Seligson Professor of Law, New York University School of Law, *COP Field Hearing on the Auto Industry*, at 2-3 (July 27, 2009) (online at cop.senate.gov/documents/testimony-072709-adler.pdf).

[436] March 2010 Oversight Report, *supra* note 22, at 4. *See also id.* at 122 (from the Additional Views of Panel member J. Mark McWatters and former Panel member Paul S. Atkins).

[437] Federal Reserve Bank of St. Louis, *Series STLFSI: Business/Fiscal: Other Economic Indicators* (Instrument: St. Louis Financial Stress Index, Frequency: Weekly) (online at research.stlouisfed.org/fred2/series/STLFSI) (accessed Jan. 3, 2011). The index includes 18 weekly data series, beginning in December 1993 to the present. The series are: effective federal funds rate, 2-year Treasury, 10-year Treasury, 30-year Treasury, Baa-rated corporate, Merrill Lynch High Yield Corporate Master II Index, Merrill Lynch Asset-Backed Master BBB-rated, 10-year Treasury minus 3-month Treasury, Corporate Baa-rated bond minus 10-year Treasury, Merrill Lynch High Yield Corporate Master II Index minus 10-year Treasury, 3-month LIBOR-OIS spread, 3-month TED spread, 3-month commercial paper minus 3-month Treasury, the J.P. Morgan Emerging Markets Bond Index Plus, Chicago Board Options Exchange Market Volatility Index, Merrill Lynch Bond Market Volatility Index (1-month), 10-year nominal Treasury yield minus 10-year Treasury Inflation Protected Security yield, and Vanguard Financials Exchange-Traded Fund (equities). The index is constructed using principal components analysis after the data series are de-meaned and divided by their respective standard deviations to make them comparable units. The standard deviation of the index is set to 1. For more details on the construction of this index, *see* Federal Reserve Bank of St. Louis, *National Economic Trends Appendix: The St. Louis Fed's Financial Stress Index* (Jan. 2010) (online at research.stlouisfed.org/ publications/ net/NETJan2010Appendix.pdf).

[438] Data accessed through Bloomberg Data Service (Jan. 3, 2011). The CBOE VIX is a key measure of market expectations of near-term volatility. Chicago Board Options Exchange, *The CBOE Volatility Index – VIX*, 2009 (online at www.cboe.com/micro/vix/vixwhite.pdf) (accessed Jan. 3, 2011).

[439] Data accessed through Bloomberg Data Service (Jan. 3, 2011).

[440] Data accessed through Bloomberg Data Service (Jan. 3, 2011).

[441] Data accessed through Bloomberg Data Service (Jan. 3, 2011).

[442] Board of Governors of the Federal Reserve System, *Federal Reserve Statistical Release H.15: Selected Interest Rates: Historical Data* (Instrument: Conventional Mortgages, Frequency: Weekly) (online at www.federalreserve.gov/releases/h15/data/Weekly_Thursday_/H15_MORTG_NA.txt) (accessed Jan. 3, 2011) (hereinafter "Federal Reserve Statistical Release H.15"); Federal Reserve Bank of St. Louis, *Series DGS10: Interest Rates: Treasury Constant Maturity* (Instrument: 10-Year Treasury Constant Maturity Rate, Frequency: Daily) (online at research.stlouisfed.org/fred2/series/DGS10) (accessed Jan. 3, 2011).

[443] Federal Reserve Bank of Minneapolis, *Measuring Perceived Risk – The TED Spread* (Dec. 2008) (online at www.minneapolisfed.org/publications_papers/pub_display.cfm?id=4120).

[444] Federal Reserve Bank of St. Louis, *What the LIBOR-OIS Spread Says* (May 11, 2009) (online at research.stlouisfed.org/publications/es/09/ES0924.pdf).

[445] Data accessed through Bloomberg Data Service (Jan. 3, 2011).

[446] Data accessed through Bloomberg Data Service (Jan. 3, 2011).

[447] Data accessed through Bloomberg Data Service (Jan. 3, 2011).

[448] Federal Reserve Statistical Release H.15, *supra* note 442; Board of Governors of the Federal Reserve System, *Federal Reserve Statistical Release H.15: Selected Interest Rates: Historical Data* (Instrument: U.S. Government Securities/Treasury Constant Maturities/Nominal 10-Year, Frequency: Weekly) (online at www.federalreserve.gov/releases/h15/data/Weekly_Friday_/H15_TCMNOM_Y10.txt) (accessed Jan. 3, 2011).

[449] The overnight AA asset-backed commercial paper interest rate spread reflects the difference between the AA asset-backed commercial paper discount rate and the AA nonfinancial commercial paper discount rate. Board of Governors of the Federal Reserve System, *Federal Reserve Statistical Release: Commercial Paper Rates and Outstandings: Data Download Program* (Instrument: AA Asset-Backed Discount Rate, Frequency: Daily)

(online at www.federalreserve.gov/DataDownload/Choose.aspx?rel=CP) (accessed Jan. 3, 2011); Board of Governors of the Federal Reserve System, *Federal Reserve Statistical Release: Commercial Paper Rates and Outstandings: Data Download Program* (Instrument: AA Nonfinancial Discount Rate, Frequency: Daily) (online at www.federalreserve.gov/DataDownload/Choose.aspx?rel=CP) (accessed Jan. 3, 2011). In order to provide a more complete comparison, this metric utilizes the average of the interest rate spread for the last five days of December.

[450] The overnight A2/P2 nonfinancial commercial paper interest rate spread reflects the difference between the A2/P2 nonfinancial commercial paper discount rate and the AA nonfinancial commercial paper discount rate. Board of Governors of the Federal Reserve System, *Federal Reserve Statistical Release: Commercial Paper Rates and Outstandings: Data Download Program* (Instrument: A2/P2 Nonfinancial Discount Rate, Frequency: Daily) (online at www.federalreserve.gov/DataDownload/Choose.aspx?rel=CP) (accessed Jan. 3, 2011); Board of Governors of the Federal Reserve System, *Federal Reserve Statistical Release: Commercial Paper Rates and Outstandings: Data Download Program* (Instrument: AA Nonfinancial Discount Rate, Frequency: Daily) (online at www.federalreserve.gov/DataDownload/Choose.aspx?rel=CP) (accessed Jan. 3, 2011). In order to provide a more complete comparison, this metric utilizes the average of the interest rate spread for the last five days of December.

[451] Federal Reserve Bank of St. Louis, *Series DGS30: Selected Interest Rates* (Instrument: 30-Year Treasury Constant Maturity Rate, Frequency: Daily) (online at research.stlouisfed.org/fred2/release?rid=18) (accessed Jan. 3, 2011). Corporate Baa rate data accessed through Bloomberg data service (Jan. 3, 2011).

[452] Loans in nonaccrual status include those that are: (a) maintained on a cash basis because of deterioration in the financial condition of the borrower; (b) full payment of principal or interest is not expected; or (c) principal or interest has been in default for 90 or more days. Federal Deposit Insurance Corporation, *Schedule RC-N – Past Due and Nonaccrual Loans, Leases, and Other Assets*, at 2 (online at www.fdic.gov/regulations/resources/call/crinst/2008-03/308RC-N032808.pdf).

[453] Federal Reserve Bank of St. Louis, *Condition of Banking: Total Net Loan Charge-offs* (online at research.stlouisfed.org/fred2/series/NCOTOT/downloaddata?cid=93) (accessed Jan. 3, 2011).

[454] Federal Reserve Bank of St. Louis, *Condition of Banking: Nonperforming Loans (Past Due 90+ Days Plus Nonaccrual)/Total Loans for All U.S. Banks* (online at research.stlouisfed.org/fred2/series/USNPTL?cid=93) (accessed Jan. 3, 2011).

[455] Federal Deposit Insurance Corporation, *Failures & Assistance Transactions* (online at www2.fdic.gov/hsob/SelectRpt.asp?EntryTyp=30) (accessed Jan. 3, 2011) (hereinafter "FDIC Failures & Assistance Transactions").

[456] The disparity between the number of and total assets of failed banks in 2008 is driven primarily by the failure of Washington Mutual Bank, which held $307 billion in assets. The 2010 year-to-date percentage of bank failures includes failures through December. The total number of FDIC-insured institutions as of September 30, 2010 is 7,760 commercial banks and savings institutions, which represents a quarter-over-quarter decline of 70 institutions and a decrease of 624 institutions since the end of the third quarter of 2008. Furthermore, there are currently 860 institutions on the FDIC's "Problem List." FDIC Failures & Assistance Transactions, *supra* note 455; Federal Deposit Insurance Corporation, *Quarterly Banking Profile, Third Quarter 2010: Statistics At A Glance*, at 5 (online at www.fdic.gov/bank/statistical/stats/2010sep/industry.pdf) (accessed Jan. 3, 2011). Asset totals have been converted into 2005 dollars using the GDP implicit price deflator. The quarterly values were averaged into a yearly value. FDIC Failures & Assistance Transactions, *supra* note 455.

[457] Data accessed through Bloomberg Data Service (Jan. 3, 2011). Spikes in both new and existing home sales in January 2009 and November 2009 correlate with the tax credits extended to first-time and repeat home buyers during these periods. After both tax credits were extinguished on April 30, 2010, existing home sales dropped to 3.8 million homes in July, their lowest level in a decade. National Association of Realtors, *July Existing-Home Sales Fall as Expected but Prices Rise* (Aug. 24, 2010) (online at www.realtor.org/press_room/news_releases/2010/08/ehs_fall).

[458] RealtyTrac, *Foreclosure Activity Decreases 21 Percent in November* (Dec. 16, 2010) (online at www.realtytrac.com/content/press-releases/foreclosure-activity-decreases-21-percent-in-november-6251) (hereinafter "RealtyTrac – Foreclosure Activity Decreases").

[459] For more information on foreclosure irregularities, *see* November 2010 Oversight Report, *supra* note 369.

[460] Data accessed through Bloomberg Data Service (Jan. 3, 2011).

[461] The most recent data available are for September 2010. *See* Standard and Poor's, *S&P/Case-Shiller Home Price Indices* (Instrument: Case-Shiller 20-City Composite Seasonally Adjusted, Frequency: Monthly) (online at

www.standardandpoors.com/indices/sp-case-shiller-home-price-indices/en/us/?indexId=spusa-cashpidff--p-us----) (accessed Jan. 3, 2011) (hereinafter "S&P/Case-Shiller Home Price Indices"); Federal Housing Finance Agency, *U.S. and Census Division Monthly Purchase Only Index* (Instrument: USA, Seasonally Adjusted) (online at www.fhfa.gov/Default.aspx?Page=87) (accessed Jan. 3, 2011) (hereinafter "FHFA Monthly Purchase Only Index"). S&P has cautioned that the seasonal adjustment is probably being distorted by irregular factors. These factors could include distressed sales and the various government programs. *See* Standard and Poor's, *S&P/Case-Shiller Home Price Indices and Seasonal Adjustment* (Apr. 2010) (online at www.standardandpoors.com/servlet/BlobServer?blobheadername3=MDT-Type&blobcol=urldata&blobtable=MungoBlobs&blobheadervalue2=inline;+filename%3DCaseShiller_SeasonalAdjustment2,0.pdf&blobheadername2=Content-Disposition&blobheadervalue1= application/pdf&blobkey=id&blobheadername1=content-type&blobwhere=1243679046081&blobheadervalue3=UTF-8). For a discussion of the differences between the Case-Shiller Index and the FHFA Index, *see* Congressional Oversight Panel, *April Oversight Report: Evaluating Progress on TARP Foreclosure Mitigation Programs*, at 98 (Apr. 14, 2010) (online at cop.senate.gov/documents/cop-041410-report.pdf).

[462] Data accessed through Bloomberg Data Service (Jan. 3, 2011). The Case-Shiller Futures contract is traded on the Chicago Mercantile Exchange (CME) and is settled to the Case-Shiller Index two months after the previous calendar quarter. For example, the February contract will be settled against the spot value of the S&P Case-Shiller Home Price Index values representing the fourth calendar quarter of the previous year, which is released in February one day after the settlement of the contract. Note that most close observers believe that the accuracy of these futures contracts as forecasts diminishes the farther out one looks. A Metropolitan Statistical Area is defined as a core area containing a substantial population nucleus, together with adjacent communities having a high degree of economic and social integration with the core. U.S. Census Bureau, *About Metropolitan and Micropolitan Statistical Areas* (online at www.census.gov/population/www/metroareas/aboutmetro.html) (accessed Dec. 10, 2010).

[463] RealtyTrac – Foreclosure Activity Decreases, *supra* note 458. The most recent data available are for November 2010.

[464] S&P/Case-Shiller Home Price Indices, *supra* note 461. The most recent data available are for October 2010.

[465] FHFA Monthly Purchase Only Index, *supra* note 461. The most recent data available are for October 2010.

[466] All data normalized to 100 in January 2000. Futures data accessed through Bloomberg Data Service (Jan. 3, 2011). S&P/Case-Shiller Home Price Indices, *supra* note 461.

[467] U.S. Department of the Treasury, *Cumulative Dividends, Interest and Distributions Report as of September 30, 2010* (Oct. 11, 2010) (online at financialstability.gov/docs/dividends-interestreports/September%202010%20Dividends%20&%20Interest%20Report.pdf); Treasury Transactions Report, *supra* note 24.

[468] The original $700 billion TARP ceiling was reduced by $1.26 billion as part of the Helping Families Save Their Homes Act of 2009. 12 U.S.C. § 5225(a)-(b) (online at www.gpo.gov/fdsys/pkg/PLAW-111publ22/pdf/PLAW-111publ22.pdf). On June 30, 2010, the House-Senate Conference Committee agreed to reduce the amount authorized under the TARP from $700 billion to $475 billion as part of the Dodd-Frank Wall Street Reform and Consumer Protection Act that was signed into law on July 21, 2010. *See Dodd-Frank Wall Street Reform and Consumer Protection Act*, Pub. L. No. 111-203 (2010) (online at www.gpo.gov/fdsys/pkg/PLAW111publ203/pdf/PLAW-111publ203.pdf); The White House, *Remarks by the President at Signing of Dodd-Frank Wall Street Reform and Consumer Protection Act* (July 21, 2010) (online at www.whitehouse.gov/the-pressoffice/remarks-president-signing-dodd-frank-wall-street-reform-and-consumer-protection-act).

[469] This figure is comprised of the $4.2 billion in net proceeds from the sale of Citigroup common stock between April 26 and December 6, 2010 as well as $2.7 billion in proceeds from the December 6 equity underwriting.

[470] Treasury Transactions Report, *supra* note 24.

[471] The $34.4 billion currently outstanding reflects the $2.6 billion in announced losses associated with the program. See Figure 42 for further details on losses associated with programs.

[472] For its CPP investments in privately held financial institutions, Treasury also received warrants to purchase additional shares of preferred stock, which it exercised immediately. Similarly, Treasury received warrants to purchase additional subordinated debt that were immediately exercised along with its CPP investments in subchapter S corporations. Treasury Transactions Report, *supra* note 24, at 14.

[473] U.S. Department of the Treasury, *Capital Purchase Program* (Oct. 3, 2010) (online at www.financialstability.gov/roadtostability/capitalpurchaseprogram.html).

[474] U.S. Department of the Treasury, *Targeted Investment Program* (Oct. 3, 2010) (online at www.financialstability.gov/roadtostability/targetedinvestmentprogram.html).

[475] U.S. Department of the Treasury, *Cumulative Dividends, Interest and Distributions Report as of November 30, 2010* (Dec. 10, 2010) (online at financialstability.gov/docs/dividends-interest-reports/November%202010%20Dividends%20&%20Interest%20Report.pdf) (hereinafter "Cumulative Dividends, Interest and Distributions Report"); Treasury Transactions Report, *supra* note 24. Treasury also received an additional $1.2 billion in participation fees from its Guarantee Program for Money Market Funds. U.S. Department of the Treasury, *Treasury Announces Expiration of Guarantee Program for Money Market Funds* (Sept. 18, 2009) (online at www.treasury.gov/press-center/press-releases/Pages/tg293.aspx).

[476] Cumulative Dividends, Interest and Distributions Report, *supra* note 475, at 20.

[477] This figure does not include banks with missed dividend payments that have either repaid all delinquent dividends, exited the TARP, gone into receivership, or filed for bankruptcy.

[478] Fifteen of these institutions made payments later. The 21 institutions also include those that have either (a) fully repaid their CPP investment and exited the program or (b) entered bankruptcy or their subsidiary was placed into receivership. Cumulative Dividends, Interest and Distributions Report, *supra* note 475, at 21.

[479] U.S. Department of the Treasury, *Frequently Asked Questions: Capital Purchase Program (CPP): Related to Missed Dividend (or Interest) Payments and Director Nomination* (online at www.financialstability.gov/docs/CPP/CPP%20Directors%20FAQs.pdf) (accessed Jan. 11, 2011).

[480] Cumulative Dividends, Interest and Distributions Report, *supra* note 475, at 17-20. Data on total bank assets compiled using SNL Financial data service (accessed Jan. 6, 2011).

[481] Treasury Transactions Report, *supra* note 24, at 13.

[482] Treasury Transactions Report, *supra* note 24, at 14. The asterisk ("*") denotes recognized losses on Treasury's Transactions Report.

[483] Capital Bank Corporation, *Schedule 14A*, at 5 (Nov. 19, 2010) (online at www.sec.gov/Archives/edgar/data/1071992/000095012310107474/g25191ddef14a.htm).

[484] Calculation of the internal rate of return (IRR) also includes CPP investments in public institutions not repaid in full (for reasons such as acquisition by another institution), such as The South Financial Group and TIB Financial Corporation. The Panel's total IRR calculation now includes CPP investments in public institutions recorded as a loss on the TARP Transactions Report due to bankruptcy, such as CIT Group Inc. Going forward, the Panel will continue to include losses due to bankruptcy when Treasury determines that any associated contingent value rights have expired without value. When excluding CIT Group from the calculation, the resulting IRR is 10.4 percent. Treasury Transactions Report, *supra* note 24.

[485] Investment date for Bank of America in the CPP.

[486] Investment date for Merrill Lynch in the CPP.

[487] Investment date for Bank of America in the TIP.

[488] Includes warrants issued under the CPP, the AGP, and the TIP.

[489] Congressional Oversight Panel, *November Oversight Report: Guarantees and Contingent Payments in TARP and Related Programs*, at 36 (Nov. 6, 2009) (online at cop.senate.gov/documents/cop-110609-report.pdf).

[490] U.S. Department of the Treasury, *FY2011 Budget in Brief*, at 138 (Feb. 2010) (online at www.treasury.gov/about/budget-performance/budget-in-brief/Documents/FY%202011%20BIB%20(2).pdf).

[491] U.S. Department of the Treasury, *MBS Purchase Program: Portfolio by Month* (online at www.financialstability.gov/docs/December%202010%20Portfolio%20by%20month.pdf) (accessed Jan. 11, 2011). Treasury has received $75.9 billion in principal repayments and $15.6 billion in interest payments from these securities. See U.S. Department of the Treasury, *MBS Purchase Program Principal and Interest Received* (online at www.financialstability.gov/docs/December%202010%20MBS%20Principal%20and%20Interest%20Monthly%20Breakout.pdf) (accessed Jan. 11, 2011).

[492] Board of Governors of the Federal Reserve System, *Federal Reserve System Monthly Report on Credit and Liquidity Programs and the Balance Sheet*, at 5 (Dec. 2010) (online at federalreserve.gov/monetarypolicy/files/monthlyclbsreport201012.pdf).

[493] *Id.* at 5.

[494] Board of Governors of the Federal Reserve System, *Factors Affecting Reserve Balances (H.4.1)* (Jan. 6, 2011) (online at www.federalreserve.gov/releases/h41/20110106/) (hereinafter "Factors Affecting Reserve Balances (H.4.1)").

[495] Board of Governors of the Federal Reserve System, *Press Release – FOMC Statement* (Nov. 3, 2010) (online at www.federalreserve.gov/newsevents/press/monetary/20101103a.htm); Federal Reserve Bank of New York,

Statement Regarding Purchases of Treasury Securities (Nov. 3, 2010) (online at www.federalreserve.gov/newsevents/press/monetary/monetary20101103a1.pdf).

[496] On August 10, 2010, the Federal Reserve began reinvesting principal payments on agency debt and agency MBS holdings in longer-term Treasury securities in order to keep the amount of their securities holdings in their System Open Market Account portfolio at their then-current level. Board of Governors of the Federal Reserve System, *FOMC Statement* (Aug. 10, 2010) (online at www.federalreserve.gov/newsevents/press/monetary/20100810a.htm).

[497] Federal Reserve Bank of New York, *FAQs: Purchases of Longer-term Treasury Securities* (Nov. 3, 2010) (online at www.newyorkfed.org/markets/lttreas_faq.html).

[498] Factors Affecting Reserve Balances (H.4.1), *supra* note 494.

[499] *See* Congressional Oversight Panel, *COP Hearing on the TARP and Executive Compensation Restrictions* (Oct. 21, 2010) (online at cop.senate.gov/hearings/library/hearing-102110-compensation.cfm).

References for Figures

[i] Figures affected by rounding. Unless otherwise noted, data in this table are from the following sources: U.S. Department of the Treasury, *Troubled Asset Relief Program Transactions Report for the Period Ending December 30, 2010* (Dec. 30, 2010) (online at www.financialstability.gov/docs/transaction-reports/12-30-10%20Transactions%20Report%20as%20of%2012-30-10.pdf); U.S. Department of the Treasury, *Troubled Assets Relief Program Monthly 105(a) Report – November 2010* (Dec. 10, 2010) (online at www.financialstability.gov/docs/November%20105(a)%20FINAL.pdf.

[ii] In June 2009, Treasury exchanged $25 billion in Citigroup preferred stock for 7.7 billion shares of the company's common stock at $3.25 per share. As of December 30, 2010, Treasury had sold the entirety of its Citigroup common shares for $31.85 billion in gross proceeds. The amount repaid under CPP includes $25 billion Treasury received as part of its sales of Citigroup common stock. The difference between these two numbers represents the $6.85 billion in net profit Treasury has received from the sale of Citigroup common stock. Total CPP repayments also include amounts repaid by institutions that exchanged their CPP investments for investments under the CDCI, as well as proceeds earned from the sale of preferred stock issued by South Financial Group, Inc., TIB Financial Corp, and the Bank of Currituck. *See* U.S. Department of the Treasury, *Troubled Asset Relief Program Transactions Report for the Period Ending December 30, 2010*, at 2, 13-15 (Dec. 30, 2010) (online at www.financialstability.gov/docs/transaction-reports/12-30-10%20Transactions%20Report%20as%20of%2012-30-10.pdf); U.S. Department of the Treasury, *Troubled Asset Relief Program: Two-Year Retrospective*, at 25 (Oct. 2010) (online at www.financialstability.gov/docs/TARP%20Two%20Year%20Retrospective_10%2005%2010_transmittal%20letter.pdf); U.S. Department of the Treasury, *Treasury Commences Plan to Sell Citigroup Common Stock* (Apr. 26, 2010) (online at www.treasury.gov/press-center/press-releases/Pages/tg660.aspx).

[iii] In the TARP Transactions Report, Treasury has classified the investments it made in two institutions, CIT Group ($2.3 billion) and Pacific Coast National Bancorp ($4.1 million), as losses. In addition, Treasury sold its preferred ownership interests, along with warrants, in South Financial Group, Inc., TIB Financial Corp., and the Bank of Currituck to non-TARP participating institutions. These shares were sold at prices below the value of the original CPP investment, at respective losses of $217 million, $25 million, and $2.3 million. Therefore, Treasury's net current CPP investment is $34.4 billion due to the $2.6 billion in losses thus far. *See* U.S. Department of the Treasury, *Troubled Asset Relief Program Transactions Report for the Period Ending December 30, 2010*, at 1-14 (Dec. 30, 2010) (online at www.financialstability.gov/docs/transaction-reports/12-30-10%20Transactions%20Report%20as%20of%2012-30-10.pdf).

[iv] The $5.0 billion AGP guarantee for Citigroup was unused since Treasury was not required to make any guarantee payments during the life of the program. U.S. Department of the Treasury, *Troubled Asset Relief Program: Two-Year Retrospective*, at 31 (Oct. 2010) (online at www.financialstability.gov/docs/TARP%20Two%20Year%20Retrospective_10%2005%2010_transmittal%20letter.pdf); U.S. Department of the Treasury, *Troubled Asset Relief Program Transactions Report for the Period Ending December 30, 2010*, at 20 (Dec. 30, 2010) (online at www.financialstability.gov/docs/transaction-reports/12-30-10%20Transactions%20Report%20as%20of%2012-30-10.pdf).

[v] Although this $5.0 billion is no longer exposed as part of the AGP, Treasury did not receive a repayment in the same sense as with other investments. Treasury did receive other income as consideration for the guarantee, which is not a repayment and is accounted for in Figure 42. See U.S. Department of the Treasury, *Troubled Asset Relief Program Transactions Report for the Period Ending December 30, 2010*, at 20 (Dec. 30, 2010) (online at www.financialstability.gov/docs/transaction-reports/12-30-10%20Transactions%20 Report%20as %20of%2012-30- 10.pdf).

[vi] AIG has completely utilized the $40 billion that was made available on November 25, 2008, in exchange for the company's preferred stock. See U.S. Department of the Treasury, *Troubled Asset Relief Program Transactions Report for the Period Ending December 30, 2010*, at 21 (Dec. 30, 2010) (online at www.financialstability.gov/docs/transaction-reports/12-30-10%20Transactions%20Report%20as%20of%2012-30- 10.pdf). It has also drawn down $7.5 billion of the $29.8 billion made available on April 17, 2009. American International Group, Inc., *Form 10-Q for the Quarterly Period Ended September 30, 2010*, at 119 (Nov. 5, 2010) (online at sec.gov/Archives/edgar/data/5272/000104746910009269/a2200724z10-q.htm). This figure does not include $1.6 billion in accumulated but unpaid dividends owed by AIG to Treasury due to the restructuring of Treasury's investment from cumulative preferred shares to non-cumulative shares. See U.S. Department of the Treasury, *Troubled Asset Relief Program Transactions Report for the Period Ending December 30, 2010*, at 21 (Dec. 30, 2010) (online at www.financialstability.gov/docs/transaction-reports/12-30-10%20Transactions%20Report%20as%20of%2012-30-10.pdf). AIG expects to draw down up to $22.3 billion in unutilized funds from the TARP as part of its plan to repay the revolving credit facility provided by the Federal Reserve Bank of New York. American International Group, Inc., *AIG Announces Plan to Repay U.S. Government* (Sept. 30, 2010) (online at www.aigcorporate.com/newsroom/2010_ September/ AIGAnnouncesPlantoRepay30Sept2010.pdf);

[vii] On May 14, 2010, Treasury accepted a $1.9 billion settlement payment for its $3.5 billion loan to Chrysler Holding. The payment represented a $1.6 billion loss from the termination of the debt obligation. See U.S. Department of the Treasury, *Chrysler Financial Parent Company Repays $1.9 Billion in Settlement of Original Chrysler Loan* (May 17, 2010) (online at www.financialstability.gov/latest/pr_05172010c.html); U.S. Department of the Treasury, *Troubled Asset Relief Program Transactions Report for the Period Ending December 30, 2010*, at 18- 19 (Dec. 30, 2010) (online at www.financialstability.gov/docs/transaction-reports/12-30- 10%20Transactions%20Report%20as%20of%2012-30-10.pdf). Also, following the bankruptcy proceedings for Old Chrysler, which extinguished the $1.9 billion debtor-in-possession (DIP) loan provided to Old Chrysler, Treasury retained the right to recover the proceeds from the liquidation of specified collateral. Although Treasury does not expect a significant recovery from the liquidation proceeds, Treasury is not yet reporting this loan as a loss in the TARP Transactions Report. As of December 30, 2010, Treasury had collected $48.1 million in proceeds from the sale of collateral. Treasury included these proceeds as part of the $26.4 billion repaid under the AIFP. U.S. Department of the Treasury, *Troubled Assets Relief Program Monthly 105(a) Report – September 2010* (Oct. 12, 2010) (online at www.financialstability.gov/docs/105CongressionalReports/September 105(a) report_FINAL.pdf); Treasury conversations with Panel staff (Aug. 19, 2010 and Nov. 29, 2010); U.S. Department of the Treasury, *Troubled Asset Relief Program Transactions Report for the Period Ending December 30, 2010*, at 18 (Dec. 30, 2010) (online at www.financialstability.gov/docs/transaction-reports/12-30- 10%20Transactions% 20Report% 20as%20of%2012-30-10.pdf).

[viii] In the TARP Transactions Report, the $1.9 billion Chrysler debtor-in-possession loan, which was extinguished April 30, 2010, was deducted from Treasury's current AIFP investment amount. U.S. Department of the Treasury, *Troubled Asset Relief Program Transactions Report for the Period Ending December 30, 2010*, at 18 (Dec. 30, 2010) (online at www.financialstability.gov/docs/transaction-reports/12-30-10%20Transactions%20Report%20as%20of%2012-30-10.pdf). See endnote vii, *supra*, for details on losses from Treasury's investment in Chrysler.

[ix] On April 5, 2010, Treasury terminated its commitment to lend to the GM special purpose vehicle (SPV) under the ASSP. On April 7, 2010, it terminated its commitment to lend to the Chrysler SPV. In total, Treasury received $413 million in repayments from loans provided by this program ($290 million from the GM SPV and $123 million from the Chrysler SPV). Further, Treasury received $101 million in proceeds from additional notes associated with this program. U.S. Department of the Treasury, *Troubled Asset Relief Program Transactions Report for the Period Ending December 30, 2010*, at 19 (Dec. 30, 2010) (online at

www.financialstability.gov/docs/transaction-reports/12-30-10%20Transactions%20Report%20as%20of%2012-30- 10.pdf).

[x] For the TALF, $1 of TARP funds was committed for every $10 of funds obligated by the Federal Reserve. The program was intended to be a $200 billion initiative, and the TARP was responsible for the first $20 billion in loan-losses, if any were incurred. The loan was incrementally funded. When the program closed in June 2010, a total of $43 billion in loans was outstanding under the TALF, and the TARP's commitments constituted $4.3 billion. The Federal Reserve Board of Governors agreed that it was appropriate for Treasury to reduce TALF credit protection from the TARP to $4.3 billion. Board of Governors of the Federal Reserve System, *Federal Reserve Announces Agreement with the Treasury Department Regarding a Reduction of Credit Protection Provided for the Term Asset-Backed Securities Loan Facility (TALF)* (July 20, 2010) (online at www.federalreserve.gov/newsevents/press/monetary/20100720a.htm).

[xi] As of January 5, 2011, Treasury had provided $106 million to TALF LLC. This total is net of accrued interest payable to Treasury. Board of Governors of the Federal Reserve System, *Factors Affecting Reserve Balances (H.4.1)* (Jan. 3, 2010) (online at www.federalreserve.gov/releases/h41/20110106/).

[xii] As of September 30, 2010, the total value of securities held by the PPIP fund managers was $19.3 billion. Non-agency residential mortgage-backed securities represented 82 percent of the total; commercial mortgage-backed securities represented the balance. U.S. Department of the Treasury, *Legacy Securities Public-Private Investment Program, Program Update – Quarter Ended September 30, 2010*, at 4 (Oct. 20, 2010) (online at www.financialstability.gov/docs/External%20Report%20-%2009-10%20vFinal.pdf).

[xiii] U.S. Department of the Treasury, *Troubled Assets Relief Program Monthly 105(a) Report – November 2010*, at 4 (Dec. 10, 2010) (online at www.financialstability.gov/docs/November%20105(a)%20FINAL.pdf).

[xiv] As of December 30, 2010, Treasury has received $593 million in capital repayments from two PPIP fund managers. U.S. Department of the Treasury, *Troubled Asset Relief Program Transactions Report for the Period Ending December 30, 2010*, at 23 (Dec. 30, 2010) (online at www.financialstability.gov/docs/transaction-reports/12- 30-10%20Transactions%20Report%20as%20 of%2012-30-10.pdf).

[xv] As of December 30, 2010, Treasury's purchases under the SBA 7(a) Securities Purchase Program totaled $368.1 million. U.S. Department of the Treasury, *Troubled Asset Relief Program Transactions Report for the Period Ending December 30, 2010*, at 22 (Dec. 30, 2010) (online at www.financialstability.gov/docs/transaction-reports/12-30-10%20Transactions%20Report%20as%20of%2012-30-10.pdf).

[xvi] Treasury will not make additional purchases pursuant to the expiration of its purchasing authority under EESA. U.S. Department of the Treasury, *Troubled Asset Relief Program: Two-Year Retrospective*, at 43 (Oct. 2010) (online at www.tinancialstability.gov/docs/TARP%20Two%20Year%20Retrospective_ 10%2005%2010_ transmittal%20letter. pdf).

[xvii] On June 23, 2010, $1.5 billion was allocated to mortgage assistance through the Hardest Hit Fund (HHF). Another $600 million was approved on August 3, 2010. U.S. Department of the Treasury, *Obama Administration Approves State Plans for $600 million of "Hardest Hit Fund' Foreclosure Prevention Assistance* (Aug. 3, 2010) (online at www.financialstability.gov/latest/pr_08042010.html). As part of its revisions to TARP allocations upon enactment of the Dodd-Frank Wall Street Reform and Consumer Protection Act, Treasury allocated an additional $2 billion in TARP funds to mortgage assistance for unemployed borrowers through the HHF. U.S. Department of the Treasury, *Obama Administration Announces Additional Support for Targeted Foreclosure-Prevention Programs to Help Homeowners Struggling with Unemployment* (Aug. 11, 2010) (online at www.financialstability.gov/latest/pr_08112010.html). In October 2010, another $3.5 billion was allocated among the 18 states and the District of Columbia currently participating in HHF. The amount each state received during this round of funding is proportional to its population. U.S. Department of the Treasury, *Troubled Asset Relief Program: Two Year Retrospective*, at 72 (Oct. 2010) (online at www.financialstability.gov/docs/TARP%20Two%20 Year%20 Retrospective_ 10%2005%2010_transmittal%20letter. pdf).

[xviii] As of December 31, 2010, a total of $103.6 million has been disbursed to 12 state Housing Finance Agencies (HFAs). Data provided by Treasury (Jan. 4, 2011).

[xix] This figure represents the amount Treasury disbursed to fund the advance purchase account of the Letter of Credit issued under the FHA Short Refinance Program. The $53.3 million in the FHA Short Refinance program is broken down as follows: $50 million for a deposit into an advance purchase account as collateral to the initial $50 million Letter of Credit, $2.9 million for the closing and funding of the Letter of Credit,

[xx] $115,000 in trustee fees, $175,000 in claims processor fees, and $156,000 for an unused commitment fee for the Letter of Credit. Data provided by Treasury (Dec. 2, 2010).

[xx] U.S. Department of the Treasury, *Troubled Asset Relief Program Transactions Report for the Period Ending December 30, 2010,* at 1-13, 16-17 (Dec. 30, 2010) (online at www.financialstability.gov/docs/transaction-reports/12-30-10%20Transactions%20Report%20as%20of%2012-30-10.pdf). Treasury closed the program on September 30, 2010, after investing $570 million in 84 CDFIs. U.S. Department of the Treasury, *Treasury Announces Special Financial Stabilization Initiative Investments of $570 Million in 84 Community Development Financial Institutions in Underserved Areas* (Sept. 30, 2010) (online at www.financialstability.gov/latest/pr_09302010b.html).

[xxi] AIG is not listed in this table because no profit or loss has been recorded to date for AIG. Its missed dividends were capitalized as part of the issuance to Treasury of Series E preferred shares and are not considered to be outstanding. Treasury currently holds non-cumulative preferred shares, meaning AIG is not penalized for non-payment. Therefore, no profit or loss has been realized on Treasury's AIG investment to date. HAMP is not listed in this table because HAMP is a 100 percent subsidy program, and no profit is expected.

[xxii] U.S. Department of the Treasury, *Cumulative Dividends, Interest and Distributions Report as of November 30, 2010* (Dec. 10, 2010) (online at www.financialstability.gov/docs/dividends-interest-reports/November%202010%20Dividends%20&%20Interest%20Report.pdf).

[xxiii] U.S. Department of the Treasury, *Cumulative Dividends, Interest and Distributions Report as of November 30, 2010* (Dec. 10, 2010) (online at www.financialstability.gov/docs/dividends-interestreports/November%202010%20Dividends%20&%20Interest%20Report.pdf).

[xxiv] U.S. Department of the Treasury, *Troubled Asset Relief Program Transactions Report for the Period Ending December 30, 2010* (Dec. 30, 2010) (online at www.financialstability.gov/docs/transaction-reports/12-30-10%20Transactions%20Report%20as%20of%2012-30-10.pdf).

[xxv] In the TARP Transactions Report, Treasury classified the investments it made in two institutions, CIT Group ($2.3 billion) and Pacific Coast National Bancorp ($4.1 million), as losses. Treasury has also sold its preferred ownership interests and warrants from South Financial Group, Inc., TIB Financial Corp., and the Bank of Currituck. This represents a $244.0 million loss on its CPP investments in these three banks. Two TARP recipients, UCBH Holdings, Inc. ($298.7 million) and a banking subsidiary of Midwest Banc Holdings, Inc. ($89.4 million), are currently in bankruptcy proceedings. As of November 26, three TARP recipients, Pierce County Bancorp, Sonoma Valley Bancorp, and Tifton Banking Company, had entered receivership. Cumulatively, these three had received $19.3 million in TARP funding. U.S. Department of the Treasury, *Troubled Asset Relief Program Transactions Report for the Period Ending December 30, 2010* (Dec. 30, 2010) (online at www.financialstability.gov/docs/transaction-reports/12-30-10%20Transactions%20Report%20as%20of%2012-30- 10.pdf).

[xxvi] This figure represents net proceeds to Treasury from the sale of Citigroup common stock to date. For details on Treasury's sales of Citigroup common stock, see endnote ii, *supra.* U.S. Department of the Treasury, *Troubled Asset Relief Program Transactions Report for the Period Ending December 30, 2010,* at 15 (Dec. 30, 2010) (online at www.financialstability.gov/docs/transaction-reports/12-30- 10%20Transactions%20Report%20as%20of%2012-30-10.pdf); U.S. Department of the Treasury, *Troubled Asset Relief Program: Two-Year Retrospective,* at 25 (Oct. 2010) (online at www.financialstability.gov/docs/TARP%20Two%20Year%20Retrospective_10%2005%2010_transmittal%20letter. pdf).

[xxvii] This figure includes $815 million in dividends from GMAC/Ally Financial preferred stock, trust preferred securities, and mandatory convertible preferred shares. The dividend total also includes a $748.6 million senior unsecured note from Treasury's investment in General Motors. U.S. Department of the Treasury, *Cumulative Dividends, Interest and Distributions Report as of November 30, 2010* (Dec. 10, 2010) (online at financialstability.gov/docs/dividends-interest-reports/November%202010%20Dividends%20&%20Interest%20Report.pdf); Data provided by Treasury (May 7, 2010).

[xxviii] Treasury received proceeds from an additional note connected with the loan made to Chrysler Financial on January 16, 2009. U.S. Department of the Treasury, *Troubled Asset Relief Program Transactions Report for the Period Ending December 30, 2010,* at 18 (Dec. 30, 2010) (online at www.financialstability.gov/docs/transaction-reports/12-30-10%20Transactions%20Report%20as%20of%2012-30- 10.pdf).

[xxix] This represents the total proceeds from additional notes connected with Treasury's investments in GM Supplier Receivables LLC and Chrysler Receivables SPV LLC. U.S. Department of the Treasury, *Troubled Asset Relief Program Transactions Report for the Period Ending December 30, 2010,* at 19 (Dec. 30, 2010) (online at

www.financialstability.gov/docs/transaction-reports/12-30-10%20Transactions%20Report%20a s%20of%2012-30- 10.pdf).

[xxx] As a fee for taking a second-loss position of up to $5 billion on a $301 billion pool of ring-fenced Citigroup assets as part of the AGP, Treasury received $4.03 billion in Citigroup preferred stock and warrants. Treasury exchanged these preferred stocks for trust preferred securities in June 2009. Following the early termination of the guarantee in December 2009, Treasury cancelled $1.8 billion of the trust preferred securities, leaving Treasury with $2.23 billion in Citigroup trust preferred securities. On September 30, 2010, Treasury sold these securities for $2.25 billion in total proceeds. At the end of Citigroup's participation in the FDIC's Temporary Liquidity Guarantee Program (TLGP), the FDIC may transfer $800 million of $3.02 billion in Citigroup Trust Preferred Securities it received in consideration for its role in the AGP to Treasury. U.S. Department of the Treasury, *Troubled Asset Relief Program Transactions Report for the Period Ending December 30, 2010*, at 20 (Dec. 30, 2010) (online at www.financialstability.gov/docs/transaction-reports/12-30-10%20Transactions%20Report%20as%20of%2012-30-10.pdf); U.S. Department of the Treasury, Board of Governors of the Federal Reserve System, Federal Deposit Insurance Corporation, and Citigroup Inc., *Termination Agreement*, at 1 (Dec. 23, 2009) (online at www.financialstability.gov/docs/Citi%20AGP%20Termination%20Agreement%20- %20Fully%20Executed%20Version.pdf); U.S. Department of the Treasury, *Treasury Announces Further Sales of Citigroup Securities and Cumulative Return to Taxpayers of $41.6 Billion* (Sept. 30, 2010) (online at financialstability.gov/latest/pr_09302010c.html); Federal Deposit Insurance Corporation, *2009 Annual Report*, at 87 (June 30, 2010) (online at www.fdic.gov/about/strategic/report/2009annualreport/AR09final.pdf).

[xxxi] As of November 30, 2010, Treasury has earned $289.6 million in membership interest distributions from the PPIP. Additionally, Treasury has earned $20.6 million in total proceeds following the termination of the TCW fund. *See* U.S. Department of the Treasury, *Cumulative Dividends, Interest and Distributions Report as of November 30, 2010*, at 14 (Dec. 10, 2010) (online at financialstability.gov/docs/dividends-interest-reports/November%202010%20Dividends%20&%20Interest%20Report.pdf); U.S. Department of the Treasury, *Troubled Asset Relief Program Transactions Report for the Period Ending December 30, 2010*, at 23 (Dec. 30, 2010) (online at www.financialstability.gov/docs/transaction-reports/12-30-10%20Transactions%20Report%20as%20of%2012-30-10.pdf).

[xxxii] Although Treasury, the Federal Reserve, and the FDIC negotiated with Bank of America regarding a similar guarantee, the parties never reached an agreement. In September 2009, Bank of America agreed to pay each of the prospective guarantors a fee as though the guarantee had been in place during the negotiations period. This agreement resulted in payments of $276 million to Treasury, $57 million to the Federal Reserve, and $92 million to the FDIC. U.S. Department of the Treasury, Board of Governors of the Federal Reserve System, Federal Deposit Insurance Corporation, and Bank of America Corporation, *Termination Agreement*, at 1-2 (Sept. 21, 2009) (online at www.financialstability.gov/docs/AGP/BofA%20-%20Termination%20Agreement%20-%20executed.pdf).

[xxxiii] Unless otherwise noted, all data in this figure are as of December 30, 2010.

[xxxiv] The term "outlays" is used here to describe the use of Treasury funds under the TARP, which are broadly classifiable as purchases of debt or equity securities (e.g., debentures, preferred stock, exercised warrants, etc.). These values were calculated using (1) Treasury's actual reported expenditures, and (2) Treasury's anticipated funding levels as estimated by a variety of sources, including Treasury statements and GAO estimates. Anticipated funding levels are set at Treasury's discretion, have changed from initial announcements, and are subject to further change. Outlays used here represent investment and asset purchases – as well as commitments to make investments and asset purchases – and are not the same as budget outlays, which under section 123 of EESA are recorded on a "credit reform" basis.

[xxxv] Although many of the guarantees may never be exercised or will be exercised only partially, the guarantee figures included here represent the federal government's greatest possible financial exposure.

[xxxvi] U.S. Department of the Treasury, *Treasury Update on AIG Investment Valuation* (Nov. 1, 2010) (online at financialstability.gov/latest/pr_11012010.html). AIG values exclude accrued dividends on preferred interests in the AIA and ALICO SPVs and accrued interest payable to FRBNY on the Maiden Lane LLCs.

[xxxvii] This number includes investments under the AIGIP/SSFI Program: a $40 billion investment made on November 25, 2008, and a $30 billion investment made on April 17, 2009 (less a reduction of $165 million representing bonuses paid to AIG Financial Products employees). As of November 1, 2010, AIG had utilized $47.5 billion of the available $69.8 billion under the AIGIP/SSFI. U.S. Department of the Treasury, *Treasury Update on AIG Investment Valuation* (Nov. 1, 2010) (online at

[xxxviii] As part of the restructuring of the U.S. government's investment in AIG announced on March 2, 2009, the amount available to AIG through the Revolving Credit Facility was reduced by $25 billion in exchange for preferred equity interests in two special purpose vehicles, AIA Aurora LLC and ALICO Holdings LLC. Board of Governors of the Federal Reserve System, *Federal Reserve System Monthly Report on Credit and Liquidity Programs and the Balance Sheet*, at 18 (Dec. 2010) (online at www.federalreserve.gov/monetarypolicy/files/monthlyclbsreport201012.pdf). These SPVs were established to hold the common stock of two AIG subsidiaries: American International Assurance Company Ltd. (AIA) and American Life Insurance Company (ALICO). As of January 6, 2011, the book value of the Federal Reserve Bank of New York's holdings in AIA Aurora LLC and ALICO Holdings LLC was $26.4 billion in preferred equity ($16.9 billion in AIA and $9.5 billion in ALICO). Federal Reserve Bank of New York, *Factors Affecting Reserve Balances (H.4.1)* (Jan. 6, 2011) (online at www.federalreserve.gov/releases/h41/20110106/).

[xxxix] This number represents the full $28.9 billion made available to AIG through its Revolving Credit Facility (RCF) with FRBNY ($20.0 billion had been drawn down as of January 5, 2011) and the outstanding principal of the loans extended to the Maiden Lane II and III SPVs to buy AIG assets (as of January 5, 2011, $12.8 billion and $13.5 billion, respectively). Federal Reserve Bank of New York, *Factors Affecting Reserve Balances (H.4.1)* (Jan. 6, 2011) (online at www.federalreserve.gov/releases/h41/20110106/); Board of Governors of the Federal Reserve System, Federal Reserve System, *Federal Reserve System Monthly Report on Credit and Liquidity Programs and the Balance Sheet*, at 16 (Dec. 2010) (online at www.federalreserve.gov/monetarypolicy/files/monthlyclbsreport201012.pdf). The amounts outstanding under the Maiden Lane II and III facilities do not reflect the accrued interest payable to FRBNY. Income from the purchased assets is used to pay down the loans to the SPVs, reducing the taxpayers' exposure to losses over time. Board of Governors of the Federal Reserve System, *Federal Reserve System Monthly Report on Credit and Liquidity Programs and the Balance Sheet*, at 15 (Nov. 2010) (online at www.federalreserve.gov/monetarypolicy/files/monthlyclbsreport201011.pdf). The maximum amount available through the RCF decreased from $34.4 billion to $28.9 billion between March and November 2010, primarily as a result of the sale of several subsidiaries. The reduced ceiling also reflects a $3.95 billion repayment to the RCF from proceeds earned from a debt offering by the International Lease Finance Corporation (ILFC), an AIG subsidiary. The balance on the RCF increased $0.7 billion between October 27 and November 24, 2010, primarily due to recapitalized interest and fees as principal repayments. Board of Governors of the Federal Reserve System, *Federal Reserve System Monthly Report on Credit and Liquidity Programs and the Balance Sheet*, at 16, 19 (Dec. 2010) (online at www.federalreserve.gov/monetary policy/ files/ monthlyclbsreport201012.pdf).

[xl] The final sale of Treasury's Citigroup common stock resulted in full repayment of Treasury's investment of $25 billion. *See* endnote ii, *supra*, for further details of the sales of Citigroup common stock. U.S. Department of the Treasury, *Troubled Asset Relief Program Transactions Report for the Period Ending December 30, 2010*, at 1, 13 (Dec. 30, 2010) (online at www.financialstability.gov/docs/transaction-reports/12-30-10%20Transactions%20Report%20as%20of%2012-30-10.pdf).

[xli] This figure represents the $204.9 billion Treasury disbursed under the CPP, minus the $25 billion investment in Citigroup identified above, $139.5 billion in repayments (excluding the amount repaid for the Citigroup investment) that are in "repaid and unavailable" TARP funds, and losses under the program. This figure does not account for future repayments of CPP investments and dividend payments from CPP investments. U.S. Department of the Treasury, *Troubled Asset Relief Program Transactions Report for the Period Ending December 30, 2010*, at 13 (Dec. 30, 2010) (online at www.financialstability.gov/docs/transaction-reports/12-30- 10%20Transactions%20Report%20as%20of%2012-30-10.pdf).

[xlii] On November 9, 2009, Treasury announced the closing of the CAP and that only one institution, GMAC/Ally Financial, was in need of further capital from Treasury. GMAC/Ally Financial, however, received further funding through the AIFP. Therefore, the Panel considers the CAP unused. U.S. Department of the Treasury, *Treasury Announcement Regarding the Capital Assistance Program* (Nov. 9, 2009) (online at www.financialstability.gov/latest/tg_11092009.html).

[xliii] This figure represents the $4.3 billion adjusted allocation to the TALF SPV. However, as of January 6, 2011, TALF LLC had drawn only $106 million of the available $4.3 billion. Board of Governors of the Federal

Reserve System, *Factors Affecting Reserve Balances (H.4.1)* (Jan. 6, 2011) (online at www.federalreserve.gov/releases/h41/20110106/); U.S. Department of the Treasury, *Troubled Asset Relief Program Transactions Report for the Period Ending December 30, 2010,* at 21 (Dec. 30, 2010) (online at financialstability.gov/latest/tg_11092009.html). On June 30, 2010, the Federal Reserve ceased issuing loans collateralized by newly issued CMBS. As of this date, investors had requested a total of $73.3 billion in TALF loans ($13.2 billion in CMBS and $60.1 billion in non-CMBS) and $71 billion in TALF loans had been settled ($12 billion in CMBS and $59 billion in non-CMBS). Earlier, it ended its issues of loans collateralized by other TALFeligible newly issued and legacy ABS (non-CMBS) on March 31, 2010. Federal Reserve Bank of New York, *Term Asset-Backed Securities Loan Facility: Terms and Conditions* (online at www.newyorkfed.org/markets/talf_terms.html) (accessed Jan. 6, 2011); Federal Reserve Bank of New York, *Term Asset-Backed Securities Loan Facility: CMBS* (online at www.newyorkfed.org/markets/cmbs_operations.html) (accessed Jan. 6, 2011); Federal Reserve Bank of New York, *Term Asset-Backed Securities Loan Facility: CMBS* (online at www.newyorkfed.org/markets/CMBS_recent_operations.html) (accessed Jan. 6, 2011); Federal Reserve Bank of New York, *Term Asset-Backed Securities Loan Facility: non-CMBS* (online at www.newyorkfed.org/markets/talf_operations.html) (accessed Jan. 6, 2011); Federal Reserve Bank of New York, *Term Asset-Backed Securities Loan Facility: non-CMBS* (online at www.newyorkfed.org/markets/TALF_recent_operations.html) (accessed Jan. 6, 2011).

[xliv] This number is derived from the unofficial 1:10 ratio of the value of Treasury loan guarantees to the value of Federal Reserve loans under the TALF. U.S. Department of the Treasury, *Fact Sheet: Financial Stability Plan*, at 4 (Feb. 10, 2009) (online at financialstability.gov/docs/fact-sheet.pdf) (describing the initial $20 billion Treasury contribution tied to $200 billion in Federal Reserve loans and announcing potential expansion to a $100 billion Treasury contribution tied to $1 trillion in Federal Reserve loans). Since only $43 billion in TALF loans remained outstanding when the program closed, Treasury is currently responsible for reimbursing the Federal Reserve Board only up to $4.3 billion in losses from these loans. Thus, the Federal Reserve's maximum potential exposure under the TALF is $38.7 billion. *See* Board of Governors of the Federal Reserve System, *Federal Reserve Announces Agreement with Treasury Regarding Reduction of Credit Protection Provided for the Term Asset-Backed Securities Loan Facility (TALF)* (July 20, 2010) (online at www.federalreserve.gov/newsevents/press/monetary/20100720a.htm); Board of Governors of the Federal Reserve System, *Factors Affecting Reserve Balances (H.4.1)* (Jan. 6, 2011) (online at www.federalreserve.gov/releases/h41/20110106/).

[xlv] No TARP resources were expended under the PPIP Legacy Loans Program, a TARP program that was announced in March 2009 but never launched. Since no TARP funds were allocated for the program by the time the TARP expired in October 2010, this or a similar program cannot be implemented unless another source of funding is available.

[xlvi] This figure represents Treasury's final adjusted investment amount in the Legacy Securities Public-Private Investment Program (PPIP). As of December 30, 2010, Treasury reported commitments of $15.1 billion in loans and $7.4 billion in membership interest associated with the PPIP. *See* U.S. Department of the Treasury, *Troubled Asset Relief Program Transactions Report for the Period Ending December 30, 2010*, at 23 (Dec. 30, 2010) (online at www.financialstability.gov/docs/transaction-reports/12-30- 10%20 Transactions %20Report%20as%20of%2012-30-10.pdf). On January 4, 2010, Treasury and one of the nine fund managers, UST/TCW Senior Mortgage Securities Fund, L.P. (TCW), entered into a "Winding Up and Liquidation Agreement." U.S. Department of the Treasury, *Winding Up and Liquidation Agreement Between the United States Department of the Treasury and UST/TCW Senior Mortgage Securities Fund, L.P.* (Jan. 4, 2010) (online at financialstability.gov/docs/TCW%20Winding%20Up%20Agmt%20 (Execution%20Copy)%20 Redacted.pdf). Treasury's final investment amount in TCW totaled $356 million. Following the liquidation of the fund, Treasury's initial $3.3 billion obligation to TCW was reallocated among the eight remaining funds on March 22, 2010. *See* U.S. Department of the Treasury, *Troubled Asset Relief Program Transactions Report for the Period Ending December 30, 2010*, at 23 (Dec. 30, 2010) (online at www.financialstability.gov/docs/transaction-reports/12-30- 10%20Transactions%20Report% 20as%20of% 2012-30-10.pdf). On October 20, 2010, Treasury released its fourth quarterly report on PPIP. The report indicates that as of September 30, 2010, all eight investment funds have realized an internal rate of return since inception (net of any management fees or expenses owed to Treasury) above 19 percent. The highest performing fund, thus far, is AG GECC PPIF Master Fund, L.P., which has a net internal rate of return of 52

percent. U.S. Department of the Treasury, *Legacy Securities Public-Private Investment Program*, at 7 (Oct. 20, 2010) (online at financialstability.gov/docs/External%20Report%20-%2009-10%20vFinal.pdf).

xlvii The total amount of TARP funds committed to HAMP is $29.9 billion. U.S. Department of the Treasury, *Troubled Asset Relief Program Transactions Report for the Period Ending December 30, 2010*, at 45 (Dec. 30, 2010) (online at www.financialstability.gov/docs/transaction-reports/12-30- 10%20Transactions%20 Report%20as%20of%2012-30-10.pdf); U.S. Department of the Treasury, *Troubled Assets Relief Program Monthly 105(a) Report – November 2010*, at 4 (Dec. 10, 2010) (online at financialstability.gov/docs/November%20105(a)%20Report.pdf). However, as of December 31, 2010, only $840.1 million in non-GSE payments have been disbursed under HAMP. Data provided by Treasury (Jan. 4, 2011).

xlviii A substantial portion of the total $81.3 billion in debt instruments extended under the AIFP has since been converted to common equity and preferred shares in restructured companies. $8.1 billion has been retained as first-lien debt (with $1 billion committed to Old GM and $7.1 billion to Chrysler). $51.4 billion represents Treasury's current obligation under the AIFP after repayments and losses. U.S. Department of the Treasury, *Troubled Asset Relief Program Transactions Report for the Period Ending December 30, 2010*, at 18 (Dec. 30, 2010) (online at www.financialstability.gov/docs/transaction-reports/12-30- 10%20Transactions%20 Report%20as%20of%2012-30-10.pdf).

xlix This figure represents Treasury's total adjusted investment amount in the ASSP. U.S. Department of the Treasury, *Troubled Asset Relief Program Transactions Report for the Period Ending December 30, 2010*, at 19 (Dec. 30, 2010) (online at www.financialstability.gov/docs/transaction-reports/12-30- 10%20Transactions%20Report%20as%20of%2012-30-10.pdf).

l U.S. Department of the Treasury, *Troubled Asset Relief Program: Two Year Retrospective*, at 43 (Oct. 2010) (online at www.financialstability.gov/docs/TARP%20Two%20Year%20Retrospective_10% 2005%2010 _transmittal%20letter. pdf).

li U.S. Department of the Treasury, *Troubled Asset Relief Program Transactions Report for the Period Ending December 30, 2010*, at 17 (Dec. 30, 2010) (online at www.financialstability.gov/docs/transaction-reports/12- 30-10%20Transactions%20Report%20as%20of%2012-30-10.pdf).

lii This figure represents the current maximum aggregate debt guarantees that could be made under the program, which is a function of the number and size of individual financial institutions participating. $286.8 billion of debt subject to the guarantee is currently outstanding, which represents approximately 57.1 percent of the current cap. Federal Deposit Insurance Corporation, *Monthly Reports Related to the Temporary Liquidity Guarantee Program: Debt Issuance Under Guarantee Program* (Dec. 21, 2010) (online at www.fdic.gov/regulations/resources/tlgp/total_issuance11-10.html). The FDIC has collected $10.4 billion in fees and surcharges from this program since its inception in the fourth quarter of 2008. Federal Deposit Insurance Corporation, *Monthly Reports Related to the Temporary Liquidity Guarantee Program: Fees Under Temporary Liquidity Guarantee Debt Program* (Dec. 21, 2010) (online at www.fdic.gov/regulations/resources/tlgp/fees.html).

liii This figure represents the FDIC's provision for losses to its deposit insurance fund attributable to bank failures in the third and fourth quarters of 2008; the first, second, third, and fourth quarters of 2009; and the first, second, and third quarters of 2010. Federal Deposit Insurance Corporation, *Chief Financial Officer's (CFO) Report to the Board: DIF Income Statement – Third Quarter 2010* (Nov. 12, 2010) (online at www.fdic.gov/about/strategic/corporate/cfo_report_3rdqtr_10/income.html). For earlier reports, *see* Federal Deposit Insurance Corporation, *Chief Financial Officer's (CFO) Report to the Board* (Sept. 23, 2010) (online at www.fdic.gov/about/strategic/corporate/index.html). This figure includes the FDIC's estimates of its future losses under loss-sharing agreements that it has entered into with banks acquiring assets of insolvent banks during these eight quarters. Under a loss-sharing agreement, as a condition of an acquiring bank's agreement to purchase the assets of an insolvent bank, the FDIC typically agrees to cover 80 percent of an acquiring bank's future losses on an initial portion of these assets and 95 percent of losses on another portion of assets. *See, e.g.*, Federal Deposit Insurance Corporation, *Purchase and Assumption Agreement – Whole Bank, All Deposits – Among FDIC, Receiver of Guaranty Bank, Austin, Texas, Federal Deposit Insurance Corporation and Compass Bank*, at 65-66 (Aug. 21, 2009) (online at www.fdic.gov/bank/individual/failed/guaranty-tx_p_and_a_w_addendum.pdf).

liv Outlays are comprised of the Federal Reserve Mortgage Related Facilities. The Federal Reserve balance sheet accounts for these facilities under federal agency debt securities and mortgage-backed securities held by the Federal Reserve. Board of Governors of the Federal Reserve System, *Factors Affecting Reserve Balances*

(H.4.1) (Jan. 6, 2011) (online at www.federalreserve.gov/releases/h41/20110106/ (accessed Jan. 6, 2011). Although the Federal Reserve does not employ the outlays, loans, and guarantees classification, its accounting clearly separates its mortgage-related purchasing programs from its liquidity programs. *See, e.g.*, Board of Governors of the Federal Reserve System, *Factors Affecting Reserve Balances (H.4.1)*, at 2 (Jan. 6, 2011) (online at www.federalreserve.gov/releases/h41/20110106/) (accessed Jan. 6, 2011).

[lv] Federal Reserve Liquidity Facilities classified in this table as loans include primary credit, secondary credit, central bank liquidity swaps, Asset-Backed Commercial Paper Money Market Mutual Fund Liquidity Facility, loans outstanding to Commercial Paper Funding Facility LLC, seasonal credit, term auction credit, the Term Asset-Backed Securities Loan Facility, and loans outstanding to Bear Stearns (Maiden Lane LLC). Board of Governors of the Federal Reserve System, *Factors Affecting Reserve Balances (H.4.1)* (Jan. 6, 2011) (online at www.federalreserve.gov/releases/h41/20110106/ (accessed Jan. 6, 2011). For further information, see the data that the Federal Reserve recently disclosed on these programs pursuant to its obligations under the Dodd-Frank Wall Street Reform and Consumer Protection Act. Board of Governors of the Federal Reserve System, *Credit and Liquidity Programs and the Balance Sheet: Overview* (May 11, 2010) (online at www.federalreserve.gov/monetarypolicy/bst.htm); Board of Governors of the Federal Reserve System, *Credit and Liquidity Programs and the Balance Sheet: Reports and Disclosures* (Aug. 24, 2010) (online at www.federalreserve.gov/monetarypolicy/bst_reports.htm); Board of Governors of the Federal Reserve System, *Usage of Federal Reserve Credit and Liquidity Facilities* (Dec. 3, 2010) (online at www.federalreserve.gov/newsevents/reform_transaction.htm).

In: TARP on the U.S. Automotive Industry...
Editors: S. E. Walcott, J. A. Capaldi

ISBN: 978-1-61324-363-3
© 2011 Nova Science Publishers, Inc.

Chapter 2

GENERAL MOTORS' INITIAL PUBLIC OFFERING: REVIEW OF ISSUES AND IMPLICATIONS FOR TARP[*]

Bill Canis, Baird Webel and Gary Shorter

SUMMARY

On November 18, 2010, General Motors Company (GM) conducted an initial public offering (IPO) of stock to investors, once again becoming a publicly traded company.

General Motors Corporation (Old GM) was a publicly traded company from 1916 until its bankruptcy in 2009. As part of restructuring, GM and Old GM combined received over $50 billion in federal assistance through the federal Troubled Asset Relief Program (TARP). In exchange for this financial support, most of Old GM's assets were sold to General Motors Company, a new corporation owned by the U.S. Treasury, the United Autoworkers (UAW) retiree health care trust fund, the governments of Canada and Ontario, and a group of bondholders.

GM is not the only company that received TARP funds as a result of the September 2008 financial crisis. More than 700 institutions received support, with the federal government taking ownership stakes in five large companies: GM, Chrysler, GMAC (now called Ally Financial), AIG, and Citigroup. The Obama Administration and GM have both indicated interest in reducing or eliminating the federal stake in GM. In October 2009, GM and its owners agreed on the desirability of launching an IPO by July 2010.

In the IPO, a portion of GM common shares was sold by its owners at a market price of $33 a share, raising $23.1 billion. The proceeds from this IPO largely went to the government and union trust owners, not to GM. The only capital GM raised itself through the IPO is from shares of preferred stock sold at the same time. The U.S. Treasury received $13.5 billion from its sale of shares, resulting in its ownership stake in GM falling from 60.8% to 33.3%. Among the other owners, the United Auto Workers' retiree health care fund and the governments of Canada and Ontario also sold part of their shares, reducing their ownership. Additional shares may be sold in the future by those owners, including the U.S. government.

---

[*] This is an edited, reformatted and augmented version of a Congressional Research Services publication, dated December 8, 2010.

The continuing strength of GM's stock price, and the related recoupment of government investments in the company, hinges on two major factors: the success of GM's restructuring and the performance of the U.S. economy, including U.S. retail auto sales. Since General Motors Company was created in 2009 with many of the assets of its predecessor company, it has closed plants, cut its hourly and salaried workforce, shed three brands, reduced debt, introduced popular new vehicles, and implemented changes in retiree legacy costs that had been a major financial drain. These changes are reflected in the successful IPO at a share price of $33. However, further strengthening of both external and internal conditions may be required for the shares to reach approximately $54, the level at which the U.S. government would be able to recoup the nominal value of its $50.2 billion investment in the company.

INTRODUCTION

In the fall of 2008 and well into 2009, collapsing world credit markets and a slowing global economy combined to create the worst market in decades for production and sale of motor vehicles in the United States and other industrial countries. U.S. light vehicle *production* fell by more than 34% in 2009 from 2008 levels, but the year-over-year fall-off was more acute for General Motors (Old GM), whose production dropped by 48%, and for Old Chrysler, whose production fell by 57%.[1] A similar pattern was reflected in U.S. light vehicle *sales*, as they fell from just over 16.5 million units in 2007 to only 10.4 million units in 2009.[2]

The production and sales slides were serious business challenges for all automakers, and rippled through the large and interconnected motor vehicle industry supply chain, touching suppliers, auto dealers, and the communities where auto-making is a major industry. Old GM and Old Chrysler were in especially precarious positions.[3] The immediate crisis that brought these two companies to bankruptcy was a loss of financial liquidity as the banking system's credit sources froze and neither company had enough internal reserves to weather the economic storm. Their liabilities exceeded their assets, and they turned to the federal government for assistance in November 2008.

Terminology: General Motors Corporation and General Motors Company

As a result of bankruptcy proceedings, there are two companies commonly referred to as "GM." Both are discussed in this report. General Motors Corporation filed for bankruptcy in June 2009, and many of its assets and liabilities remain under the jurisdiction of the U.S. Bankruptcy Court for the Southern District of New York as part of the bankruptcy estate. In this report, that company is referred to as "Old GM." In July 2009, the majority of Old GM's assets and some of its liabilities were purchased by a new entity that was subsequently renamed "General Motors Company." The U.S. Treasury Department is its largest shareholder, and it is an entirely new legal entity. In this report, it is referred to as "GM."

While not the focus of this report, Chrysler also went through bankruptcy in 2009, and the pre-bankruptcy entity is referred to as "Old Chrysler." The company created in June 2009 is referred to in this report as "Chrysler."

In December 2008 and the early months of 2009, both automakers received federal financial assistance from the Bush and Obama Administrations. As discussed later in this report, that funding was a lifeline that enabled them to begin restructuring their operations, a process that was ultimately completed in bankruptcy court.

Alone among the world's major automakers, Old GM and Old Chrysler filed for bankruptcy in the summer of 2009 and, with oversight from the Obama Administration as well as the bankruptcy court, restructured their operations in an attempt to become more competitive companies. Both companies are now governed by newly constituted boards of directors. GM's new board members and chairman were chosen by the U.S. Treasury Department. Both companies have sizable ownership stakes by the federal government and the United Auto Workers (UAW).[4]

As auto markets improved in 2010, so too did GM's balance sheet and its outlook. GM paid off a $6.7 billion federal loan ahead of time, and the new management team indicated that it would like to float stock so that GM would be a publicly traded company.

This report analyzes the progress that General Motors Company has made since it was created from the sale of the bankrupt Old GM in July 2009 and the major issues related to its November 18, 2010, initial public offering (IPO).[5]

GENERAL MOTORS' CAPITAL CRISIS IN 2008-2009

General Motors Corporation was a publicly traded company from 1916 until it filed for bankruptcy in June 2009.[6] It faced a capital crisis in 2008 and 2009 because the normal avenues for raising capital were unavailable: auto sales were plummeting; the company had limited success in selling off assets; its efforts to cut costs were affected by the long timeline required to determine the efficacy of such steps; and sources of capital in the open market were frozen by the financial meltdown. As a consequence, the company's executives tried to arrange federal bridge loans beginning in the fall of 2008.[7] As Old GM's then-Chief Executive Officer (CEO) Fritz Henderson stated in the company's bankruptcy court filing:

> By the fall of 2008, [Old GM] was in the midst of a severe liquidity crisis, and its ability to continue operations grew more and more uncertain with each passing day. The Company previously has recognized the need for bold action to modify and transform its operations and balance sheet to create a leaner, more efficient, productive and profitable business; and it had expended a tremendous amount of resources and effort, on operational, strategic partnering, and financial fronts, to accomplish this task. Unfortunately, because of the continuing and deepening recession, aggravated by the collapse of Lehman Brothers Holdings on September 15, 2008, GM was not able to achieve its objective. As a result of the economic crisis, the Company was compelled to seek financial assistance from the federal government.[8]

When capital markets are functioning normally, companies might arrange for debt financing through a major investment bank. In 2007, Ford Motor Company's then-new president and CEO, Alan Mulally, prompted Ford to borrow $23.5 billion to finance a restructuring of the company, which was then seen to be in financial peril. Private capital was still available at that time, allowing Ford to mortgage all of its assets to obtain a large loan.

An article in *Fortune* described the precarious position that led Ford to refinance its operations:

> When Mulally arrived in September 2006, he took over a company on the verge of collapse. Ford lost $12.6 billion that year and another $2.7 billion in 2007. Mulally put up every asset, including the blue-oval trademark, as collateral to borrow $23.5 billion to keep the company afloat. Then he set about his mission of creating a global Ford, both in terms of the vehicles it produces and how it produces them.[9]

As Old GM's bankruptcy filing indicated, these avenues for raising capital were not available in the late fall of 2008. There were a number of long-simmering issues, both internal and external to GM, however, that lay behind its financial difficulties.

- **Decline in the U.S. auto market.** In 2008 and the first half of 2009, U.S. auto sales were in a freefall, ultimately dropping further than at any time in three decades. The 2009 combined sales of Old GM and GM fell by 30% (compared with 2008 sales), a much steeper decline than any other automaker, except the combined sales of Old Chrysler and Chrysler.[10] The decline in sales further dried up financial resources that Old GM could have utilized.
- **Steady loss of U.S. market share.** General Motors—which at its peak sold 51% of all autos in the United States—saw its market share slide, dropping from over 28% in 2000 to under 20% in 2009 (**Table 1**).

Table 1. Top Sellers of Light Vehicles in the United States
Share of units sold

Company	2000	2009
General Motors	28.1%	19.8%
Toyota	9.3%	17.0%
Ford	23.1%	16.1%
Honda	6.6%	11.0%
Chrysler	11.7%	8.9%

Source: "U.S. Light Vehicle Sales," *Market Data Book, Automotive News*, 2002, and "U.S. Car and Light Truck Sales by Make, 12 Months, 2009," *Automotive News*, January 5, 2010.

Notes: Ford data do not include Volvo, Land Rover, and Jaguar; GM data do not include Saab. Sales in 2000 are for Old GM and Old Chrysler. Sales in 2009 are the combined sales of Old GM/GM and Old Chrysler/Chrysler.

- **Break-even point for car making was too high.** The break-even point is the volume of sales at which net sales (i.e., gross sales less discounts, returns, and freight costs) equal its costs.[11] For Old GM, that point required a higher level of U.S. motor vehicle sales. In 2009, Old GM said that the U.S. market would need to hit a rate of 11.5 million to 12 million vehicle sales a year for it to break even.[12] Yet U.S. sales in 2009 were only 10.4 million units, and are forecast by IHS Global Insight and others to be about 11.4 million units in 2010.[13]

- **Exceptional labor and retiree health care costs.** The Detroit 3 automakers (Old GM, Ford, and Old Chrysler) negotiated contracts with the UAW over the years that expanded benefits for union workers to a level the companies could not sustain when imported vehicles began to take large shares of the U.S. market. Old GM estimated that its retiree health care and pension costs added $1,500 to the cost of every U.S.-made vehicle, and exceeded the cost of the steel used in the vehicles.[14] Old GM had obligations of nearly $30 billion to fund retiree health care and pension funds.[15]
- **Corporate culture.** It was alleged at the time of bankruptcy that Old GM's corporate executives had been too bureaucratic and out of touch with U.S. car buyers' preferences. The Auto Task Force at the Treasury Department, which oversaw restructuring of Old GM (and Old Chrysler), repeatedly said that changing GM's senior executive corps and the internal corporate culture would be one of the most important steps in Old GM's transformation to a more competitive company. The Obama Administration's firing of Old GM's then-chairman and CEO, Rick Wagoner, in 2009, and its appointment of new board members and a new chairman and CEO, were intended, in part, to emphasize to all stakeholders the importance of cultural change.
- **Erratic gasoline prices.** In 2008, gasoline prices rose to over $4 a gallon in many parts of the United States, adversely affecting demand for large vehicles with low fuel efficiency. These vehicles, such as pickup trucks and SUVs, had been critical to Old GM's profitability.[16]

U.S. GOVERNMENT LOANS AND BANKRUPTCY

The initial U.S. government loans to Old GM were made by the Bush Administration in December 2008. At that time, Old GM received $13.4 billion from the U.S. Treasury, the first of several loans made through the Troubled Asset Relief Program (TARP), which was authorized by the Emergency Economic Stabilization Act[17] (EESA) in the fall of 2008 to address the ongoing financial crisis. The TARP statute specifically authorizes the Secretary of the Treasury to purchase troubled assets from "financial firms," the definition of which did not mention manufacturing companies.[18] According to the U.S. Treasury Department,

> The overriding objective of EESA was to restore liquidity and stability to the financial system of the United States in a manner which maximizes overall returns to the taxpayers. Consistent with the statutory requirement, Treasury's four portfolio management guiding principles for the TARP are: (i) protect taxpayer investments and maximize overall investment returns within competing constraints; (ii) promote stability for and prevent disruption of financial markets and the economy; (iii) bolster market confidence to increase private capital investment; and (iv) dispose of investments as soon as practicable, in a timely and orderly manner that minimizes financial market and economic impact.[19]

The authorities within TARP are very broad, and when Congress did not pass any specific auto industry loan legislation,[20] the Bush Administration turned to TARP for funding, arguing that to not provide any assistance to Old GM (and Old Chrysler) would make the recession much worse. At the time, President Bush reportedly said:

Under ordinary economic circumstances, I would say this is the price that failed companies must pay, and I would not favor intervening to prevent the auto makers from going out of business. But these are not ordinary circumstances. In the midst of a financial crisis and a recession, allowing the U.S. auto industry to collapse is not a responsible course of action.[21]

When the Obama Administration took office, it built on this precedent. Old GM received additional loans from TARP of $2 billion in April and $4 billion in May 2009. These loans kept Old GM's operations alive as it went through a drastic restructuring prompted by the Obama Administration's Auto Task Force.[22] (A detailed list of the approximately $50 billion in TARP assistance for combined GM can be found in the **Appendix**.)

Old GM's Viability Plan of February 2009, which was a U.S. Treasury requirement to obtain additional loans after the initial loan of December 2008, laid out a plan of recovery based on changes in operations, labor costs, and other factors. President Obama rejected that plan at the end of March 2009, saying it was insufficient for a total recovery of the company. The Administration gave Old GM two months, until June 1, to devise a more thorough restructuring and thereby qualify for more federal aid.[23]

Throughout the spring of 2009, Old GM worked with various stakeholders, including the UAW, bondholders, creditors, dealers, and suppliers, to devise a new restructuring plan that would be approved by the Auto Task Force and avert bankruptcy. While the company succeeded in reaching tentative agreements with most stakeholders, a group of creditors would not agree to the terms offered, thus prompting GM to file for bankruptcy on June 1, 2009.

During the bankruptcy proceedings, the government provided a final installment from TARP: a $30 billion loan to facilitate the transformation to a new, smaller company, bringing total federal loans related to GM to more than $50 billion. While much of this $30 billion was used by GM during the restructuring process, a majority of it was not used, and $16.4 billion remained in an escrow account on September 30, 2009.[24]

POST-BANKRUPTCY GENERAL MOTORS

A new company emerged in July 2009, after just 40 days in federal bankruptcy proceedings. New GM began with smaller U.S. operations than its predecessor company and a major presence overseas. As shown in **Table 2**, GM operates as three divisions: GM North America (GMNA), GM Europe (GME) and GM International Operations (GMIO). Nearly 50% of GM's vehicle sales are outside North America and Europe, primarily in developing countries in Asia. In China alone in 3Q 2010, GM sold 567,000 vehicles, 27% of all its worldwide sales. While GM sells more vehicles through GMIO, its North American sales are more lucrative as the larger cars, pickup trucks, and SUVs sold in North America are more profitable than the smaller vehicles sold elsewhere in the world.

**Table 2. General Motors Company
3Q 2010 Results by Region**

	GMNA	GME	GMIO	Total
Vehicle Units Sold	661,000	391,000	1,014,000	2,065,000
Net Revenue	$21.5 billion	$5.7 billion	$8.7 billion	$35.9 billion[a]
Earnings	$2.1 billion	$-0.6 billion	$0.6 billion	$2.1 billion

Source: GM Earnings Chart Set, November 10, 2010.
Notes: Earnings are before taxes and interest.
a. According to GM, after intercompany transfers, corporate and other eliminations, net revenue in the 3Q 2010 was $34.1 billion.

GM differed in a number of important ways from the Old GM:[25]

- *Employment was cut.* Old GM had 91,000 U.S. employees in 2008; new GM had 75,000 after bankruptcy. Its worldwide employment fell from 243,500 to 209,000 during the same time period.
- *Plants were closed.* Old GM announced that, of its 47 U.S. plants (in 2008), 13 would close by 2010. The closed plants and machinery remained with Old GM.
- *Brands were shed.* Pontiac, Saturn, and Hummer brands were terminated, and Saab was sold to a Dutch company.
- *Health care costs for retired U.S. union workers were transferred to the UAW.* Old GM reached agreement with the UAW in 2007 to transfer the financial responsibility for UAW retiree health care to the union's VEBA (Voluntary Employee Beneficiary Association), thus removing $30 billion in obligations. Similar agreements were reached with Ford and Old Chrysler. The Detroit 3 agreed to fund the VEBAs with cash or stock. The union made additional concessions in 2009 negotiations. The restructuring agreement gave the VEBA a significant ownership stake in GM because the company did not have the financial resources to provide cash.
- *Many expensive liabilities were jettisoned.* Left with Old GM were environmental liabilities estimated at $350 million for polluted properties, including Superfund sites; certain tort liability claims, including those for some product defects and asbestos; and contracts with suppliers with whom GM would not be doing business.

The federal government was the majority owner of the company that emerged from the bankruptcy process, as the majority of the TARP loans made to GM were converted into an initial 60.8% government ownership stake. In addition, $6.7 billion of the TARP loans remained outstanding after the bankruptcy and the federal government received $2.1 billion in preferred stock.[26] Following positive financial results in the quarters after emerging from bankruptcy, GM used cash in the escrow account that held its TARP borrowings to pay off the $6.7 billion in outstanding loans by April 2010.[27] The $2.1 billion in preferred stock is scheduled to be repurchased by GM following GM's IPO.[28]

ELEMENTS OF U.S. GOVERNMENT OWNERSHIP

In addition to its ownership of GM, the U.S. government has acquired large ownership stakes in Chrysler, GMAC/Ally Financial Citigroup, and AIG through TARP funds and other assistance during the financial crisis. It has sold its stake in Citigroup, but retains larges stakes in the other companies. **Table 3** details these government ownership stakes in these companies.

Table 3. Companies with Large Government Ownership Stakes (Data current through December 7, 2010)

Company	Government Ownership Share	Total TARP Funds Received[a]	Amount Recouped by the Treasury	TARP Outlays Still to Be Repaid to the Treasury	Outstanding TARP Funds Converted to Ownership Stakes
GM[b]	33.3%	$50.2 billion	$20.9 billion[c]	$2.1 billion	$27.2 billion
Chrysler	9.9%	$10.9 billion	$2.8 billion[d]	$5.1 billion	$3.5 billion
GMAC/Ally Financial	56.3%	$17.2 billion	$0	$13.3 billion	$3.9 billion
AIG	79.8%	$47.5 billion	$0	$47.5 billion	$0[e]

Source: U.S. Treasury, Troubled Asset Relief Program: Monthly 105(a) Report—October 2010, November 10, 2010; U.S. Treasury, Troubled Asset Relief Program: Dividends and Interest Report, November 10, 2010; U.S. Treasury, Troubled Asset Relief Program: Transaction Report, November 30, 2010; Chrysler Group LLC, Third Quarter 2010 Financial Statement, November 8, 2010.

a Some of these companies received commitments greater than the reported amounts, or other TARP assistance. These figures are actual dollars received. For GM and Chrysler, the figures include amounts received both before and after their respective bankruptcy filings.
b The U.S. government ownership stake in GM was 60.8% prior to the GM IPO on November 18, 2010. The U.S. government share of GM fell to 36,9% after the IPO. It fell further to 33.3% when the underwriters exercised their option and sold their overallotment of shares on November 26, 2010.
c Includes repayments, interest, dividends and fees; see Appendix for detailed accounting.
d $1.9 billion recouped from assets remaining after the bankruptcy of Old Chrysler; $403 million principal repaid for warranty and supplier support loans; and $484 million in interest, dividends, and fees.
e Government ownership of AIG results from a Federal Reserve loan that predates TARP.

Government operation of these companies has generally not been the goal of these shareholdings. Their purpose was to compensate taxpayers for assistance given to the companies while not saddling the companies with large liabilities that could hinder their recovery. The Obama Administration laid out four core principles to guide the management of the government's ownership stakes:

- The government has no desire to own equity any longer than necessary, and will seek to dispose of its ownership interests as soon as practicable.

- In exceptional cases where the government feels it is necessary to respond to a company's request for substantial assistance, the government will reserve the right to set up-front conditions to protect taxpayers, promote financial stability, and encourage growth.
- After any up-front conditions are in place, the government will manage its ownership stake in a hands-off, commercial manner.
- As a common shareholder, the government will only vote on core governance issues, including the selection of a company's board of directors and major corporate events or transactions.[29]

Compared with the other companies in which the government has a significant ownership stake, GM was unusual in that it was not publicly traded and was majority-owned by the federal government. The size of the ownership stake gave the U.S. Treasury Department the largest stake in the company's outcome, as well as the power to direct the company's actions, if it so chose.

The fact that GM was not publicly traded after bankruptcy proceedings complicated to some degree the disposal of the ownership stake. With publicly traded companies, it is relatively straightforward to simply sell the government's shares on the open market, although in a large stock sale some strategy is required to avoid flooding the market with shares and thereby driving down the price. The government's stake in GM could have been sold directly to a willing buyer, but a negotiated sale might have led to claims that the government was not getting a fair price. GM's size and prominence, as well as its anticipated need for future access to the equity market, made an initial public offering a logical course of action.

ISSUES ARISING IN THE GM IPO

The GM stock offering was one of many such offerings in 2010, and competed with other companies for global investor capital.[30] The largest previous IPO in U.S. history was credit card company VISA, Inc., in 2008, at $19.7 billion.[31] GM's IPO raised $23.1 billion, making it the largest-ever U.S. IPO.[32] As the U.S. Treasury begins to divest its federal ownership stake in General Motors Company, a number of public policy and finance issues arise.

IPOs in the U.S. Auto Industry

Although the IPO market has been a major source of funds for U.S. startups for decades, the auto industry in general has not been part of this Wall Street funding process. In the past 60 years, there have been only two U.S. automaker IPOs: Ford Motor Company in 1956 and Tesla Motors in June 2010.

Ford Motor Company

When it moved to become a publicly traded company in 1956, Ford had been in business for 53 years as a privately held company controlled by members of the Ford family. Henry

Ford, the company's founder, strongly opposed making his company publicly held. He believed he would surrender too much control over the company's operations to the vagaries of the stock market and that such financing relieved the company of the need to cut internal waste and costs.[33]

Nine years after Henry Ford's death, Ford Motor Company issued what was then the largest-ever stock offering. According to one author who has chronicled the company and the Ford family, "people stood in lines outside brokerage houses to buy Ford stock, thus owning a piece of the company that still had an almost magical quality for the average American." The 1956 IPO represented 22% ownership in the company at the time. Offered publicly at $64.50, Ford shares closed at $69.50 on the first day of trading.[36]

Tesla Motors

The most recent automaker to have issued an IPO was Tesla Motors in June 2010. Tesla is a new entrant to the auto-making industry, founded in 2003 by a group of engineers in California's Silicon Valley who wanted to produce all-electric vehicles. Its first product, the Tesla Roadster, debuted in 2008, with a retail price of $109,000. The company has sold about 1,000 of these two-seater sports cars in the two years since production began. The Model S, a four-door sedan planned for 2012, at less than half the price of the Roadster, will be built at the former GM-Toyota NUMMI[37] plant in Fremont, CA, which Tesla purchased in May 2010.

A Different View of Publicly Traded Stock

The founders of Old GM did not have the same reservations as Henry Ford about publicly traded stock: it has been owned by stockholders for most of its existence. The original General Motors Corporation was founded in 1908,[34] and held that name until it filed for bankruptcy in 2009. Its stock was traded continuously during that period, falling to a low of 71 cents per share on the last day it traded publicly.[35]

Having yet to turn a profit in its seven years, Tesla Motors needed capital to fund its expansion and research and development in electric vehicles. It raised capital from three sources:

- • A $465 million federal loan[38] from the U.S. Department of Energy for building the Model S sedan.
- A joint agreement with Toyota in which Tesla hopes to learn modern manufacturing techniques from Toyota while Toyota learns more about electric vehicle technology. Toyota invested $50 million in the venture.[39]
- An IPO priced at $17 a share (above the anticipated range of $14 to $16) that raised $226 million on June 29, 2010.[40] By December 6, 2010, Tesla shares had risen steadily to just over $30 a share.

What Is an IPO?

This section discusses the basics of an IPO, the attendant Securities and Exchange Commission (SEC) new securities registration process, and the contours of the GM IPO.

The Basics of an Initial Public Offering

An IPO occurs when a company sells common shares to investors in the public for the first time. In general, an IPO has several benefits. It offers owners of a closely held company, such as post-bankruptcy GM, a mechanism for selling part or all of their investment. It provides the issuer with a stock market listing, enabling it to raise additional capital through further stock offerings. It creates publicly traded shares that the issuer can use for incentive compensation or management retention. GM officials cited an additional benefit of a public stock offering: reducing the stigma that some vehicle buyers were said to attach to the company's products due to its ownership by the U.S. government.

When a company decides to conduct an IPO, it selects an intermediary or intermediaries to facilitate such a transaction. Intermediaries are usually investment banks that have experience in helping firms "go public." The investment banks that lead an IPO are known variously as managing underwriters, lead underwriters, or bookrunners.

Key duties performed by the lead underwriters in the facilitation of an IPO include (1) helping the issuing company to prepare and file the necessary securities public offering registration statements with the SEC; (2) providing advice on the valuation of the company and the pricing of the securities issue; and (3) helping to assemble (as well as participate in) a group of investment banks and brokerage firms, the underwriting syndicate, whose aim is to sell shares from the IPO to the investing public.

Led by Morgan Stanley and JP Morgan, other underwriters of the GM IPO included Bank of America/Merrill Lynch, Goldman Sachs, Barclays Capital, Credit Suisse, Deutsche Bank, RBC Capital Markets, Citigroup Global Markets, Barclays Capital, Banco Bradesco BBI S.A., CIBC World Markets, Commerz Markets, BNY Mellon Capital Markets, ICBC International Securities Limited, Itau BBA USA Securities, Lloyds TSB Bank, China International Capital Corporation Hong Kong Securities, Loop Capital Markets, the Williams Capital Group, Soleil Securities Corporation, Scotia Capital (USA), Piper Jaffray, SMBC Nikko Capital Markets, Sanford C. Bernstein & Co., Cabrera Capital Markets, CastleOak Securities, GF Global Trading, C.L. King & Associates, CRT Investment Banking, FBR Capital Markets, and Gardner Rich. With a total of 35 underwriters, the GM IPO had an unusually large underwriting syndicate.[41] Included in the syndicate were several female- and minority-owned brokerage firms, including Loop Capital Markets of Chicago and Williams Capital Group of New York.[42]

Depending on the nature of their contract with an IPO issuer, bookrunners generally either (1) absorb some of the risk of the issue by guaranteeing an offer price on the securities issue, known as a "best effort deal" or (2) collectively purchase the shares from a company's IPO and then resell them to the investing public, known as a "bought deal." Based on the language in its initial August 2010 securities registration statement filed with the SEC, GM had a "bought deal" contract with its bookrunners.[43]

The IPO Registration Process

With a few exceptions, the Securities Act of 1933[44] (subsequently referred to as the 1933 act) requires that before securities are sold to the public, an issuer must register the securities through a document filed with the SEC. That document is aimed at providing the investing public with reliable and timely financial and business information about the company. The most common registration statement is known as Form S-1, which bookrunners typically assist the issuer in preparing and filing.

There are two parts to Form S-1. The initial part is known as the prospectus, which contains information on the issuer, the securities being offered, the manner of distribution, and the issuer's audited and unaudited financial statements as required by the 1933 act's disclosure rules. The prospectus is the primary marketing document for an IPO and is also known as a preliminary prospectus or a red herring. A preliminary prospectus can be issued to prospective investors for information purposes only while the SEC is reviewing Form S-1.

The remaining part of Form S-1 contains additional information on the issuer and the offering. This includes other expenses associated with the offering, recent sales of unregistered securities, information on the indemnification and compensation of the issuer's directors and officers, various exhibits, and financial statement schedules. This section does not have to be provided to prospective investors.

Issuers and their underwriters may need to amend the registration statement in response to SEC deficiency memoranda that request that additional information be included. This back and forth often means that SEC approval of an IPO registration statement can take several months. This process ends when the SEC declares a company's registration statement "effective." The company may then be considered a public entity that is entitled to offer securities.

After this final SEC approval, the issuer's management and underwriters mount a "road show," a weeks-long promotional tour in which an issuer's prospects are touted to prospective institutional investor buyers of the offering, such as mutual funds, hedge funds, and pension funds. (GM's senior management, especially CEO Dan Akerson, was prominently featured in the road show.) During and after a road show, the issue's underwriters also endeavor to "build the book" on the offering—the process of gauging the level of investor interest and pricing sentiment. Generally, issuers and underwriters strive for a share price that results in an IPO being significantly oversubscribed, meaning that there is much more demand than there are available shares. However, pricing involves a balancing act of sorts: if it is too low and the offer is heavily oversubscribed, then an issuer can "leave a lot of money on the table"—but if it is too high and the offer is greatly undersubscribed, the underwriters can take substantial financial hits.[45]

After arriving at an overall valuation for the issuer and assessing potential supply and demand for the shares, the lead underwriters then arrive at a price range for the offering. Members of an IPO syndicate generally offer certain allocations of the shares to institutional investor clients. Typically, the last share orders are due the afternoon of the day before the stock is set to be offered, which is usually the day on which the exact price of the offering is announced. IPOs are often underpriced, meaning that they tend to exhibit large jumps in share price from the initial offering price when they start their first day of stock market trading.

Key Elements of GM's IPO

On November 17, 2010, GM proposed pricing its common stock at $33 a share and its Series B convertible preferred stock[46] at $50 a share with a coupon rate of 4.75%. The next day, November 18, the securities began trading on both the New York Stock Exchange and the Toronto Stock Exchange at those prices. The common stock quickly rose to nearly $36, but closed its first day at $34.19.

Before trading began GM's underwriters received 478 million shares of the common stock for a total of $15.77 billion, and 87 million shares of the preferred stock for $4.35 billion. In addition, the underwriters exercised a 30-day overallotment option to purchase up to 71.7 million additional shares of common stock for $2.37 billion and an additional 13 million shares of the preferred stock for $650 million. The underwriters will reportedly receive aggregate fees from their sale of the preferred stock of up to $137.5 million. For selling the common stock, the underwriters reportedly received a fee of 0.75%. According to some estimates, the IPO's lead underwriters, JP Morgan, and Morgan Stanley, each earned about $40 million.[47] The 0.75% represented a steep discount from the 2% to 3% underwriting fee that is often charged for large IPOs.[48] (As a general rule, the fees tend to be inversely related to a deal's size, with smaller deals being subject to higher percentage fees.)[49]

On November 18, 2010, GM officials reported that about 90% of the IPO shares were held in North America.[50] GM's Chief Financial Officer, Chris Liddell, told the press that nearly $4 billion of the shares were sold to retail investors in the IPO.[51] A number of foreign entities also received substantial allotments. SAIC Motor Corporation, GM's Chinese automotive partner, reportedly acquired a $500 million stake, and Saudi Arabian Prince Alwaleed Bin Talal, and the Kingdom Holding Company, of which he is the majority owner, reportedly acquired a similar amount.[52]

Reasons for Issuing the IPO in Fall 2010

According to a Treasury Department report to Congress, GM, the U.S. government and other shareholders agreed on October 15, 2009, that the government would prompt the issuance of an IPO by July 10, 2010, "unless the Corporation is already taking steps and proceeding with reasonable diligence to effect an IPO." Moreover, the U.S. Treasury hired Lazard Frères & Co. in early 2010 as a paid adviser in exploring a GM IPO. On June 10, 2010, the Treasury issued a press release stating "[The] exact timing of the offering will be determined by [New] GM in light of market conditions and other factors, but will not occur before the fourth quarter of this year."[53]

Aside from the desire of the federal government to begin selling its shares in the automaker in 2010, GM wanted to eliminate any perception that its vehicles are inferior due to the federal government's ownership stake. Edward Whitacre Jr., who became the company's chairman in 2009 and will remain in that role until the end of 2010, told reporters in August 2010 that he wanted the Treasury Department to sell its entire 61% stake in GM at the time of the IPO, because the company was being hurt by the stigma of being known as "Government Motors."[54]

In addition to addressing negative consumer perceptions, GM had other reasons for proceeding with an IPO in the last half of 2010:

- *Profitability and cash flow were positive.* In the second and third quarters of 2010, GM has posted its largest quarterly profits since 2004: in the third quarter, it recorded a net income of $2.0 billion on sales of $34.1 billion, up from $865 million on $31.5 billion in sales in the first quarter of 2010. Its cash flow was $2.8 billion in Q2 and $1.4 billion in Q3. GM sees earnings growth continuing, however at a slower pace. In its November filing with the SEC, GM notes that it expects Q4 earnings "at a significantly lower level than that of each of the first three quarters, due to the fourth quarter having a different production mix, new vehicle launch costs (in particular the Chevrolet Cruze and Volt) and higher engineering expenses for future products."[55]

- *GM has achieved a new, lower break-even point.* Whereas Old GM needed a strong U.S. auto market to make a profit or break even, GM has lowered its cost structure. GM says its break-even point in the United States is industry-wide annual sales of 10.5 million to 11 million units.[56] Analysts estimate U.S. sales of 11.44 million units in 2010, implying that the company's domestic operations are profitable.[57]

- *North American operations have turned the corner.* Q3 2010 earnings in North American operations (before interest and taxes) were $2.1 billion, an increase from the first and second quarters and a turnaround from a $3.4 billion loss in Q4 2009. Old GM's North American operations had not turned in a strong performance. As one reporter noted, "in an ironic reversal of what had become common at GM in years past, North American operations are the engine of current corporate earnings."[58]

- *Growth in many foreign markets is strong.* GM notes that it is well positioned in a number of high-growth foreign markets, particularly China, where it is the top automaker and where a quarter of its worldwide sales originated in 2009.[59] Chinese auto sales for 2010 May reach a record-breaking 17 million units.[60] GM expects its position in China, India, Brazil, and other overseas growth markets to help fuel its turnaround. (The one exception to this strong overseas performance is GM in Europe, where it continues to have negative earnings.)

- *GM's new vehicles are seen as high-quality.* Measurements of vehicle quality include market share trends, and third-party customer satisfaction ratings. Data suggest that GM has improved on these benchmarks.

  Some GM vehicles did well in an independent customer survey conducted by the American Customer Satisfaction Index (ACSI). In 2010, GM's Buick ranked second on the list, and GM's Cadillac was tied with Mercedes-Benz in third place. Both GM makes received higher satisfaction ratings than any Japanese models. As ACSI said in its release of the results, "It was not long ago when Detroit's products were clustered at the bottom of the industry. Although very few automakers improved this year, the domestic ones are either steady or have lost less in customer satisfaction compared to international competition. In this sense, the near future looks good for Ford and General Motors. Satisfied customers tend to do more repeat business, generate good word-of-mouth and don't require greater price incentives to come back."[61]

- *New management has changed the direction of the company.* When the Treasury took the major ownership interest in GM in July 2009, it appointed five new directors to the board and selected a new chairman, Edward Whitacre Jr. (the retired chairman and CEO of AT&T). These changes at the top created an actively engaged board of directors that has reportedly often challenged GM staff initiatives. In December 2009, the board replaced then-CEO Fritz Henderson, turning his management duties over to Whitacre, and reassigned Chief Financial Officer Ray Young, replacing him with Chris Liddell from Microsoft. The board has overseen the downsizing of both salaried and hourly employment. On September 1, 2010, Chairman and CEO Whitacre stepped down as CEO, and will retire as chairman at the end of the year. The new CEO (and chairman-designee) is Daniel Akerson, a GM board member and former managing director at the Carlyle Group, a Washington, DC-based private equity firm.

- *Recent labor agreements have placed GM at near-parity with transplant labor costs.* Contracts negotiated with the UAW in 2007 and revised in 2009 have reduced labor costs, which for many years favored the lower-wage, non-union Japanese and European transplant auto manufacturers in the United States. According to the Center for Automotive Research (CAR), GM's total labor costs, including benefits, stand at $58.15 an hour in 2010, compared with Toyota's total labor costs of $56.16 an hour. CAR notes that when new skilled and entry-level workers are hired at GM in the next few years, the lower hourly pay and benefits required by the UAW contract will further reduce GM's total labor costs to just over $48 an hour, well under what Toyota, Honda, and other non-U.S. manufacturers pay.[62] As mentioned earlier in this report, GM has shifted many of the costs of the UAW retiree health care plan to the UAW's VEBA, reducing GM's costs for supporting UAW retiree health care.

- *In 2010, the stock market has been relatively strong and the economy improving slowly.* The general economic environment affects the success of an IPO, in addition to the company's balance sheet. Indications of a healthier labor market and stronger consumer spending are generally positive for auto sales, which may have helped bolster the offering price.

Risks in the Future Valuation of Government Shares

There are economic and business factors that may negatively influence the performance of GM stock, potentially leading to a lower stock price in the future and the possibility that the U.S. Treasury would not recoup its full investment in GM. In its filings with the SEC, GM provided an analysis of the factors that could adversely affect its stock performance going forward. In the S-1, GM notes that "any of the following risks could materially adversely affect our business, financial condition, or results of operations. In such case, the trading price of our securities could decline, and you may lose all or part of your original investment."[63]

Among the internal and external risk factors GM cites in its prospectus are the following highlights. *Quotations below are taken from the discussion of risk factors in GM's SEC Registration (S-1 filing), unless otherwise noted.*

Internal Risks
- **Perception of product quality and innovation.** "Our ability to achieve long-term profitability depends on our ability to entice consumers to consider our products when purchasing a new vehicle." The prospectus says GM had lost market share "in part, due to negative public perceptions of our products" and that GM's ability to

successfully market smaller cars, hybrids, and electric and other energy-efficient vehicles, such as the Chevrolet Volt that debuted this fall, will affect GM's stock price.

- **Ability to further reduce costs.** Ongoing cost reduction and productivity improvement remain keys to sustained profitability, especially in North American and European operations. "Reducing costs may prove difficult due to our focus on increasing advertising and our belief that engineering expenses necessary to improve the performance, safety and customer satisfaction of our vehicles are likely to increase." In addition, the prospectus says costs could rise if dealer terminations and consolidations do not meet their targeted savings.
- **Generating adequate cash flow.** Automakers require substantial liquidity to invest in R&D and produce and market new vehicles. The prospectus states that GM has adequate liquidity now to operate its business, but that in the future, "inadequate cash flow could materially adversely affect our business operations."
- **Restructuring of GM European operations.** GM's large European operations have not been restructured as the North American operations were last year. The prospectus notes that "we cannot be certain that we will be able to successfully complete any of these restructurings."
- **Funding of the GM defined benefit pension plans.** According to the prospectus, GM's pension plans for its U.S. and non-U.S. hourly and salaried employees were underfunded by $27.4 billion. The prospectus stated that "we may need to make significant contributions to our U.S. pension plan in 2014." On December 2, 2010, GM made a $4 billion contribution to both the salaried and hourly pension plans.[64]
- **Labor union resistance and additional VEBA payments.** Most hourly workers at GM facilities in the United States, Canada, and Europe are covered by collective bargaining agreements. The contract with the UAW expires in 2011, and "while the UAW has agreed to a commitment not to strike prior to 2015, any UAW strikes, threats of strikes, or other resistance in the future could materially adversely affect our business as well as impair our ability to implement further measures to reduce costs and improve production efficiencies."
GM and the UAW agreed in the 2007 and 2009 contracts that the hourly workers'retiree health plan would be turned over to a VEBA and managed by a UAW trustee. GM is still obligated to make payments to the VEBA going forward, including $1.4 billion in each of 2013, 2015, and 2017.
- **New management team.** The departure of Chairman Ed Whitacre Jr. at the end of the year will leave GM headed by Dan Akerson, who has limited auto industry experience. Akerson has served on the GM board since July 2009, but his previous experience was in the telecom industry and private equity management.

External Risks
- **Auto sales volume and financing.** GM's business is sensitive to the pace of auto sales in the United States and its major markets. Deterioration in U.S. retail auto sales could affect investors'views of GM's stock. In addition, GM's customers and dealers depend on adequate capital to finance auto sales. Earlier this year, GM purchased AmeriCredit so it would once again have a captive finance company, but it

is not known if this new financing entity will close the gap in financing needs for GM dealers and consumers.[65]
- **Price of gasoline and raw materials.** When gasoline sold for more than $4 a gallon in 2008, many consumers turned away from the large, highly profitable vehicles that GM produces. A renewed increase in gasoline prices could adversely affect GM's market share and profitability again. In addition, substantial increases in the prices of raw materials could reduce profitability.
- **Government-imposed costs.** GM foresees a wide range of new regulatory costs in major markets around the world, especially associated with government-mandated greenhouse gas emissions reductions, vehicle safety, and fuel economy.
- **Executive compensation limits.** Under federal law,[66] compensation to the top level of GM executives has been reduced since the company received TARP funds. According to the prospectus, the continuing salary caps may interfere with GM's ability to retain and hire employees "whose expertise is required to execute our business plan while at the same time developing and producing vehicles that will stimulate demand for our products."
- **International economic trends.** The majority of GM's sales take place outside the United States, so its future financial success hinges on global economic trends, especially in China, Brazil, and India. Economic downturns, costly new government mandates, and political and economic instability in overseas markets will affect GM's financial standing.

RECOUPING U.S. GOVERNMENT FUNDS INVESTED IN GM

As detailed in the **Appendix**, the U.S. government through TARP has aided the combined Old GM and GM with more than $50 billion in loans since December 2008. Of this amount, $7.4 billion was repaid in installments, completed in April 2010, and approximately $0.8 billion has been paid in interest, dividends, and fees as of the end of October 2010. An additional $2.1 billion of the loans was converted into shares of preferred stock, which are held by the U.S. Treasury and are slated to be repaid in December 2010. The approximately $40.7 billion remaining was effectively converted into an initial 60.8% equity stake. The TARP authorization to purchase new assets or make new commitments expired on October 3, 2010, but Treasury has continuing authority to manage the equity in GM and other TARP assets.

The November 18, 2010, sale of 358.5 million GM shares returned $11.7 billion dollars to the government, and the sale of another 58.8 billion overallotment shares returned another $1.8 billion. With this sale of overallotment shares, the government now holds approximately 500 million shares or 33% of GM, with approximately $27.2 billion to be recouped. In order for the government's share to be worth this $27.2 billion, and thus for the government to recoup the nominal value[67] of its investment in GM,[68] the entire company's market capitalization would have to be approximately $81.6 billion. To achieve this market capitalization, the GM stock price would have to rise from the $33 per share price in the IPO to approximately $54 per share. Adjusted for inflation, the reported market value of Old GM approached $81.6 billion in only one year of the last decade. **Table 4** presents the market value of GM for the past 10 years.

Table 4. Market Value of General Motors, 2000-2010

Date	Market Capitalization (nominal value, $ billions)	Market Capitalization (real value, $ billions in 2010)
2010 (New GM IPO)[a]	$49.5	$49.5
2009	$2.2	$2.2
2008	$10.6	$10.7
2007	$18.1	$19.0
2006	$11.9	$12.9
2005	$16.0	$17.9
2004	$27.3	$31.5
2003	$17.9	$21.2
2002	$47.5	$57.6
2001	$48.1	$59.2
2000	$63.8	$80.1

Source: *Fortune* magazine, annual ranking of Fortune 500 firms, 2000-2009; U.S. Treasury, *Troubled Asset Relief Program: Transaction Report*, November 22, 2010. Inflation adjustment by CRS using the Consumer Price Index from the Bureau of Labor Statistics.

Notes: Market capitalization reflects the outstanding number of shares of common stock multiplied by the price per share. *Fortune* publishes its listing in May of each year, based on market prices on particular dates in March.

a. The IPO was issued on November 18, 2010.

CONCLUSION

After credit markets tightened and the recession reduced auto sales in the fall of 2008, General Motors restructured its operations through bankruptcy and began operations as a new company in July 2009. The Bush and Obama Administrations used TARP funds to provide capital to General Motors during this time, in exchange for a majority ownership stake in the company. Without the federal assistance, GM would not have been able to pay creditors, suppliers or workers and would have most likely entered bankruptcy earlier with a less certain outcome. TARP support enabled it to reorganize itself in a more orderly manner.

Both the Obama administration and GM's senior management have been eager to reduce the federal ownership stake in the company. Not long after GM emerged as a new company after bankruptcy, GM and the U.S. Treasury agreed that there should be an initial public offering of new GM stock in the latter half of 2010. While the proceeds from the sale of stock would go primarily to GM's post-bankruptcy government and union owners, issuing an IPO was the first step in removing GM from government ownership.

The GM IPO on November 18, 2010, was deemed a success by most financial observers. In the days prior to the offering, market interest seemed strong, so GM raised its target price from the mid-20s per share to $33 a share and it sold slightly above that price immediately following the IPO. To date, its range has been between the IPO price and $35.99 per share. The steadiness of its stock price is a sign of investor confidence in the company's outlook.

The federal government, the governments of Canada and Ontario and the UAW VEBA trust still own more than half of GM. It is expected that these shareholders will sell their remaining shares over the course of the next year or more.

An unanswered question is whether the federal government will recoup the $50.2 billion investment it made in GM. As of December 8, 2010, the federal government had recouped $20.87 billion in principal and had received $0.76 billion in fees and dividends, for a total recoupment of $21.6 billion. How much additional funding the federal government will recoup depends on the internal GM factors described in this report, external factors such as the strength of the economic recovery and the auto sales market, as well as the Treasury Department's timing in selling its sizeable, remaining shareholding.

APPENDIX. FEDERAL FINANCIAL SUPPORT FOR GENERAL MOTORS THROUGH THE TROUBLED ASSET RELIEF PROGRAM

Table A-1. Chronology of Federal Aid

Date	Recipient/Source	Amount ($ in billions)
December 2008	Old GM	$13.40
April 2009 May 2009	Old GM Old GM	$2.00 $4.00
June 2009	GM Warranty Program Old GM/GM	$0.36 $30.10
April 2009-April 2010 Total Funds Loaned	Old GM Supplier Receivablesa	$0.29 $50.15
Recoupment of Principal		
July 2009	Repayment for Warranty Program	$0.36
November 2009 December 2009/January 2010	Partial repayment of Supplier Receivables loans Partial debt repayment	$0.14 $1.03
February 2010 March 2010	Partial repayment of Supplier Receivables loans Partial debt repayment	$0.10 $1.00
April 2010	Final debt repayment Final repayment of Supplier Receivables loans	$4.68 $0.06
November 2010 Total	Proceeds from sale of common equity	$13.5 $20.87
Interest, Dividends, and Fees Paid		
December 2008-April 2009	Interest on Old GM loans	$0.14
April 2009-April 2010 March 2010	Interest for GM Supplier Receivables Additional Note for GM Supplier Receivables Program	$0.01 $0.05
October 2009-April 2010 September 2009-present (ongoing quarterly payments)	Interest on GM loans Dividends on Preferred Stock	$0.34 $0.22
Total		$0.76

Sources: U.S. Department of the Treasury, Troubled Asset Relief Program (TARP), Transactions Reports, various dates, and Troubled Asset Relief Program (TARP), Dividends and Interest Report, various dates.

Note: In December 2008, the U.S. Treasury provided $884 million to assist GM in GMAC's rights offerings, separate from the $13.4 billion loaned for GM's operations. While this was provided to GM, it assisted GMAC and is generally tallied as GMAC assistance.

a. The original April 2009 Automotive Supplier Support Program commitment was $3.5 billion for use with GM suppliers. This commitment was reduced to $2.5 billion in July 2009. Ultimately approximately $290 million of the $2.5 billion commitment was used.

End Notes

[1] Other automakers' U.S. production fell as well: Toyota's by 28%, Honda's by 27%, and Ford's by 13%. Source: "North American Car and Truck Production," *Automotive News*, January 11, 2010. GM and Chrysler sales in 2008 were made by Old GM and Old Chrysler; 2009 sales include sales made by both entities before they filed for bankruptcy as well as sales made by new GM and new Chrysler after bankruptcy.

[2] U.S auto sales for most of the decade 2000-2009 were above 16 million units per year. Ward's, *Ward's Motor Vehicle Facts & Figures 2009*, "U.S. Retail Sales of Cars and Trucks."

[3] For a full analysis of the decline in U.S. and other industrial country auto manufacturing during the recent recession, see CRS Report R41154, *The U.S. Motor Vehicle Industry: A Review of Recent Domestic and International Developments*, by Bill Canis and Brent D. Yacobucci.

[4] After the GM IPO, the federal government owns 33.3% of GM (and 9.85% of Chrysler). The Voluntary Employee Beneficiary Association (the UAW's retiree health care plan) owns 10.7% of GM (and 67.7% of Chrysler). The Canadian and Ontario governments own 9.3% of GM (and the Canadian government owns 2.46% of Chrysler).

[5] Chrysler is not expected to seek an IPO until 2011 or later; this report does not discuss Chrysler's turnaround.

[6] William J. Holstein, *Why GM Matters: Inside the Race to Transform an American Icon* (Walker & Company, 2009), p. 4.

[7] A bridge loan is a temporary, short-term loan made to a borrower, with the expectation that it will be repaid quickly. At Investorwords.com, http://www.investorwords.com/581/bridge_loan.html.

[8] Affidavit of Frederick A. Henderson Pursuant to Local Bankruptcy Rule 1007-2, U.S. Bankruptcy Court, Southern District of New York, filed June 1, 2009. [9] Alex Taylor III, "Can This Car Save Ford?," *Fortune*, April 22, 2008.

[10] *Automotive News*, "US Car and Light Truck Sales by Make—12 Months 2009," January 5, 2010, and "US Car and Light Truck Sales by Make—12 Months 2008," January 12, 2009.

[11] *InvestorWords.com*, http://www.investorwords.com/575/break_even_point.html.

[12] Jeff Green and Caroline Salas, "GM Said to Speed Cutbacks to Lower Break-Even Point," *Bloomberg*, April 22, 2009, at http://www.bloomberg.com/apps/news?sid=aOloQhPHrqX0&pid=newsarchive.

[13] U.S. auto sales forecast, "Forecast and Analysis: Latest Developments," *IHS Global Insight*, November 29, 2010.

[14] Julie Appleby and Sharon Silke Carty, "Ailing GM Looks to Scale Back Generous Health Benefits," *USA Today*, June 23, 2005.

[15] Bill Visnic, "UAW Cornered on VEBA?," *Edmunds*, February 27, 2009, at http://www.autoobserver.com/2009/02/uaw-cornered-on-veba.html.

[16] Affidavit of Frederick A. Henderson, part of General Motors filing in the U.S. Bankruptcy Court, Southern District of New York, June 1, 2009, pp. 18-19.

[17] P.L. 110-343, 122 Stat. 3765.

[18] P.L. 110-343, Division A, Section 3.

[19] TARP, "Monthly 105(a) Report to Congress," U.S. Department of the Treasury, July 2010, p. 10.

[20] In December 2008, the House of Representatives passed H.R. 7321, authorizing the use of certain Department of Energy funds as bridge loans to GM and Chrysler. Passed 237-170, the bill was not acted upon in the Senate. For a complete description of Congress's consideration of auto industry loan legislation in the fall of 2008, see CRS Report R40003, *U.S. Motor Vehicle Industry: Federal Financial Assistance and Restructuring*, coordinated by Bill Canis.

[21] John D. McKinnon and John D. Stoll, "U.S. Throws Lifeline to Detroit," *Wall Street Journal*, December 20, 2008.

[22] The Auto Task Force is chaired by Treasury Secretary Geithner and composed of officials from a wide range of federal agencies, including the departments of Labor, Commerce, and Transportation. On a day-to-day basis, the task force was managed for most of 2009 by Steven Rattner, the cofounder of a private equity firm. Since July 13, 2009, it has been managed by Ron Bloom, a former investment banker and one-time adviser to the United Steelworkers union

[23] Old Chrysler's Viability Plan was also rejected by the Obama Administration, and it was given 30 days to restructure.

[24] General Motors Company, *Form 10-Q Quarterly Report*, April 7, 2010, p. 37.

[25] Old GM—General Motors *Corporation*—remains in bankruptcy and is officially the Motors Liquidation Company, with the assets and liabilities that were not attached to the new General Motors *Company*.

[26] This preferred stock is an equity instrument, but it does not confer any control over the company and typically has a set dividend rate to be paid by the company; thus it is similar economically to debt.

[27] The SIGTARP report states, referring to GM's repayment of $6.7 billion in TARP loans, that "all of these payments were made, with Treasury's permission, using funds from the escrow account that held TARP funds provided to GM." "Quarterly Report to Congress," Office of the Special Inspector General for the Troubled Asset Relief Program (SIGTARP), July 21, 2010, p. 108.

[28] U.S. Treasury, "General Motors to Repurchase Treasury Preferred Stock," press release, October 28, 2010, http://financialstability.gov/latest/pr_10282010.html.

[29] U.S. Treasury, "FACT SHEET: Obama Administration Auto Restructuring Initiative," press release, June 1, 2009, http://www.financialstability.gov/latest/05312009_gm-factsheet.html.

[30] Robert Snell and David Shepardson, "GM Faces Rocky 'Road Show' on Stock Offering," *Detroit News*, August 20, 2010.

[31] "GM Files for IPO; Could Raise $10 Bln," *Wall Street Journal*, August 18, 2010.

[32] The banks which were selected to underwrite and market the GM IPO have a 30-day option to buy up to 71.7 million additional shares of common stock and 13 million shares of mandatory convertible junior preferred stock, which will convert to common shares in 2013. When these options are exercised, the GM IPO will reach $23.1 billion. "General Motors Company Prices Offering of Common and Preferred Stock," GM Press Release, November 17, 2010.

[33] Henry Ford discussed his views on ownership in his autobiography, *My Life and Work*, printed by Doubleday, 1922. See chapter XII, "Money—Master or Servant?," p. 169 *et seq.* Also see "Henry Ford Never Wanted His Company to Go Public," *Automotive News*, June 15, 2003.

[34] General Motors Fact Sheet, http://www.gm.com/corporate/about/gm_fact_sheet.jsp.

[35] On Friday, May 29, 2009, GM stock in after-hours trading sold for 71 cents per share. Source: "After 93 Years, G.M. Shares Go Out on a Low Note," *New York Times*, May 29, 2009, http://dealbook.blogs.

[36] Quote and information on the IPO are from "Henry Ford Never Wanted His Company to Go Public," *Automotive News*, June 15, 2003. The article cites information on the IPO which is taken from *Henry: A Life of Henry Ford II*, by Walter Hayes, Grove Publishing, June 1990.

[37] The GM-Toyota joint venture—NUMMI—stood for New United Motor Manufacturing, Inc.

[38] The Energy Independence and Security Act (P.L. 110-140, sec. 136) authorized up to $25 billion for loans from the U.S. Department of Energy to companies making cars and components in U.S. factories that increase fuel economy at least 25% above 2005 fuel economy levels. The Consolidated Security, Disaster Assistance, and Continuing Appropriations Act (P.L. 110-329, sec. 129), appropriated $7.51 billion to cover the subsidy ($7.5 billion) and administrative costs ($10 million) of the loans. For more information on this program, see CRS Report RL34743, *Federal Loans to the Auto Industry Under the Energy Independence and Security Act*, by Bill Canis and Brent D. Yacobucci.

[39] Tesla Motors, "Tesla Motors and Toyota Motor Corporation Intend to Work Jointly on EV Development, TMC to Invest in Tesla," press release, May 20, 2010.

[40] Eric Wesoff, "Update: Tesla Stock Price Falls Below IPO Price," *Greentechmedia*, July 6, 2010, http://www.greentechmedia.com/articles/read/tesla-ipo-gentlemen-start-your-drivetrains/.

[41] Shanny Basar, "Record Bookrunner Club Prepares GM Float," *Financial News*, August 19, 2010, available at http://www.efinancialnews.com/story/2010-08-19/gm-ipo-bookrunners.

[42] Walter Hamilton and Nathaniel Popper, "Access to General Motors Stock Offering Won't Include Many of its Rescuers," *Los Angeles Times*, November 16, 2010.

[43] Available at http://www.sec.gov/Archives/edgar/data/1467858/000119312510192195/ds1.htm.

[44] 15 U.S.C. §§ 77a *et seq.*

[45] During the road show, institutional investors begin to place orders for the stock, with each willing investor indicating how much it would be interested in purchasing at various prices. While one investor may offer to buy 40,000 shares at $29 a share, another may offer to acquire 70,000 shares at $26 a share. Chrissie Thompson, "Ins and Outs of the Stock Sale," *Detroit Free Press*, November 4, 2010, at http://www.freep.com/article/20101104/BUSINESS01/11040618/First-GM-execs-will-make-their-pitch-then-investors-will-help-set-a-price.

[46] The Series B preferred stock will convert to common stock in 2013. GM Series A Preferred Stock was previously issued to stakeholders during the bankruptcy, including the U.S, Treasury.

[47] "M. Stanley, JPMorgan Could Make $40 Million Each from GM's IPO's IPO," *Reuters*, November 18, 2010.

[48] See, e.g., Aaron Lucchetti, et al., "GM Will Pay a Cut-Rate Price to Do Its New IPO," *Wall Street Journal*, June 12, 2010, available at http://online.wsj.com/article/ NA_WSJ_PUB:SB 1000142405274 8703509404 575300430351563768.html. "Goldman Sachs Undercuts Rivals in GM IPO as It Loses Top Role," *Businessweek*, August 16, 2010, available at http://www.businessweek.com/news/2010-08- 16/goldman-sachs-undercuts-rivals-in-gm-ipo-as-it-loses-top-role.html, and "Taxpayers on GM Off Ramp with IPO," *The Windsor Star*, August 19, 2010, available at http://www.driving.ca/windsor/Taxpayers+ ramp+with/3417484/story.html?cid=megadrop_story. There are reports that one of the underwriters, Goldman Sachs, offered to take the cut-rate 0.75% underwriters fee, which was lower than those proposed by other banks that joined the syndicate, and that subsequently U.S. Treasury officials imposed those terms on the other underwriters, who originally were going to get heftier fees. Nick Bunkley and Bill Vlasic, "General Motors Files for an Initial Public Offering," *The New York Times*, August 18, 2010. In a joint bookrunner IPO like that being conducted by GM, bookrunners typically receive 30% to 40% of the revenue from the gross spread. Yunchun Hu, "Multiple Bookrunners in IPOs," *University of Florida PhD Dissertation*, 2007, http://marriottschool.byu.edu/emp/boyer/financeseminar/s07_08/bookrunners_0903_2007.pdf.

[49] Some explain the underwriters' willingness to accept such comparatively low fees in terms of the prestige it affords them in being part of such a highly visible deal and how it is likely to place them in a favorable position to take part in anticipated follow-on GM stock offerings.

[50] "Alwaleed's Kingdom Buys $500 Million GM Stake in IPO," *Bloomberg*, November 23, 2010.

[51] "GM Stock Makes Strong Debut," *CNNMoney.com*, November 18, 2010, "Even after GM, Plenty of Cash to Go Around," *Reuters*, November 18, 2010.

[52] Ibid. The IPO's underwriters reportedly met with a number of sovereign wealth funds and private investors in the Middle East and Asia, but as in the case of the Kuwait Investment Authority, the country's sovereign wealth fund, reports indicate that they secured no such commitments.

[53] "Quarterly Report to Congress," Office of the Special Inspector General for the Troubled Asset Relief Program (SIGTARP), July 21, 2010, p. 108.

[54] "GM Getting a New CEO—Again," *CNNMoney.com*, August 12, 2010.

[55] GM's S-1A Registration Statement, filed with the SEC on November 17, 2010, p. 8.

[56] "Our Competitive Strengths," *Form S-1 Registration Statement*, filed by General Motors Company with the Securities and Exchange Commission, August 18, 2010, p. 3.

[57] U.S. auto sales forecast, "Forecast and Analysis: Latest Developments," *IHS Global Insight*, November 29, 2010.

[58] "Best of 2010 May Already Be Behind GM," *Edmunds Auto Observer*, August 12, 2010.

[59] In 2009, China surpassed the United States for the first time to become the world's largest retail auto market.

[60] The forecast that 17 million cars will be sold in China in 2010 was made by the Ministry of Industry and Information Technology. "China's October Passenger Car-Sales Rise on Incentives," *Bloomberg*, November 9, 2010.

[61] Statement of Claes Fornell, founder of the ACSI, "ACSI: Detroit Tops Auto Industry for the First Time Ever," ASCI, August 17, 2010, http://www.theacsi.org/images

[62] McAlinden, Sean, Executive Vice President and Chief Economist, Center for Automotive Research, "Picking Up the Pieces: Restructuring of the North American Automotive Industry," presented at CAR Management Briefing Seminars, Acme, MI, August 4, 2010.

[63] General Motors Company, "Risk Factors," *Form S-1 Registration Statement*, August 18, 2010, p. 13.

[64] "GM Makes $4 Billion Pension Plan Contribution," General Motors Press Release, December 2, 2010.

[65] For dealer and consumer financing, GM intends to continue to utilize Ally Financial (formerly GMAC), the majority of which is owned by the federal government. According to the GM prospectus, Ally's credit rating has been downgraded in recent years.

[66] Required of TARP-assisted companies by Section 111 of the Emergency Economic Stabilization Act of 2008, P.L. 110-343.

[67] The nominal value is the value of the stock at the time it was originally traded; the real value indexes it for inflation.

[68] It should be noted that, under the TARP statute, CBO and OMB perform additional calculations taking into account the time value of money and market risk in arriving at a budget estimate of the costs of TARP. Thus, even if the sales of GM stock return a nominal amount of money equal to the amount of the government loans, the loans may still show a budgetary cost.

Chapter 3

TROUBLED ASSET RELIEF PROGRAM: AUTOMAKER PENSION FUNDING AND MULTIPLE FEDERAL ROLES POSE CHALLENGES FOR THE FUTURE[*]

United States Government Accountability Office

WHY GAO DID THIS STUDY

Over $81 billion has been committed under the Troubled Asset Relief Program (TARP) to improve the domestic auto industry's competitiveness and long-term viability. The bulk of this assistance has gone to General Motors (GM) and Chrysler, who sponsor some of the largest defined benefit pension plans insured by the federal Pension Benefit Guaranty Corporation (PBGC). As part of GAO's statutorily mandated oversight of TARP, this report examines:

1) the impact of restructuring on GM's and Chrysler's pension plans;
2) the impact of restructuring on auto supply sector pension plans;
3) the impacts on PBGC and plan participants should auto industry pension plans be terminated; and
4) how the federal government is dealing with the potential tensions of its multiple roles as pension regulator, shareholder, and creditor.

To conduct this study, GAO interviewed officials at GM, Chrysler, a labor union, a supplier association, the Departments of the Treasury and Labor, and PBGC; and reviewed relevant statutes, reports, and documents concerning the automakers' restructuring and pension plan funding.

---

[*] This is an edited, reformatted and augmented version of the United States Government Accountability Office's publication, dated April 2010.

Treasury and PBGC generally agreed with the report's findings. Their technical comments and the technical comments provided by GM, Chrysler, and Delphi, were incorporated as appropriate.

WHAT GAO FOUND

The new GM and the new Chrysler that were established during each company's bankruptcy process in the summer of 2009 assumed sponsorship for all the old companies'U.S. defined benefit plans. Although the pension plans have been maintained, their future remains uncertain. According to current company projections, large contributions may be needed to comply with federal pension funding requirements within the next 5 years.

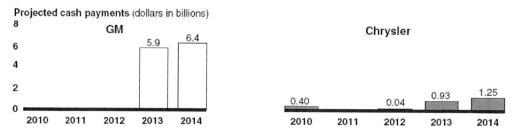

Source: GAO analysis of GM and Chrysler funding projections for all U.S. qualified defined benefit pension plans each sponsors, based on valuation methods for required contributions defined under the Pension Protection Act.

Officials at the Department of the Treasury, which oversees TARP, expect both GM and Chrysler to return to profitability. If this is the case, then the companies will likely be able to make the required payments and prevent their pension plans from being terminated. However, if GM and Chrysler were not able to return to profitability and their pension plans were terminated, PBGC would be hit hard both financially and administratively. In early 2009, prior to the new companies assuming sponsorship, PBGC estimated that its exposure to potential losses for GM's and Chrysler's plans to be about $14.5 billion.

Meanwhile, automaker downsizing and the credit market crisis have created significant stress for suppliers and their pensions. During 2009, there was a rise in the number of supplier bankruptcies, liquidations, and pension plan terminations. In July, the nation's largest auto parts supplier, Delphi Corporation, terminated its pension plans with expected losses to PBGC of over $6.2 billion. Across the auto sector as a whole, in January 2009, PBGC estimated that unfunded pension liabilities totaled about $77 billion, with PBGC's exposure for potential losses due to unfunded benefits of about $42 billion, leaving plan participants to bear the potential loss of the $35 billion difference through reduced benefits.

Moreover, until Treasury either sells or liquidates the equity it acquired in each of the companies in exchange for the TARP assistance, its role as shareholder creates potential tensions with its role as pension regulator and overseer of PBGC in its role as pension insurer. In particular, tensions could arise if decisions must be made between allocating funds to company assets (thereby protecting shareholders, including taxpayers) or to pension fund assets (thereby protecting plan participants). As GAO reported previously, better communication with Congress and others about TARP interests could help mitigate such tensions.

ABBREVIATIONS

AIFP	Automotive Industry Financing Program
ERISA	Employee Retirement Income Security Act of 1974
GM	General Motors Company
IRS	Internal Revenue Service
PBGC	Pension Benefit Guaranty Corporation
PPA	Pension Protection Act of 2006
TARP	Troubled Asset Relief Program
UAW	International Union, United Automobile, Aerospace and Agricultural Implement Workers of America
VEBA	Voluntary Employee Beneficiary Association

April 6, 2010

Congressional Committees

Domestic auto manufacturers remain sponsors of some of the largest private defined benefit plans in the United States. The fate of these pension plans affects not only the benefits of current and future auto company retirees, but also the financial well-being of the Pension Benefit Guaranty Corporation (PBGC)[1]—the federal corporation that insures private sector defined benefit plans. During the past year, the U.S. automotive industry has undergone major restructuring, including the bankruptcy reorganization of two of the country's largest auto manufacturers and re-emergence as new companies—General Motors Company (GM) and Chrysler Group, LLC (Chrysler)—and the continued consolidation in the auto supply industry. Since 2008, the federal government has committed to provide over $81 billion under the Troubled Asset Relief Program (TARP) to assist the automobile industry.[2] These funds, along with loans from the Canadian government and concessions from nearly every stakeholder (including labor unions), were intended to allow the companies time to restructure to improve their competitiveness and long-term viability, which is critical to the future of both the companies and their pension plans. In exchange for this funding, the federal government acquired partial ownership in and made loans to the new GM and the new Chrysler that were established during the bankruptcy process. Treasury's new role as a shareholder adds an unprecedented and extraordinary element to the previously established government responsibilities of regulator and its relationship to PBGC as insurer.

Under our statutorily mandated responsibilities for providing timely oversight of TARP, we are continuing to report on the federal government's assistance to the U.S. automotive industry.[3,4] In this report, we focused on the impact of the recent restructuring on auto industry pension plans and the government's role in overseeing those plans and PBGC's role in insuring these plans. Specifically, our review focused on the following questions:

1) How has restructuring affected GM's and Chrysler's pension plans and the outlook for the plans going forward?
2) How has restructuring affected auto supply sector pension plans?
3) What are the impacts on PBGC and plan participants should auto industry pension plans be terminated in the next 5 years?
4) How is the federal government dealing with the potential tensions between its multiple roles as pension regulator and insurer, and its new roles as shareholder and creditor?

To describe how restructuring has affected GM's and Chrysler's pension plans and the plans' funding going forward,[5] we interviewed officials from each automaker. They provided us with an overview of their pension plans as well as a number of documents, including detailed actuarial information about their PBGC-insured pension plans. We interviewed Department of Treasury (Treasury) officials who are responsible for overseeing the assistance to GM and Chrysler (referred to as Treasury's "auto team") in Treasury's program office for TARP, the Office of Financial Stability.

These officials provided information on Treasury's involvement in the restructurings and how it considered future plan funding when structuring the financing packages for the companies. We interviewed other Treasury officials, as well as officials at PBGC, and the Department of Labor (Labor). We also interviewed the International Union, United Automobile, Aerospace and Agricultural Implement Workers of America (UAW), which represents a significant number of the participants in the collectively bargained pension plans, and asked for their views on restructuring efforts and their effect on pension plans. Additionally, we reviewed materials related to restructurings, including corporate annual reports and bankruptcy documents, as well as relevant federal laws and regulations, and other materials related to defined benefit plans and plan funding, such as pension consulting briefs.

To describe how restructuring has affected the auto supply sector and its pensions, we interviewed officials from PBGC, Treasury, and the Motor and Equipment Manufacturers Association. We also reviewed materials related to key production parts suppliers in the auto industry, including corporate annual reports, bankruptcy filings, PBGC press releases, and industry publications.

To determine the potential consequences of plan termination for PBGC and plan participants, and to describe the tensions and challenges faced by the federal agencies responsible for the regulation and oversight of qualified defined benefit plans,[6] we interviewed officials from GM, Chrysler, UAW, PBGC, and the board representatives for PBGC's Board of Directors, comprised of the Secretaries of Commerce, Labor, and Treasury, the primary agencies charged with pension regulation and overseeing PBGC. We requested additional actuarial information from the automakers in certain instances and reviewed bankruptcy documents related to the individual automaker restructurings. We also reviewed relevant federal laws and regulations, and past GAO reports that addressed the topics of pension plan termination and managing multiple roles under TARP.

To ensure the technical accuracy of the information contained in the report, we asked representatives of GM, Chrysler, and Delphi to review portions of a draft of this report. We conducted this performance audit between September 2009 and April 2010, in accordance with generally accepted government auditing standards. Those standards require that we plan and perform the audit to obtain sufficient, appropriate evidence to provide a reasonable basis for our findings and conclusions based on our audit objectives. We believe the evidence obtained provides a reasonable basis for our findings and conclusions based on our audit objectives.

BACKGROUND

The domestic auto industry—including automakers, dealerships, and automotive parts suppliers—contributes substantially to the U.S. economy, but has faced financial challenges in recent years. According to the Congressional Research Service, more than 435,000 U.S. automotive manufacturing jobs have been eliminated since 2000—an amount equal to about 3.3 percent of all manufacturing jobs in 2008.[7] The employment level first dipped below 1 million in 2007 and fell to 880,000 workers in 2008. The Detroit-based automotive manufacturers—GM, Chrysler, and the Ford Motor Company—have seen their share of the domestic market drop from 64.5 percent in 2001 to 47.5 percent in 2008. Prior to restructuring, GM and Chrysler reported losses in 2008 totaling $31 billion and $8 billion, respectively.

TARP Assistance for the Auto Sector

Concerned that the collapse of a major U.S. automaker could pose a systemic risk to the nation's economy, in December 2008, Treasury established the Automotive Industry Financing Program (AIFP) under TARP. Through June 2009, $81.1 billion in AIFP funding has been made available to assist the auto industry. The largest part of the program's funding—about $62 billion—was provided to help GM and Chrysler fund their operations while they restructured. In exchange for this funding, the Treasury has become part-owner of the two new companies that reemerged, receiving 60.8 percent of the equity in the new GM and 9.85 percent of the equity in the new Chrysler, and has a debt interest of about $14 billion in loans between the two.[8] Given the large taxpayer investments in GM and Chrysler, in a recent report, we recommended that Treasury report to Congress on how it plans to assess and monitor the companies' performance to help ensure the companies are on track to repay their loans and to return to profitability. In response, Treasury said the agency intends to develop an approach for reporting on its investments in the auto industry that strikes an appropriate balance between its goal of transparency and the need to avoid compromising either the competitive positions of these companies or Treasury's ability to recover taxpayer funds.[9] More broadly, we also previously recommended that Treasury better communicate to external stakeholders, including Congress, about its TARP strategies and activities to improve the integrity, accountability, and transparency of the program. In response to this recommendation, Treasury noted that it was implementing a communication strategy to provide key congressional stakeholders more current information about its TARP activities.[10]

AIFP also established the Auto Supplier Support Program—a mechanism to extend credit to auto suppliers. Under this program, Treasury committed to fund up to $3.5 billion in loans to special purpose entities created by new GM and new Chrysler for the purpose of ensuring payment to suppliers. The program was designed to ensure that automakers receive the parts and components they need to manufacture vehicles and that suppliers have access to liquidity on their receivables.[11] According to Treasury officials, the program will terminate in April 2010.

Restructuring in the Auto Sector

As a condition of receiving federal financial assistance, GM and Chrysler were also required to develop restructuring plans to identify how the companies planned to achieve and sustain long-term financial viability.[12]

GM

Prior to restructuring, GM was a publicly traded company that employed about 240,000 people worldwide. It had manufacturing facilities in 34 countries and sold more than a dozen brands of vehicles in about 140 countries. GM's core U.S. brands are Buick, Cadillac, Chevrolet, and GMC; other brands included Daewoo, Holden, Hummer, Opel, Pontiac, Saab, Saturn, Vauxhall, and Wuling.

GM filed for Chapter 11 bankruptcy protection on June 1, 2009, and on July 5, 2009, the bankruptcy court approved the sale of substantially all of old GM's assets to a newly formed company, referred to as "new GM." The new GM assumed sponsorship of both of old GM's U.S. qualified defined benefit plans.

Chrysler

Prior to restructuring, Chrysler was a privately held company that employed about 54,000 people worldwide, including manufacturing facilities in four countries and vehicles assembled under contract in four others. Chrysler's major brands include Dodge, Chrysler, and Jeep.

Chrysler filed for Chapter 11 bankruptcy protection on April 30, 2009, and on June 9, 2009, the bankruptcy court approved the sale of substantially all of old Chrysler's assets to a newly formed company, referred to as "new Chrysler." The new Chrysler assumed sponsorship of all Chrysler's U.S. qualified defined benefit plans.

To implement the restructuring plans, both companies filed voluntary petitions for reorganization under Chapter 11 of the U.S. Bankruptcy Code. During the bankruptcy process, newly organized companies for both GM and Chrysler were established in the summer of 2009. These new companies purchased substantially all of the operating assets of the previous companies, while the old companies, which retained very few assets but most of the liabilities, continued in bankruptcy. The new companies also streamlined operations and substantially reduced their debt. Changes included reductions in the number of brands and models, closing factories and dealerships, and reducing their hourly and salaried workforces through early retirements, buyouts, and layoffs.

Automakers are highly dependent on a large motor vehicle parts supply industry. The auto supply chain consists of networks of suppliers, transportation carriers, fabrication sites, assembly locations, distribution centers, and locations by which components, services, information and products flow. The supply chain starts with suppliers who assemble raw components into more complex components which are processed or combined with additional components and eventually brought together by top-level suppliers to manufacture end products for use by the automaker. Each level in the supply chain depends on the financial health of the other for its survival.

The U.S. auto supply sector became unstable as the domestic market share of the global automotive marketplace declined, prices for raw materials and petroleum increased, and production cuts ensued. These financial pressures affected various levels of the supply chain, leading some suppliers to file for bankruptcy, including the nation's largest U.S. auto supplier, Delphi Corporation (a spin off of GM), which filed for bankruptcy in 2005.[13]

Private Sector Pension Plans

About one-half of all U.S. workers participate in some form of employer-sponsored retirement plan, typically classified either as a defined benefit or as a defined contribution plan. Defined benefit plans generally offer a fixed level of monthly retirement income based upon a participant's salary, years of service, and age at retirement, regardless of how the plan's investments perform. In contrast, benefit levels for those with defined contribution plans depend on the contributions made to individual accounts (such as 401(k) plans) and the performance of the investments in those accounts, which may fluctuate in value. Over the last two decades, much of the private sector pension coverage has moved away from traditional defined benefit plans in favor of defined contribution plans and hybrid defined benefit plans,[14] thereby increasing portability for workers as they change jobs, but also shifting the risk and burden of financing retirement from employers to employees.

Delphi

Delphi evolved as part of GM until it was spun off as a separate entity in 1999. By 2005, the company employed more than 185,000 workers in 38 countries, making it one of the largest suppliers in the world. However, on October 8, 2005, Delphi Corporation and its U.S. subsidiaries filed for Chapter 11 bankruptcy protection. Four years later, most of Delphi's U.S. and foreign operations were sold to a new entity, known as "new Delphi," on October 6, 2009.

The former Delphi Corporation sponsored six defined benefit plans for its U.S.-based workers. Despite efforts to keep the pension plans ongoing, on July 31, 2009, PBGC terminated all six of Delphi's U.S. qualified defined benefit plans.

For more details on Delphi, see appendix I.

Table 1. Defined Benefit Plans Sponsored by New GM and New Chrysler

Short plan name	Full plan name	Number of participants[a]	Collectively bargained plan[b]	Plan liabilities (dollars in millions)[c]	Plan status[d]
GM's plans					
Hourly Plan	General Motors Hourly-Rate Employees Pension Plan	505,289	Yes	(plan-level data not publicly available)	Open, but plan terms modified for certain newhires as of 10/15/2007[e]
Salaried Plan	General Motors Retirement Program for Salaried Employees	197,098	No	(plan-level data not publicly available)	Plan closed and frozen for certain participants 1/1/2007[f]
Total GM		702,387	-	$98.1[g]	
Chrysler's plans					
UAW Pension Plan	Pension Agreement between Chrysler LLC and the UAW	134,689	Yes	14,003	Open
Chrysler Pension Plan	Chrysler LLC Pension Plan	44,329	No	2,973	Closed 12/31/2003
Salaried Employees' Retirement Plan	Chrysler LLC Salaried Employees' Retirement Plan	46,217	Yes (for some)	2,567	Closed 12/31/2003
AMC Plan	American Motors Union Retirement Income Plan	10,693	Yes	809	Closed 12/31/1996
Jeep Plan	Jeep Corporation - UAW Retirement Income Plan	8,960	Yes	1,288	Open
Chrysler IUE Pension Plan	Pension Agreement Between Chrysler LLC and the International Union of Electronic, Electrical, Salaried, Machine and Furniture Workers	4,011	Yes	205	Frozen 3/31/2002

Short plan name	Full plan name	Number of participants[a]	Collectively bargained plan[b]	Plan liabilities (dollars in millions)[c]	Plan status[d]
Executive Salaried Employees' Retirement Plan	Chrysler LLC Executive Salaried Employee's Retirement Plan	2,867	No	1,478	Closed 12/31/2003
Subsidiaries' Pension Plan	Chrysler LLC Subsidiaries' Pension Plan	1,693	No	22	Open
Chrysler UPGWA/Guards Pension Plan	Pension Agreement between Chrysler LLC and the United Plant Guard Workers of America	985	Yes	41	Frozen 9/30/2005
GEMA UAW Pension Plan	Global Engine Manufacturing Alliance UAW Pension Plan	220	Yes	1	Open
Total Chrysler		254,664[h]	-	$23,387	

Source: GM and Chrysler documents.

[a] GM participant data are as of September 30, 2008, and Chrysler participant data are as of January 1, 2008, (the most recent data available at the time of our study).

[b] A collectively bargained plan is a plan in which contributions to the plan or benefits paid by the plan (or both) are subject to the collective bargaining process. At least some or all of the employees covered by the plan are members of a collective bargaining unit that negotiates the contributions or benefits (or both).

[c] Data on plan liabilities are based on "projected benefit obligations" as measured in accordance with Financial Accounting Standards. GM data are as of December 31, 2008, and Chrysler data are as of January 1, 2009.

[d] "Closed" indicates closed to new hires, but active employees continue to accrue benefits; "frozen" indicates no employees are actively accruing benefits, sometimes called a "hard freeze"; future benefit accruals ceased as of the date indicated (unless otherwise noted). In all cases, the plan has not been terminated.

[e] The hourly plan was amended to provide a new cash balance benefit for all hourly new hires (except skilled trades) after October 15, 2007.

[f] Employees hired between January 1, 2001, and December 31, 2006, participated in a cash balance benefit under the plan, and this benefit was frozen as of December 31, 2006. Employees hired before January 1, 2001, received accrued defined benefits, and such benefits were frozen as of January 1, 2007, when a new lower defined benefit formula was implemented.

[g] Total includes a small amount of obligations (1-2 percent) for GM's unqualified salaried plan, but are the only GM data publicly available.

[h] Total simply sums participant totals across each plan and does not represent unique participants within Chrysler plans. For example, according to Chrysler officials, most Chrysler Pension Plan participants also participate in the Salaried Employees Retirement Plan and, thus, would be counted twice in the data.

Domestic automakers sponsor some of the largest private sector defined benefit plans. According to a financial publication, as of year-end 2007, GM sponsored the largest defined benefit plans by a considerable margin, with nearly 60 percent more benefit obligations than the plan sponsor ranked second: AT&T, Inc.[15] The Ford Motor Company ranked fifth. At the time, Delphi, the auto supplier that spun off from GM in 1999, ranked 18th. Chrysler was not included in the publication's list, but, as of the beginning of 2008, it had about one-fourth of GM's benefit obligations, and would have ranked in the top 10 if its total benefit obligations were included on this list. Based on data gathered for previous GAO reports, in 2004, the plans sponsored by GM and Chrysler represented roughly 7 percent of the liabilities, 7 percent of the assets, and 2.5 percent of the total participants of the entire defined benefit system.[16] The defined benefit plans that continue to be sponsored by the new GM and the new Chrysler are summarized in table 1. Unlike the new GM and new Chrysler, the "new Delphi" that emerged from Delphi's bankruptcy reorganization did not assume sponsorship of the company's pension plans. After Delphi froze its hourly pension plan in November 2008,[17] some Delphi hourly employees began to accrue credited service in the GM hourly pension plan according to the terms of agreements negotiated with various unions, while other Delphi employees did not receive similar treatment. PBGC terminated all six of Delphi's U.S. qualified defined benefit plans in July 2009.

Federal Oversight of Private Sector Pensions

Three federal agencies are charged with responsibility for overseeing and regulating tax-qualified private sector pension plans: the Internal Revenue Service (IRS), an agency within Treasury; the Employee Benefits Security Administration, an agency within Labor; and PBGC, a government corporation.[18] Two overlapping statutory sources provide the basis for this oversight: the Internal Revenue Code,[19] and the Employee Retirement Income Security Act of 1974 (ERISA).[20] These laws specify, among other things, the standards of fiduciary responsibility for managing these plans, minimum funding requirements, the requirements for reporting information to the federal government and plan participants, and plan termination insurance.

PBGC was created by ERISA in 1974 as a federal guarantor of most private sector defined benefit plans and currently insures the pension income of nearly 44 million workers in over 29,000 plans. PBGC is a self-financing entity, funding its operations through insurance premiums paid by the plan sponsors, money earned from investments, and funds received from terminated pension plans. It is governed by a three-member board of directors consisting of the Secretary of Labor as the Chair, and the Secretaries of Commerce and Treasury as the remaining members. The board of directors is ultimately responsible for providing policy direction and oversight of PBGC's finances and operations, but the board members often rely on their representatives to conduct much of the work on their behalf. Currently, the board representatives for the members are the Assistant Secretary of Labor for the Employee Benefits Security Administration, the Under Secretary for Economic Affairs at the Department of Commerce, and the Assistant Secretary of the Treasury for Financial Institutions.

PBGC administers two separate insurance programs for private sector defined benefit plans: a single-employer program and a multiemployer program.[21] The single-employer program covers about 34 million participants in about 28,000 plans.[22] The multiemployer program covers about 10 million participants in about 1,500 collectively bargained plans that are maintained by two or more unrelated employers. If a multiemployer pension plan is underfunded and unable to pay guaranteed benefits when due, PBGC will provide financial assistance to the plan, usually a loan, so that retirees continue receiving their benefits. However, if a single-employer pension plan is underfunded and certain criteria are met, the plan sponsor may request termination of the plan (referred to as a "distress" termination),[23] and PBGC will pay retirees'benefits as they become due, up to certain limits as prescribed under statute and related regulations (see appendix II). PBGC may also initiate an "involuntary" termination under certain circumstances, such as when the possible long-run loss to PBGC is expected to increase unreasonably if the plan is not terminated.[24] As of the end of fiscal year 2009, PBGC had terminated and trusteed a total of 4,003 single-employer plans.[25]

We designated PBGC's single-employer pension insurance program as "high risk" in 2003, including it on our list of major programs that need urgent attention and transformation.[26] The program remains high risk due to an ongoing threat of losses from the termination of underfunded plans. As of September 2009, PBGC had an accumulated deficit that totaled $22 billion, a $10.8 billion increase since September 2008.

NEW GM AND NEW CHRYSLER ASSUMED SPONSORSHIP OF PENSION PLANS IN RESTRUCTURING, BUT FACE FUTURE FUNDING CHALLENGES

As new companies, GM and Chrysler have streamlined their operations and have substantially less debt than their predecessors; nevertheless, the future viability of the companies and their pension plans is unclear. The bankruptcy agreements that provided for establishment of the new companies specified that they would assume sponsorship of the previous companies'U.S. qualified defined benefit plans, and made only one significant change to pension benefits. However, prior to the change in sponsorship, many of the pension plans had been closed to new hires or had ceased benefit accruals.[27] Moreover, since 2008, the funded status of the pension plans has been declining, and within the next 5 years, both companies project that, based on current estimates, they may need to make large contributions to their plans to comply with federal minimum funding requirements.

Restructuring Shifted Sponsorship of GM and Chrysler Defined Benefit Plans with Prior Changes Mostly Intact

As a result of restructuring, sponsorship for all GM and Chrysler U.S. defined benefit plans shifted to the new companies. But beyond the shift in sponsorship, the only significant change to pension benefits that occurred was the elimination of a future pension benefit increase that was to compensate UAW retirees for increased required contributions to their retiree health care plans, beginning in 2010.[28] For the most part, the terms of the restructuring called for current levels of employee benefits— including pension benefits—to remain in place for at least 1 year. Specifically, the master sale agreements for both companies stipulate that, in general, union employees are to be provided employee benefits that are "not less favorable in the aggregate" than the benefits provided under the employee pension and welfare benefit plans, and contracts and arrangements currently in place; nonunion employees are to receive current levels of compensation and benefits until at least 1 year after the date the agreements are signed.

More significant changes affecting GM's and Chrysler's pensions were made prior to last year's restructuring. For example, over the past decade, several of GM's and Chrysler's pension plans had been modified or closed to new hires, or had stopped allowing further benefit accruals. GM's salaried plan was closed and benefit accruals ceased for certain employees, while 4 of Chrysler's ten plans have been closed to new hires, and 2 other Chrysler plans have ceased benefit accruals (also referred to as being "hard frozen").[29] Nevertheless, new collective bargaining agreements were put in place in 2007 for both GM's and Chrysler's UAW-negotiated plans, calling for annual increases to the pension benefits for their participants.[30] In addition, both GM and Chrysler had implemented numerous attrition programs for both union and nonunion employees that provided various opportunities for early retirement and other types of added benefits as incentives to help mitigate the effects of downsizing. For a listing of attrition programs offered by these companies since 2004, see appendix III.

Funded Status of GM and Chrysler Pension Plans Has Been Declining

As illustrated in figure 1, the funded status of GM and Chrysler pension plans has been declining since 2008. This is due, in part, to the economic downturn, which has brought significant financial stress to many sectors of the economy, including the auto industry. The significant decline in the stock market decreased the value of certain assets (such as equities) and increased the value of others (such as bonds), while low interest rates tended to increase liabilities.[31] Fluctuations in liabilities may also be caused by changes to actuarial assumptions or other types of gains and losses.[32] However, in the case of GM and Chrysler, certain other factors are at play as well.

Similarly, Chrysler's downsizing efforts also predate TARP. For example, its decision to eliminate four models within its three primary brands dates back to November 2007, and the company has implemented various attrition programs to accomplish this.[35] Due in part to these programs, over the past few years, Chrysler's pension liabilities have fluctuated while plan assets have been declining (see fig. 3). For example, Chrysler's UAW plan reported a $900 million increase in liabilities from 2007 to 2008, and the plan's 2008 valuation report noted that the cost of special termination benefits during 2008 were nearly $390 million. Total liabilities for the Chrysler Pension Plan increased by a smaller margin overall from 2007 to 2008, but the plan's 2008 valuation report noted that nearly $195 million in additional costs were being recorded due to special early retirements, added service costs, and curtailment loss.

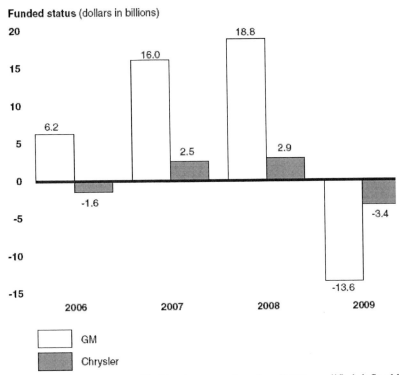

Source: GAO analysis of documents provided by the automakers for all U.S. qualified defined benefit plans each sponsors.

Note: Funded status reflects measurements in accordance with Financial Accounting Standards. For each year, the data for GM's plans are as of December 31 of the preceding year; the data for Chrysler's plans are as of January 1 of the year cited. GM's data include a small amount of obligations (1-2 percent) for the unqualified salaried plan, but are the only GM data publicly available.

Figure 1. Trends in the Funded Status of GM's and Chrysler's Pension Plans (2006- 2009).

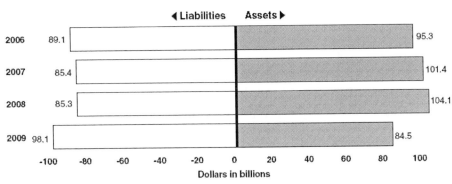

Source: GAO analysis of GM documents for both U.S. qualified defined benefit plans sponsored by GM.

Note: Plan liabilities (based on "projected benefit obligations") and assets reflect measurements in accordance with Financial Accounting Standards. For each year, the data are as of December 31 of the preceding year. Data include a small amount of obligations (1-2 percent) for GM's unqualified salaried plan, but are the only GM data publicly available.

Figure 2. Trends in GM's Pension Plans' Liabilities and Assets.

For example, a reduction in the number of workers is one key factor affecting the funded status of both companies' plans. Large numbers of workers have left employment as product lines are eliminated and plants are shut down. When workers are forced to leave their jobs before becoming eligible to retire, the liabilities for their expected future benefits will usually be less than previously recorded. However, for those workers who are eligible to retire early and choose to do so under the enhanced provisions of one of the numerous attrition programs, the liabilities for their expected future benefits will usually be greater than previously recorded. In other words, more workers will retire early and with more benefits than previously anticipated in the company's valuation of future benefit obligations.

GM began its downsizing even before its TARP-related restructuring efforts reduced the number of its North American brands from eight to four. According to a GM news release, approximately 66,000 U.S. hourly workers left the company under a special attrition program between 2006 and 2009.[33] Often the lump-sum payments and buyouts offered by these programs were paid from company assets, but when these benefits are paid from pension assets, there can be an impact on the plan's financial status.[34] GM noted that the attrition programs implemented between 2006 and 2009 contributed to an increase of estimated plan obligations during this period and—along with other factors, such as discount rate changes—played a role in the recent increase in GM's pension liabilities (see fig. 2).

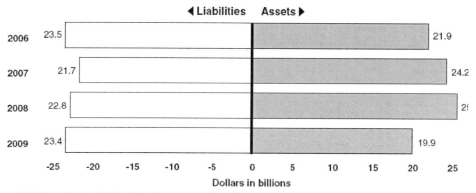

Source: GAO analysis of Chrysler documents for all U.S. qualified defined benefit plans sponsored by Chrysler.

Note: Plan liabilities (based on "projected benefit obligations") and assets reflect measurements in accordance with Financial Accounting Standards. For each year, the data are as of January 1 of the year cited.

Figure 3. Trends in Chrysler's Pension Plans' Liabilities and Assets.

Other factors that have affected the funded status of both GM's and Chrysler's plans are the special arrangements made with other companies in conjunction with acquisitions and divestitures.[36] For example, when an auto parts supplier, the former Delphi Corporation, was spun off from GM in 1999, the transaction included a negotiated agreement with various unions for a benefit guarantee for certain employees in the event that Delphi's hourly pension plan would be frozen or terminated.[37] When the company froze its hourly plan on November 30, 2008, as agreed, GM began providing covered employees with up to 7 years of credited service in the GM hourly plan while they continued to work at Delphi. Under this negotiated benefit guarantee, GM also agreed that upon plan termination, once PBGC determined the benefit to be paid subject to its guarantee limits, GM would pay eligible covered employees the difference to "top up" the benefit to the level provided under Delphi's hourly plan. Following the termination of Delphi's hourly plan in July 2009, GM estimated that the cost of implementing this benefit guarantee for all covered unions would be approximately $1.0 billion. In addition to the benefit guarantee for Delphi employees still in the Delphi hourly plan, in the fall of 2008, GM's hourly plan assumed responsibility for $2.7 billion in liabilities and $0.6 billion in assets from Delphi's plan, thereby increasing the GM plan's funding deficit by $2.1 billion.[38]

When Chrysler was sold by Daimler in 2007, the transaction included an agreement with Daimler to help protect the funded status of Chrysler's pension plans.[39] As part of this transaction, PBGC negotiated an agreement whereby Daimler provided a $1 billion termination guarantee and Chrysler made $200 million in additional pension contributions. Subsequently, in April 2009, this agreement was replaced by a new arrangement requiring Daimler to begin making annual contributions, even though the plans had not terminated. Under this arrangement, Daimler agreed to make payments totaling $600 million to Chrysler's pension plans over a 3-year period, with $200 million due in June 2009, 2010, and 2011. In addition, if the Chrysler pension plans were to terminate before August 2012 and are trusteed by PBGC, Daimler is to pay an additional $200 million to the PBGC insurance program.

Both Automakers Project Large Contributions to Plans Will Be Required within the Next Five Years

Although projections of plan funding are inherently sensitive to underlying assumptions, GM and Chrysler currently estimate that they may need to make large contributions to their pension plans within the next 5 years in order to meet minimum funding requirements.[40] They also may need to manage the funded status of their plans in order to avoid certain plan benefit restrictions and potential additional liabilities that may occur if the plans are determined to be "at risk."[41]

While useful as indicators of the financial pressures that could lie ahead, the funding projections provided by GM and Chrysler are subject to much uncertainty because of factors that could result in changes in the size or timing of needed contributions to meet future years' funding requirements. For example, projections are particularly sensitive to the future economic environment, especially with respect to future interest rates and asset returns. Also, GM or Chrysler could make additional voluntary contributions to their plans, or funding rules could be affected by changes in legislation.

To strengthen pension funding, the Pension Protection Act of 2006 (PPA) made sweeping changes to plan funding requirements, effective for plan years beginning in 2008.[42] For example, the act included provisions that raised the funding targets for defined benefit plans, reduced the period for "smoothing" assets and liabilities, and restricted sponsors' ability to substitute credit balances for cash contributions. At the same time, as we have reported previously, the act did not fully close potential plan funding gaps, and it provided funding relief to plan sponsors in troubled industries.[43] In addition, in the face of a weakened economy, the Worker, Retiree, and Employer Recovery Act of 2008 provided plan sponsors with further relief from the changes,[44] as did IRS guidance in 2009 concerning interest rates that could be used to value plan liabilities in some cases.[45] Legislative proposals that would make additional changes to funding requirements are currently being considered.[46]

Nevertheless, according to GM's projections utilizing valuation methods defined under PPA, large cash contributions may be needed to meet its funding obligations to its U.S. pension plans beginning in 2013 (see fig. 4). GM officials told us that cash contributions are not expected to be needed for the next few years because it has a relatively large "credit balance" based on contributions made in prior years that can be used to offset cash contribution requirements that would otherwise be required until that time.[47] As of October 1, 2008, GM had about $36 billion of credit balance in its hourly plan and about $10 billion in its salaried plan. However, once these credit balances are exhausted, GM projects that the contributions needed to meet its defined benefit plan funding requirements will total about $12.3 billion for the years 2013 and 2014, and additional contributions may be required thereafter. In its 2008 year-end report, GM noted that due to significant declines in financial markets and deterioration in the value of its plans' assets, as well as the coverage of additional retirees, including Delphi employees, it may need to make significant contributions to its U.S. plans in 2013 and beyond.[48]

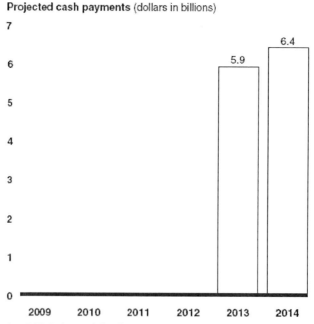

Source: GAO analysis of GM planned funding projections for both U.S. qualified defined benefit plans sponsored by GM.

Note: Funding projections reflect audited data as of December 31, 2008 (the most recent publicly available at the time of our study). Projections utilize valuation methods for required contributions defined under PPA, and include any temporary funding relief as provided by the Worker, Retiree, and Employer Recovery Act of 2008.

Figure 4. Projected Calendar Year Contributions to GM's Pension Plans (2009-2014).

Similarly, Chrysler's management expects that contributions to meet minimum funding requirements may begin to increase significantly in 2013, but are projected to be relatively minimal until then (see fig. 5). Chrysler, like GM, intends to use credit balances to offset the contribution requirements for some of its plans. As of end-of-year 2009, Chrysler had credit balances of about $3.5 billion for its UAW Pension Plan and about $1.9 billion across the other eight plans for which it provided funding information. In addition, Chrysler also has $600 million in payments from Daimler to help meet its funding requirements over the next few years.[49] Nevertheless, Chrysler's funding projections reveal that about $3.4 billion in contributions may be needed to meet its funding requirements over the 2009 to 2015 period.[50]

In addition, both GM and Chrysler may need to manage the funded status of their plans in order to avoid incurring an "at-risk" status or triggering certain benefit restrictions. If a plan's funding level falls below certain specified thresholds, then it must use special "at-risk" actuarial assumptions to determine its minimum funding requirements and, in most cases, increase its contributions.[51] For example, the most recent annual funding notice for the GM hourly plan reveals that the plan is in at-risk status for plan year 2008.[52,53]

Also, if a plan's funding level falls below certain specified thresholds, then certain restrictions may be placed on the benefits provided by the plan, such as lump sum withdrawals and plant shutdown benefits (see table 2).[54]

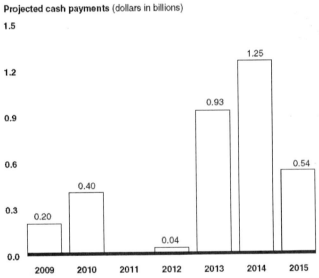

Source: GAO analysis of Chrysler planned funding projections for all U.S. qualified defined benefit plans sponsored by Chrysler.

Note: Funding projections include unaudited data for nine of Chrysler's ten plans provided to GAO in February 2010 (no information was provided for one plan). Projections utilize valuation methods for required contributions defined under PPA. For six of the nine plans with data, the projections explicitly included any temporary funding relief as provided by the Worker, Retiree, and Employer Act of 2008, except for a provision relating to adjustments, or "smoothing," to the value of plan assets.

Figure 5. Projected Calendar Year Contributions to Chrysler's Pension Plans (2009-2015).

Table 2. Benefit Restrictions Based on a Plan's Funded Status

If a plan's funded status:[a]	Then, there is a restriction against:
At least 80 percent, but would be less than 80 percent taking the amendment into account	•plan amendments to increase benefits
At least 60 percent, but less than 80 percent	•50 percent benefits paid in a lump sum (i.e., accelerated benefit payments)
At least 60 percent, but would be less than 60 percent, taking the unpredictable contingent event benefit into account	•unpredictable contingent event benefits (i.e., shutdown benefits)
Less than 60 percent	•future benefit accruals (i.e., accruals are frozen) •all lump sum payments (i.e., acceleratedbenefit payments) •unpredictable contingent event benefits (i.e., shutdown benefits)

Source: GAO analysis.

[a] Funded status described here is based on the "adjusted funding target attainment percentage." This percentage is the ratio of a plan's assets, reduced by any credit balances, to the value of the plan's liabilities (referred to as the "funding target attainment percentage") adjusted by adding the value of certain annuities. Special rules apply in bankruptcy.

ECONOMIC STRESS IN AUTO INDUSTRY HAS ENDANGERED AUTO SUPPLIER PENSIONS

Automaker restructuring, the credit market crisis, and the global recession have created significant economic stress across the auto supply industry. Federal efforts to aid the supply sector through a program that provided GM and Chrysler with funding to guarantee supplier payments benefited the automakers' top-level direct suppliers, but did little to support component and raw material suppliers. The restructuring of GM and Chrysler amid this difficult economic environment has had a ripple effect throughout the auto supply sector, likely contributing to the recent wave of supplier bankruptcies and pension plan terminations.

Automaker Restructuring and Current Economic Conditions Have Created Significant Financial Stress for Suppliers

The auto supply sector is highly dependent on the success of the automakers that it supplies. For years, the auto supply sector has felt the impact of the problems facing the domestic auto market, including declining vehicle sales, and deep production cuts—resulting in overcapacity within the industry. In 2004, the Department of Commerce reported that the possibility of relying on increased auto sales that automatically translate into increased orders and components for U.S. suppliers no longer existed because U.S. automobile manufacturers had shifted from providing a ready market for many domestic suppliers of parts and components to operating on a global basis. The result of this shift was that automotive parts suppliers had to find niches in the global supply chains of U.S. auto companies or their foreign competitors to succeed.

Many auto suppliers broadened their sales base to remain competitive. With the domestic share of the market in decline, these suppliers diversified their business models to include just-in-time manufacturing capacity or sold their products to multiple automakers in North America, Europe, and Asia. For example, at the time it filed for bankruptcy, the U.S. auto parts supplier, Delphi Corporation, employed more than 185,000 workers in 38 countries in 2004, making it one of the largest suppliers in the world.[55] Still, according to a 2009 industry report, just 7 of the 29 U.S.- based suppliers listed among the top 100 global suppliers sold the majority of their products in North America. Suppliers serving the large U.S. automakers also have considerable overlap, with as many as 80 percent supplying parts to one or more automaker. For example, Chrysler reported that 96 percent of its top 100 suppliers also served either GM or Ford. Similarly, 27 of GM's top 39 suppliers also served as major suppliers for Chrysler. While this crossover allowed suppliers to spread their risk among domestic automakers, the impact of the global economic downturn affected many suppliers, and left suppliers that sold primarily to GM and Chrysler particularly vulnerable when the automakers filed for bankruptcy.

The recent global credit crisis and the rapid decline in auto sales left many of the nation's auto parts suppliers under significant stress with limited access to credit and facing growing uncertainty about their future business prospects. For example, GM's and Chrysler's decision to slow production by temporarily shutting down some U.S. operations in late 2008 led to interruptions in suppliers' operations and cash flow. As a result, many suppliers were left with excess inventory, were not paid for products they had shipped to automakers, and lacked the liquidity needed to settle their debts with their raw material and component suppliers. Concerns over the ability of the organizations to continue operations and, among other things, collect their receivables and pay their bills when due, led some suppliers to receive a "going concern" qualification from their auditors.[56] Lenders restricted credit and cash flow to suppliers, limiting their liquidity at the time when it was needed most. With limited cash flow, the suppliers experienced increasing pressure from their raw material and component suppliers. According to Chrysler, 43 percent of its suppliers had received requests from their suppliers for some form of payment term compression. Chrysler recognized the liquidity shortfall in the supplier network as a significant threat to its successful restructuring, and identified supplier insolvencies and supply chain disruptions as key risks to the critical assumptions in its restructuring plan. Another industry report indicated that at least 500 suppliers in North America (or 30 percent of the estimated 1,700 direct suppliers in the U.S.) may be at high risk of insolvency due to the effect of reduced volumes and the lack of credit availability. This credit crunch also affected bankrupt companies, which found securing financing to restructure their companies increasingly difficult.

Federal Assistance Program Helped Avert Catastrophe, but Provided Limited Support to Smaller Suppliers

In an effort to help stabilize the auto supply base, in March 2009, also under TARP, Treasury established the Auto Supplier Support Program, which initially dedicated up to $5 billion in government-backed guarantees to GM and Chrysler for supplier payments in order to give suppliers the confidence they needed to keep shipping parts, paying their employees, and continuing operations. Treasury had rejected appeals from the auto supply sector for direct aid to assist a broader portion of the supplier industry because, according to Treasury officials, it had become clear that the vast network of suppliers had to engage in a substantial restructuring and capacity reduction to achieve long-term viability. The program was to ensure that GM and Chrysler received the parts and components they needed to manufacture vehicles and suppliers had access to credit from lenders. Under the program, any supplier that shipped directly to GM or Chrysler on qualifying commercial terms could be eligible to participate. Treasury left it up to the automakers to determine which suppliers qualified for the assistance. According to GM, 74 percent of its 1,300 suppliers were eligible for the program, but only 28 percent of its suppliers (38 percent of its eligible suppliers) received funds under the program.[57] Nearly half of the $947.8 million in program funds that GM dispersed went to 31 of its top 40 suppliers.[58] Shortly after the program began, Treasury reduced the amount of funding available under this program to $3.5 billion, at the request of the automakers. According to Treasury officials, the automakers made this request because conditions had changed: they no longer needed to maintain their prebankruptcy supply capacity, credit markets had opened up, and suppliers' access to capital had improved.

The program, as administered, helped a portion of the industry survive the downturn in production and vehicle sales, but did little to improve supplier access to traditional sources of capital, according to a leading auto supply industry group. The group noted that the program supported suppliers by making funds available to purchase receivables for parts already shipped by participating suppliers, but that many troubled suppliers who had no outstanding debts to the automakers were excluded. According to Treasury officials, the program was not designed to address liquidity for troubled suppliers who were unable to move their inventory and had no receivables, including from GM and Chrysler, due to the extended shutdowns at the manufacturing plants. However, the group also noted that the suppliers who participated in the program were generally satisfied with the outcome, and that the supply sector as a whole believed that without the government's action, the effect of automakers' restructuring would have been catastrophic for suppliers.

Suppliers Have Experienced a Wave of Bankruptcies and Pension Plan Terminations

Bankruptcy reorganizations and liquidations occur frequently in the volatile automotive supply sector, but the number of bankruptcies has recently increased. Some suppliers have gone bankrupt multiple times in a decade, while other suppliers have remained in bankruptcy proceedings for years before successfully emerging as a new entity. For example, the "new Delphi" (Delphi Automotive, LLP) emerged in 2009 after the former Delphi had been in bankruptcy proceedings for 4 years. Auto suppliers experienced a rise in the number of bankruptcies, liquidations, and pension plan terminations in 2008 and 2009. In November 2009, a survey by the Original Equipment Suppliers Association (Association)—a leading auto supply industry group—found that a majority of suppliers anticipated a 20 percent decline in their revenue and operating profits on a year-to-year basis. The Association also reported that at least 43 U.S. based auto suppliers had filed for Chapter 11 bankruptcy protection between January and December 2009. Moreover, it was reported that an additional 200 U.S. suppliers had begun the liquidation process by selling off their assets to other suppliers or private equity companies. Chrysler reported that the proportion of its suppliers that were financially troubled had more than doubled, from 10 percent in October 2008 to 22 percent in February 2009, with the troubled suppliers accounting for $6.6 billion of the company's annual business. In addition, in the summer of 2009, a consultant group estimated that as many as 30 percent of North American suppliers were at high risk of failure. According to Treasury officials, many of Chrysler's troubled suppliers had difficulty accessing credit because of their concentrated exposure to Chrysler.

In the summer of 2009, the auto supply sector was also expected to shrink significantly through mergers and consolidation in order to survive. According to the Association's survey of its membership in June 2009, auto suppliers were operating at 46.4 percent capacity. In its restructuring plan, Chrysler stated that industry conditions required substantial and coordinated restructuring of the supply base, and that automakers must concentrate their business in "surviving" suppliers. GM projected a 30 percent reduction in the number of suppliers, stating that such compression would allow GM to build and manage a competitive supply base. Several industry consultants noted that the path to long-term viability would require suppliers to reduce their number by 30 to 40 percent and secure more business from Asian and European transplant automakers. However, by early 2010, there were signs that the economic conditions for suppliers may have begun to stabilize. The Association's January 2010 and March 2010 surveys of its membership reported increased optimism across the sector, especially among larger companies.

Table 3. Funded Status of Selected Suppliers' Defined Benefit Pension Plans (2008)

Dollars in millions		
Supplier name	In bankruptcy proceedings in 2009	Unfunded pensionliabilities
Delphi Corporation	Xa	$5,264.0
Honeywell International		3,526.0
Goodyear Tire & Rubber		2,129.0
Eaton Corporation		1,614.0
Johnson Controls, Inc.		402.0
TRW Automotive Holdings		361.0
Visteon	X	326.0
Lear Corporation	X	254.7
American Axle and Manufacturing Holdings, Inc.		254.5
Tenneco, Inc.		169.0
Dana Holding Corporation		149.0
Cooper-Standard Holdings	X	89.1
BorgWarner, Inc.		87.1
Hayes Lemmerz International	Xa	70.8
Dura Automotive Systems, Inc.		65.3
ArvinMeritor, Inc.		42.0
Modine Manufacturing Company		35.3
Accuride	X	26.8
Total		$14,865.6

Source: GAO analysis of recent corporate annual reports and filings. Data are for fiscal years ending in 2008 or 2009.
[a] Suppliers with pension plans that have been terminated and trusteed by PBGC.

Many U.S.-based auto suppliers sponsor defined benefit plans that are insured by PBGC. Each company failure could potentially result in PBGC having to assume responsibility for its pension plans, and PBGC officials told us that they are monitoring about 35 large auto suppliers. Even before last year's restructuring of GM and Chrysler, suppliers (like many other employers) were experiencing significant underfunding of their defined benefit plans. Table 3 shows 18 auto suppliers we identified that reported a combined $14.9 billion in unfunded pension liabilities in 2008.

In 2009, several of GM and Chrysler's suppliers filed for bankruptcy, and in some cases, PBGC intervened and assumed trusteeship of the companies' defined benefit plans. For example, in July 2009, PBGC terminated and assumed responsibility for the pension plans of 70,000 workers and retirees of the former Delphi Corporation, citing Delphi's inability to afford to maintain the plans. More specifically, according to PBGC officials, the key factors that led to this action were Delphi's failure to fund its pensions during bankruptcy, and the company's imminent sale and liquidation of its assets as it left bankruptcy protection. Other suppliers avoided bankruptcy, but still felt the effects of the slumping auto industry. For example, American Axle and Manufacturing Holdings, Inc., an auto part supplier that narrowly averted bankruptcy in 2009, estimated that the GM and Chrysler factory shutdowns had cost the company $100.6 million in sales and $29.3 million in operating income.

While some recent reports have indicated that the outlook for the automakers and suppliers may be improving, the ability of suppliers to fund their defined benefit plans in the future will rest, in part, on the continued viability of the automakers. Moreover, any revival in the auto supply sector may come too late for workers who have already had their pension plans terminated and their benefits reduced to the PBGC benefit guarantee levels.[59]

BOTH PBGC AND PLAN PARTICIPANTS INCUR LOSSES WHEN UNDERFUNDED PLANS ARE TERMINATED

When an underfunded defined benefit plan is terminated, the PBGC bears the costs of any unfunded liabilities up to the guaranteed benefit amounts defined by ERISA, while plan participants bear the loss of benefits beyond these guaranteed amounts that would go unpaid.[60] According to Treasury officials, there is no indication that any of GM's or Chrysler's defined benefit plans will be terminated. Nevertheless, to hypothetically examine the potential impact if their plans were to be terminated, we explored how PBGC and plan participants would have been affected had the plans been terminated when these companies filed for bankruptcy in 2009, and the factors at play that could change that picture if the plans were to be terminated 5 years later.

PBGC's Exposure Signals Potential Impacts on Both its Deficit and its Resources

Following the termination of an underfunded defined benefit plan, PBGC generally incurs losses that affect its deficit, as well as its resources. With respect to its deficit, the amount of loss to the single-employer fund is equal to the value of the unfunded guaranteed benefits required to be paid under ERISA.[61] Although this is generally considerably less than the total value of unfunded liabilities in a large auto sector pension plan, the loss can still be substantial. With respect to its resources, PBGC must assume responsibility for administering the terminated plan, including continuing benefit payments to retirees, determining the assets and liabilities of the plan as of the date of termination, calculating the guaranteed and nonguaranteed benefit amounts owed each participant in the plan, and keeping participants informed. When plans are large and complex, this can be an enormous task, requiring years to complete.

PBGC's Deficit-Related Exposure

Each year, PBGC assesses its exposure to losses from underfunded pension plans sponsored by financially weak companies. Its estimates of exposure are based on companies with credit ratings below investment grade or that meet one or more of the criteria for financial distress. PBGC classifies the plans sponsored by these companies as "reasonably possible" terminations.[62] At the end of fiscal year 2009, PBGC estimated that its exposure from reasonably possible terminations was approximately $168 billion, up from $47 billion a year earlier.[63] A significant part of this increase was due to the dramatic increase in exposure related to manufacturing, which PBGC attributed primarily to changes in the auto industry, as well as primary and fabricated metals (see fig. 6).

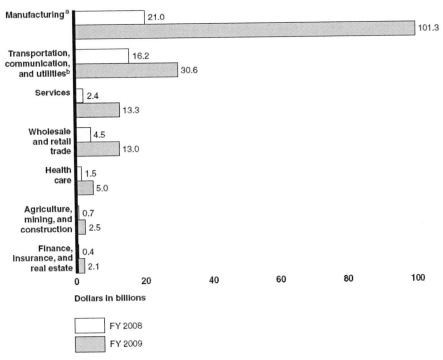

Source:
[a] For fiscal years 2008 and 2009, manufacturing exposure was primarily from automobiles, auto parts, and primary and fabricated metals.
[b] For fiscal years 2008 and 2009, transportation exposure was primarily from airlines.

Figure 6. PBGC's Estimate of Possible Exposure to Loss by Industry.

In May 2009, PBGC reported that unfunded pension liabilities across the auto industry as a whole totaled about $77 billion as of January 31, 2009, and accounted for about $42 billion of PBGC's total exposure of $168 billion.[64] This means that, should all the auto industry's underfunded plans insured by PBGC be terminated and trusteed, PBGC would be required to cover about $42 billion of the benefit amounts promised, adding to its deficit. Between the end of fiscal years 2008 and 2009, the deficit in PBGC's single-employer insurance program doubled in size from $10.7 billion to $21.1 billion.[65] Should all the underfunded auto industry plans fail, PBGC's January 2009 estimate indicated that its end of fiscal year 2009 deficit could triple in size. An increase of this magnitude would have implications not just for PBGC's accumulated deficit, but for its overall funding going forward, as the auto industry is responsible for contributing a significant portion of PBGC's premiums each year. According to PBGC's most recent data book, the motor vehicle equipment industry accounted for about 1.2 percent of all insured plans under the single-employer insurance program in 2007, but 6.1 percent of all insured participants and 7.3 percent of all premiums.

With respect to PBGC's exposure for GM's and Chrysler's pension plans in particular, PBGC calculated its potential exposure prior to when the new companies assumed sponsorship of the plans. Before the change in sponsorship, PBGC estimated that its exposure for GM's unfunded guaranteed benefits would be about $9.0 billion, and that its exposure for Chrysler's unfunded guaranteed benefits would be about $5.5 billion (see table 4).

Table 4. PBGC's Estimates of Potential Exposure for GM's and Chrysler's Pension Plans in Early 2009

	Estimated unfunded benefit liabilities	Estimated unfunded guaranteed benefit liabilities	Estimated unfunded nonguaranteed benefit liabilities	Estimated number of participants
GM	$27.3	$9.0	$18.3	673,286
Chrysler	10.4	5.5	4.9	249,251
Total	$37.7	$14.5	$23.2	922,537

Source: PBGC estimates, calculated on a termination liability basis.

Notes: GM estimates are as of January 31, 2009; Chrysler estimates are as of April 30, 2009—the most recent PBGC estimates available. Totals exclude pension plans that are fully funded. PBGC officials note that volatility in plan asset returns and valuation discount rates may cause significant changes in these estimates over time.

Even without the change in sponsorship, actual losses to PBGC could be substantially different, as estimates of exposure are inherently difficult to calculate. For example, the significant volatility in plan underfunding and sponsor creditworthiness over time makes long-term estimates of PBGC's expected claims difficult. Moreover, there is a time lag in making these estimates. Estimates of exposure are generally based on company reports filed as of December 31 of the previous year. Thus, the dramatic increase in PBGC's aggregate reasonably possible exposure between fiscal years 2008 and 2009 depicted in figure 6 was primarily due to the deterioration of credit quality and poor asset returns that occurred during calendar year 2008. Subsequent changes in economic conditions (such as the steady rise in equity returns since March 2009) were not yet reflected in these estimates. In addition, actual losses due to terminated plans depend on PBGC's liability only for unfunded guaranteed benefits, but this is not factored into the estimates because it is difficult to determine the extent and effect of the limits on guaranteed benefits prior to actual termination.[66]

However, PBGC's exposure for unfunded guaranteed benefits in the auto supply sector has already begun to materialize. Over the past year, the plans of several large suppliers were terminated and trusteed by PBGC, and PBGC estimates that the unfunded guaranteed benefits that it will be required to pay to participants in the plans of these large suppliers will exceed $6.6 billion (see table 5). The estimate for the pension plans of the former Delphi Corporation alone is over $6.2 billion.

To help protect against further exposure, according to PBGC's 2009 annual report, the agency was continuing to monitor the auto industry and negotiate settlements for additional pension protections in several auto-related corporate downsizing cases. For example, in the case of Visteon Corporation, a large automotive supplier, PBGC negotiated an agreement in January 2009 that required Visteon to provide over $55 million in additional protections to workers at closed facilities by making cash contributions to the plan, a letter of credit to PBGC, and a guaranty by certain affiliates of certain contingent pension obligations. Similarly, in the case of Cooper Tire & Rubber Company, PBGC negotiated a deal in August 2009 that required the plan sponsor to strengthen the plan by $62 million, in connection with a plant closing in Albany, Georgia. According to PBGC, such protections can help prevent plan termination or, in the event that the plan does terminate, reduce the losses to the insurance program and participants.[67]

Table 5. Auto Supplier Pension Plans Terminated and Trusteed by PBGC, May 2009–January 2010

Supplier	Estimated unfunded benefit liabilities	Estimated unfunded guaranteed benefit liabilities	Estimated unfunded nonguaranteed benefit liabilities	Estimated number of participants
Delphi Corporation				
•Hourly Plan	$4,500.0	$3,800.0	$700.0	47,176
•Salaried Plan	2,700.0	2,200.0	500.0	20,203
•Other plans	65.0	60.0	5.0	2,229
Metaldyne Corporation	157.0	153.0	4.0	10,771
Hayes-Lemmerz International	94.4	93.7	0.7	4,786
Foamex LP	79.0	76.0	3.0	5,504
Fluid Routing Solutions Inc.	29.7	24.9	4.8	2,400
Proliance International, Inc.	17.0	17.0	0.0	1,620
Contech U.S., LLC	13.6	12.0	1.6	532
Stant Manufacturing, Inc.	9.0	8.9	0.1	900
Total	$7,664.7	$6,445.5	$1,219.2	96,121

Source: GAO analysis of PBGC estimated data for each plan as of February 2010.

PBGC's Resource-Related Exposure

If PBGC were to become trustee of GM's and Chrysler's auto plans, the impact on its resources would be unprecedented. As illustrated in figure 7, the number of participants and trust fund assets that PBGC is responsible for managing would increase dramatically. Moreover, in addition to their sheer size, these plans have many of the characteristics that contribute to complexity and delays in processing, such as a history of mergers, complicated benefit formulas, movement of participants and assets across plans, and large numbers of participants subject to one or more of the legal limits on guaranteed benefits.[68]

Among plans terminated and trusteed by PBGC, the average number of participants per plan is just under 1,000,[69] but most of GM's and Chrysler's plans far exceed this average. For example, as of the end of September 2008, GM's hourly plan had over 500,000 participants, and its salaried plan had nearly 200,000. Based on counts as of the beginning of 2008 (the most recent available), Chrysler's UAW Plan had about 135,000 participants, and the Chrysler Pension Plan had about 44,000 participants. Only two of Chrysler's ten plans had less than 1,000 participants. Taken together, the number of participants in these two companies' pension plans is equal to about 40 percent of all the participants in all the plans terminated and trusteed by PBGC since the agency was established in 1974. Even more striking, taken together, the amount of assets in these two companies' pension plans exceeds—by a considerable margin—the total amount of assets that PBGC is currently managing for all the plans it has trusteed combined (see fig. 6).

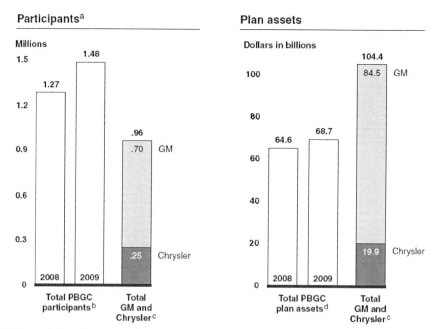

Source: GAO analysis of PBGC and automakers' documents.
[a] Participant data for PBGC and the automakers is summed by plan; therefore, employees who participate in more than one plan are counted multiple times.
[b] PBGC data includes participants in all plans terminated and trusteed under the single-employer insurance program. (A very small number of payees—fewer than 200—are from multiemployer plans that were terminated and trusteed prior to October 1980. Since October 1980, PBGC no longer assumes trusteeship or pays benefits to participants of terminated multiemployer plans.)
[c] Automaker data include all U.S.-based defined benefit plans under each company's sponsorship. GM's participant data are as of September 30, 2008, and Chrysler's participant data are as of January 1, 2008 (most recent data available). Data on plan assets reflect measurements in accordance with Financial Accounting Standards. GM data are as of December 31, 2008; Chrysler data are as of January 1, 2009.
[d] PBGC data includes assets for all plans terminated and trusteed under the single-employer insurance program.

Figure 7. Size of GM's and Chrysler's Plans Compared with Total PBGC-Trusteed Plans.

In addition to their large size, GM's and Chrysler's plans have many of the characteristics that, as delineated in a previous report,[70] contribute to complexity and delay in processing. For example, both GM and Chrysler have long histories of acquisitions, mergers, and divestitures, stretching over the past century (see appendix V). To determine the potential impact on any current or future retirees or beneficiaries of the plan, documentation concerning each change must be obtained, along with data about any affected employees. An employee's movement from one plan to another also can cause complexity in benefit calculations. Even within a plan, tiers can be created that treat some employees differently and make benefit calculations more complicated. For example, at both GM and Chrysler, different formulas were created for employees based on such things as the date employees began participating in their plans or whether or not they contributed to their plans.

Delays also result when PBGC must adjust participants'benefits to comply with legal requirements. PBGC guarantees participants'benefits only up to certain limits, specified under ERISA and related regulations.[71] Among GM's and Chrysler's plans, certain provisions and characteristics of participants suggest that many would likely be subject to one or more of these limits should the plans be terminated, as discussed further in the next section. Recent changes in the law added new provisions concerning the treatment of certain events, such as plant shutdowns and attrition programs (referred to as "unpredictable contingent events").[72] PBGC has begun to grapple with some of these complexities following the termination of the Delphi plans, as many of the benefits provided by the Delphi plans reflect negotiations with UAW and are similar to benefits provided by UAW plans across the auto sector.

In its 2009 annual report, PBGC noted that it has been taking steps to prepare for the possible trusteeship of large auto industry plans by defining the changes to its infrastructure that would be needed to handle the increase in workload. The types of changes examined as part of this effort included expanded contracts, additional staff, and increased capacity in its information technology system.

High Earners and Early Retirees Are Most at Risk for Reduced Benefits

When ERISA's guarantees do not cover all pension benefits promised by an underfunded plan that is terminated, those participants whose benefits are reduced share in the losses from the plan's termination. In many cases involving terminated and trusteed plans, participants'full benefit amounts are guaranteed and their benefits are not reduced as a result of the termination. But in cases involving complex plans with generous benefit structures such as GM's and Chrysler's, large numbers of participants are likely to have benefits subject to the guarantee limits and, depending on the extent of plan underfunding at termination, these participants would be at risk of having their benefits reduced as a result. When PBGC calculated its exposure across the auto sector as a whole in January 2009—prior to the shift in sponsorship of GM's and Chrysler's plans to the new companies—PBGC estimated that about $35 billion in unfunded liabilities would be nonguaranteed benefits; that is, plan participants would bear losses for about $35 billion in benefits not funded by the company and not guaranteed by PBGC if all the at-risk underfunded plans across the sector were terminated. Of this $35 billion, about half ($18 billion) was attributable to GM's plans, and another $5 billion was attributable to Chrysler's plans.

Participants most often affected by the application of guaranteed benefit limits are high earners whose benefits exceed the maximum limit,[73] those who take early retirement, and those whose benefits increased due to recent plan amendments. We were unable to obtain precise data on the number of GM and Chrysler plan participants whose benefits might be reduced due to these limits; however, GM and Chrysler pension plans provide several options for early retirement, with supplemental benefits to those who retire before age 62 as a bridge to Social Security benefits. Under one type of guarantee limit (the accrued-at-normal limit),[74] any supplements being provided to retirees as of the date of plan termination, and any supplements to be provided to future retirees, would not be guaranteed. According to PBGC officials, a significant number of GM and Chrysler participants could be vulnerable to having their benefits reduced due to this limit should the pension plans be terminated. In addition, retirees whose benefits reflect increases in the 5 years prior to the date of plan termination could be subject to another type of guarantee limit (the phase-in limit).[75] For example, if GM's and Chrysler's plans had been terminated in 2009, this limit would have affected the increases in benefits provided in the 2007 UAW contracts negotiated with both GM and Chrysler, causing only a part of those increases to be guaranteed.[76] The increases included as benefit enhancements offered as part of recent attrition programs would be subject to the phase-in limit, as well.[77]

Although many participants would likely lose some portion of their nonguaranteed benefits if the automakers' plans were terminated, not all would be at equal risk. This is because when a pension plan is terminated and trusteed by PBGC, ERISA specifies that the remaining assets of the plan and any funds recovered for the plan from company assets be allocated to participant benefits according to a certain priority order (see appendix VI).[78] Due to this allocation process, if GM and Chrysler plans were terminated, participants who were retired (or eligible to retire) for at least 3 years would be most likely to have some or all of their nonguaranteed benefits paid, while those participants who retired early— especially those who retired under one of the special attrition programs— would be most at risk for having their benefits reduced.[79]

Passage of Time Would Shift Termination Losses for PBGC and Plan Participants

The exposure to loss from plan termination would shift over time, but it is unclear whether PBGC or plan participants would be better off as a result. Hypothetically, if plans were to terminate 5 years into the future—in 2014 instead of 2009—overall losses could either increase or decrease, and how those losses would be shared between PBGC and plan participants would likely shift as well. For example, plan assets could grow or diminish over time, depending on investment returns and employer contributions. Plan liabilities could also grow or diminish over time, depending on interest rates, ages of participants, and whether benefits are revised in future years. In addition, more participants could acquire vested benefits over time, increasing liabilities; while more benefits would have been paid over time, decreasing liabilities.

How the losses due to unfunded benefits would be shared between PBGC (for guaranteed benefits) and plan participants (for nonguaranteed benefits) could also shift over time. For example, participants' monthly amount of guaranteed benefits would increase over time for three main reasons: (1) more workers would be eligible to retire with more generous benefits, based on years of service; (2) the maximum limits are updated each year and thus would increase, and people would grow older, so the cutbacks due to this limit would grow smaller; and (3) the benefit reductions due to the phase-in limit would be phased out. This increase in the monthly amount of guaranteed benefits would tend to shift costs from participants to PBGC. Meanwhile, over time, more participants will have been retired (or eligible to retire) for 3 years or more, and thus have benefits eligible for higher priority status in the asset allocation process.[80] In addition to shifting the distribution of benefits to be paid among different groups of participants, this could also cause more of the plan's remaining assets to be allocated to guaranteed benefits within this priority category, with less available to cover nonguaranteed benefits, resulting in a shift in costs from PBGC to plan participants.

Taking all these factors into account, it is unclear whether the passage of time would increase or decrease the overall cost of unfunded guaranteed benefits to be paid by PBGC compared with the loss of unfunded nonguaranteed benefits to be borne by plan participants. Clearly, improvements in the financial well-being of the companies and their pension plans would serve the best interests of both PBGC and plan participants.

BALANCING MULTIPLE FEDERAL ROLES MAY CREATE TENSIONS AND CHALLENGES

As a result of GM's and Chrysler's restructuring, the federal government has assumed new roles vis-à-vis the automakers as part-owner and lender, in addition to its traditional role as pension regulator.[81] On behalf of the U.S. taxpayer, Treasury has an interest, as a shareholder, in the financial well-being of the companies, as well as the viability of their pension plans.[82] These interests may diverge at times. Although Treasury has established policies designed to separate these interests, the perception of a conflict could arise, for example, should choices need to be made regarding the allocation of funds from the companies to their pension plans.

Treasury Has Established Various Structures to Mitigate Any Risk Related to Conflicts

Under normal circumstances, transparency and disclosures to the public related to agency actions can often mitigate risks related to conflicts of interest. But, in this case, because this involves private companies and business sensitive information, Treasury is less able to rely on transparency and disclosure in its dealings with the automakers to mitigate any potential conflicts of interest. Nevertheless, as we have previously reported, what Treasury's goals are for its investment in Chrysler and GM, among other things, is important information for Congress and the public to have.[83] Although Treasury provides public information on TARP activities, including AIFP, through its legally mandated monthly reports to Congress, transaction reports, and others, these reports do not provide information on the indicators

Treasury may use in assessing the goals for its auto investments and the status of the automakers' pensions. Identifying these indicators for Congress, and sharing as much of this information as possible, while still respecting the sensitivity of certain business information, could help Congress and the public better understand whether the investment in the auto companies has been successful and help mitigate potential or perceived conflicts of interest.

Recognizing the potential for interested parties to perceive conflicts, Treasury has taken several other steps to mitigate its risk. First, to guide its oversight of the investments going forward and limit its involvement in the day-to-day operations of the companies, Treasury developed four core principles: (1) acting as a reluctant shareholder, for example, by not owning equity stakes in companies any longer than necessary; (2) not interfering in the day-to-day management decisions; (3) ensuring a strong board of directors; and (4) exercising limited voting rights. According to Treasury officials, use of these core principles defines the operating boundaries of the federal role within its ownership context by limiting the reach and ability of the government to exert its powerful influence on the business and operational matters of these companies. Officials noted that the core principle of not interfering in day-to-day decisions has been particularly helpful in dealing with political pressures related to business operations. For example, officials said that Treasury's auto team received about 300 congressional letters in 2009 regarding day-to-day management issues involving GM and Chrysler. Several of these letters asked about company decisions and strategies, or called on Treasury to exert influence on the companies' business decisions. Some letters lobbied either in favor of or against a certain practice or activity. Other letters have been passed along on behalf of a particular constituent concern. Treasury officials said that, because of their core principle, most of the time they can simply reply to such letters by reiterating their policy of not getting involved with the companies' business decisions, and as a result, they have been able to avoid having to respond to these pressures.

Second, to implement these core principles, Treasury established a protective barrier between the Treasury officials (beneath the Secretary level) who make policy-related decisions with respect to investments in the automakers and the Treasury officials who are responsible for regulating pensions or overseeing the operations of PBGC. In theory, this barrier prevents Treasury in its role as owner from interacting with Treasury in its role as pension regulator or overseer of PBGC. Treasury officials stated that, in the management of its investment in GM and Chrysler, the Treasury auto team does not communicate with the IRS or PBGC.

Given the importance of balancing its competing interests as regulator and part-owner, and mitigating the appearance of conflicts between these interests, it is essential that Treasury ensure that it has an adequate number of staff with the appropriate skills and expertise to carry out its various tasks. Because of earlier reductions in the number of Treasury staff working on the AIFP and Treasury's stated plans to disband the team focused exclusively on managing Treasury's stake in the auto industry, we recently recommended that Treasury ensure it has the expertise needed to adequately monitor and divest the government's investments in Chrysler and GM.[84] We believe that ensuring sufficient staffing continues to be essential, particularly in light of the circumstances discussed here. Subsequent to our making this recommendation, Treasury officials said they hired two additional analysts dedicated solely to monitoring Treasury's investments in Chrysler and GM, and planned to hire one more.

Despite These Efforts, Tensions May Remain

The steps taken to mitigate any risks likely to result should conflicts of interest arise—adoption of the core principles and establishment of a protective barrier—may help, but the tensions inherent in Treasury's multiple roles remain. This can be illustrated by the conflicting pressures that would likely be brought to bear in two critical and interrelated contexts: (1) how to respond to a decline in pension funding; and (2) how to decide when to sell the government's shares of stock.

Treasury officials told us they expect both GM and Chrysler to return to profitability. If this is the case, and the companies are able to make the required contributions to their pension plans as they become due, then Treasury's multiple roles are less likely to result in any perceived conflicts. However, if the funding of any of GM's or Chrysler's defined benefit plans declines below certain funding levels set out in statute,[85] the company may request a waiver—that is, request permission from IRS (within Treasury) to reduce its required contributions to its plans over an extended period. Despite Treasury's protective barrier and the autonomy of IRS to grant or refuse such a waiver request apart from any influence from other units within Treasury, some may still perceive a possible tension between Treasury's interest in the value of its shareholder investment and Treasury's interest, through its oversight of PBGC, in ensuring the viability of the pension plans.

In addition, Treasury has been clear that it wants to divest its shares as soon as practicable, but it must weigh a variety of factors when making the decision about when and how this should happen. Treasury officials said that on the basis of their analysis of the companies' future profitability, they believe that both GM and Chrysler will be able to attract sufficient investor interest for Treasury to sell its equity. However, circumstances that may appear advisable as to the best time to sell from a shareholder perspective— that is, which would maximize the return on the taxpayer's investment— could be at odds with the best interests of plan participants and beneficiaries. For example, Treasury could decide to sell its equity stake at a time when it would maximize its return on investment, but when the companies' pension plans were still at risk.

Finally, in the event that the companies do not return to profitability in a reasonable time frame, Treasury officials said that they will consider all commercial options for disposing of Treasury's equity, including forcing the companies into liquidation, which would likely mean that the companies' pension plans would be terminated and decisions would need to be made about the allocation of remaining company assets. In such circumstances, although there is a protective barrier preventing Treasury in its role as shareholder from interacting with Treasury in its role overseeing the PBGC, it may be difficult for the agency to make certain decisions without some perceiving a tension between these two separate roles.

CONCLUDING OBSERVATIONS

Treasury's substantial investment and other assistance, as well as loans from the Canadian government and concessions from nearly every stakeholder, including the unions, have made it possible for Chrysler and GM to stabilize and survive years of declining market share and the deepest recession since the Great Depression. However, because of the ongoing challenges facing the auto industry—including the still recovering economy and weak demand for new vehicles—the ultimate impact that the assistance will have on the companies' profitability and long-term viability remains uncertain. This, too, is the case for the companies' pensions. The companies' ability to make the large contributions that would be required based on current projections is mostly dependent on their profitability. Treasury officials who oversee TARP expect both automakers to return to profitability. Ultimately, much of the automaker recovery is not only dependent on how well the automakers turn their companies around but also how well the overall economy and employment levels improve.

The suppliers' future is even more complex. GM and Chrysler are expected to continue to reduce the number of suppliers that they use going forward. Suppliers have diversified their client base to include many other domestic and international automakers to minimize the impact of such cuts, but this has caused their viability to be more dependent on a global economic recovery, which has been slow. As a result, supplier bankruptcies and pension plan terminations may continue for the near future.

In light of these conditions, the risks to PBGC and participants in auto sector pension plans remain significant. PBGC estimated its exposure for unfunded guaranteed benefits across the sector to be about $42 billion as of January 31, 2009, and the exposure for plan participants for unfunded nonguaranteed benefits to be about $35 billion. The federal government and its institutions, the automakers, and the unions have all made a concerted effort to ensure that GM and Chrysler do not fail. But, should the automakers not return to profitability, interests may no longer be aligned. Treasury officials said that they will consider all commercial options for disposing of Treasury's equity, including liquidation; this would likely mean terminating the companies' pension plans, and allocating remaining company assets. In such circumstances, it would be difficult for Treasury to make any decisions that would trade off the value of its investment against the expense of the pension funds, potentially exposing the government either to loss of its TARP investment or to significant worsening of PBGC's financial condition. This is not a choice the government wants to face, but this risk and its attendant challenges remain real.

We recently recommended that Treasury should regularly communicate to Congress about TARP activities, including the financial health of GM and Chrysler.[86] This would include information on the companies' pensions as an integral part of the companies' financial health. Treasury already provides some information on its investments in the automakers through its monthly reports to Congress. In response to our previous recommendations, Treasury said that it intended to develop an approach for reporting on its investments in the auto industry that strikes an appropriate balance between transparency and the need to avoid compromising the competitive positions of the companies, and that it was implementing a communication strategy to provide key congressional stakeholders more current information about its TARP activities. These reports could provide a vehicle to report publicly available information on the financial status of the automakers' pensions. Such disclosure could help mitigate the potential or perceived tensions that could arise with the federal government's multiple roles with respect to the automakers and, when the time comes, could shed light on how Treasury's decision to divest will impact the companies' pension plans.

AGENCY COMMENTS AND OUR EVALUATION

We obtained written comments on a draft of this report from the Department of the Treasury (see appendix VIII) and from PBGC (see appendix IX). Treasury generally agreed with our findings, but reiterated the importance of striking an appropriate balance in its public reporting between its goal of transparency and the need to avoid compromising the competitive positions of the companies or its ability to recover funds for taxpayers. Treasury noted that it already provides "a wealth of information" about AIFP on its Web site, and also provides periodic updates to oversight bodies, including GAO. It further noted that it will provide additional reports on its investments in Chrysler and GM as circumstances warrant, but that it will not communicate confidential business information due to the potential to negatively affect the value of the investments. Treasury concluded that, given its role as a shareholder, it would be inappropriate for it to report separately on the assets and liabilities in the automakers' pension plans to Congress and the public.

We understand the importance of protecting the automakers' proprietary interests. However, as we pointed out in our report, Treasury's role is multifaceted, serving not only as a shareholder and creditor for Chrysler and GM, but also as a regulator of pensions. As a creditor of these companies, Treasury should know and disclose the pension commitments, which represent liabilities for these companies. These liabilities must be taken into account when evaluating the financial status of these companies. GM and Chrysler are already required to disclose certain information about the status of their pensions in publicly available reports. By including this publicly available information on the status of the automakers' pension plans in its reports to Congress, Treasury could provide a more complete picture of the companies' financial health and help mitigate any perceived tensions between the various roles that the Treasury currently plays as shareholder, creditor, and pension regulator without compromising the companies' competitive positions.

Both Treasury and PBGC provided technical comments, which are incorporated into the report where appropriate. In addition, we received technical comments on certain segments of the draft report from GM, Chrysler, and Delphi, and have incorporated their comments where appropriate, as well.

We are sending copies of this report to other interested congressional committees and members, the Acting Director of PBGC, the Secretary of Labor, the Secretary of the Treasury, and other interested parties. In addition, the report is available at no charge on the GAO Web site at http://www.gao.gov.

If you or your staff have any questions concerning this report, please contact Barbara Bovbjerg at (202) 512-7215 (bovbjergb@gao.gov) or A. Nicole Clowers at (202) 512-2843 (clowersa@gao.gov). Contact points for our offices of Congressional Relations and Public Affairs may be found on the last page of this report. GAO staff who made key contributions to this report are listed in appendix X.

Gene L. Dodaro
Acting Comptroller General
of the United States

List of Committees

The Honorable Daniel K. Inouye
Chairman
The Honorable Thad Cochran
Vice Chairman
Committee on Appropriations
United States Senate

The Honorable Christopher J. Dodd
Chairman
The Honorable Richard C. Shelby
Ranking Member
Committee on Banking, Housing,
and Urban Affairs
United States Senate

The Honorable Kent Conrad Chairman
The Honorable Judd Gregg
Ranking Member
Committee on the Budget
United States Senate

The Honorable Max Baucus
Chairman
The Honorable Charles E. Grassley
Ranking Member
Committee on Finance
United States Senate

The Honorable David R. Obey
Chairman
The Honorable Jerry Lewis
Ranking Member
Committee on Appropriations
House of Representatives

The Honorable John M. Spratt, Jr.
Chairman
The Honorable Paul Ryan
Ranking Member
Committee on the Budget
House of Representatives

The Honorable Barney Frank
Chairman

The Honorable Spencer Bachus
Ranking Member
Committee on Financial Services
House of Representatives

The Honorable Sander M. Levin
Acting Chairman
The Honorable Dave Camp
Ranking Member
Committee on Ways and Means
House of Representatives

APPENDIX I: THE DELPHI STORY

Both as the former Delphi, prior to bankruptcy, and now as the "new Delphi," postbankruptcy, the Delphi Corporation has been a leading global supplier of mobile electronics and transportation systems, including powertrain, safety, thermal, controls and security systems, electrical/electronic architecture, and in-car entertainment technologies. Delphi evolved as part of General Motors (GM) until it was spun off as a separate entity in 1999. At the time it filed for Chapter 11 bankruptcy in 2005, the company employed more than 185,000 workers in 38 countries, making it one of the largest suppliers in the world.

The former Delphi Corporation sponsored six defined benefit plans for its U.S.-based workers:

- the Delphi Hourly-Rate Employees Pension Plan;
- the Delphi Retirement Program For Salaried Employees;
- the Packard-Hughes Interconnect Bargaining Retirement Plan;
- the Packard-Hughes Interconnect Non-Bargaining Retirement Plan;
- the ASEC Manufacturing Retirement Program; and
- the Delphi Mechatronic Systems Retirement Program.

Following Delphi's spin off from GM in 1999, GM agreed with its unions, including the International Union, United Automobile, Aerospace and Agricultural Implement Workers of America (UAW), to offer pension protections for certain employees in the event that Delphi's pension plans would be frozen or terminated. Specifically, under the agreement, GM agreed with three unions to provide certain former GM employees retired from Delphi certain pension benefits that would otherwise not be paid by Delphi or by the Pension Benefit Guaranty Corporation (PBGC) upon plan termination. Salaried and certain other union-represented employees did not receive similar contractual commitments from GM with respect to their pensions or other postemployment benefits, and they are suffering the full impact of their Delphi plans having been frozen and terminated.

In addition, GM agreed to provide transfer rights for certain Delphi hourly UAW-represented employees in the United States. Specifically, it provided these employees with "flowback" opportunities to transfer to GM as appropriate job openings became available at

GM. GM employees in the U.S. had similar opportunities to transfer to Delphi. The original flowback agreement provided that, when an employee transferred, the employee would be eligible for pension benefits which reflected the transferring employee's combined years of credited service. The parties did not transfer pension assets or liabilities in order to accomplish this. Rather, pension responsibility between Delphi and GM was allocated on a pro-rata basis based upon the employee's credited service at each company.

After Delphi and its U.S. subsidiaries filed for bankruptcy in 2005, there were extensive efforts involving negotiations between Delphi, GM, and other stakeholders to keep the pension plans ongoing. On September 30, 2008, the company froze its salaried plan, the ASEC Manufacturing Retirement Program, the Delphi Mechatronic Systems Retirement Program and the Packard Hughes Interconnect Non-Bargaining Retirement Plan. The company also reached agreement with its labor unions allowing it to freeze the accrual of traditional benefits under its hourly plan, effective as of November 30, 2008.

Delphi received the consent of its labor unions and approval from the court to transfer certain assets and liabilities of Delphi's hourly plan to GM's hourly plan. The first transfer involved liabilities of approximately $2.6 billion and assets of approximately $486 million (about 90 percent of the estimated $540 million of assets initially scheduled to be transferred). It was anticipated that the remaining assets would be transferred by March 29, 2009, upon finalizing the related valuations. In exchange for the first transfer, Delphi's reorganization plan released GM from all claims that could be brought by its creditors with respect to, among other things, the spin off of Delphi, any collective bargaining agreements to which the former Delphi was a party, and any obligations to former Delphi employees.

Although the first transfer had the effect that no contributions were due under the hourly plan for the plan year ended September 30, 2008, Delphi still had a funding deficiency of $56 million for the salaried plan and an approximate $13 million funding deficiency for its other pension plans for the plan year ending September 30, 2008. Delphi applied to the Internal Revenue Service (IRS) for a waiver of the obligation to make the minimum funding contribution to the salaried plan by June 15, 2009, and requested permission, instead, to pay the amount due in installments over the following 5 years. However, Delphi abandoned the waiver request when it became clear that it could not afford to maintain the salaried plan and that GM was not going to assume it.

In the second phase of the transfer, Delphi expected to transfer substantially all of the remaining assets and liabilities of the hourly plan to GM. In exchange for the second transfer, GM was to receive a $2 billion administrative claim when Delphi emerged from bankruptcy. In its 2008 annual report, Delphi was cognizant that the second pension transfer to GM was contingent upon its emergence from Chapter 11 under a modified plan of reorganization. If these conditions were not satisfied and the second transfer did not take place, it would likely be unable to fund its U.S. pension obligations. Specifically, Delphi stated that

> " . . . due to the impact of the global economic recession, including reduced global automotive production, capital markets volatility that has adversely affected our pension asset return expectations, a declining interest rate environment, or other reasons, our funding requirements have substantially increased since September 30, 2008. Should we be unable to obtain funding from some other source to resolve these pension funding obligations, either Delphi or the Pension Benefit Guaranty Corporation (the "PBGC") may initiate plan terminations."

Delphi's financial difficulties continued, and when the second transfer of pension assets and liabilities to GM was not implemented on July 31, 2009, PBGC terminated all six of Delphi's U.S. qualified defined benefit plans. PBGC assumed responsibility for the plans on August 10, 2009. According to PBGC, this step was necessary because Delphi had stated that it could not afford to maintain its pension plans and GM, which itself had reorganized in bankruptcy earlier in the year, had stated that it was unable to afford the additional financial burden of the Delphi pensions. PBGC stated that the Delphi pension plans were $7 billion underfunded when they terminated the plans. PBGC estimates that it will make up about $6 billion of that shortfall using PBGC funds. Following PBGC's takeover of the plans, on October 6, 2009, in accordance with Delphi's plan of reorganization, the former company sold its U.S. and foreign operations to a new entity, Delphi Automotive LLP, with the exception of four UAW sites in the United States and its steering business, which were sold to GM.

PBGC has acknowledged that the calculation of benefits for former Delphi plan participants will be a difficult, lengthy process due to the plans' complex benefit structures and the availability of documentation for all the mergers and acquisitions that have taken place throughout the life of the plans. On its Web site, PBGC stated that it could take 6 to 9 months from Delphi's date of trusteeship before it adjusted benefits to estimated PBGC benefit amounts. Moreover, PBGC noted that it could take several years to fully review the plan and finally determine all benefit amounts.

APPENDIX II: LEGAL LIMITS ON PBGC GUARANTEED BENEFITS

To help protect the retirement income of U.S. workers with private sector defined benefit plans, PBGC guarantees participant benefits up to certain limits specified under the Employee Retirement Income Security Act of 1974 (ERISA) and related regulations. These limits include the phase-in limit, the accrued-at-normal limit, and the maximum limit, as illustrated below in figure 8.

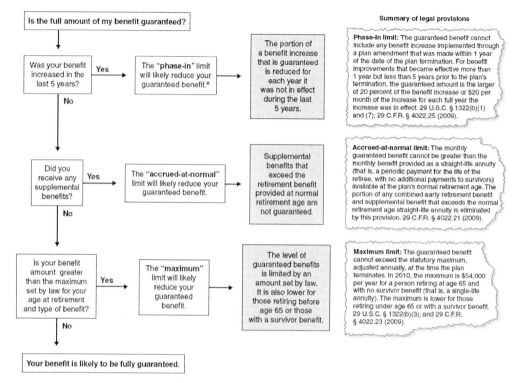

Source: GAO analysis of ERISA, PBGC's implementing regulations and related documents.
a Benefit increases subject to phase-in limits also include "unpredictable contingent event benefits" (such as shutdown benefits). In addition, in cases involving bankruptcy, the date the bankruptcy petition was filed is treated as the termination date of the plan.

Figure 8. Determining If a Participant's Guaranteed Benefit Is Subject to Legal Limits.

APPENDIX III: RECENT ATTRITION PROGRAMS AT GM AND CHRYSLER

Table 6. Recent Attrition Programs at GM

Plan/program	Description	Estimated impact on pension obligations[a]
Hourly Plan		
2006 Special Attrition Program	Hourly UAW employees and select Delphi UAW employees were offered the following: •Lump-sum payment of $35,000 for normal or early voluntary retirement (paid from company assets). •"Mutually satisfactory retirement" for age 50 and 10 years of service and preretirement leave for select employees, depending on plant location. •Buyout of $140,000 for employees with 10 or more years of service and $70,000 for employees with less than 10 years of service (paid from company assets).	$1.2 billion decrease in obligations (34,400 acceptances)

2008 Special Attrition Program	About 74,000 UAW-represented employees and 2,300 other union-represented employees were offered the following: • Lump sum payment for retirement-eligible employees ($45,000 for production and $62,500 for skilled trade) funded from plan assets. Lump sum payable as an annuity, if elected. • "Mutually satisfactory retirement" for age 50 and 10 or more years of service. • Preretirement leave for employees with 26-29 years of service. • Buyout of $140,000 for employees with 10 or more years of service, and $70,000 for employees with less than 10 years of service (paid from company assets).	$0.8billion increase in obligations (18,700 acceptances)
Special Attrition Program 3.0 (February 2009)	About 57,000 hourly UAW employees were offered the following: • $45,000 incentive value offered to production and skilled employees for normal/voluntary retirement and buyout. Incentive included $25,000 vehicle voucher plus $20,000 cash. • "Mutually satisfactory retirement" for age 55 with 10 or more years of service, and age 50 with 10 or more years of service for select closed or closing plants. All cash payments were funded from company assets.	$1.2 billion increase in obligations (February and June programs combined) (7,000 acceptances in February program)
Special Attrition Program 3.1 (June 2009)	About 50,000 hourly UAW employees were offered the following: • Normal/voluntary retirement incentive value of $45,000 (production) and $70,000 (skilled). Incentive included $25,000 vehicle voucher. • Buyout incentive value of $70,000 for those with less than 10 years of service; $105,000 for those with 10 to 20 years of service; and $140,000 for those with 20 or more years of service. Incentive included $25,000 vehicle voucher. • Preretirement leave offered to employees with 28and 29 years seniority. • "Mutually satisfactory retirement" for age 50 and 10 or more years of service. All cash payments were funded from company assets.	(6,000 acceptances in June program)
Salaried Plan		
2008 Salaried Window Retirement Program	Voluntary retirement offers were extended to certain U.S. salaried employees, as follows: • 6-month cash lump sum payment from the pension plan for all retirement-eligible employees (age 62 and older) who elect to retire or for employees under age 55 who will receive reduced benefits. Lump sum payable as an annuity, if elected. • Enhanced window retirement factors for employees ages 55 to 61 who are eligible but do not elect the lump sum payment.	$0.3billion increase in obligations (3,700 acceptances)
2009 Salaried Window Retirement and Involuntary Severance Program (June 2009)	Offers were extended to about 5,700 salaried employees for retirements targeted for October 1, 2009, as follows: • Unreduced pension benefits for participants age 58and older as of October 1, 2009; participants ages 53-57 would receive enhanced window retirement benefits. • Severance program provides monthly base salary payments up to 6 months (if classified) or 12 months (if executive). Severance payments to be paid from company assets.	$0.5 billion increase in obligations (3,000 acceptances)

Source: GM documents.

[a] Estimated impact is based on measurements of pension obligations in accordance with Financial Accounting Standards. The measurements reflect remeasurements performed around the time of the respective attrition programs and changes in a number of variables that are incorporated into the remeasurement calculations, such as changes in present-value discount rates. All data included in this column are approximations.

Table 7. Recent Attrition Programs at Chrysler

Plan/program	Description	Estimated impact[a]
Incentive Program for Retirement (2006-2009)	•Normal retirement eligibility (that is, 30 or more years of service, or combination of age and years of service = 85), or age 60 with 10 or more years of service, or age 65 with one or more year of service. •$50,000 lump sum payment plus $25,000 vehicle purchase voucher.[b]	$1,067 million increase in obligations(10,956 acceptances)[c]
Special Early Retirement (2006-2009)	•Age 55-62 with 10 or more years of service and not otherwise eligible for IPR.[d] •Normal retirement benefit with no age reduction factor applied (in certain labor markets, nonviable age reduced to 50). •No lump sum.	$401 million increase in obligations (3,141 acceptances)
Enhanced Voluntary Termination of Employment (2007-2009)	•$75,000 lump sum payment plus $25,000 vehicle purchase voucher (per "Plant Closure Agreements"- $100,000 plus $25,000 vehicle purchase voucher).[b]	$57 million decrease in obligations (7,636 acceptances)
Other miscellaneous programs (2006-2008)		$184 million increase in obligations (438acceptances)

Source: Chrysler documents.

[a] Estimated impact is based on measurements of pension obligations in accordance with Financial Accounting Standards. The measurements reflect remeasurements performed around the time of the respective attrition programs and changes in a number of variables that are incorporated into the remeasurement calculations, such as changes in present-value discount rates. Data for 2006-2008 are based on actual numbers; data for 2009 are based on projected numbers, across all ten U.S. qualified defined benefit plans, as appropriate.

[b] Lump sum payments during 2008 paid with pension plan assets; payments before 2008 and after 2008 paid with company assets.

[c] Also includes data for the Separation Incentive Program.

[d] In 2008, the retirement age was 53 instead of 55 for certain salaried nonunion employees.

APPENDIX IV: PRODUCT LINES AND FACILITIES BEING ELIMINATED

Table 8. GM Product Lines and Facilities Being Eliminated

Product line	Current status	Location of plant shutdowns
Pontiac Vibe	Production ceased at the end of August 2009.	The New United Motor Manufacturing Incorporated facility (known as "Nummi")jointly operated by GM and Toyota in Fremont, CA, to close.
Pontiac	Production of the last Pontiac model will cease by the end of December 2010.	None identified to date.

Product line	Current status	Location of plant shutdowns
Hummer	In February 2010, GM announced that the sale of Hummer to Sichuan Tengzhong Heavy Industrial Machinery Co., Ltd. could not be completed and there would be an orderly wind-down of Hummer operations. Currently approximately 850 units of the H3 model are being produced for a fleet customer. H3 production will cease at the end of June 2010. All other Hummer production ceased at the end of September 2009.	None identified to date.
Chevy Kodiak and GMC Topkick	Production ceased at the end of July 2009.	None identified to date.
Saturn	Following Penske Automotive Group's decision to terminate discussions to acquire Saturn in September 2009, GM announced that it would be winding down the Saturn brand and dealership network. Production ceased at the end of December 2009.	None identified to date.
Saab	Purchased by Spyker Cars, NV, on February 23, 2010.	The previously announced wind down of Saab operations has ended. Saab and Spyker will operate under the Spyker (AMS:SPYKR) umbrella, and Spyker will assume responsibility for Saab operations.
Manufacturing plants	Total number of assembly, powertrain, and stamping facilities in the United States to be reduced from 47 in 2008 to 34 by the end of 2010 and 33 by 2012.	• Powertrain castings plant in Massena, NY, closed in May 2009. • Stamping plant in Grand Rapids, MI, closed in May 2009. • Assembly plant in Wilmington, DE, closed in July 2009. • Assembly plant in Pontiac, MI, closed in September 2009. • Stamping plant in Mansfield, OH, closed in January 2010. • Powertrain engine plant in Livonia, MI, to close by July 2010. • Powertrain components plant in Fredericksburg, VA, to close by August 2010. • Powertrain plants: Flint North components plant and Willow Run Site, MI; and Parma, OH, components plant to close by August 2010. • Stamping plant in Indianapolis, IN, to close by December 2011. • Stamping plant and assembly plant in Shreveport, LA, to close by June 2012.
Parts	Three parts distribution centers closed.	• Parts distribution centers in Boston, MA; Columbus, OH; and Jacksonville, FL, closed on December 31, 2009.

Source: GM documents.

Table 9. Chrysler Product Lines and Facilities Being Eliminated

Product line	Current status	Location of plant shutdowns
Dodge Magnum and the Chrysler Pacifica, Crossfire, and PT Cruiser convertible.	Announced in November 2007 that these four models were to be eliminated from the product portfolio through 2008. Subsequently announced that the PT Cruiser would remain in production.	Production at several North American assembly and powertrain plants to be cut, which combined with other actions, was expected to reduce the number of hourly jobs by 8,500 to 10,000 people through 2008. See May 2009 updated list of plant closings provided below in last row of this table.
Dodge Ram pick-up truck	Announced in June 2009 that production would end effective July 10, 2009.	•St. Louis Assembly Plant North in Fenton, MO. See also below.
Service and parts operations	List of plants scheduled for closing, as of May 2009.	•St. Louis Assembly Plant South in Fenton, MO, closed October 2008. •Assembly plant in Newark, DE, closed in December 2008. •St. Louis Assembly Plant North in Fenton, MO, was to close by the end of September 2009. Production to be moved to Warren Truck Assembly plant. •Conner Avenue Assembly Plant in Detroit, MI, was to close in December 2009. •Stamping plant in Twinsburg, OH, was to close in March 2010. Existingvolume to be transferred to Warren Stamping and Sterling Stamping plants. •Assembly plant in Sterling Heights, MI; engine plant in Kenosha, WI; and axle plant in Detroit, MI, to closeat the end of December 2010.

Source: Chrysler documents.

APPENDIX V: HISTORY OF MAJOR ACQUISITIONS AND DIVESTITURES

	GM	Chrysler
1900s	Founded September 16, 1908. 1908:Acquired Oldsmobile and Reliance Motor Truck Company. 1909:Acquired Cadillac; Oakland Motor Car Company; Rapid Motor Vehicle Company(later renamed GMC Truck); and Champion (later renamed AC Spark Plug Company).	
1910s	1918:Acquired McLaughlin Motor Company(later renamed General Motors) and United Motor Corporation. 1919:Acquired Fisher Body; Dayton Wright Company; Guardian Frigerator (later renamed Frigidaire); and Saginaw Malleable Iron Company (renamed Saginaw Products Company).	

	GM	Chrysler
1920s	1925: Acquired Vauxhall Motors, Ltd., based in Luton, England. 1929: Acquired Adam Opel Corporation, located in Rüsselsheim, Germany; and Allison Engineering Company.	Founded June 6, 1925. 1928: Acquired Dodge.
1930s	1930: Acquired Electro-Motive Engineering Corporation. 1931: Acquired Holden's Motor Body Builders Limited; merged with GM's Australia Proprietary, Limited, to form Holden's Limited, located in Melbourne, Australia. 1933: Acquired a controlling interest in North American Aviation; merged with GM's General Aviation division.	
1940s		
1950s	1953: Acquired Euclid, Inc.	1957: Acquired Ensamblaje Venezolana, soon renamed Chrysler de Venezuela S. A. 1959: Acquired Chrysler South Africa Ltd.
1960s	1968: Sold most of Euclid; renamed remaining facilities the Terex Division.	1963: Acquired Chrysler Hellas S. A., Greece. 1965: Acquired the outboard engine business of West Bend Company of Hartford, Wisconsin and the Lone Star Boat Company of Plano, Texas, forming the Chrysler BoatCorporation. 1967: Acquired Redisco, Inc., from American Motors Corporation and integrated it with Chrysler Credit to form Chrysler Financial Corporation. Also acquired 77 percent of Barreiros Diesel S. A. (Spain), and increased interest in Chrysler do Brasil (Brazil) to 92 percent.
1970s	1973: Merged Allison Engineering with Detroit Diesel.	1970: Control of Rootes Group equity reached 73percent; the company renamed Chrysler United Kingdom Ltd. 1976: Sold the Airtemp Division to Fedders Corporation. 1978: Sold the Chrysler Europe Division.
1980s	1981: Sold Terex Division. 1984: Acquired Electronic Data Systems Corporation. 1985: Acquired Hughes Aircraft Company; merged with Delco Electronics to form a new subsidiary called Hughes Electronics. 1988: Spin off of Detroit Diesel. 1989: Purchased 50 percent equity in Saab Automobile AB of Sweden; later purchased the remaining 50 percent to become sole owner in 2000.	1980: Sold the Marine Division. 1981: Sold the Defense Division to General Dynamics. 1984: Reorganized into a holding company that included Chrysler Motors, Chrysler Financial, Gulfstream Aerospace and Chrysler Technologies. 1987: Acquired American Motors Corporation (and Jeep) for $800 million.

Appendix V. (Continued)

	GM	Chrysler
1980s	1981: Sold Terex Division. 1984: Acquired Electronic Data Systems Corporation. 1985: Acquired Hughes Aircraft Company; merged with Delco Electronics to form a new subsidiary called Hughes Electronics. 1988: Spin off of Detroit Diesel. 1989: Purchased 50 percent equity in Saab Automobile AB of Sweden; later purchased the remaining 50 percent to become sole owner in 2000.	1980: Sold the Marine Division. 1981: Sold the Defense Division to General Dynamics. 1984: Reorganized into a holding company that included Chrysler Motors, Chrysler Financial, Gulfstream Aerospace and Chrysler Technologies. 1987: Acquired American Motors Corporation (and Jeep) for $800 million.
1990s	1993: Sold Allison Gas Turbine. 1996: Sold Electronic Data Systems Corporation. 1997: Sold Hughes Aircraft to Raytheon. 1999: Spin off of Delphi; acquired exclusive rights to the Hummer brand name from AM General Corporation.	1998: Merged with Daimler-Benz AG; operated as "Chrysler Group," a business unit of DaimlerChrysler AG.
2000s	2002: Acquired the bulk of Korean automaker Daewoo Motor's automotive assets and created a new company called GM Daewoo Auto & Technology. 2003: Sold Hughes Electronics. 2005: Sold Electro-Motive Diesel. 2006: Divested majority ownership in its financing unit, General Motors Acceptance Corporation (now known as GMAC). 2007: Sold Allison Transmission. 2009: Acquired five U.S.-based components plants from Delphi.	2007: Just over 80 percent of Chrysler and its related financial services business sold to Cerberus Capital Management for $7.4 billion. 2008: Spin off of Chrysler Financial Corporation.

Source: GM's and Chrysler's Web sites.

APPENDIX VI: ALLOCATION OF ASSETS TO PARTICIPANT BENEFITS

When a pension plan is terminated and trusteed by PBGC, ERISA specifies that the remaining assets of the plan and any funds recovered for the plan during the bankruptcy proceedings be allocated to participant benefits according to six priority categories (see table 10).[1]

---

[1] 29 U.S.C. §§ 1322(c) and 1344.

Table 10. Priority Categories for Allocating Participant Benefits

Priority category 1	Accrued benefits derived from voluntary employee contributions.
Priority category 2	Accrued benefits derived from mandatory employee contributions.
Priority category 3	Annuity benefits that have been in pay status for at least 3years before the plan's termination date, or could have been in pay status for at least 3years before the plan's termination date had the participant chosen to retire at his or her earliest possible retirement date; however, benefits subject to the phase-in limitation (that is, benefit increases made within the last 5 years) are excluded. These benefits can be either guaranteed or nonguaranteed.
Priority category 4	Other guaranteed benefits, and certain nonguaranteed benefits.[a]
Priority category 5	Other vested nonguaranteed benefits that a participant is entitledto under the plan; however, benefits that result solely due to the termination of the plan—which are deemed "forfeitable"—are excluded.
Priority category 6	All other benefits under the plan. This category includes nonvested benefits and "grow-in"benefits, which are benefits that are provided in some situations where the company continues to operate after the plan is terminated.

Source: GAO analysis of PBGC documents.

Note: The distribution of plan assets is based on type of benefit, not retirement status, and many participants have benefits in more than one category.

[a] Specifically, the nonguaranteed benefits included in priority category 4 are those that are nonguaranteed because they are subject to the aggregate benefits limitation for participants in more than one plan that has been terminated with insufficient funds, or because they are subject to special provisions applicable to substantial owners (that is, those owning more than 10 percent of the company).

Funds recovered from bankruptcy proceedings are also allocated using these priority categories, but unlike plan assets, recoveries are required to be shared between participants'unfunded nonguaranteed benefits and PBGC's costs for unfunded guaranteed benefits.[2] As a result, recoveries are often more advantageous for participants than residual plan assets. PBGC allocates the participants'portion of the recoveries beginning with the highest priority category in which there are unfunded nonguaranteed benefits, and then to each lower priority category, in succession.[3]

---

[2] In cases when a plan's unfunded nonguaranteed benefits exceed $20 million, the total amount to be shared depends on the actual amount recovered. In all other cases, the amount to be shared is determined by an average of PBGC's recoveries over a 5-year period. ERISA section 4022(c).

[3] If the assets are not sufficient to pay for all benefits in a category, the assets are distributed among the participants according to the ratio that the value of each participant's benefit in that priority category bears to the total value of all benefits in that category. Within each priority category (except priority category 5), assets are allocated first to the participant's "basic-type" benefits (which include benefits that are guaranteed by PBGC, or that would be guaranteed but for the maximum and phase-in limits), and then to the participant's "nonbasic-type" benefits (which include all other benefits). If the plan assets available for allocation to priority category 5, which includes benefits subject to the phase-in limit, are insufficient to pay for all benefits in that category, the assets are allocated by date of plan amendment, oldest to newest, until all plan assets available for allocation have been exhausted.

APPENDIX VII: PBGC EXAMPLE BENEFIT CALCULATIONS

PBGC prepared example benefit calculations to illustrate how termination of the automaker pension plans might impact participant benefits, depending on the participant's situation (see table 11). The calculations assume that plan assets and recoveries are not sufficient to fund nonguaranteed benefits beyond a portion of those benefits in priority category 3 (that is, of those retired or eligible to retire for at least 3 years), and they focus on those who would lose the most under such situations. Although an early retiree eligible for priority 3 status would lose the least, all early retirees under age 62 as of the date of plan termination would lose a sizeable portion of their benefits until age 62 because their supplements are not guaranteed. The person who retired early under a special attrition program or plant shutdown benefit would lose even more, as the enhanced benefits under the special program would also not be guaranteed, reducing the person's lifetime benefit by more than half. Finally, the person not yet eligible to retire would lose the most. Compared to the benefits promised under the plan, he would not be able to retire for 5 more years and his payment would be less than a quarter of the amount promised. Over time, in general, more employees will be eligible to retire and qualify for priority 3 status, and the amount of retirees' monthly guaranteed benefits will increase.

Table 11. Examples of Participants' Benefit Reductions If an Automaker Hourly Plan Were Terminated

	Plan benefit	PBGC benefit if plan terminates in 2009[a]	Changes to PBGC benefit if plan terminates 5 years later (in 2014)
Example 1: Employee retires early in 2009 Age 53 with 33 years of service (eligible for priority category 3)			Employee retires early in 2014 Age 58 with 38 years of service (eligible for priority category 3)
Benefit until age 62	$3,200	$1,750[b]	Incremental increase in PBGC benefit
Benefit after age 62	1,750	1,750	Incremental increase in PBGC benefit
Example 2: Employee retires early in 2009 Age 50 with 30 years of service (not eligible for priority category 3)			Employee retires early in 2014 Age 55 with 35 years of service (eligible for priority category 3)
Benefit until age 62	3,200	1,500	Incremental increase in PBGC benefit
Benefit after age 62	1,500	1,500	Incremental increase in PBGC benefit
Example 3: Employee retires early under special attrition program (or plant shutdown) in 2009 (0 percent phase-in) Age 55 with 25 years of service (not eligible for priority category 3)			Employee retires early under special attrition program (or plant shutdown) in 2009 (100 percent phase-in) Age 55 with 25 years of service (eligible for priority category 3)
Benefit until age 62	2,600	600	No loss of benefit enhancements due to phase in, substantial increase in PBGC benefit
Benefit after age 62	1,400	600	No loss of benefit enhancements due to phase in, substantial increase in PBGC benefit
	Plan benefit	PBGC benefit if plan terminates in 2009[a]	Changes to PBGC benefit if plan terminates 5 years later (in 2014)
Example 4: Employee not yet retired when plan terminates in 2009 Age 49 with 29 years of service (not eligible for priority category 3)			Employee retires early in 2014 Age 54 with 34 years of service (eligible for priority category 3)

	Plan benefit	PBGC benefit if plan terminates in 2009[a]	Changes to PBGC benefit if plan terminates 5 years later (in 2014)
Benefit until age 62	3,200 (beginning at age 50 with 30 years of service)	700 (beginning at age 55)	Eligible to retire, benefits not deferred, substantial increase in PBGC benefit
Benefit after age 62	1,600	700	Substantial increase in PBGC benefit

Source: GAO analysis of PBGC documents.

a PBGC example calculations, assuming plan assets and recoveries are not sufficient to pay nonguaranteed benefits beyond a portion of priority category 3.

b PBGC benefit if priority category 3 is 70 percent funded. If more than 70 percent funded, part of the temporary supplement is payable, and could increase up to $2,750 if 100 percent funded.

APPENDIX VIII: COMMENTS FROM THE DEPARTMENT OF THE TREASURY

DEPARTMENT OF THE TREASURY
WASHINGTON, D.C. 20220

March 26, 2010

Thomas J. McCool
Director, Center for Economics
Applied Research and Methods
U.S. Government Accountability Office
441 G Street, N.W.
Washington, D.C. 20548

Dear Mr. McCool:

The Treasury Department (Treasury) appreciates the opportunity to review the GAO's latest draft report on Treasury's Troubled Asset Relief Program (TARP), titled *Troubled Asset Relief Program: Automakers' Pension Funding and Multiple Federal Roles Pose Challenges for the Future* (Draft Report). Treasury welcomes the recognition by the GAO that Treasury through TARP investments has helped make "it possible for Chrysler and GM to stabilize and survive years of declining market share and the deepest recession since the Great Depression." There is important work ahead and the GAO's Draft Report is constructive as Treasury continues to implement its Automotive Industry Financing Program (AIFP).

Although the Draft Report contains no new recommendations, it suggests that Treasury should not only report publicly on the auto investments but also on the "status of the automakers' pensions." As we have stated previously, in addition to providing a wealth of information on the AIFP on FinancialStability.gov and periodic updates to the oversight bodies, Treasury will provide additional reports regarding the status of its investments in the automotive companies as circumstances warrant. Treasury recognizes the importance, as noted by the GAO in its various reports, of striking an appropriate balance in its public reporting between our goal of transparency and the need to avoid compromising either the competitive positions of these automotive companies or Treasury's ability to recover funds for taxpayers. It would be inappropriate for Treasury in our capacity as a shareholder to separately report on the pension assets and liabilities under the GM and Chrysler pension plans, and we suggest directing these questions to GM and Chrysler.

Once again, Treasury appreciates the opportunity to review the Draft Report. Treasury also appreciates the GAO's close oversight of TARP as Treasury develops and implements its policies to stabilize the financial system. We look forward to continuing this constructive dialogue.

Sincerely,

Herbert M. Allison, Jr.
Assistant Secretary for Financial Stability

APPENDIX IX: COMMENTS FROM PBGC

Pension Benefit Guaranty Corporation
1200 K Street, N.W., Washington, D.C. 20005-4026

Office of the Director

March 26, 2010

Gene L. Dodaro
Acting Comptroller General of the United States
U.S. Government Accountability Office
Washington, D.C. 20548

Dear Mr. Dodaro:

Thank you for the opportunity to comment on the draft version of your report entitled, "Troubled Asset Relief Program: Automaker Pension Funding and Multiple Federal Roles Pose Challenges for the Future."

We appreciate GAO's calling attention to the automakers' defined benefit pension plans, their funded status, and the risk of loss faced by plan participants and PBGC's single-employer insurance program if these plans are terminated in the future. As the report correctly points out, improvements in the financial condition of the companies and their pension plans will strengthen retirement security for plan participants and reduce PBGC's exposure to loss. The report also serves to highlight the complexity of the environment in which PBGC operates as it strives to fulfill its mission. PBGC is actively monitoring the financial health of plan sponsors in the auto industry, as well as related corporate transactions that may affect defined benefit pension plans.

Under a separate cover, we have provided suggested technical corrections and other changes to further clarify aspects of the report.

GAO has consistently reported on matters affecting the retirement security of the American people, and we especially appreciate GAO's work in highlighting the challenges PBGC faces in "Protecting America's Pensions."

Sincerely,

Vincent K. Snowbarger
Acting Director

End Notes

[1] 29 U.S.C. §1302.

[2] The Emergency Economic Stabilization Act of 2008 authorized TARP, Pub. L. No. 110-343, Div. A, §§ 101-136, 122 Stat. 3765, 3767-3800 (codified at 12 U.S.C. §§ 5201-5241).

[3] GAO is required to report at least every 60 days on findings resulting from, among other things, oversight of TARP's performance in meeting the purposes of the act, the financial condition and internal controls of TARP,

the characteristics of both asset purchases and the disposition of assets acquired, TARP's efficiency in using the funds appropriated for the program's operation, and TARP's compliance with applicable laws and regulations. 12 U.S.C. § 5226(a).

[4] For more information on the restructuring of GM and Chrysler companies overall, see GAO, *Troubled Asset Relief Program: Continued Stewardship Needed as Treasury Develops Strategies for Monitoring and Divesting Financial Interests in Chrysler and GM*, GAO-10-151 (Washington, D.C.: Nov. 2, 2009); GAO, *Auto Industry: Summary of Government Efforts and Automakers' Restructuring to Date*, GAO-09-553 (Washington, D.C.: Apr. 23, 2009); and GAO, *Auto Industry: A Framework for Considering Federal Financial Assistance*, GAO-09-242T (Washington, D.C.: Dec. 4, 2008).

[5] While a portion of TARP funds for the auto industry have been used to assist GMAC LLC and Chrysler Financial, the former financing divisions of GM and Chrysler respectively, we did not review the effect of restructuring on the pension plans of these finance companies as they are now separate legal entities.

[6] To qualify for preferential tax treatment, pension plans must satisfy certain requirements related, for example, to minimal funding, vesting, and accounting. 26 U.S.C. § 401. Employers may deduct their contributions to qualified plans. Although such contributions are a form of compensation to them, employees do not claim such contributions as income for tax purposes, but the income from pensions is considered taxable when pension benefits are received.

[7] Michaela D. Platzer and Glennon J. Harrison, *The U.S. Automotive Industry: National and State Trends in Manufacturing Employment*. (Washington, D.C.: Congressional Research Service, 2009).

[8] Treasury also received $2.1 billion in preferred stock in GM.

[9] GAO-10-151.

[10] GAO, *Troubled Asset Relief Program: March 2009 Status of Efforts to Address Transparency and Accountability Issues*, GAO-09-504 (Washington, D.C.: Mar. 31, 2009); and GAO, *Troubled Asset Relief Program: June 2009 Status of Efforts to Address Transparency and Accountability Issues*, GAO-09-658 (Washington, D.C.: June 17, 2009).

[11] The remaining funds have been used: (1) for the Warranty Commitment Program, which provided funds to Chrysler and GM, but have been repaid in full; and (2) to provide assistance to GM's and Chrysler's financing divisions, now spun off as separate legal entities.

[12] For a more detailed discussion of Chrysler and GM restructuring efforts, see GAO-09-553 and GAO-10-151.

[13] For further details on Delphi, see appendix I.

[14] Hybrid plans are legally defined benefit plans, but they contain certain features that resemble defined contribution plans.

[15] Rob Kozlowski, "The List: Funded Status of the Largest Defined Benefit Plans," *Financial Week*, June 16, 2008.

[16] See GAO-08-817 and GAO, *Defined Benefit Pensions: Survey Results of the Nation's Largest Private Defined Benefit Plan Sponsors*, GAO-09-291 (Washington, D.C.: Mar. 30, 2009).

[17] A plan freeze is a plan amendment that closes the plan to new entrants and may or may not reduce future benefit accruals for some or all active plan participants. A "hard freeze," referenced here, occurs when the plan is closed to new entrants and participants no longer accrue additional benefits. For other freeze types and a discussion of their effects, see: GAO, *Defined Benefit Pensions: Plan Freezes Affect Millions of Participants and May Pose Retirement Income Challenges*, GAO-08-817 (Washington, D.C.: July 21, 2008).

[18] PBGC is a wholly-owned government corporation—that is, the federal government does not share ownership interests with nonfederal entities. As such, PBGC must prepare annual budgets, produce audited financial statements, and submit a management report to Congress each year. 31 U.S.C. §§ 9101(3)(J), 9103, 9105 and 9107.

[19] 26 U.S.C. §§ 1-9834. The Internal Revenue Code is also referred to sometimes as simply "the tax code."

[20] Pub. L. No. 93-406, 88 Stat. 829 (codified as amended at 29 U.S.C. §§ 1001- 1461).

[21] Unlike defined benefit plans, defined contribution plans are not covered by PBGC insurance. 29 U.S.C. § 1321(B)(1).

[22] A single-employer plan is a plan that is established and maintained only by employers in a single controlled group. Single-employer plans can be established unilaterally by the sponsor or through a collective bargaining agreement with a labor union.

[23] 29 U.S.C. § 1341(c).

[24] 29 U.S.C. § 1342(a).

[25] If a plan has sufficient assets, a plan sponsor may voluntarily terminate the plan without it being trusteed by PBGC (referred to as a "standard termination"). In such cases, the sponsor generally purchases a group annuity contract with an insurance company or makes lump sum payments so that participants are paid all the benefits

accrued under the plan up to the date of termination. 29 U.S.C. § 1341(b). With respect to collectively bargained plans, there can be no distress or standard termination until the collective bargaining obligation has been rejected or modified—either through negotiated resolution or court order authorizing rejection of the agreement through the Bankruptcy Code. 11 U.S.C. § 1113 and 29 U.S.C. § 1341(a)(3).

[26] GAO, *Pension Benefit Guaranty Corporation Single-Employer Insurance Program: Long-Term Vulnerabilities Warrant "High Risk" Designation*, GAO-03-1050SP (Washington, D.C.: July 23, 2003).

[27] See table 1 in the Background section for details.

[28] In 2007, both GM and Chrysler had reached agreements with UAW to transfer responsibility for retiree health care of UAW members to new independent voluntary employee beneficiary associations (VEBA) that were created to manage retiree health plans starting on January 1, 2010. As part of the funding arrangement for these new VEBAs, members would have to pay an additional monthly contribution toward their medical benefits, but the automakers agreed to increase members' pension benefits by a corresponding amount once these added payments were to begin. This pension benefit increase became known as the VEBA "pension pass-through." During the restructuring negotiations with GM and Chrysler, however, this benefit increase was eliminated before it was ever implemented.

[29] See table 1 in the Background section for details.

[30] The 2007 UAW plan benefit increases included a $2.65 or 5.1 percent increase (per month, per year of credited service) in the active basic benefit, a $2.00 increase in the retiree basic benefit, and a retiree lump sum payment paid from the pension plan, among other changes.

[31] Liability valuations reflect the time value of money—that a dollar in the future is worth less than a dollar today. Using a lower interest rate would increase the present value of a stream of payments, while using a higher interest rate would decrease the present value of a stream of payments.

[32] Throughout this report, we have characterized the value of plan assets and plan liabilities based on available information obtained from financial statements and public filings. It is often the case that the value of assets and liabilities from these sources are substantially different than the value of assets and liabilities at the point of plan termination. We have reported previously that there are many factors that can increase plan liabilities immediately before plan termination, such as economic factors, benefit increases, and earlier-than-anticipated retirements. See GAO, *Pension Plans: Hidden Liabilities Increase Claims Against Government Insurance Program*, GAO/HRD-93-7 (Washington, D.C.: Dec. 30, 1992).

[33] For a listing of recent GM attrition programs and their estimated impact on plan liabilities, see appendix III. For a detailed summary of recent GM plant closings, see appendix IV.

[34] From the perspective of the company's consolidated financial statement, it makes little difference whether payments are made from plan or company assets; but from the participant's perspective, if the level of plan assets has been diminished, it could have a significant impact on future benefits should the plan be terminated.

[35] For a listing of recent Chrysler attrition programs and their impact on plan liabilities, see appendix III. For a detailed summary of recent Chrysler plant closings, see appendix IV.

[36] Most GM divestitures have resulted in no future pension benefit accruals for the affected employees under the GM plan at the time of divestiture, with only limited impact on the GM plan going forward. See appendix V for a summary of key acquisitions and divestitures since GM and Chrysler were founded.

[37] According to GM officials, Delphi salaried employees were never eligible for any pension benefit guarantees.

[38] In exchange for GM's agreement to assume this liability from the Delphi hourly plan, Delphi and its creditors released GM from all potential litigation arising out of the original 1999 Delphi spin off. For further details on the Delphi story, see appendix I.

[39] Chrysler merged with Daimler-Benz AG in 1998 and was operated as a separate business unit called "Chrysler Group" until it was sold in 2007.

[40] Statutorily prescribed pension funding requirements for single-employer plans specify how much a sponsor must contribute to its defined benefit plans each year. 26 U.S.C. §§ 412 and 430. In general, the minimum required contribution reflects the value of the plan's assets compared with the plan's benefit obligations, as measured by the present value of all benefits accrued or earned as of the beginning of the plan year (the plan's funding target) and the present value of all benefits that are expected to accrue or be earned under the plan during the plan year (the target normal cost).

[41] 26 U.S.C. §§ 430 and 436.

[42] Pub. L. No. 109-280, §§ 101-107, 120 Stat. 780, 784-820.

[43] GAO, *High Risk Series: An Update*, GAO-07-310 (Washington, D.C.: Jan. 31, 2007), 85.

[44] Pub. L. No. 110-458, 122 Stat. 5092.

[45] In March 2009, the IRS issued guidance clarifying that under Notice 2008-21, for a calendar year plan with a January 1, 2009, valuation date, the IRS would not challenge the use of the monthly yield curve for January 2009, or any one of the four months immediately preceding January 2009. Since interest rates were much higher on October 1, 2008, than on January 1, 2009, using the October 1, 2008, yield curve for the discount rate would significantly reduce required contributions for the 2009 plan year. Also, in September 2009, the IRS issued guidance providing automatic approval for a new choice of interest rates for 2010, regardless of what choices were made for earlier plan years (as codified in new regulations effective October 15, 2009).

[46] 401(k) Fair Disclosure and Pension Security Act of 2009, H.R. 2989, 111th Cong. tit. III (as reported by H.R. Comm. on Ways and Means, July 31, 2009) and American Workers, State, and Business Relief Act of 2010, H. R. 4213, 111th Cong. tit. III (as passed by Senate, March 10, 2010). Yet another factor that could affect funding projections is future labor negotiations. Both GM and Chrysler have plans that are collectively bargained with UAW, and the result of future negotiations could increase or decrease projected liabilities.

[47] 26 U.S.C. § 430(f). Credit balances can be earned when a sponsor contributes more to its pension plans than required. Under certain conditions, sponsors can use these balances to offset required contributions until the balances are exhausted. Prior to PPA, credit balances could be augmented because they accrued interest at a rate determined by the plan to reflect the time value of money. PPA delineated two types of credit balances: so-called "carryover balances," generated under prior law, and "prefunding balances," generated after passage of the act. PPA also established certain standards on the use of credit balances, such as a requirement that balances be adjusted based on market conditions. Further, if a plan's funded ratio (determined with a reduction of assets in the amount of any carryover balance) is at least 80%, the plan sponsor may generally use its credit balance to offset any required contribution. The credit balances we refer to with respect to GM and Chrysler are specifically "carryover balances."

[48] The 2008 data on projected cash contributions are the latest publicly available data. GM was to file quarterly and annual financial reports for the period ending December 31, 2009, with the Securities and Exchange Commission by March 31, 2010. However, GM submitted a "notification of late filing" with the Commission and officials told us they plan to file the reports sometime in April 2010.

[49] As noted earlier, Daimler agreed to make installment payments of $200 million in 2009, 2010, and 2011 (for a total of $600 million).

[50] Chrysler expected to provide its 2009 audited annual financial statement to Treasury and its other shareholders by April 2010. Chrysler plans to file quarterly and annual financial reports with the Securities and Exchange Commission beginning with its 2010 audited annual financial statements, which will be publicly available.

[51] 26 U.S.C. § 430(i). Once it is fully phased in, the test for determining if a plan is at risk will be whether its funding target attainment percentage for the preceding year, not applying at-risk requirements, is less than 80 percent and its funding target attainment percentage for the preceding year, applying at-risk requirements, was less than 70 percent. 26 U.S.C. § 430(i)(4).

[52] Plans determined to be "at risk" are required to use actuarial assumptions that result in a higher value of plan liabilities and, thus, require additional funding by the plan sponsor. 26 U.S.C. § 430(i)(1)(A)(i) and (i)(1)(B). For example, plans in "at-risk" status are required to assume that all workers eligible to retire in the next 10 years will do so as soon as they can, and that they will take their distribution in whatever form would create the highest cost to the plan, without regard to whether those workers actually do so.

[53] The notice for the GM's hourly plan covers the plan year beginning October 1, 2008, and ending September 30, 2009. GM's estimated plan funding requirements of $12.3 billion for the years 2013 and 2014 reflect funding needs for both its hourly and its salaried pension plans combined, including consideration of its hourly pension plan being in "at-risk" status. GM's salaried pension plan is not "at risk."

[54] 26 U.S.C. §§ 436(b) and (d).

[55] For further details on Delphi, see appendix I.

[55] For further details on Delphi, see appendix I.

[56] A "going concern" qualification is a reflection of the auditor's substantial doubt of the audited company's ability to remain in operation. Organizational weaknesses including overcapacity and high wage agreements, when combined with questions about their ability to continue as a going concern may have the effect of triggering loan and bond defaults and making it difficult for suppliers to raise new capital.

[57] In a hearing before the Senate Committee on Banking, Housing, and Urban Affairs in October 2009, a representative of nearly 700 parts suppliers testified that administrative obstacles, bank restrictions, and limitations on the types of receivables eligible for assistance had created a significant gap between those suppliers eligible to participate and those suppliers able to participate in the program. Restoring Credit to Manufacturers: Hearing Before the S. Comm. on Banking, Housing and Urban Affairs, 110th Cong. (2009)

(statement of David Andrea, Vice President, Industry Analysis and Economics, Motor and Equipment Manufacturers Association).

[58] According to GM, the 31 top suppliers that participated in the Treasury program accounted for less than 2 percent of GM's North American 2009 adjusted present value.

[59] For further details on PBGC's guaranteed benefit limits, see appendix II.

[60] This describes the situation when an underfunded defined benefit plan covered by PBGC's single-employer insurance program is terminated and benefits are paid subject to certain limits. 29 U.S.C. § 1322. If a plan is covered by PBGC's multiemployer insurance program, PBGC will provide financial assistance, but it will not trustee the plan or pay unfunded guaranteed benefits. 29 U.S.C. § 1341a. Also, while PBGC insures most defined benefit plans, it does not insure some categories, such as defined benefit plans sponsored by governments or churches. In addition, PBGC does not insure defined contribution plans. 29 U.S.C. § 1321(b)(1)-(3).

[61] 29 U.S.C. § 1361.

[62] For PBGC to classify a plan as a "reasonably possible" termination, it must have $5 million or more of underfunding, as well as meet additional criteria, such as that it has filed for bankruptcy, has requested a funding waiver, has missed a minimum funding contribution, or has a bond rating that is below-investment grade for Standard & Poor's or Moody's. At even higher risk are those companies PBGC classifies as "probables," which are those that PBGC deems likely to terminate in the future. For more information on this topic, see GAO, *Private Pensions: Questions Concerning the Pension Benefit Guaranty Corporation's Practices Regarding Single-Employer Probable Claims*, GAO-05-991R (Washington, D.C.: Sept. 9, 2005).

[63] PBGC's exposure to loss ultimately may be less than these amounts because of the limits on guaranteed benefits, as specified under ERISA and related regulations (see appendix II). However, calculations taking into account these limits are not specifically factored into PBGC's estimates of exposure, *per se*, because it is difficult to prospectively determine the precise extent and effect of the limits prior to a plan's actual termination.

[64] PBGC calculates estimates of exposure by using information such as the reports submitted to IRS and corporate annual reports. Although guaranteed benefit limit calculations are not part of PBGC's estimate of its exposure, *per se*, its estimate nevertheless attempts to approximate the losses it would incur under ERISA upon a plan's termination. 29 U.S.C. § 1361. Also, PBGC officials noted that these estimates can change substantially over time due to volatility in discount rates and plan asset values.

[65] PBGC holds assets in two categories of funds: the trust funds and the revolving funds. The trust funds hold assets acquired from terminated plans; the revolving funds consist of premium receipts. Separate funds are maintained for the single-employer and the multiemployer programs. 29 U.S.C. § 1305.

[66] Following termination of a plan insured under the single-employer program, the net liability assumed by PBGC is equal to the present value of the future guaranteed benefits payable by PBGC less amounts provided by the plan's assets and amounts recoverable by PBGC from the plan sponsor and members of the plan sponsor's controlled group, as defined by ERISA. 29 U.S.C. § 1301(a)(14).

[67] 29 U.S.C. § 1362(e), which authorizes PBGC to assess plan liability when there is a substantial cessation of operations by an employer.

[68] See GAO, *Pension Benefit Guaranty Corporation: More Strategic Approach Needed for Processing Complex Plans Prone to Delays and Overpayments*, GAO-09-716 (Washington, D.C.: Aug. 17, 2009).

[69] GAO-09-716.

[70] GAO-09-716.

[71] 29 U.S.C. § 1322(b)(1), (3) and (7), and 29 C.F.R. §§ 4022.21, 4022.24 and 4022.25 (2009). These guarantee limits are commonly referred to as the maximum limit, the "accrued-atnormal" limit, and the phase-in limit. For further details, see appendix II.

[72] PPA amended ERISA to provide a special phase-in rule for shutdown benefits and other unpredictable contingent event benefits. 29 U.S.C. § 1322(b)(8). PBGC intends to issue a separate rule to implement this section of the law, but the proposed rule has not yet been published.

[73] In 2009, the maximum monthly guarantee limit for those age 65 with no survivor benefit was $4,500, or $54,000 annually. Retirees who are under age 65 as of the date of plan termination could be subject to a maximum limit on their monthly benefit that is considerably lower. For example, in 2009, the monthly maximum limit for a retiree age 60 was $2,925, and for a retiree age 50, just $1,575.

[74] For more details about the accrued-at-normal limit, see appendix II.

[75] For more details about the phase-in limit, see appendix II.

[76] In addition, this limit would have eliminated the additional $300 monthly benefit provided to certain post-65 retirees and surviving spouses in GM's salaried plan in exchange for elimination of their company-sponsored retiree health care.

[77] For a list of recent GM and Chrysler attrition programs, see appendix III.

[78] 29 U.S.C. §§ 1322(c) and 1344.

[79] After benefits derived from employee contributions are paid, benefits of those retired (or eligible to retire) for at least 3 years are given priority status in this allocation process (priority category 3). In terminations of large complex plans, plan assets typically are depleted with the payment of benefits in this priority category. (See GAO-09-716, table 4.) For PBGC's example benefit calculations that illustrate how termination of the automaker pension plans might impact participant benefits, see appendix VII.

[80] For examples of this impact on participant benefits, see appendix VII.

[81] The IRS oversees the tax qualified status of pension plans and the Secretary of the Treasury serves as one of the three members on PBGC's board of directors. 26 U.S.C. § 401(a) and 29 U.S.C. § 1302(d). In addition, PBGC provides insurance for most private defined benefit plans. 29 U.S.C. § 1321.

[82] Previous reports have discussed the conflicts of interest that could be created by having the government both regulate and hold an ownership interest in an institution or company. See GAO, *Troubled Asset Relief Program: The U.S. Government Role as Shareholder in AIG, Citigroup, Chrysler, and General Motors and Preliminary Views on its Investment Management Activities*, GAO-10-325T (Washington, D.C.: Dec. 16, 2009); GAO, *Troubled Asset Relief Program: Status of Efforts to Address Transparency and Accountability Issues*, GAO-09-296 (Washington, D.C.: Jan. 30, 2009); and GAO, *Troubled Asset Relief Program: Additional Actions Needed to Better Ensure Accountability, Integrity, and Transparency*, GAO-09-161 (Washington, D.C.: Dec. 2, 2008).

[83] GAO-10-151.

[84] GAO-10-151.

[85] 26 U.S.C. §§ 412 and 430.

[86] GAO-10-151.

In: TARP on the U.S. Automotive Industry...
Editors: S. E. Walcott, J. A. Capaldi

ISBN: 978-1-61324-363-3
© 2011 Nova Science Publishers, Inc.

Chapter 4

TROUBLED ASSET RELIEF PROGRAM: CONTINUED STEWARDSHIP NEEDED AS TREASURY DEVELOPS STRATEGIES FOR MONITORING AND DIVESTING FINANCIAL INTERESTS IN CHRYSLER AND GM[*]

United States Government Accountability Office

WHY GAO DID THIS STUDY

The Department of the Treasury (Treasury) provided $81.1 billion in Troubled Asset Relief Program (TARP) aid to the U.S. auto industry, including $62 billion in restructuring loans to Chrysler Group LLC (Chrysler) and General Motors Company (GM). In return, Treasury received 9.85 percent equity in Chrysler, 60.8 percent equity and $2.1 billion in preferred stock in GM, and $13.8 billion in debt obligations between the two companies.

As part of GAO's statutory responsibilities for providing oversight of TARP, this report addresses (1) steps Chrysler and GM have taken since December 2008 to reorganize, (2) Treasury's oversight of its financial interest in the companies, and (3) considerations for Treasury in monitoring and selling its equity in the companies. GAO reviewed documents on the auto companies' restructuring and spoke with officials at Treasury, Chrysler, and GM, and individuals with expertise in finance and the auto industry.

WHAT GAO RECOMMENDS

GAO recommends that the Secretary of the Treasury ensure the expertise needed to monitor Treasury's investment in Chrysler and GM remains in place, report to Congress on its general approach for monitoring the companies' performance, and have a plan for

---

[*] This is an edited, reformatted and augmented version of the United States Government Accountability Office's publication, dated November 2009.

evaluating the optimal method and timing for divesting Treasury's equity. Treasury generally agreed with GAO's findings, conclusions, and recommendations.

WHAT GAO FOUND

Chrysler and GM have made changes since December 2008 to address key challenges to achieving viability, but the ultimate effect of these changes remains to be seen. The companies have eliminated a substantial amount of their long-term debt, reduced the number of brands and models of vehicles they sell, rationalized their dealership networks, and lowered production costs and capacities by reducing the number of factories and employees. It is difficult to fully assess the impact of these changes because of the short amount of time that has passed since reorganization and the low level of new vehicle sales. Moreover, Chrysler and GM are revaluing their assets and liabilities based on their reorganizations in 2009 and expect to prepare financial statements based on this effort in the coming months.

Treasury does not plan to be involved in the day-to-day management of Chrysler and GM, but it plans to monitor the companies' performance. Treasury developed several principles to guide its role as a shareholder, including the commitment that although Treasury reserves the right to set upfront conditions to protect taxpayers and promote financial stability, Treasury will oversee its financial interests in a hands-off, commercial manner. The conditions that Treasury set for the companies include requiring that a portion of their vehicles be manufactured in the United States and that they report to Treasury on the use of the TARP funding provided. Treasury officials told us that they are also requiring that Chrysler and GM submit financial information on a regular basis and that they plan to meet with the companies' top management on a regular basis to discuss the companies' financial condition.

Treasury should make certain that its current approach for monitoring and selling its equity in Chrysler and GM fully addresses all important considerations financial and industry experts identified. For example, Treasury initially hired or consulted with a number of individuals with experience in investment banking or equity analysis to help assess Chrysler's and GM's financial condition and develop financing packages for the companies. Many of these individuals have recently left as the restructuring phase of Treasury's work has been completed. Treasury will need to ensure these staff and any staff that depart in the future are replaced as needed with similarly qualified personnel. Also, Treasury does not currently contract with or employ outside firms with specialty expertise for its work with the auto industry but may need to do so in the future, to make sure sufficient expertise is available to oversee the government's significant financial interests in Chrysler and GM. In addition, although Treasury officials told us they are considering all options for divesting the government's ownership interests, including an initial public offering or private sale, they have focused primarily on a series of public offerings for GM and have not identified criteria for determining the optimal time and method to sell. Regardless of the option pursued, however, Treasury is unlikely to recover the entirety of its investment in Chrysler or GM, given that the companies' values would have to grow substantially above what they have been in the past.

ABBREVIATIONS

AIFP	Automotive Industry Financing Program
COP	Congressional Oversight Panel
EESA	Emergency Economic Stabilization Act
GM	General Motors Company
NAS	National Academy of Sciences
OFS	Office of Financial Stability
SEC	Securities and Exchange Commission
TARP	Troubled Asset Relief Program
UAW	International Union, United Automobile, Aerospace and Agricultural Implement Workers of America

November 2, 2009
Congressional Committees

After authorizing more than $80 billion in financial assistance to the ailing domestic automotive industry since December 2008, the Department of the Treasury (Treasury) is in the unprecedented position of having ownership stakes in two of the nation's three largest auto manufacturers—Chrysler Group LLC (Chrysler) and General Motors Company (GM).[1] Although most automakers experienced declining sales in the last couple of years as the economy slipped into a recession, the current economic conditions have particularly hurt the sales of Chrysler and GM, resulting in significant financial losses and necessitating the use of billions of dollars of borrowed money or cash reserves to keep operating. In December 2008, the chief executive officers of Chrysler and GM testified before Congress that without federal assistance, their companies would likely run out of the cash needed to keep operating.

Concerned that the collapse of one, or both, of these companies could pose a systemic risk to the nation's economy, the previous Administration established the Automotive Industry Financing Program (AIFP) under the Troubled Asset Relief Program (TARP) in December 2008.[2] Through AIFP, Treasury provided loans to help Chrysler and GM continue operating as the companies restructured. In exchange for the funding it provided,

Treasury received 9.85 percent equity in the new Chrysler,[3] 60.8 percent equity and $2.1 billion in preferred stock in the new GM, and about $13.8 billion in debt obligations between the two companies.[4] The companies still struggle to remain competitive with other automakers and to regain market share.

We have previously reported that in a market economy the federal role in aiding industrial sectors should generally be of limited duration and establish clear limits on the extent of government involvement. Regarding assistance to the auto industry, we have noted that Treasury should have a plan for ending its financial involvement with Chrysler and GM that indicates how it will both sell its equity and ensure adequate repayment for the financial assistance it provided.[5] The current Administration has stated that it is a "reluctant shareholder" in Chrysler and GM, but that it would be irresponsible to "[give] away the equity stake to which taxpayers were rightly entitled."[6] As such, Treasury has said that in managing its equity it will seek to exit as soon as practicable, maximize return on investment, and foster strong companies that can be independently viable.

As part of our statutorily mandated responsibilities for providing timely oversight of TARP, we are continuing to monitor Treasury's assistance to the auto industry, including how Treasury is managing its equity in Chrysler and GM and how it plans to sell this equity.[7] This report will explore the following issues related to Treasury's ownership of Chrysler and GM: (1) steps Chrysler and GM have taken since December 2008 to reorganize, (2) Treasury's oversight of its financial interests in Chrysler and GM, and (3) important considerations for Treasury in monitoring and selling its equity in the companies.

SCOPE AND METHODOLOGY

To identify steps Chrysler and GM have taken since December 2008 to reorganize, we reviewed information on the companies' finances and operations, including financial statements, select documents from their bankruptcy proceedings, and company-provided data, and interviewed representatives of the companies.

To determine how Treasury will monitor its financial interests in Chrysler and GM, we reviewed transaction documents related to the restructuring of Chrysler and GM that Treasury was a party to, such as the secured credit agreements and shareholders' agreements, which set forth Treasury's rights with regard to the companies and certain requirements the companies must comply with. We also reviewed information on Treasury's plans for overseeing its ownership interests in the companies, including White House and Treasury press releases, and testimony statements. In addition, we interviewed officials from Treasury's Office of Financial Stability (OFS), which was established to administer TARP, about their plans to monitor the government's financial interests, including Treasury's enforcement of the reporting requirements that were established for Chrysler and GM. We did not, however, independently verify the processes and procedures Treasury has established to monitor and enforce the reporting requirements.[8]

To identify important considerations for Treasury in monitoring and determining how and when to sell its equity in Chrysler and GM, we conducted a review of the academic literature on government ownership of private entities, including both domestic and international cases of private equity investments, privatization, and nationalization, and reviewed analyses of the potential future value of Chrysler and GM and Treasury's equity stake. We also interviewed individuals with expertise in the financial condition of domestic automakers, principles of corporate restructuring, and government ownership of private entities. The financial and business experts whose opinions are represented in this report were selected from a list of experts identified for us by the National Academy of Sciences (NAS) for our earlier report on challenges facing Chrysler and GM.[9] Of the panel of experts we interviewed for that report, we contacted a subset whose expertise was particularly relevant to structuring an exit strategy. In addition to individuals identified by NAS, we spoke with individuals NAS experts themselves identified as being knowledgeable in this area. We also added two experts with investment experience specifically in the auto industry. We chose experts in government management of investments in private companies by identifying former federal government officials who were involved in well-known cases of government assistance to private entities, such as the federal assistance provided to Chrysler in 1979. We conducted individual semistructured interviews with these individuals, both in person and by telephone. Once this review was completed, we analyzed the content of the literature and the interviews for recurring themes and summarized these common results. A list of the individuals we spoke with is provided in appendix I.

We conducted this performance audit from August 2009 to November 2009 in accordance with generally accepted government auditing standards. Those standards require that we plan and perform the audit to obtain sufficient, appropriate evidence to provide a reasonable basis for our findings and conclusions based on our audit objectives. We believe that the evidence obtained provides a reasonable basis for our findings and conclusions based on our audit objectives.

BACKGROUND

Treasury's decision to provide substantial amounts of funding to the auto industry—more than 12 percent of the TARP funds authorized to date— and to accept equity in the companies as a form of repayment for a portion of the assistance reflects Treasury's view of the importance of the industry to the financial health of the United States as a whole. The auto industry— including automakers, dealerships, and automotive parts suppliers— contributes substantially to the U.S. economy by, for example, directly employing about 1.7 million people, according to industry and government data.[10] To help stabilize this industry and avoid economic disruptions, Treasury authorized $81.1 billion through AIFP from December 2008 through June 2009 for the following purposes.

- **Funding to support automakers during restructuring.** Treasury has provided financial assistance to Chrysler and GM to support their restructuring as they attempt to return to profitability. This assistance was provided in loans and equity investments in the companies.
- **Auto Supplier Support Program.** Under this program, Chrysler and GM received funding for the purpose of ensuring payment to suppliers. The program was designed to ensure that automakers receive the parts and components they need to manufacture vehicles and that suppliers have access to liquidity on their receivables.
- **Warranty Commitment Program.** This program was designed to mitigate consumer uncertainty about purchasing vehicles from the restructuring automakers by providing funding to guarantee the warranties on new vehicles purchased from them. Funds were provided to Chrysler and GM under this program but have been repaid in full because both were able to continue to honor consumer warranties.
- **Funding to support automotive finance companies.** Treasury has provided funding to support Chrysler Financial and GMAC LLC, financial services companies whose businesses include providing consumer financing for vehicle purchases and dealer financing for inventory. Chrysler Financial is following Treasury's directive to liquidate its business and is planning to wind down its operations by the end of 2011. GMAC has agreed to provide Chrysler customers and dealers with financing for retail and wholesale purchases.

Table 1. TARP Funding Provided to the Auto Industry, as of September 20, 2009

(Dollars in billions)

Description of Company funding		Authorized amount	Repayments of principal	Interest and dividend payments	Amount and form of future repayments
Chrysler	Loans to Chrysler for general business purposes and restructuring	$12.5	0	0.052	A total of up to $7.1 billion will be repaid as a term loan, including $5.1 billion to be repaid within 8 years and $2 billion to be repaid within 2.5 years. Treasury also received a 9.85 percent equity share in the new Chrysler. Treasury also has $5.4 billion of debt in the old Chrysler, but it is not clear at this time whether this amount will be repaid.[a]
	Supplier Support Program loan	1.0	0	0.002	Amounts provided are due to be repaid by April 2010.
	Warranty Commitment Program loan	0.28	0.28	0.003	All funds have been repaid.
	Total	$13.8	0.23	0.06	
General Motors	Loans to GM for general business purposes and restructuring	49.5	0	0.168	A total of $6.7 billion will be repaid as a term loan. Treasury also received $2.1 billion in preferred stock, and 60.8 percent equity in the new GM. Treasury also has $986 million debt in the old GM, which it does not expect to be repaid.
	Supplier Support Program loan	2.5	0	0.004	Amounts provided are due to be repaid by April 2010.
	Warranty Commitment Program loan	0.361	0.361	0	All funds have been repaid.
	Loan to participate in GMAC rights offering	0.884	0	0.009	Treasury exchanged this loan for a portion of GM's equity in GMAC. As a result, Treasury holds a 35.4 percent common equity interest in GMAC. The GM loan was terminated but GM paid $9 million in interest on the loan to participate in GMAC rights offering before the loan was terminated.
	Total	$53.24	0.36	0.18	

(Dollars in billions)

Description of Company funding		Authorized amount	Repayments of principal	Interest and dividend payments	Amount and form of future repayments
Chrysler Financial	Loan funded through Chrysler LB Receivables Trust	1.5	1.5	0.007	Loan repaid in full plus about $7 million in interest.[b]
GMAC	Preferred stock and convertible preferred stock	12.5	Not applicable	0.43	Treasury may convert $7.5 billion of its preferred shares to common shares upon specific events such as public offerings.
Total		$81.1	$2.1	$0.68	

Source: GAO analysis of Treasury information.

Note: Numbers are affected by rounding.

[a] The $5.4 billion is composed of the original remaining loan and additional amounts provided as bankruptcy financing. Payment of this amount is contingent on receipt of distributions from Chrysler Financial in an amount equal to the greater of $1.375 billion or 40 percent of distributions.

[b] In lieu of warrants, Treasury received an additional note from Chrysler Financial. The initial aggregate principal amount of the note was $15 million, which Chrysler Financial has repaid.

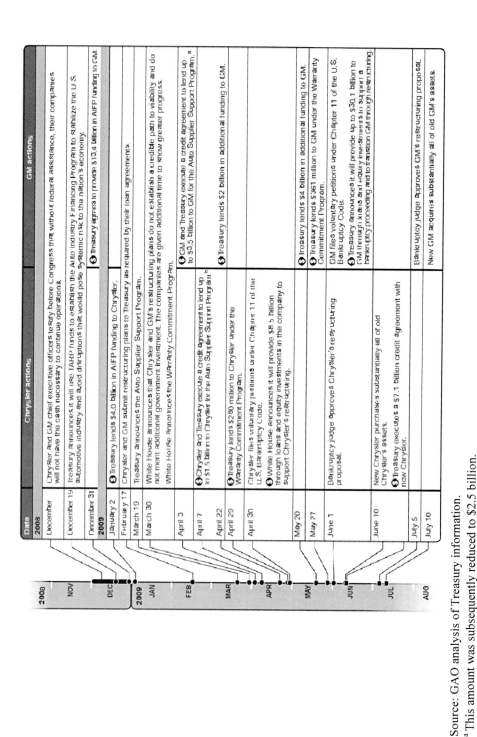

Source: GAO analysis of Treasury information.

[a] This amount was subsequently reduced to $2.5 billion.
[b] This amount was subsequently reduced to $1 billion.

Figure 1. Key Events in Treasury's Assistance to the Auto Industry and Chrysler's and GM's Restructuring.

Table 1 provides information on the funding levels Treasury authorized under AIFP, the amounts Chrysler, GM, and the finance companies have repaid, and Treasury's plans to be repaid or otherwise compensated for the outstanding funds. Treasury officials have said the agency does not intend to provide more funding to Chrysler or GM.

As a condition of the initial federal financial assistance provided in December 2008 and January 2009, the Bush Administration required that Chrysler and GM develop restructuring plans that would, among other things, identify how the companies plan to achieve and sustain long-term financial viability. President Obama rejected the restructuring plans that Chrysler and GM submitted in February 2009, and required the companies to develop more aggressive plans. After reviewing the revised plans, the President announced in April 2009 and June 2009 that the government would provide additional financial assistance to support Chrysler's and GM's restructuring efforts, respectively. To effectuate the restructuring plans, both companies filed voluntary petitions for reorganization under Chapter 11 of the U.S. Bankruptcy Code. Through the bankruptcy process, the newly organized Chrysler and GM purchased substantially all of the operating assets of the old companies. In June 2009 and July 2009, respectively, the new Chrysler and new GM emerged from the bankruptcy process with substantially less debt and with streamlined operations. The old companies, which retained very few assets but most of the liabilities, remain in bankruptcy, where their remaining liabilities are being dealt with. These liabilities include a portion of the loans Treasury provided to the companies prior to bankruptcy in the amounts of $5.4 billion for Chrysler and $986 million for GM. As noted, Treasury has stated that it has no plans to provide additional assistance to Chrysler and GM. Figure 1 describes other key events in the funding and restructuring of the auto companies.

CHRYSLER AND GM HAVE ADDRESSED SOME CHALLENGES IMPORTANT TO ACHIEVING VIABILITY, BUT THE EFFECT OF THESE ACTIONS REMAINS TO BE SEEN

Since the condition of the domestic auto industry first came to the forefront of national attention in December 2008, Chrysler and GM have made changes to address key challenges to achieving viability, but the effect that these actions will have on the companies remains to be seen. As we previously reported, a number of operational and financial challenges stand in the way of Chrysler's and GM's return to profitability.[11] Some of these challenges are beyond the companies' control, such as current economic conditions and limited credit availability. However, other factors the companies can exert more control over include the companies' debt levels, dealership networks, and production costs and capacity. Aided by substantial government assistance and bankruptcy reorganization, they have begun to address a number of these challenges. Although the companies' restructuring efforts started before receiving government assistance under TARP, our analysis focuses on the period between first receiving TARP assistance (around the end of 2008) and after bankruptcy reorganization (June 2009 and July 2009 for Chrysler and GM, respectively). The following are some key challenges that Chrysler and GM have begun to address.

- **Reducing debt.** Through the bankruptcy process, Chrysler and GM eliminated a substantial amount of their long-term financial liabilities, including debt owed to bank lenders and bondholders. In our previous work, we discussed the importance of reducing debt for companies to achieve long-term viability. By reducing the amount the companies pay in interest expense, cash flow is improved, freeing up more money for research and development and other activities that can help the businesses prosper. The precise amount of the companies' total debt reduction is not known because the value of some debts will not be determined until the companies' post-reorganization accounting is complete. However, some reduced or eliminated debts whose values are known include $6.9 billion of secured bank debt owed by old Chrysler, of which $2 billion was repaid and none carried forward to new Chrysler; $5.9 billion of secured bank debt owed by old GM, substantially all of which was repaid by old GM, leaving new GM with none of this debt; substantial reductions of the companies' monetary obligations to the trusts established to provide health care benefits to retirees of the International Union, United Automobile, Aerospace and Agricultural Implement Workers of America (UAW); and about $27 billion in unsecured GM bondholder debt and $2 billion in unsecured Chrysler obligations, which stayed as a liability of the old GM and old Chrysler, leaving new GM and new Chrysler with none of this debt.

- **Reducing the number of brands and models.** GM is reducing its North American brands from eight to four.[12] In November 2007, Chrysler announced it would eliminate four models within its three primary brands—Chrysler, Dodge, and Jeep—and in October 2009 it announced that it would create a fourth brand by splitting the Ram brand out of the Dodge brand. As we have previously reported, advantages of reducing brands and models include eliminating costs such as factory tooling and product development, reducing intracompany competition for sales of similar models, and allowing more focus and resources on the remaining models' quality, image, and performance.

- **Rationalizing dealership networks to align with sales volumes.** Both Chrysler and GM have made cuts to their dealership networks since yearend 2008. As we reported in April, the companies' dealer networks were too large to be supported by recent sales levels. As of April 2009, Chrysler, Ford, and GM dealerships—most of which are independently owned and operated—were more numerous and, in general, sold half or fewer vehicles per dealership than dealerships selling vehicles from foreign automakers. Higher sales per store allow for a greater return on the dealer's fixed costs of running the business, allowing for more investment in facilities and advertising—which ultimately benefits the automaker by improving the price for which its cars are sold. As of June 30, 2009, shortly after the new Chrysler emerged from bankruptcy, Chrysler had reduced its U.S. dealerships to 2,382, a reduction of about 28 percent from the yearend 2008 level of 3,298.[13] As of July 2009, when the new GM emerged from bankruptcy, its number of dealers had declined to 6,039 through normal attrition, down from 6,375 at year-end 2008. GM is executing "wind-down" agreements with another approximately 1,300 dealerships and expects another 600 Saturn, Saab, or Hummer dealerships to be transferred to another manufacturer or be phased out. With additional normal attrition, GM expects to have between

3,600 and 3,800 dealerships by the end of 2010, which will represent a 44 percent reduction from 2008 year-end numbers.

- **Reducing production costs and capacity.** Both companies have made reductions in their production costs and capacity since year-end 2008, according to company-provided information. In our April report, we noted such reductions are important because the companies'pre-reorganization cost structures were not sustainable given the decline in their sales and market shares in recent years.[14] Table 2 shows the reductions the companies made between year-end 2008 and the dates they emerged from bankruptcy. In addition to the reductions made during these time periods, the companies implemented restructuring efforts prior to 2008 and plan additional reductions in the future. For instance, Chrysler closed two factories, reduced a number of shifts, and cut nearly 29,000 hourly, salaried, and supplemental employees between year-end 2006 and yearend 2008. GM announced in September 2009 that it will add a third shift at three U.S. assembly plants as part of a plan to close other plants to increase the efficiency of its manufacturing operations. Chrysler and GM have also reached agreements with the UAW, in accordance with the terms of the companies'prebankruptcy loans from Treasury, which will result in further reductions in production costs. Under these terms, the companies were required to use their best efforts to reduce total compensation paid to U.S. employees, including wages and benefits, to be comparable with the total compensation Honda, Nissan, or Toyota pays to employees at their U.S. facilities. The companies were also required to use their best efforts to make changes to work rules to be comparable with the work rules of Honda's, Nissan's, or Toyota's U.S. facilities. Changes the UAW agreed to as part of restructuring included cancellation of cost-of-living adjustments for current workers and restructuring of skilled trade classifications, among other things.

Table 2. Changes to Chrysler's and GM's U.S. Production Costs and Capacity

Production capacity[a]	Chrysler			GM		
	Year-end 2008	After reorganization	Percent reduction	Year end 2008	After reorganization	Percent reduction
Factories	21	20[b]	4.8%	47	34	27.7%
Hourly employees	24,135	21,082	12.6%	61,999	54,391	12.3%
Salaried employees	10,691	10,307	3.6%	29,655	27,091	8.6%

Source: GAO presentation of Chrysler and GM data.
[a] According to Treasury, these numbers will likely continue to change in the future, since the companies'restructuring efforts are not complete.
[b] Four additional factories that remain with old Chrysler are planned for future closure.

Whether and to what extent these changes will improve Chrysler's and GM's profitability and long-term viability remains to be seen. Many elements of a company's financial statements are also used in measures of financial health, but neither Chrysler nor GM has finalized new financial statements based on their reorganization. Chrysler and GM have agreed to provide certain financial information, as outlined in agreements between Chrysler and its shareholders, including Treasury, and between GM and the Securities and Exchange

Commission (SEC). Consistent with the agreements, Chrysler and GM plan to complete the process of determining the fair value of the assets and liabilities transferred to the new companies for their audited 2009 year-end financial statements, which they expect to complete by April 2010 and March 2010, respectively.[15] Chrysler will provide its 2009 audited annual financial statement to Treasury and its other shareholders, and GM will provide its 2009 audited annual financial statement to SEC, where it will also be available to the public. Chrysler will begin filing quarterly and annual financial reports with SEC beginning with its 2010 audited annual financial statements, which will be publicly available through SEC. Before audited annual financial statements are filed with SEC, Chrysler and GM will make other select information publicly available.

Moreover, whether enough time has passed for the impact of the structural changes to be seen is unlikely, especially given that the automakers have not completed restructuring, the economy is still recovering, and new vehicle purchases remain at low levels. For instance, although the federal Car Allowance Rebate System program resulted in a sales spike in August,[16] September sales returned to historically low levels. These and other challenges are likely to delay the companies' recovery beyond what it would be under more favorable economic circumstances.

TREASURY DOES NOT PLAN TO BE INVOLVED IN CHRYSLER'S OR GM'S DAY-TO-DAY OPERATIONS OR MANAGEMENT, BUT IT PLANS TO CLOSELY MONITOR THE COMPANIES' PERFORMANCE

Treasury, which has a sizable financial stake in Chrysler and GM, does not plan to be involved in the day-to-day management of the companies, but it has established certain requirements that will be in effect as long as it holds debt or equity in the companies.[17] Treasury has distinct rights as both a creditor and an equity owner. Its rights as a creditor are documented in the secured credit agreements, which set forth the terms and provisions of the loans Treasury provided to new Chrysler and new GM. Its rights as an equity owner are documented in a number of transactional documents related to the formation of the new Chrysler and the new GM, including shareholders' agreements, equity registration rights agreements, and organizational documents. Treasury's role as an equity owner focuses on monitoring the financial health of the companies in order to protect the value of Treasury's equity stake.[18] Treasury developed several principles to guide its role as an equity owner, including the commitment that, although Treasury reserves the right to set up-front conditions to protect taxpayers and promote financial stability, Treasury plans to oversee its financial interests in a commercial manner, in which it will focus primarily on maximizing its return and take a hands-off approach to day-to-day management. Treasury plans to reserve its involvement for major transactions such as the sale of a controlling share of the companies. Treasury's role as a creditor is not as clearly delineated, but much like in its role as equity owner, Treasury has said it will focus on monitoring the companies' financial health.

Conditions set by Treasury in the credit agreements include requiring that the companies comply with provisions applicable to companies receiving TARP assistance, in accordance with the Emergency Economic Stabilization Act (EESA), as well as other requirements that are specific to Chrysler and GM.[19] According to the agreements, Chrysler and GM must do the following:

- **Produce a portion of their vehicles in the United States.** Chrysler must either manufacture 40 percent of its U.S. sales volume in the United States or its U.S. production volume must be at least 90 percent of its 2008 U.S. production volume. GM agrees to use its commercially reasonable best efforts to ensure that the volume of manufacturing conducted in the United States is consistent with at least 90 percent of the level envisioned in GM's business plan.
- **Comply with the executive compensation requirements of EESA.**[20] These requirements state that bonuses or incentive compensation paid to any of the senior executive officers or the next 20 most highly compensated employees based on materially inaccurate earnings must be repaid, no golden parachute payments may be made to a senior executive officer or any of the next five most highly compensated employees, compensation in excess of $500,000 per executive may not be deducted for tax purposes, and the companies must establish a compensation committee of independent directors to review employee compensation plans and the risks posed by these plans.
- **Have an expense policy that is in compliance with TARP standards for compensation and corporate governance.** The policy must govern hosting and sponsoring for conferences and events, travel accommodations and expenditures, office or facility renovations and relocations, and entertainment and holiday parties, among other things.
- **Report to Treasury on the use of government funds.** The companies are to provide Treasury with a report each quarter setting forth in reasonable detail the actual use of the TARP funding they received upon exiting from bankruptcy.
- **Have internal controls to ensure compliance with the requirements.** The companies are to promptly establish internal controls to provide reasonable assurance of compliance in all material respects with each of the credit agreement's requirements for executive privileges and compensation, aircraft, expenses, and the Employ American Workers Act.[21] The companies must also have documentation of these controls and the companies' compliance with them.
- **Report on events related to pension plans.** The companies must report to Treasury if actions occur that could result in the companies failing to meet the minimum funding requirements for their pension plans, or if the companies plan to terminate any of their plans.[22]

To protect the value of its equity share and the likelihood of loan repayment, Treasury has also established requirements under which the companies must report financial information, and it intends to use this information to closely monitor the financial condition of Chrysler and GM. The financial reporting requirements are set forth in Treasury's credit agreements with the companies and other agreements that specify the rights of the companies and their shareholders, which include Treasury and other parties.[23] GM is also subject to additional reporting requirements related to the reserve portion of its loan from Treasury that is being held in escrow.[24] Treasury has agreed with the companies on additional financial, managerial, and operating information, which the companies will provide in monthly reporting packages, along with items specified in the agreements. Tables 3 and 4 provide details on Chrysler's and GM's reporting requirements.

Table 3: Chrysler's Financial Reporting Requirements

Requirements Treasury established as creditor
Until repayment of the loan, Chrysler must provide to Treasury • its consolidated balance sheet and the related consolidated statements of income and cash flow, on a quarterly and annual basis, and • updates to its schedules of real property, mortgaged property, pledged equity and notes, subsidiaries, and mortgage filing offices (beginning in 2010).
Requirements Treasury established as equity owner
As long as Treasury holds its initial membership shares in Chrysler, Chrysler must provide • public reports containing quarterly and annual financial information, and • quarterly and annual financial reports to the Securities and Exchange Commission (beginning with its 2010 audited annual financial statements). As long as Treasury holds more than 5 percent equity, Chrysler must provide to Treasury • monthly, quarterly, and annual management financial reports summarizing results of the company for the period and comparing these results with the annual budget, and • unaudited quarterly and audited annual balance sheets and related statements of income and cash flow.

Source: GAO presentation of Treasury information.

Table 4. GM's Financial Reporting Requirements

Requirements Treasury established as creditor
Until repayment of the loan, GM must provide to Treasury • its consolidated balance sheet and the related consolidated statements of income and cash flow, on an annual (audited) and quarterly basis (unaudited), • copies of any financial statements or reports GM is required to file with the Securities and Exchange Commission, and • other information that Treasury might periodically request.
Until the balance of GM's escrow account reaches zero or the escrow account's expiration on June 30, 2010, GM must provide to Treasury • biweekly 13-week forecasts, • monthly liquidity status reports, and • monthly budgets covering a 5-year period.
Requirements Treasury established as equity owner
As long as Treasury owns at least 10 percent of GM's common stock, GM must provide to Treasury • all financial statements, budgets, reports, liquidity statements, materials, data, and other information pursuant to Section 5 of the credit agreement, and • a monthly report, the format and content of which Treasury has the right to specify.

Source: GAO presentation of Treasury information.

According to Treasury officials, they plan to review and analyze the reports they receive under creditor and equity owner requirements to identify areas of concern, such as actual market share lagging behind the projected market share, an excess of inventory, or other signs that business is foundering. Treasury does not have authority to direct the companies to take specific actions to address such findings, but Treasury said it plans to notify the companies' management and the Secretary of the Treasury if it sees any cause for concern in the financial reports. In addition to reviewing financial information, Treasury's team of staff responsible for overseeing AIFP (subsequently referred to as the auto team) plans to meet monthly via teleconference and quarterly in person with the companies' top management to discuss the companies' progress against their restructuring plans. Important findings that result from the review of financial reports or management meetings will also be conveyed to key staff in OFS and other Treasury offices with responsibilities for managing TARP investments. Treasury also intends to use financial reports as a basis for decisions on how and when to sell its equity in the companies, as discussed below.

While Treasury has stated that it plans to manage its investments in Chrysler and GM in a hands-off manner and will not interfere in day-to-day operations of the companies, Chrysler and GM will be subject to requirements regarding compensation, expenses, and reporting that other auto companies are not. For example, as discussed above, each company is subject to certain requirements about the vehicles it is to produce, such as the requirement to produce a portion of its vehicles in the United States. In addition, Chrysler's shareholders, including Treasury, have agreed that Fiat's equity stake in Chrysler will increase if Chrysler meets certain benchmarks, such as producing a vehicle that achieves a fuel economy of 40 miles per gallon or producing a new engine in the United States.[25] Treasury officials stated that they established such up-front conditions not solely to protect Treasury's financial interests as a creditor and equity owner but also to reflect the Administration's views on responsibly utilizing taxpayer resources for these companies. While Treasury has stated it does not plan to manage its stake in Chrysler or GM to achieve social policy goals, these requirements and covenants to which the companies are subject indicate the challenges Treasury has faced and likely will face in balancing its roles.

TREASURY'S APPROACH FOR MONITORING AND SELLING ITS OWNERSHIP INTEREST IN CHRYSLER AND GM DOES NOT FULLY ADDRESS ALL IMPORTANT CONSIDERATIONS EXPERTS IDENTIFIED

Treasury's general goals of exiting as soon as practicable, maximizing return on investment, and improving the strength and viability of Chrysler and GM are reasonable but possibly competing, according to the group of financial and industry experts we spoke with. For example, if Treasury sells its stake as soon as practicable, it may not maximize its return because too little time may have elapsed to demonstrate to investors the companies' potential for future profitability. Similarly, maximizing return on investment might require actions that do not contribute to making the companies strong and viable—for example, if Chrysler or GM does not return to profitability, Treasury may need to act to liquidate the companies, with the proceeds divided among its shareholders and creditors, to maximize its return on investment. Treasury will ultimately have to address these inherent trade-offs, decide which goal is most important, and then manage its interest in a way that prioritizes that goal over others. Treasury officials told us that they have considered these trade-offs and scenarios, including the worst-case scenario of Chrysler and GM not attaining long-term viability, and that they intend to balance these competing goals when deciding when and how to exit.

Treasury's current approach for monitoring its equity in Chrysler and GM does not fully address the considerations that our group of experts identified as important. In particular:

- **Retain necessary expertise.** Experts stressed that it is critical for Treasury to employ or contract with individuals with experience managing and selling equity in private companies. Individuals with investment, equity, and capital market backgrounds should be available to provide advice and expertise on the oversight and sale of Treasury's equity. This is crucial because prior to TARP, Treasury did not typically buy and sell stakes in private companies, so it has needed to employ appropriate personnel and to retain consultants, such as investment bankers and private equity analysts and firms, who are knowledgeable about such investment decisions. One expert we interviewed noted that housing such individuals in a program office created specifically and solely to oversee the government's investment in the companies could be beneficial. Program staff would be devoted solely to this purpose, and staff turnover would be low so that institutional knowledge would be preserved over the life of the program. The literature also stressed the importance of designating staff to oversee equity sales.

In assessing Chrysler's and GM's financial condition and future prospects and putting together financing packages for the companies, Treasury hired or consulted with a number of individuals with experience in investment banking, equity analysis, and the auto industry, but it has not established a program office to oversee its investment in the auto companies. As with the rest of the TARP programs, OFS oversees the investment in the auto companies. Some OFS employees work exclusively on the automotive companies, while others divide their time among multiple TARP programs. While the auto team has experienced a significant decline in its number of staff, and presently has limited engagements with outside firms with specialty expertise such as investment banking or equity analysis to assist in its management of its investment in the auto companies, Treasury officials stated that the rest of OFS is available to "backfill" as necessary and acts as a program office for Treasury's investment in the auto industry. However, OFS is not a dedicated program office for overseeing

Treasury's investment in Chrysler and GM, in that it has responsibilities for Treasury's investments in other companies. Treasury officials also stated that the reduction in the number of staff on the auto team has been a reflection of the team's reduced workload now that the intensive process of restructuring the companies is over and that the size of the team required for monitoring the government's investment is smaller than for a restructuring process.

Because of the particular needs of the auto companies and the unprecedented nature of providing such assistance, Treasury hired or contracted with a number of individuals with expertise in the auto industry, equity investment, and relevant areas of law throughout the first half of calendar year 2009 as Treasury assessed Chrysler's and GM's financial condition, assembled financing packages for the companies, and helped with restructuring efforts. When Treasury was heavily involved in the restructuring of the companies, Treasury's auto team consisted of 12 professional staff and 4 administrative staff, and it used the services of investment banking, consulting, and law firms. Since those agreements have been finalized and the workload has declined, two-thirds of the original professional staff has left, leaving Treasury with 4 of the original professional staff dedicated to auto issues, other OFS staff who have also helped monitor these investments, and limited use of investment or industry consultants. The leader of the auto team, who also serves as a senior adviser to the President on the auto industry, was recently appointed Senior Counselor for Manufacturing Policy, requiring him to split his time between the auto team and his new role. Moreover, Treasury officials told us that there will likely be additional staff reductions in the future because they plan to disband the auto team over time as other OFS staff assume the role of monitoring the financial condition of the companies. In commenting on a draft of this report, Treasury officials stated that in light of recent and expected staff turnover, they are prepared to hire personnel from within Treasury or externally to fill Treasury's monitoring function. Nonetheless, given the wind-down of the auto team— and the associated loss of dedicated staff with industry- and company-specific knowledge and expertise—we are concerned that Treasury may not have sufficient expertise to actively oversee and protect the government's ownership interests, including determining when and how to divest these interests.

In general, Treasury has faced challenges hiring the full complement of staff necessary to administer the TARP programs, in part because qualified candidates can often find a more competitive salary with a financial regulator, which has the authority to establish its own compensation programs without regard to certain requirements applicable to executive branch agencies. We have reported on the importance of Treasury documenting the skills and competencies it needs to administer the program and continuing to expeditiously hire personnel.[26] The quality of human capital policies and practices including, but not limited to, hiring affects the control environment. A strong control environment will depend, in part, on the managerial and other staff hired.[27] Treasury has made progress in hiring staff to administer TARP duties, but Treasury officials have not formally evaluated whether the staffing level to oversee AIFP is appropriate for their current and projected needs. Officials said that they had considered future needs and determined that Treasury's monitoring role could be achieved with fewer staff. In response to a request for documentation of their evaluation of staffing needs, Treasury provided us with a document showing the current and projected number of staff working on AIFP, but this document did not show how Treasurydetermined the appropriate number of staff or areas of expertise that would be needed for future workloads. In commenting on a draft of this report, Treasury officials stated that they had not had difficulty hiring qualified professionals to work on the auto team and did not anticipate having difficulties finding qualified staff in the future should the need arise for additional hiring.

- **Monitor and communicate company, industry, and economic indicators**. All of the experts we spoke with emphasized the importance of monitoring company indicators such as financial and operating performance, automotive industry-wide indicators such as vehicle sales, and broader economic indicators such as interest rates and consumer spending. Monitoring these indicators allows investors, including Treasury, to determine how well the companies, and in turn the investment, are performing in relation to the rest of the industry. It also allows an investor to determine how receptive the market would be to an equity sale, something that contributes to the price at which the investor can sell. Some experts also noted that Treasury should assign an individual with expertise in investment banking or private equity to be in charge of monitoring these metrics, which Treasury officials told us they had done. In addition to monitoring the investment, communicating a clearly articulated vision for TARP programs is important, as we have previously reported.

Understanding the different TARP programs and the distinct rationale for each can be difficult for Congress, the markets, and the public, because many of the programs address specific developments and have similar guidelines and terms. Specifically for AIFP, what Treasury's goals are for its investment in Chrysler and GM, and in turn, which indicators and metrics are necessary to determine progress in achieving these goals, is important information for Congress and the public to have. Although Treasury provides public information on activities in the TARP programs, including AIFP, through its legally mandated monthly reports to Congress, transaction reports, and others, these reports do not provide information on the indicators Treasury plans to use in assessing its goals for its auto investments. Identifying these indicators for Congress, and sharing as much of this information as possible, while still respecting the need for certain business sensitive information not to be released, could help Congress and the public better understand whether the investment in the auto companies has been successful.

Treasury's auto team plans to closely monitor the performance of Chrysler and GM by way of financial reports from the companies such as balance sheets and liquidity statements, which, in general, measure the financial health of a company at the time of the statement. It also plans to monitorindustry and broader economic indicators. The auto team plans to use this information to alert Chrysler and GM management to any problematic areas in the companies, and to help determine the best time and strategy for divesting the government's interest. Finally, Treasury officials have not informed Congress which components of the reporting package will be shared or how they plan to use the information contained in these packages to assess and monitor the companies' performance. In commenting on a draft of this report, Treasury noted that it will not make the components of these reports public because the release of certain information could put Chrysler and GM at a competitive disadvantage, thereby harming the potential recovery of taxpayer funds. Treasury further noted that the companies will publicly report on certain financial information—similar to what publicly traded companies report—in the future.

- **To the extent possible, determine the optimal time and method to divest**. One of the key components of an exit strategy is determining how and when to sell the investment. Given the many different ways to dispose of equity—through public sales, private negotiated sales, all at once, or in batches—experts noted that the seller's needs should inform decisions on which approach is most appropriate. For example, if an investor is interested in selling quickly but the company has not demonstrated the level of performance necessary for a successful initial public offering (IPO), in which the company first sells stock to the public, the investor should consider other sale options, such as a private sale. According to experts, a successful IPO requires that the companies show signs of earnings growth and future profitability, something that will take a considerable amount of time for Chrysler and GM, as they only recently emerged from bankruptcy. Attracting investors to the market is essential because lack of sufficient investor interest may result in depressed value of shares. Experts noted that a convergence of factors related both to financial markets and to the company itself create an ideal window for an IPO; this window can quickly open and close and cannot easily be predicted. This requires constant monitoring of up-to-date company, industry, and economic indicators when an investor is considering when and how to sell. As Treasury evaluates these indicators, considering all possible sale strategies is important.

Members of the auto team said that they plan to consider indicators such as profitability and prospects, cash flow, market share, and market conditions to determine the optimal time and method of sale. The ultimate decision on when and how to sell will be made by the Secretary of the Treasury, but auto team staff will be in charge of monitoring these indicators and recommending a strategy to the Secretary and Assistant Secretary for Financial Stability. Although Treasury officials said they plan to consider all options for selling the government's ownership stakes in Chrysler and GM, they noted that they believe the most likely scenario for GM is to dispose of Treasury's equity in the company through a series of public offerings. Treasury has publicly discussed the possibility of selling part of its equity in the company through an IPO that would occur sometime in 2010. However, by publicly discussing a method and a time for a sale of GM shares now, the extent to which Treasury is using the indicators to inform method and timing decisions is unclear. Moreover, two of the experts we spoke with said GM might not be ready for a successful IPO by 2010, because it may be too early for the company to have demonstrated sufficient progress to attract investor interest, and two other experts noted that 2010 would be the earliest possible time for an IPO. For Chrysler, Treasury officials noted that the department is more likely to consider a private sale because its equity stake is smaller, and several of the experts we interviewed noted that non-IPO options could be possible for Chrysler, given the relatively smaller stake Treasury has in the company (9.85 percent, versus its 60.8 percent stake in GM) and the relative affordability of the company. In commenting on a draft of this report, Treasury officials stated that they were aware of the diversity of opinions on divesting the government's interest in the auto companies and would make an appropriate determination to maximize the taxpayers' return. To achieve the maximum return for taxpayers, Treasury also said it plans not to disclose more information about its strategy to divest its ownership interests than is necessary.

Treasury officials said that on the basis of their analysis of the companies' future profitability, they believe that Chrysler and GM will be able to attract sufficient investor interest for Treasury to sell its equity. With regard to the possibility that there may not be sufficient investor interest, Treasury officials said they would monitor the financial markets and the companies' operations in order to identify any issues that could affect profitability, and work with the companies' boards of directors and management to address them. In the event that the companies do not return to profitability in the time frame Treasury has projected, Treasury officials said that they will consider all commercial options for disposing of Treasury's equity, including liquidation.

- **Manage investments in a commercial manner**. Experts emphasized the importance of Treasury resisting external pressures to focus on public policy goals over focusing on its role as a commercial investor. For example, some experts said that Treasury should not let public policy goals such as job retention interfere with its goals of maximizing its return on investment and making Chrysler and GM strong and viable companies. They said that this is especially important because making the companies financially strong and competitive may require reducing the number of employees. Nevertheless, one expert suggested that Treasury should consider public policy goals and include the value of jobs saved and other economic benefits from its investment when calculating its return, since these goals, though not important to a private investor, are critical to the economy.

As long as Treasury maintains ownership interests in Chrysler and GM, it will likely be pressured to influence the companies' business decisions. Treasury has said that it plans to manage its investment in Chrysler and GM in a commercial way. Yet Treasury faces external pressures, such as to prioritize jobs over maximizing its return. For example, Congress is currently considering a number of bills to restore automotive dealers' contracts terminated in restructuring, and Treasury officials noted that they receive frequent calls from Members of Congress expressing concern about dealership closings. To protect Treasury's investment from these external pressures, a recent Congressional Oversight Panel report recommended that Treasury hold its equity interests in the auto companies in a trust managed by an independent trustee.[28] Treasury officials told us they cannot currently establish a trust managed by independent trustees because of a requirement in EESA that states that troubled assets are subject to the supervision of the Secretary of the Treasury.[29] The officials stated that if Treasury created a trust with the assets managed by independent trustees, the Secretary would not be able to exercise his authority over the assets as required by law. Congress is considering legislation that would authorize and require the Secretary to transfer to a limited liability company all equity in TARP recipients in which the government has a certain equity interest as a result of TARP assistance. The bills further provide that the equity is to be managed in trust for the benefit of taxpayers.[30] Treasury officials told us they believe their planned approach for managing Treasury's equity in Chrysler and GM is sufficient for now.

Regardless of the sales strategies used, the companies will have to grow substantially in order to reach values at which Treasury would recover the entirety of its equity investment upon sale of its equity, which Treasury and others consider to be unlikely. On the basis of our analysis, shown in table 5, we estimate that Chrysler and GM would need to have a market capitalization of $54.8 billion and $66.9 billion, respectively, for Treasury to earn enough on the sale of its equity to break even.[31] A recent Congressional Oversight Panel report reached similar conclusions on what the companies would have to be worth.[32] As a point of reference for these values, in 1997, the last year Chrysler was a publicly traded company, its market capitalization value ranged between $23.1 billion and $31.7 billion, and in 1998, when it merged with Daimler, it was valued at an estimated $37 billion. GM, at its peak in 2000, had a market capitalization of $57 billion.[33] In commenting on a draft of this report, Treasury officials noted that the companies' past equity values are not comparable to today's equity values because the companies have substantially restructured their balance sheets through bankruptcy. Although we recognize the changes the companies have experienced in recent years, we believe this information provides a sense of the magnitude of growth that will be required of the companies.

Treasury's own analysis suggests that the circumstances necessary for the companies to reach market capitalizations high enough for Treasury to fully recover its equity investment are unlikely. Treasury officials also noted that considering the companies' enterprise values—a measure of a business's total value, including the value of equity and debt—in addition to equity value is important, because enterprise value takes into account the likelihood of repayment of loans and other obligations extended to the companies as well as the value of equity stakes.[34]

However, these estimates do not take into account other benefits and costs that are more difficult to measure, such as the impact of Treasury's investment on jobs and local and national economies and the opportunity costs Treasury incurred in providing financial assistance. The impact on the economy is difficult to measure because, according to the Council of Economic Advisors, it involves predicting what employment and economic performance would have been without government investment. Nevertheless, a more comprehensive analysis that takes these effects into account would yield a richer picture of the value of Treasury's net investment and net return, especially given that the government's goal upon first providing assistance to the auto industry was to prevent economic disruption.

CONCLUSIONS

Treasury's substantial investment and other assistance, including loans from the Canadian government and concessions from the UAW, have contributed to the current stability of Chrysler and GM. However, because of the challenges continuing to face the auto industry—including the still recovering economy and weak demand for new vehicles—the ultimate impact that the assistance will have on the companies' profitability and long-term viability is uncertain. Although the immediate crisis of helping Chrysler and GM maintain solvency has passed for now and Treasury has no plans for further financial assistance to the companies, the significant sums of taxpayer dollars that are invested in these companies warrant continued oversight. It is critical that Treasury remain focused on protecting the government's interest in the coming months as Chrysler and GM work to become profitable. However, most of the original staff on Treasury's auto team either have left Treasury or may do so in the future. Treasury officials told us that OFS personnel will continue to provide oversight. Given the substantial decline in the number of staff and lack of dedicated staff for this oversight moving forward, however, we are concerned whether Treasury will continue to have the needed expertise to provide oversight of the use of government funds, assess the financial condition of the auto companies, and develop strategies to divest the government's interests. Monitoring industry conditions and determining when to divest will require a certain expertise, including a robust monitoring function through which detailed financial data from Chrysler and GM are reviewed on a regular basis. Transparency as to how the companies are being monitored also will be important to ensuring accountability and providing assurances that the taxpayers' investment— including both the loans to and equity in the companies—is being appropriately safeguarded. While we recognize that not all information that the companies report to Treasury should be made public because of concerns about disclosing proprietary information in a competitive market, Treasury's approach for evaluating the success of the AIFP should be as transparent as possible, given the large taxpayer investment.

Table 5. Value of Chrysler and GM Equity Required for Treasury to Recoup Its Investment

(Dollars in billions)

Description of funding	Treasury investment	Amount in term loans and preferred stock	Equity stake (percent)	Amount equity stake must be worth to recoup equity investment (*investment–loans and preferred stock*)	Equity value of company necessary to recoup investment (amount equity must be worth/60.8 percent for GM and 9.85 percent for Chrysler)
Total loans to Chrysler	$12.5	$7.1	9.85	$5.4[a]	$54.8
Loans to Chrysler prior to bankruptcy	4.0				
Loans to Chrysler after bankruptcy	8.5				
Total loans to GM	49.5	8.8	60.8	40.7	66.9
Loans GM prior to bankruptcy	19.4				
Loans to GM after bankruptcy	30.1				

Source: GAO analysis of Treasury information.

[a] This value does not take into account any repayments Treasury will receive from the payment-in-kind interest that will accumulate over the life of the $7.1 billion loan, ($17 million per quarter), the additional $288 million note, or the value of Treasury's interest in Chrysler Financial's equity (the greater of $1.375 billion or 40 percent of the equity). These figures together would be worth $833 million, thereby reducing the amount Treasury's equity stake would have to be worth from $5.4 billion to $4.6 billion, and reducing the equity value Chrysler would have to attain from $54.8 billion to $46.7 billion.

While Treasury has stated that it plans to review all possible options for divesting itself of its ownership interest in Chrysler and GM, Treasury officials have focused primarily on an IPO for GM, both in our discussions with them and in their public statements. However, given the complexity of the economy and the financial markets, considering all of the options in the context of the companies' financial progress and current financial conditions will be important for Treasury. The past year has indicated the extent to which a company's financial situation can change within a period as short as a few months. Given the fluidity of conditions and the number of factors that will need to be considered when determining how and when to divest, it is important that Treasury identify the criteria it will use to evaluate the optimal method and timing for selling the government's ownership stake. Determining when and how to divest the government's ownership stake will be one of the most important decisions Treasury will have to make regarding the federal assistance provided to the domestic automakers, as this decision will affect the overall return on investment that taxpayers will realize from aiding these companies. Currently, the value of the companies would have to grow tremendously for Treasury to approach breaking even on its investment, requiring that Treasury temper any desire to exit as quickly as possible with the need to maintain its ownership interest long enough for the companies to demonstrate sufficient financial progress. Therefore, it is important that Treasury be able to explain why and how it decided to divest when the time arrives, and clearly established criteria will help Treasury communicate this decision to Congress and the public at the appropriate time to prevent this disclosure from negatively affecting the full recovery for taxpayers.

RECOMMENDATIONS FOR EXECUTIVE ACTION

To improve the stewardship of the federal government's substantial financial investment in the auto industry, we recommend that the Secretary of the Treasury take the following three actions:

- Ensure that the department has the expertise needed to adequately monitor and divest the government's investment in Chrysler and GM, and obtain needed expertise in areas where gaps are identified. In addressing any existing or future expertise gaps, Treasury should consider both in-house and external expertise.
- Report to Congress on how it plans to assess and monitor the companies' performance to help ensure the companies are on track to repay their loans and to return to profitability. In reporting to Congress, Treasury should balance the need for transparency with the need to protect certain proprietary information that would put the companies at a competitive disadvantage or negatively affect Treasury's ability to recover the taxpayers' investments.
- Develop criteria for evaluating the optimal method and timing for divesting the government's ownership stake in Chrysler and GM. In applying these criteria, Treasury should evaluate the full range of available options, such as IPOs or private sales.

AGENCY COMMENTS AND OUR EVALUATION

We provided a draft of this report to the Department of the Treasury for review and comment. Treasury generally agreed with the report's findings, conclusions, and recommendations, and provided written comments, which are reprinted in appendix II. Treasury also provided technical comments and clarifications via e-mail, which we incorporated as appropriate. In their technical comments, Treasury officials emphasized that they believe they have individuals within OFS who can provide the needed oversight of the government's investments in Chrysler and GM. We added Treasury's views on its current staffing and expertise levels to the final report. While we recognize that OFS employs a number of qualified individuals who have worked on the government's efforts to stabilize the auto industry, we nevertheless remain concerned about the loss of industry- and company-specific knowledge and expertise that Treasury has experienced and will continue to experience with the wind-down of the auto team. Such knowledge and expertise will be critical as Treasury monitors the financial health of Chrysler and GM and develops plans to divest its ownership interests in these companies. We are pleased that Treasury—in both its written and technical comments—commits to continue to take steps to assess and maintain the expertise required to monitor and manage Treasury's investments in these companies.

In their written and technical comments, Treasury officials also stressed the need to strike a balance between the goal of transparency and the need to avoid compromising the competitive positions of Chrysler and GM or the government's ability to recover its investments. We recognize the need to strike this balance and added language to the final report, including one of our recommendations, to acknowledge this difficult trade-off. We believe our revised recommendation that Treasury report to Congress on its plans to monitor the performance of the companies provides Treasury with sufficient flexibility to strike the appropriate balance.

We also provided relevant portions of a draft of this report to SEC, Chrysler, and GM for their review and comment. SEC, Chrysler, and GM provided technical comments and clarifications that we incorporated as appropriate.

We are sending copies of this report to other interested congressional committees and members, the Department of the Treasury, and others. The report also is available at no charge on the GAO Web site at http://www.gao.gov.

If you or your staff have any questions about this report, please contact Katherine Siggerud at (202) 512-2834 or siggerudk@gao.gov or A. Nicole Clowers at (202) 512-2843 or clowersa@gao.gov. Contact points for our Offices of Congressional Relations and Public Affairs may be found on the last page of this report. GAO staff who made major contributions to this report are listed in appendix III.

Gene L. Dodaro
Acting Comptroller General
of the United States

List of Committees

The Honorable Daniel K. Inouye
Chairman
The Honorable Thad Cochran
Vice Chairman
Committee on Appropriations
United States Senate

The Honorable Christopher J. Dodd
Chairman
The Honorable Richard C. Shelby
Ranking Member
Committee on Banking, Housing,
and Urban Affairs
United States Senate

The Honorable Kent Conrad
Chairman
The Honorable Judd Gregg
Ranking Member
Committee on the Budget
United States Senate

The Honorable Max Baucus
Chairman
The Honorable Charles E. Grassley
Ranking Member
Committee on Finance
United States Senate

The Honorable David R. Obey
Chairman
The Honorable Jerry Lewis
Ranking Member
Committee on Appropriations
House of Representatives

The Honorable John M. Spratt, Jr.
Chairman
The Honorable Paul Ryan
Ranking Member
Committee on the Budget
House of Representatives

The Honorable Barney Frank
Chairman
The Honorable Spencer Bachus
Ranking Member
Committee on Financial Services
House of Representatives

The Honorable Charles B. Rangel
Chairman
The Honorable Dave Camp
Ranking Member
Committee on Ways and Means
House of Representatives

APPENDIX I:
FINANCIAL AND INDUSTRY EXPERTS GAO INTERVIEWED

Name	Affiliation
John Casesa	Casesa Shapiro Group
Justin Mirro	Moelis & Company
Thomas Maloney	Deutsche Bank
Warren Estey	Deutsche Bank
Rod Lache	Deutsche Bank
Henry Miller	Miller Buckfire
Durc Savini	Miller Buckfire
Eric Selle	J.P.Morgan
Himanshu Patel	J.P.Morgan
Charles Bowsher	Former Comptroller General of the United States
William Isaac	Former Chairman of the Federal Deposit Insurance Corporation

Source: GAO.

APPENDIX II: COMMENTS FROM THE DEPARTMENT OF THE TREASURY

DEPARTMENT OF THE TREASURY
WASHINGTON, D.C. 20220

October 23, 2009

Thomas J. McCool
Director, Center for Economics
Applied Research and Methods
U.S. Government Accountability Office
441 G Street, N.W.
Washington, D.C. 20548

Dear Mr. McCool:

The Treasury Department (Treasury) appreciates the opportunity to review the GAO's latest report on Treasury's Troubled Asset Relief Program (TARP), entitled *Auto Industry: Continued Stewardship Needed as Treasury Develops Strategies for Monitoring and Divesting Financial Interests in Chrysler and GM*. Treasury welcomes the recognition by the GAO that Treasury through TARP investments has "contributed to the stability of Chrysler and GM." There is important work ahead and the GAO's recommendations are constructive as Treasury continues to implement its Auto Industry Financing Program.

Treasury continues to assess and take steps to maintain the expertise required to adequately monitor and manage Treasury's interests in Chrysler and GM. In addition, Treasury will continue to monitor and evaluate the performance of Chrysler and GM with a view toward determining the appropriate method and timing for divesting Treasury's interests in the auto companies. Treasury also intends to develop an approach for reporting on its investments in the auto industry that strikes an appropriate balance between our goal of transparency and the need to avoid compromising either the competitive positions of these companies or Treasury's ability to recover funds for taxpayers.

Once again, Treasury appreciates the opportunity to review this report and the GAO's thoughtful recommendations. Treasury also appreciates the GAO's close oversight of TARP as Treasury develops and implements its policies to stabilize the financial system. We look forward to continuing this constructive dialogue.

Sincerely,

Duane Morse
Chief Risk and Compliance Officer
Office of Financial Stability

End Notes

[1] Prior to bankruptcy reorganization, the companies' legal names were Chrysler LLC and General Motors Corporation. Chrysler Group LLC and General Motors Company are new legal entities that were created through the bankruptcy process to purchase the operating assets of the pre-reorganization companies. The new companies also received some of the debts of the pre-reorganization companies, including a portion of the loans Treasury provided to the companies prior to bankruptcy filing. Throughout this report, in cases where such a distinction is important, we refer to the pre-reorganization companies as "old Chrysler" and "old GM," and the post-reorganization companies as "new Chrysler" and "new GM." The third domestic automaker, Ford Motor Company, has not requested assistance from Treasury.

[2] The Emergency Economic Stabilization Act of 2008 (EESA), Pub. L. No. 110-343, 122 Stat. 3765 (2008), codified at 12 U.S.C. §§ 5201 et. seq., originally authorized Treasury to buy or guarantee up to $700 billion in troubled assets. The Helping Families Save Their Homes Act of 2009, Pub. L. No. 111-22, Div. A, Title IV, § 402(f), 123 Stat. 1632, 1658 (2009), codified at 12 U.S.C. 5225(a)(3), amended the act and reduced the maximum allowable amount of outstanding troubled assets under the act by almost $1.3 billion, from $700 billion to $698.741 billion.

[3] Treasury's share in the company will become 8 percent if Fiat, another of Chrysler's shareholders, meets fuel efficiency-related performance targets and is granted additional equity.

[4] Other parties that received equity stakes in the reorganized companies include the Canadian government, which provided financial assistance to the companies, and the auto workers union's health care trust, which agreed to accept equity in the company in exchange for future monetary contributions.

[5] GAO, *Troubled Relief Asset Program: June 2009 Status of Efforts to Address Transparency and Accountability*, GAO-09-658 (Washington, D.C.: June 17, 2009).

[6] Ron Bloom, Senior Advisor, U. S. Department of the Treasury, written testimony before the Congressional Oversight Panel, Regarding Treasury's Automotive Industry Financing Program, July 27, 2009.

[7] See our previous reports on TARP assistance to the auto industry: GAO, *Auto Industry: Summary of Government Efforts and Automakers'Restructuring to Date*, GAO-09-553 (Washington, D.C.: Apr. 23, 2009); *Auto Industry: A Framework for Considering Federal Financial Assistance*, GAO-09-247T (Washington, D.C.: Dec. 5, 2008); *Auto Industry: A Framework for Considering Federal Financial Assistance*, GAO-09-242T (Washington, D.C.: Dec. 4, 2008); and GAO-09-658. EESA requires GAO to report at least every 60 days on findings resulting from, among other things, oversight of TARP's performance in meeting the purposes of the act, the financial condition and internal controls of TARP, the characteristics of both asset purchases and the disposition of assets acquired, TARP's efficiency in using the funds appropriated for the program's operation, and TARP's compliance with applicable laws and regulations. This is the ninth report issued in compliance with that mandate.

[8] We are currently conducting a coordinated review with the Special Inspector General for TARP on U.S. government oversight of and interaction with companies in which the government has provided "exceptional assistance." As part of this review, we will examine the internal controls Treasury has established to manage its portfolio of investments and its interaction with the institutions, which include Chrysler and GM.

[9] GAO-09-553.

[10] See National Automobile Dealers Association, "NADA Data 2009: Economic Impact of America's New-Car and New-Truck Dealers" (McLean, Va.: 2009) and United States Department of Labor, Bureau of Labor Statistics, Table B-12: Employees on Non-farm Payrolls by Detailed Industry, August 2009.

[11] GAO-09-553.

[12] Most recently, in October 2009, GM reached an agreement to sell its Hummer brand to a Chinese company, which is slated to take over operations in 2012.

[13] Chrysler began downsizing its operations prior to filing for bankruptcy. For instance, at year-end 2006, it had 3,749 dealerships.

[14] GAO-09-553.

[15] Under an agreement between new GM and the Securities and Exchange Commission (SEC), new GM will file by March 31, 2010, a quarterly financial report for the third quarter of 2009 and an annual financial report for 2009. According to SEC, because GM is a newly formed entity with only five shareholders, it is not required to file periodic or current reports. Also, according to SEC, it does not have any written or oral agreements with Chrysler, which was not a public company prior to its reorganization and is not currently a public company, on future filing requirements.

[16] The Car Allowance Rebate System is more commonly referred to as Cash for Clunkers.

[17] Our discussion focuses on the financial assistance Treasury provided to fund the companies'operations and restructuring because it represents the most substantial portion of the assistance the companies received. It does not address the conditions of the smaller amounts provided under the Supplier Support Program and the Warranty Commitment Program.

[18] The Congressional Oversight Panel was created as part of TARP to review the current state of financial markets and the regulatory system. The panel is empowered to hold hearings, review official data, and write reports on actions taken by Treasury and financial institutions and their effect on the economy. The Congressional Oversight Panel issued a report on federal assistance provided to the auto industry in September 2009. See Congressional Oversight Panel, *September Oversight Report: The Use of TARP Funds in the Support and Reorganization of the Domestic Automotive Industry* (Washington, D.C.: Sept. 9, 2009).

[19] As noted, GAO and the Special Inspector General for the Troubled Asset Relief Program are conducting coordinated work on Treasury's oversight of Chrysler's and GM's compliance with these requirements.

[20] Section 111 of EESA, as amended by the American Recovery and Reinvestment Act of 2009, Pub. L. No. 111-5, Div. B, Title VII, 123 Stat. 115, 516-520 (2009), codified at 12 U.S.C § 5221, prescribes certain standards for executive compensation and corporate governance for recipients of financial assistance under TARP. Treasury

published an interim final rule setting forth the applicable compensation and corporate governance standards (74 Fed. Reg. 28,394, June 15, 2009, codified at 31 C.F.R. Part 30).

[21] The Employ American Workers Act was included in the American Recovery and Reinvestment Act of 2009, Pub. L. No. 111-5, Div. A, Title XVI, § 1611, 123 Stat. 115, 305 (2009).

[22] GAO has ongoing work reviewing the state of the automakers'pension plans and the potential liabilities to the federal government should the plans be terminated. We plan to issue this report in early 2010.

[23] In the case of Chrysler, the corresponding document is the Amended and Restated Limited Liability Company Operating Agreement of Chrysler Group LLC, and in the case of GM, the corresponding document is the Shareholders Agreement by and among General Motors Company, United States Department of the Treasury, 7176384 Canada Inc., and UAW Retiree Medical Benefits Trust. Chrysler's and GM's reporting requirements are not identical because each agreement was negotiated separately and, in the case of the operating and shareholders'agreements, with the input of the shareholders.

[24] Of the $30.1 billion that Treasury provided to GM at its bankruptcy filing, $16.4 billion was held in escrow to be accessed by GM on an as-needed basis with the consent of Treasury. As of October 5, 2009, GM had requested and received $3 billion from the escrow account.

[25] As part of its reorganization, Chrysler arranged an alliance with the Italian automaker Fiat, whereby Fiat is contributing intellectual property and "know-how" to Chrysler in exchange for a 20 percent equity share in the reorganized company. Fiat will have the right to earn up to 15 percent in additional equity in three tranches of 5 percent each in exchange for meeting performance metrics, including introducing a vehicle produced at a Chrysler factory in the United States that performs at 40 miles per gallon; providing Chrysler with a distribution network in numerous foreign jurisdictions; and manufacturing state-of-the-art, next-generation engines at a U.S. Chrysler facility. Fiat will also hold an option to acquire up to an additional 16 percent fully diluted equity interest in the restructured Chrysler. Fiat may exercise this option and exceed 50 percent ownership in Chrysler once Treasury's loan has been repaid in full.

[26] GAO, *Troubled Asset Relief Program: Status of Efforts to Address Transparency and Accountability Issues*, GAO-09-296 (Washington, D.C.: Jan. 30, 2009).

[27] GAO, *Standards for Internal Control in the Federal Government*, GAO/AIMD-00-21.3.1 (Washington, D.C.: November 1999).

[28] Congressional Oversight Panel, *September Oversight Report: The Use of TARP Funds in the Support and Reorganization of the Domestic Automotive Industry* (Washington, D.C.: Sept. 9, 2009).

[29] "In order to provide the Secretary with flexibility to manage troubled assets in a manner designed to minimize cost to taxpayers, the Secretary is authorized to establish vehicles, subject to supervision by the Secretary, to purchase, hold, and sell troubled assets and issue obligations." Pub. L. No. 110-343, Sec. 101(c)(4), codified at 12 U.S.C. § 5211(c)(4).

[30] In order for a trust to be established, the government would have to have at least a 15 percent ownership in the company as a result of TARP assistance in the House bill and at least a 20 percent ownership interest as a result of TARP assistance in the Senate bill. See H.R. 3594, 111th Cong. (2009) and S. 1280, 111th Cong. (2009).

[31] Our analysis included all funds Treasury has provided to the auto companies that will be repaid through a combination of debt and equity. We assume that new Chrysler and new GM will repay all debts, and that the debts of old Chrysler and old GM will not be repaid, including $5.4 billion to old Chrysler and $986 million to old GM. As a result, Treasury's equity will have to be worth its total investments minus projected repayments of principal and preferred stock. This analysis excludes funds provided for the Supplier Support Program and the Warranty Commitment Program, since these funds were issued as loans and will be paid back as such. In addition, this analysis does not take into account the cost or opportunity cost to Treasury of lending, any interest Treasury should or could charge to the automakers on the portion of its investment that has been converted into equity, the present value of the investment, or the value of any social costs or benefits resulting from the investment. If Fiat achieves its operating goals and earns an additional 15 percent equity, Treasury's equity stake will decline to 8 percent, meaning that Chrysler's total equity value would need to reach $57 billion for Treasury to recoup its investment.

[32] Congressional Oversight Panel, *September Oversight Report: The Use of TARP Funds in the Support and Reorganization of the Domestic Automotive Industry*.

[33] Evercore Group, LLC, the financial services company that estimated GM's future value for the bankruptcy court, concluded that new GM would be worth between $59 billion and $77 billion in 2012.

[34] In June, the Congressional Budget Office (CBO) estimated that the federal government would recoup only 27 percent of its initial investment in the auto industry. CBO's analysis relies on data from the auto companies

prior to bankruptcy to estimate the likelihood of repayment in the future. Chrysler and GM had poor credit ratings and significant debts prior to bankruptcy, so the average projected repayment is only 27 cents on the dollar.

CHAPTER SOURCES

Chapter 1 - This is an edited, reformatted and augmented version of a Congressional Oversight Panel's publication, No. 110-343, dated January 13, 2011.

Chapter 2 - This is an edited, reformatted and augmented version of a Congressional Research Services publication, R41401, dated December 8, 2010.

Chapter 3 - This is an edited, reformatted and augmented version of the United States Government Accountability Office's publication, GAO-10-492, dated April 2010.

Chapter 4 - This is an edited, reformatted and augmented version of the United States Government Accountability Office's publication, GAO-10-151, dated November 2009.

INDEX

A

access, 4, 6, 20, 26, 39, 44, 45, 46, 55, 56, 70, 139, 160, 173, 174, 213
accommodations, 221
accountability, vii, 1, 70, 159, 229
accounting, 16, 62, 69, 78, 138, 175, 203, 218
acquisitions, 168, 181, 191, 204
activism, 58
actual output, 19
adjustment, 29, 148
age, 161, 182, 192, 193, 194, 200, 201, 206
agencies, 12, 20, 150, 158, 164, 225
agency actions, 183
agricultural sector, 92
American Recovery and Reinvestment Act of 2009, 236, 237
annual rate, 13, 77
appetite, 62
Appropriations Act, 151
Argentina, 43
asbestos, 23, 137
Asia, 136, 152, 173
assessment, 4, 34, 53, 66
assets, vii, 4, 5, 6, 14, 20, 23, 43, 45, 51, 58, 60, 64, 70, 76, 81, 89, 131, 132, 133, 135, 138, 147, 151, 156, 160, 164, 166, 167, 168, 169, 170, 171, 172, 174, 176, 177, 179, 180, 182, 183, 185, 186, 187, 190, 191, 192, 193, 194, 198, 199, 200, 201, 203, 204, 205, 206, 207, 210, 217, 220, 228, 235, 236, 237
AT&T, 144, 164
audit, 158, 213
authorities, 135
authority, 2, 6, 58, 78, 89, 91, 92, 147, 222, 225, 228
Automobile, 157, 158, 189, 197, 198, 211, 218, 236
automobiles, 6, 14, 21, 177
automotive sector, 63
autonomy, 185

B

bail, 69
balance sheet, 19, 44, 45, 50, 52, 54, 58, 68, 81, 133, 145, 222, 226, 228
bank debt, 218
bank failure, 76
bank financing, 4
banking, 10, 38, 51, 56, 73, 132, 224
banking sector, 10
bankruptcies, 57, 64, 68, 70, 71, 156, 172, 174, 186
bankruptcy, vii, 2, 4, 5, 6, 7, 8, 14, 15, 19, 21, 23, 24, 25, 32, 33, 34, 39, 41, 62, 65, 68, 69, 70, 71, 82, 83, 84, 89, 131, 132, 133, 134, 135, 136, 137, 138, 139, 140, 141, 148, 150, 151, 152, 156, 157, 158, 160, 161, 164, 165, 172, 173, 174, 175, 176, 189, 190, 191, 192, 198, 199, 206, 212, 215, 217, 218, 219, 221, 226, 228, 230, 235, 236, 237, 238
banks, 4, 8, 10, 15, 47, 48, 64, 72, 73, 74, 76, 79, 81, 141, 151, 152
bargaining, 163
base, 13, 46, 59, 173, 175, 186, 193
basis points, 44, 73, 74, 89
batteries, 23
benchmarks, 65, 144, 223
beneficiaries, 181, 185
benefits, 14, 15, 23, 26, 38, 52, 63, 70, 135, 141, 145, 156, 157, 163, 165, 166, 168, 171, 172, 176, 178, 179, 180, 181, 182, 183, 186, 189, 190, 191, 192, 193, 198, 199, 200, 201, 203, 204, 206, 207, 218, 219, 228, 229, 237
bias, 5, 59
bleeding, 49

Index

blogs, 151
board members, 58, 60, 133, 135, 164
Boat, 197
bondholders, vii, 24, 131, 136, 218
bonds, 5, 74, 166
bonuses, 221
borrowers, 45, 61, 89
branching, 38
Brazil, 13, 19, 20, 22, 43, 144, 147, 197
breakdown, 17
break-even, 2, 20, 24, 36, 134, 144
breast cancer, 68
Bureau of Labor Statistics, 148, 236
business cycle, 20
business model, 10, 19, 48, 51, 63, 173
business strategy, 3, 22, 44
businesses, 42, 43, 44, 45, 48, 77, 213, 218
buyer, 8, 62, 139
buyers, 6, 12, 24, 66, 68, 135, 141, 142

C

CAD, 36
calculus, 50
candidates, 60, 225
capital markets, 10, 44, 45, 47, 50, 66, 68, 133, 190
capital outflow, 54
cash, 8, 18, 20, 26, 31, 34, 37, 55, 56, 77, 83, 137, 143, 146, 163, 169, 170, 173, 179, 193, 205, 211, 218, 222, 227
cash flow, 34, 143, 146, 173, 218, 222, 227
category b, 199
Census, 77
central bank, 72
certificate, 44
challenges, 4, 59, 61, 63, 64, 91, 132, 158, 159, 186, 210, 212, 217, 220, 223, 225, 229
Chicago, 72, 141
China, 5, 13, 19, 20, 22, 43, 136, 141, 144, 147, 152
City, 77, 87
clarity, 47, 50, 54
classes, 51, 70
clients, 142
close relationships, 51
closure, 33, 219
collateral, 89, 134
collective bargaining, 68, 146, 163, 166, 190, 203, 204
commerce, 63
commercial, 12, 38, 58, 74, 139, 174, 185, 186, 210, 220, 227, 228
commercial bank, 74

communication, 157, 159, 186
communities, 132
compensation, 16, 92, 141, 142, 147, 166, 203, 219, 221, 223, 225, 236
competing interests, 184
competition, 22, 61, 144, 218
competitive supply, 175
competitiveness, vii, 19, 155, 157
competitors, 4, 14, 16, 23, 44, 172
complement, 225
complexity, 25, 179, 181, 231
compliance, 203, 221, 236
composition, 42
compression, 173, 175
conflict, 29, 65, 66, 183
Congressional Budget Office, vii, 1, 237
consent, 190, 237
consolidation, 57, 157, 175
construction, 68
consulting, 158, 224
Consumer Price Index, 148
consumers, 4, 6, 22, 42, 44, 45, 51, 63, 92, 145, 146, 147
controversial, 3
convergence, 226
conversations, 48, 49, 54, 59
conviction, 70
corporate governance, 221, 236
corporate restructuring, 212
cost, 4, 10, 11, 13, 14, 19, 20, 22, 24, 37, 38, 44, 47, 50, 52, 55, 62, 69, 89, 91, 135, 144, 146, 153, 166, 169, 176, 183, 204, 205, 219, 237
cost saving, 19
cost structures, 219
covering, 222
credit market, 4, 5, 55, 67, 132, 148, 156, 172, 174
credit rating, 20, 38, 45, 51, 152, 177, 238
creditors, 9, 23, 39, 64, 65, 70, 83, 136, 148, 190, 204, 223
creditworthiness, 178
culture, 135
currency, 5
customers, 8, 38, 43, 51, 52, 56, 62, 144, 146, 213

D

Daewoo, 160, 198
Daimler-Benz, 25, 198, 204
debentures, 10
debt service, 54
debts, 63, 173, 174, 218, 235, 237, 238
defects, 137

Index

deficiency, 142, 190
deficit, 165, 169, 176, 178
defined benefit pension, vii, 146, 155, 156
delinquency, 44
Department of Commerce, 164, 172
Department of Energy, 34, 35, 140, 150, 151
Department of Labor, 158, 236
deposits, 44, 45, 49, 55
depth, 10, 43
developing countries, 136
developing nations, 22
direct cost, 5
direct costs, 5
directives, 58
directors, 8, 16, 57, 58, 60, 66, 68, 70, 82, 133, 139, 142, 144, 164, 184, 207, 221, 227
disclosure, 67, 142, 183, 186, 231
disposition, 10, 15, 47, 70, 203, 236
distress, 165, 204
distribution, 6, 26, 30, 70, 82, 142, 161, 183, 195, 199, 205, 237
diversification, 51
diversity, 227
divestiture, 204
domestic credit, 5
domestic markets, 68
downsizing, 145, 156, 166, 168, 179, 236
draft, 158, 187, 225, 226, 227, 228, 232

E

early retirement, 160, 166, 182
earnings, 13, 34, 35, 43, 44, 50, 54, 58, 63, 64, 144, 221, 226
economic activity, 14, 51
economic crisis, 133
economic downturn, 10, 166, 173
economic growth, 57, 92
economic indicator, 225, 226, 227
economic performance, 67, 229
Ecuador, 43
e-mail, 232
emergency, 4, 7, 14
Emergency Economic Stabilization Act, 3, 91, 135, 152, 202, 211, 220, 235
emerging markets, 13, 19
employee compensation, 221
employees, 11, 19, 20, 32, 58, 62, 64, 70, 137, 146, 147, 161, 163, 164, 166, 168, 170, 173, 180, 181, 189, 190, 192, 193, 194, 200, 203, 204, 210, 219, 221, 224, 227
employers, 161, 165, 176, 203
employment, 6, 14, 51, 67, 137, 145, 159, 168, 186, 229

employment levels, 186
energy, 145
Energy Independence and Security Act, 151
enforcement, 212
engineering, 144, 146
England, 197
environment, 7, 145, 169, 172, 190, 225
equipment, 23, 64, 178
equities, 166
equity, viii, 4, 7, 9, 10, 14, 15, 17, 21, 25, 26, 29, 30, 31, 32, 34, 35, 36, 37, 38, 39, 42, 43, 46, 47, 48, 50, 52, 57, 61, 64, 65, 68, 71, 80, 138, 139, 145, 146, 147, 149, 151, 156, 159, 174, 178, 184, 185, 186, 197, 198, 209, 210, 211, 212, 213, 214, 220, 221, 222, 223, 224, 225, 226, 227, 228, 229, 230, 236, 237
equity market, 14, 53, 139
erosion, 14
Europe, 13, 21, 22, 136, 144, 146, 173, 197
evidence, 52, 53, 158, 213
evolution, 32
exchange rate, 31
exclusion, 4, 69
execution, 21, 37
executive branch, 225
exercise, 8, 18, 24, 25, 26, 29, 30, 31, 32, 36, 37, 59, 62, 63, 84, 228, 237
expenditures, 88, 221
expertise, viii, 147, 184, 209, 210, 212, 224, 225, 229, 231, 232
exposure, 24, 25, 38, 49, 50, 51, 53, 54, 64, 78, 156, 175, 177, 178, 179, 181, 182, 186, 206
extraordinary conditions, 5

F

fabrication, 161
factories, 10, 33, 151, 160, 210, 219
fear, 6, 60
federal aid, 136
federal assistance, vii, 131, 148, 211, 213, 231, 236
federal government, viii, 3, 6, 25, 39, 78, 88, 89, 131, 132, 133, 137, 139, 143, 149, 150, 152, 155, 157, 158, 164, 183, 186, 203, 212, 231, 237
Federal Government, 91, 237
federal law, 147, 158
Federal Reserve Board, 7
financial condition, 145, 186, 202, 210, 212, 221, 224, 229, 231, 236
financial crisis, 4, 5, 38, 57, 64, 92, 131, 135, 136, 138
financial data, 229

financial distress, 177
financial institutions, 5, 8, 15, 54, 69, 85, 92, 236
financial markets, 5, 73, 92, 135, 170, 226, 227, 231, 236
financial performance, 34, 65
financial reports, 205, 220, 222, 223, 226
financial resources, 134, 137
financial sector, 3, 4, 6, 48, 64, 65
financial stability, vii, 1, 57, 71, 139, 210, 220
financial support, vii, 131
financial system, 3, 69, 78, 88, 91, 92, 135
fiscal year 2009, 165, 177, 178
fixed costs, 14, 25, 218
flexibility, 15, 232, 237
flooding, 139
force, 36, 59, 151
Ford, 5, 6, 11, 16, 20, 23, 32, 50, 52, 57, 133, 134, 135, 137, 139, 140, 144, 150, 151, 159, 164, 173, 218, 235
foreclosure, 44, 53, 54, 63, 77, 78, 92
foreign exchange, 5
formation, 15, 220
formula, 34, 163
franchise, 8, 44, 45, 46, 51
fraud, 53
freedom, 37
fuel efficiency, 14, 135, 236
fuel prices, 4
funding, 4, 5, 6, 7, 21, 34, 44, 45, 46, 49, 50, 55, 56, 57, 68, 78, 81, 82, 89, 133, 135, 139, 149, 155, 156, 157, 158, 159, 164, 165, 169, 170, 171, 172, 174, 178, 185, 190, 203, 204, 205, 206, 210, 211, 213, 214, 215, 217, 221, 230
funds, vii, 1, 4, 5, 6, 9, 16, 25, 26, 29, 36, 39, 44, 57, 60, 61, 64, 68, 70, 71, 79, 88, 89, 131, 135, 138, 139, 142, 147, 148, 150, 151, 152, 156, 157, 159, 164, 174, 182, 183, 186, 187, 191, 198, 199, 203, 206, 213, 214, 217, 226, 236, 237

G

GAO, vii, viii, 71, 155, 156, 158, 164, 167, 168, 170, 171, 172, 175, 179, 180, 187, 192, 199, 201, 202, 203, 204, 206, 207, 209, 210, 215, 216, 219, 222, 230, 232, 234, 236, 237
GDP, 5
General Motors, v, vii, viii, 1, 3, 9, 14, 39, 40, 41, 131, 132, 133, 134, 136, 137, 139, 140, 144, 148, 149, 150, 151, 152, 155, 157, 162, 189, 196, 198, 207, 209, 211, 214, 235, 237
Georgia, 179
Germany, 25, 197

global economy, 132
global recession, 10, 172
governance, 38, 58, 60, 139, 237
government funds, 15, 221, 229
government intervention, 2, 4, 39, 58, 63, 66, 67
governments, vii, 31, 131, 149, 150, 206
grants, 36
Great Depression, 185
Greece, 197
greed, 83, 148
greenhouse, 147
growth, 5, 14, 20, 22, 43, 45, 50, 51, 52, 57, 139, 144, 226, 228
guidance, 15, 169, 205
guidelines, 58, 60, 63, 226
guiding principles, 57, 135

H

harmful effects, 63
Harvard Law School, 92
health, vii, 11, 14, 19, 26, 37, 50, 73, 131, 135, 137, 145, 146, 150, 161, 165, 186, 187, 204, 207, 213, 218, 219, 220, 226, 232, 236
health care, vii, 14, 19, 26, 37, 131, 135, 137, 145, 150, 165, 204, 207, 218, 236
health care costs, 26, 135
Henry Ford, 140, 151
hiring, 11, 225
history, 38, 179
holding company, 7, 39, 44, 47, 52, 197, 198
home ownership, 92
homes, 77
Hong Kong, 141
House, 92, 150, 188, 189, 233, 234, 237
House of Representatives, 150, 188, 189, 233, 234
housing, 14, 38, 39, 51, 77, 91, 224
human, 225
human capital, 225
hybrid, 23, 161

I

ideal, 226
image, 22, 218
images, 152
improvements, 13, 14, 21, 49, 183
income, 15, 43, 54, 78, 80, 144, 161, 164, 176, 191, 203, 222
income tax, 15
independence, 59, 68
Independence, 151
India, 13, 14, 19, 20, 144, 147

individuals, viii, 82, 209, 210, 212, 224, 232
industrial sectors, 211
industries, 4, 169
inflation, 36, 147, 152
information technology, 181
infrastructure, 181
institutions, 4, 8, 48, 54, 68, 69, 70, 72, 76, 80, 81, 82, 131, 186, 236
integrity, 159
intellectual property, 237
interest rates, 14, 51, 72, 166, 169, 182, 205, 225
intermediaries, 141
internal controls, 202, 221, 236
internal rate of return, 85
Internal Revenue Service, 157, 164, 190
intervention, vii, 1, 3, 4, 34, 38, 39, 60, 62, 65, 66, 67, 68, 69
investment bank, 7, 29, 32, 133, 141, 151, 210, 224, 225
investments, vii, 1, 2, 3, 5, 7, 8, 10, 15, 18, 25, 34, 36, 39, 47, 48, 55, 62, 64, 65, 66, 67, 68, 69, 79, 80, 81, 82, 83, 132, 135, 159, 161, 164, 184, 186, 187, 212, 213, 223, 224, 226, 227, 231, 232, 236, 237
investors, vii, 5, 42, 46, 47, 52, 54, 60, 61, 83, 131, 141, 142, 143, 146, 151, 152, 223, 225, 226
IPO, vii, 1, 2, 4, 10, 16, 21, 22, 24, 25, 26, 29, 31, 32, 34, 35, 36, 37, 45, 47, 48, 49, 52, 54, 59, 60, 61, 64, 65, 69, 131, 132, 133, 137, 138, 139, 140, 141, 142, 143, 145, 147, 148, 150, 151, 152, 226, 227, 231
IPR, 194
issues, 3, 39, 53, 54, 58, 60, 62, 134, 139, 184, 212, 224, 227

J

Japan, 14
jurisdiction, 132
justification, 2, 39

K

Kuwait, 152

L

labor force, 19
labor market, 145, 194
labor markets, 194
laws, 164, 203, 236
laws and regulations, 203, 236
layoffs, 160
lead, 26, 61, 65, 141, 142, 143

legislation, 6, 135, 150, 169, 228
lending, 5, 7, 8, 16, 38, 42, 45, 51, 55, 71, 72, 73, 237
lifetime, 200
light, 13, 14, 32, 63, 132, 143, 184, 186, 225
light trucks, 14
limited liability, 15, 228
liquidate, 3, 213, 223
liquidity, 20, 44, 49, 54, 55, 89, 132, 133, 135, 146, 160, 173, 174, 213, 222, 226
lithium, 23
litigation, 23, 204
loan guarantees, 25
loans, viii, 2, 4, 6, 10, 25, 26, 29, 31, 32, 34, 35, 36, 37, 39, 47, 53, 55, 61, 62, 64, 65, 69, 74, 75, 89, 133, 135, 136, 137, 138, 147, 149, 150, 151, 153, 157, 159, 185, 209, 211, 213, 217, 219, 220, 228, 229, 230, 231, 235, 237

M

machinery, 137
magnitude, 48, 178, 228
major issues, 133
majority, 2, 9, 10, 23, 25, 26, 29, 32, 36, 37, 48, 53, 60, 64, 69, 81, 132, 136, 137, 139, 143, 147, 148, 152, 173, 174, 198
management, 4, 8, 12, 16, 21, 25, 26, 31, 39, 43, 45, 47, 48, 49, 51, 53, 54, 57, 58, 66, 68, 133, 138, 141, 142, 144, 146, 148, 170, 184, 203, 210, 212, 220, 222, 224, 226, 227
manufacturing, 16, 23, 135, 140, 150, 159, 160, 173, 174, 177, 219, 221, 237
manufacturing companies, 135
market capitalization, 48, 147, 228
market discipline, 67
market economy, 70, 211
market position, 61
market share, 4, 12, 13, 14, 19, 20, 21, 22, 23, 32, 43, 44, 51, 58, 61, 63, 134, 144, 145, 147, 161, 185, 211, 219, 222, 227
marketing, 56, 63, 142
marketplace, 4, 6, 67, 69, 161
materials, 147, 158, 222
matter, iv, 24, 29, 70
MCP, 7, 47, 59
measurements, 167, 168, 180, 194
medical, 204
membership, 175, 222
Mercedes-Benz, 144
mergers, 175, 179, 181, 191
metals, 177
methodology, 35, 37, 48
Mexico, 43

Microsoft, 145
middle class, 16
Middle East, 152
mission, 134
models, 6, 32, 144, 160, 166, 196, 210, 218
modifications, 52
moral hazard, vii, 1, 3, 4, 62, 64, 67, 69, 70
mortgage-backed securities, 5
multiples, 48

N

NAS, 211, 212
net investment, 229
New York Stock Exchange, 16, 143
North America, 10, 11, 13, 20, 33, 43, 51, 83, 84, 136, 143, 144, 146, 150, 152, 168, 173, 175, 196, 197, 206, 218

O

Obama, 6, 14, 64, 131, 133, 135, 136, 138, 148, 151
Obama Administration, 6, 14, 64, 131, 133, 135, 136, 138, 148, 151
obstacles, 50, 205
officials, viii, 15, 23, 141, 143, 150, 152, 155, 158, 160, 163, 170, 174, 175, 176, 178, 182, 184, 185, 186, 204, 205, 206, 209, 210, 212, 217, 222, 223, 224, 225, 226, 227, 228, 229, 231, 232
OFS, 48, 92, 211, 212, 223, 224, 229, 232
operations, 3, 4, 5, 8, 14, 19, 20, 22, 38, 42, 43, 44, 45, 46, 47, 51, 54, 58, 59, 62, 66, 71, 133, 134, 136, 140, 144, 145, 146, 148, 150, 159, 160, 161, 164, 165, 173, 184, 191, 195, 196, 206, 212, 213, 217, 219, 223, 227, 236
opportunities, 50, 52, 63, 70, 166, 189
opportunity costs, 229
optimism, 10, 49, 175
overlap, 63, 173
oversight, vii, viii, 43, 59, 66, 91, 92, 133, 155, 157, 158, 164, 184, 185, 187, 202, 209, 212, 224, 229, 232, 236
ownership, 2, 7, 8, 9, 10, 14, 15, 18, 25, 26, 29, 34, 37, 38, 39, 42, 50, 57, 58, 60, 131, 133, 137, 138, 139, 140, 141, 143, 144, 148, 151, 157, 184, 198, 203, 207, 210, 211, 212, 225, 227, 228, 231, 232, 237
ownership structure, 26

P

Pacific, 82, 83
pacing, 13
parallel, 31
parity, 145
participants, viii, 2, 4, 25, 68, 82, 92, 155, 156, 158, 162, 163, 164, 165, 166, 176, 177, 178, 179, 180, 181, 182, 183, 185, 186, 191, 193, 199, 203
peer group, 48
Pension Benefit Guaranty Corporation, vii, 155, 157, 189, 190, 204, 206
pension plans, vii, viii, 18, 20, 23, 146, 155, 156, 157, 158, 161, 164, 165, 166, 169, 170, 175, 176, 177, 178, 179, 180, 182, 183, 185, 186, 187, 189, 190, 191, 200, 203, 205, 207, 221, 237
permit, 70
petroleum, 161
pitch, 152
plants, 19, 23, 33, 62, 64, 132, 137, 168, 174, 193, 195, 196, 198, 219
platform, 8, 16, 32, 48, 56, 62, 66
policy, 30, 64, 164, 184, 221, 227
policy choice, 64
portability, 161
portfolio, 2, 45, 49, 50, 54, 67, 135, 196, 236
portfolio investment, 67
portfolio management, 135
potential output, 19
precedent, 64, 66, 136
preparation, iv, 62
present value, 204, 206, 237
preservation, 60, 65, 66
president, 133
President, 5, 7, 16, 25, 135, 136, 217, 225
President Obama, 16, 25, 136, 217
prestige, 152
prevention, 66
principles, 8, 21, 37, 54, 58, 59, 61, 65, 66, 70, 138, 184, 185, 210, 212, 220
private firms, 3
private ownership, 2
privatization, 212
production costs, 210, 217, 219
professionals, 225
profit, 2, 14, 61, 79, 80, 140, 144
profit margin, 14
profitability, 10, 13, 15, 22, 32, 44, 46, 49, 51, 55, 58, 61, 62, 64, 71, 135, 145, 146, 147, 156, 159, 185, 186, 213, 217, 219, 223, 226, 227, 229, 231
project, 22, 165
protection, 89, 160, 161, 174, 176
public policy, 139, 227

R

ramp, 152
rate of return, 85
raw materials, 147, 161
real estate, 38, 42
real property, 222
recession, 14, 133, 135, 136, 148, 150, 185, 190, 211
recognition, 64
recommendations, iv, 67, 186, 210, 232
recovery, 1, 2, 3, 14, 15, 21, 23, 25, 34, 37, 50, 51, 54, 55, 68, 78, 83, 136, 138, 149, 186, 220, 226, 231
recreational, 52
reform, 65, 66, 67, 91, 92
regulations, 158, 165, 181, 191, 192, 205, 206
rejection, 204
relief, 169, 170, 171
remediation, 23
reporters, 143
reputation, 54, 63
requirements, 8, 56, 156, 164, 165, 169, 170, 171, 181, 190, 203, 204, 205, 212, 220, 221, 222, 223, 225, 236, 237
researchers, 20, 67
reserves, 132, 210, 211, 220
resistance, 146
resolution, 204
resources, 3, 26, 29, 63, 69, 78, 89, 133, 176, 179, 218, 223
response, 8, 44, 54, 62, 92, 142, 159, 186, 225
restrictions, 8, 15, 63, 70, 92, 169, 171, 205
restructuring, vii, viii, 4, 8, 11, 14, 19, 22, 23, 24, 25, 26, 37, 39, 65, 68, 131, 132, 133, 135, 136, 137, 155, 157, 158, 159, 160, 165, 166, 168, 172, 173, 174, 175, 176, 183, 203, 204, 209, 210, 212, 213, 214, 217, 219, 220, 223, 224, 228, 236
retail, 7, 19, 42, 43, 47, 51, 52, 55, 132, 140, 143, 146, 152, 213
retention rate, 44, 46
retirement, 23, 161, 182, 191, 192, 193, 194, 199
retirement age, 194
revenue, 20, 32, 51, 52, 58, 137, 152, 174
risk, vii, 1, 2, 3, 18, 21, 24, 44, 45, 46, 50, 51, 52, 54, 62, 63, 64, 65, 67, 69, 72, 73, 74, 89, 141, 145, 153, 161, 165, 169, 171, 173, 175, 181, 182, 184, 185, 186, 205, 206
risk factors, 145
risk profile, 54
risks, 4, 50, 54, 56, 65, 66, 69, 70, 145, 173, 183, 185, 186, 221
rules, 15, 34, 63, 142, 169, 172, 219
Russia, 13, 14, 19, 20, 22

S

safety, 69, 146, 147, 189
Saudi Arabia, 143
savings, 37, 146
science, 62
scope, 2, 45, 66
Secretary of the Treasury, 135, 164, 187, 207, 209, 222, 227, 228, 231
securities, 7, 39, 45, 71, 89, 141, 142, 143, 145
Securities Act of 1933, 142
security, 90, 189
Senate, 5, 92, 150, 188, 205, 233, 237
sensitivity, 184
settlements, 44, 53, 179
shareholders, 7, 9, 18, 24, 37, 39, 52, 58, 60, 64, 65, 67, 143, 149, 156, 205, 212, 219, 220, 221, 223, 236, 237
shortfall, 173, 191
showing, 225
signs, 175, 222, 226
Silicon Valley, 140
small firms, 16
smoothing, 169, 171
social costs, 237
social policy, 223
Social Security, 182
solution, 8
South Africa, 197
Spain, 197
specific knowledge, 225, 232
spending, 14, 78, 92, 145, 225
spin, 44, 161, 189, 190, 204
stability, 3, 10, 44, 61, 62, 135, 229
stabilization, 57, 89
staffing, 184, 225, 232
stakeholders, 30, 39, 48, 67, 135, 136, 152, 159, 186, 190
standard deviation, 71
state, 9, 10, 15, 92, 221, 236, 237
states, 6, 8, 19, 20, 21, 39, 44, 45, 53, 62, 69, 146, 151, 228
statutes, 155
steel, 135
stigma, 141, 143
stock price, 14, 22, 132, 145, 146, 147, 149
stockholders, 16, 140
strategic management, 66
stress, 7, 39, 54, 71, 156, 166, 172, 173
stretching, 181
structural changes, 220

structure, 14, 19, 22, 26, 38, 44, 46, 47, 144
structuring, 158, 212
subsidy, 67, 70, 151
succession, 199
Sun, 85
Superfund, 137
supervision, 228, 237
supplier, 6, 33, 56, 57, 138, 155, 156, 161, 164, 168, 172, 173, 174, 176, 179, 186, 189
suppliers, 5, 6, 9, 56, 62, 64, 132, 136, 137, 148, 150, 156, 158, 159, 161, 172, 173, 174, 175, 176, 179, 186, 189, 205, 206, 213
supply chain, 132, 161, 172, 173
survival, 2, 161
Sweden, 197, 198
systemic risk, 159, 211

T

takeover, 25, 191
talent, 8
target, 82, 148, 172, 204, 205
taxes, 14, 29, 137, 144
taxpayers, vii, 1, 2, 3, 6, 7, 9, 15, 16, 18, 21, 22, 23, 24, 25, 36, 37, 38, 48, 49, 50, 57, 61, 62, 65, 67, 68, 69, 70, 135, 138, 139, 156, 187, 210, 211, 220, 227, 228, 229, 231, 237
technical comments, 156, 187, 232
techniques, 140
technologies, 26
technology, 8, 23, 26, 30, 31, 140
telephone, 213
tension, 185
tensions, viii, 155, 156, 158, 185, 186, 187
tenure, 44
threats, 67, 146
time frame, 70, 185, 227
time periods, 219
Title I, 235
Title IV, 235
Title V, 236
TMC, 151
Toyota, 11, 16, 23, 43, 134, 140, 145, 150, 151, 194, 219
trade, 186, 193, 219, 223, 232
trade-off, 223, 232
tranches, 25, 34, 237
transactions, 44, 45, 47, 49, 58, 82, 139, 220
transformation, 135, 136, 165
transparency, vii, 1, 59, 66, 92, 159, 183, 186, 187, 231, 232
transplant, 145, 175
transportation, 161, 177, 189
Treasury Secretary, 6, 150

treatment, 8, 9, 59, 67, 70, 164, 181, 203
trust fund, vii, 131, 179, 206
turnover, 224, 225

U

U.S. Department of the Treasury, 149, 150
U.S. economy, 64, 71, 92, 132, 159, 213
U.S. history, 16, 139
U.S. Treasury, vii, 74, 75, 131, 132, 133, 135, 136, 138, 139, 143, 145, 147, 148, 150, 151, 152
underwriting, 16, 141, 143
uniform, 8
unions, 157, 164, 168, 185, 186, 189, 190
United, v, vii, 6, 13, 14, 19, 20, 21, 23, 26, 30, 32, 42, 43, 51, 52, 58, 79, 84, 131, 132, 133, 134, 135, 144, 145, 146, 147, 151, 152, 155, 157, 158, 163, 187, 188, 189, 191, 194, 195, 196, 197, 209, 210, 211, 213, 218, 221, 223, 232, 233, 234, 236, 237
United Kingdom, 43, 197
United States (USA), v, 6, 13, 14, 19, 20, 21, 23, 26, 30, 32, 42, 43, 51, 52, 58, 132, 134, 135, 141, 144, 145, 146, 147, 150, 152, 155, 157, 187, 188, 189, 191, 195, 209, 210, 213, 221, 223, 232, 233, 234, 236, 237
universe, 48

V

valuation, 7, 25, 29, 34, 35, 36, 37, 48, 62, 66, 67, 141, 142, 156, 166, 168, 170, 171, 178, 205
variables, 50, 194
vehicles, 2, 6, 12, 13, 14, 20, 23, 26, 30, 32, 33, 51, 52, 56, 88, 132, 134, 135, 136, 140, 143, 144, 146, 147, 160, 174, 186, 210, 213, 218, 221, 223, 229, 237
Venezuela, 197
Vice President, 152, 206
vision, 57, 225
volatility, 45, 56, 72, 178, 190, 206
vote, 58, 60, 139
voting, 58, 184
vulnerability, 6

W

wages, 11, 26, 219
waiver, 185, 190, 206
Washington, 86, 91, 145, 203, 204, 206, 207, 236, 237
waste, 140
wealth, 5, 68, 152, 187
welfare, 166

well-being, 157, 183
White House, 5, 61, 62, 212
wholesale, 43, 55, 213
Wisconsin, 197
workers, 5, 10, 11, 26, 37, 62, 70, 135, 137, 145, 146, 148, 159, 161, 164, 168, 173, 176, 179, 183, 189, 191, 205, 219, 236
workforce, 19, 132
workload, 181, 224
worldwide, 13, 20, 136, 137, 144, 160

Y

yield, 36, 205, 229